MW00779428

Reno's Big Gamble

Image and Reputation in
the Biggest Little City

Alicia Barber

University Press of Kansas

© 2008 by the University Press of Kansas

Published by the University Press of Kansas (Lawrence, Kansas 66045), which
was organized by the Kansas Board of Regents and is operated and funded by
Emporia State University, Fort Hays State University, Kansas State University,
Pittsburg State University, the University of Kansas, and Wichita State University

Library of Congress Cataloging-in-Publication Data
Barber, Alicia.
Reno's big gamble : image and reputation in the biggest little city / Alicia Barber.
p. cm.
Includes bibliographical references and index.
ISBN 978-0-7006-1594-0 (cloth : alk. paper)
1. Reno (Nev.)—History. 2. Reno (Nev.)—Economic conditions.
3. Tourism—Nevada—Reno—History. I. Title.
F849.R4B37 2008
979.3'55—dc22
2008027416

British Library Cataloguing-in-Publication Data is available.

Printed in the United States of America

10 9 8 7 6 5 4 3 2 1

The paper used in this publication is recycled and contains 30 percent
postconsumer waste. It is acid free and meets the minimum requirements
of the American National Standard for Permanence of Paper
for Printed Library Materials Z39.48-1992.

For my parents

CONTENTS

ACKNOWLEDGMENTS

So many have contributed, in ways both wonderfully broad and minutely focused, to my research and mental health as I wrote and endlessly revised this manuscript. Thanks to my academic mentors: the American Studies faculty at the University of Texas at Austin, especially Steven Hoelscher, Jeff Meikle, and Mark Smith; Shelley Fisher-Fishkin at Stanford; and Gunther Peck at Duke. Martha Norkunas was and remains an inspiration. Cary Cordova, Danielle Sigler, Kim Hewitt, Joel Dinerstein, and Tim Davis sustained me and this project through graduate school and beyond with their intellectual insights and friendship.

My research in Reno was eased through the expertise and generosity of the Nevada Historical Society's Lee Brumbaugh, Eric Moody, Michael Maher, and Marta Gonzalez-Collins. In Special Collections at the University of Nevada–Reno, my heartfelt thanks to Bob Blesse and Kathy Totton. Nevada state archivist Guy Rocha was enormously generous with time and materials, as were local experts Karl Breckenridge, Neal Cobb, Philip Earl, and Dennis Myers. I received critical input and feedback from a number of current and former faculty members at the University of Nevada–Reno, including James Hulse, James McCormick, Bill Eadington, Tom King, and Paul Starrs. My colleagues at the university have been sources of illuminating conversation and encouragement, especially Jen Huntley-Smith and Jen Hill. Nevada Historical Society history curator Mella Harmon began as a valuable research contact and has become a treasured friend and colleague. I could have no better models for combining scholarly achievement with compassionate leadership and teaching excellence than the remarkable Scott Casper, of the Department of History, and Phil Boardman, of the Core Humanities Program, both at the University of Nevada–Reno, where I feel enormously grateful to have found a home.

At the University Press of Kansas, I owe Nancy Jackson an enormous debt for her early support of my manuscript and Kalyani Fernando and Fred Woodward another debt for not giving up on me. Lastly, there is a reason authors profusely thank their families in these acknowledgments; no one else could withstand the years of agonized conversations, the gnashing of teeth, and the sporadic fits of despair and manic inspiration. I thank my parents, Peter and Karen, my sister, April, and my brother, Thomas, for their support, insight, and assistance through the years. And finally, to Mark: I was "almost" finished with this book when we met, "practically" finished with it when we got engaged, and "nearly" finished with it when we married. With our second anniversary now behind us, I thank you for your patience, love, and support and welcome the opportunity to demonstrate to you that I am actually sane.

Reno's Big Gamble

INTRODUCTION

Becoming "The Biggest Little City"

Character is like a tree and reputation like its shadow.
The shadow is what we think of it; the tree is the real thing.
Abraham Lincoln

In June 1999, public radio personality Garrison Keillor visited the campus of the University of Nevada–Reno, for a live broadcast of his popular variety show, *A Prairie Home Companion*. As usual when taking his show on the road, he began with a description of his host city's history. Reno, Keillor intoned, "was a Western town, it was a mining town, it had the nickname of 'Sin Central.'... It was a place where you could do things that were illegal elsewhere in America, which seemed to be the function of Nevada then and now." In fact, he claimed, Nevada "to this day, among all the lower forty-eight states ... is the least known, the least inhabited, the most wild, the most strange country that we have in America." He then ventured an explanation for the city's offbeat offerings: "The gambling and the brothels and the liquor laws, the divorce industry, the marriage industry, the boxing, all as I say serve a useful function in a Puritan society. Everybody needs a place to go to do things and to see things that you would not want to see in your own hometown, and that's Reno." At these final words, the local audience erupted into enthusiastic applause, hoots, and laughter. As Keillor indicated, and as his listeners well knew, Nevada is best known as a place for visitors to shed their inhibitions, their morality, and, somewhat less willingly, their paychecks. As orchestrated by generations of willing state legislators, it was no mistake that Nevada became the primary outlet for mainstream America's suppressed desires.[1]

That legacy was visible just blocks from where Keillor spoke that night, witnessed in the clamor of bells ringing out jackpots; in the barrage of quarters clanking into metal trays specifically engineered to amplify the sound of each coin falling; in the strains of rock music blaring from casino entrances where barkers called out to passersby; in the cocktails flowing

1

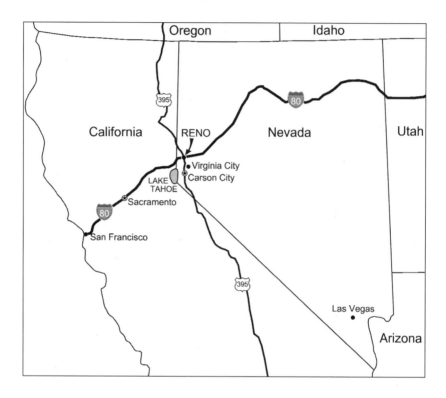

twenty-four hours a day; in the streams of people hurrying from casino to casino, clutching to their chests colorful plastic cups full of nickels and dimes; and in the blazing neon arch proclaiming Reno as "The Biggest Little City in the World."

To most Reno residents, the city's reputation as a decadent and even sordid tourist town is a source of bemusement as well as frustration. Whether new arrivals or fifth-generation natives, locals are intensely aware of outside impressions of their city. Most have a completely different experience of Reno than its predominant image would suggest. Despite the raucous appearance of its central tourist district, Reno has housed a fairly conventional residential community since its founding in 1868, growing to a population in the year 2007 of just over 200,000, with approximately 400,000 living in the metropolitan area. It may feature slot machines in the supermarkets and more all-you-can-eat buffets per capita than the average American town, but Reno's anomalies are far outnumbered by the similarities of its residential neighborhoods, schools, churches, suburban developments, and playgrounds to those of any other mid-sized city.

In recognition of this dichotomy, Nevada historian James Hulse has described the city as consistently "schizophrenic," split between the "two Renos" of the casino landscape and the respectable university town, which operate in close proximity but on different planes.[2] However, as distinctive as these communities may seem, the division between the two has never been so clear cut. Throughout its history, Reno's residential and tourist landscapes have been closely integrated, sometimes overlapping, and often inseparable. Even now, Reno's city center does not cater to tourists alone. This, too, is a product of its history. Unlike the Las Vegas strip, which transitioned directly from desert to resort, Reno had more than sixty years under its belt before the legalization of gambling in 1931 began to transform its existing downtown into a gambling mecca. Even today, just blocks away from Reno's flashy casinos, one encounters the county courthouse and city hall, a post office, a performing arts center, a movie theater, the county library, independent bars and restaurants, and, since 1885, the University of Nevada–Reno. The city's current skyline features apartment buildings and office buildings, hotel and bank towers—all the structures of a residential community standing proudly alongside those of the tourist industry.

In this respect, Reno is not unlike many other contemporary American cities where tourist and residential spaces overlap and intertwine.[3] In Seattle, San Francisco, and Boston, for instance, many components of the everyday urban landscape double as popular features of the tourist experience, unlike a wide array of western resort towns that present more obvious distinctions, both economic and aesthetic, between the two. But the specific appearance of downtown Reno, with its neon facades and souvenir shops, is certainly distinct. After all, a casino is a very different attraction than San Francisco's Haight-Ashbury district, Boston's Faneuil Hall, or Seattle's Pike Place Market. Unlike these commercial landscapes, a casino district can seem less compatible with the desired attributes of a hometown, and because it is such a visible departure, the reputation of that area, Reno's city center—or "epitome district," to use Grady Clay's term—has long shaped common perceptions of the entire city.[4]

Unfortunately for Reno, that reputation has frequently been far from positive. The image of the city as a site of escapist fun, as described by Keillor, is the most generous spin on Reno's role in American society. But the predominant opinion has often been much less flattering. In 1999, as Keillor spoke, Reno's gaming industry was clearly struggling, and the "dingy, desultory properties" of its downtown, as described by a casino industry commentator just one month earlier, reflected the financial strain.[5] A number of established casinos had closed down in the past decade, some remaining boarded shut for years with no plans for reopening. Souvenir and T-shirt shops, pawnshops, liquor stores, and a small but visible homeless population lent a seedy quality to many central streets, causing city officials understandable concern about Reno's future as a tourist destination.

At that time, a primary reason for the visible decline was increasing competition from other gaming destinations, the most obvious, although not the most direct, being Las Vegas. Reno may once have been known as "Sin Central," but it was long ago surpassed in the national imagination by "Sin City," its upstart successor to the south. By the turn of the new millennium, Las Vegas had set a standard of scale, fantasy, and opulence that no other gaming destination could begin to imitate. Even with some recent multimillion dollar additions to the skyline, including an eighty-lane bowling stadium and Victorian-themed casino, Reno's skyline could still in no way compete with the excessive monuments of its downstate neighbor. Constrained by the spatial limitations of a preexisting residential community, Reno's casino core featured no rooftop roller coasters, no full-scale dueling battleships, no choreographed dancing fountains or towering replicas of Egyptian pyramids arrayed in an unbroken sequence to form a solid entertainment landscape.

More direct competition for Reno's tourist attractions stemmed from the riverboat and Indian casinos emerging across the country, from the Pequot tribe's Foxwood Casino Resort in Connecticut to the unlikely highrise hotel casinos of Tunica, Mississippi, to the increasing number of Native American–run casinos throughout the state of California. Faced with the cutting-edge technologies and marketing strategies of such enterprises, most appearing since 1990, Reno seemed in danger of dismissal as the relic of a previous generation. What had worked for the city in an earlier era no longer appeared to be succeeding. By the end of the twentieth century, Reno had developed the reputation of an also-ran at a time when uniqueness was more than ever a tourist destination's most prized possession. Although representing a very small fraction of the city's total area, the deteriorating casino district gave the entire city a bad name, prompting concern about its overall respectability and inspiring the dismay of Reno's residential population, as they witnessed the literal and figurative battering of their hometown.

But the explanation for Reno's fraying reputation involved more than the relatively recent factors of economic competition and aesthetic decline. Indeed, the process by which a place develops a reputation is gradual and complex. Civic reputation, the governing impression of a city or town from the outside, is just one factor in the creation of place identity, a concept that has at least two other components: the sense of place as experienced by residents and the promoted image as disseminated by city marketers.

Sense of place has been widely discussed in literary and environmental circles, as writers from Wallace Stegner to Annie Dillard and Wendell Berry have described and eloquently explored the attachment of individuals, themselves included, to specific locales and regions. Deeply personal, such a connection, called "topophilia" by some, is often inspired by the natural environment, but as any dedicated urbanite knows, it can just as easily be rooted in a beloved neighborhood or a familiar skyline. To J. B. Jackson, sense of place is "a sense of being at home in a town or city," a sentiment that develops over a period of increasing familiarity. In recent years, urban planners and architects have often cited the creation of a sense of place as one of their primary goals in an increasingly impersonal and homogenized world.[6]

On the opposite end of the spectrum of place identity is the promoted image. This formulation is aspirational and idealistic, embodying how officials would best like a place to be perceived. As a professional activity, place promotion has developed over time from boastful editorials in daily newspapers and city directories and the construction of landmarks like the St. Louis Arch, to professionally crafted slogans, brochures, and pamphlets, to the sophisticated "branding" strategies of contemporary media campaigns. The promoted image may change over time, based on official assessments of a city's strengths, weaknesses, and most direct competition. At their most successful, city slogans, like "The City of Brotherly Love," might enter into the national lexicon; identifying what specific responses such familiarity might breed is a task for market researchers employed by tourist bureaus everywhere. Promoters cannot control how a place will be perceived by outsiders, although they may certainly try, particularly through manipulation of the mass media. As Stephen P. Hanna writes, "Representations of places in media play crucial roles in the development and definition of those places." Peter Borsay agrees: "Image is about power. Those who can control the way a place is represented can control the place itself."[7]

Awareness of the powerful relationship between place and image has been a key factor in the recent urban revitalization of postindustrial cities like Cleveland and Pittsburgh, whose leaders have attempted to update their cities' images through a combination of place marketing and redevelopment.[8] Concern for competition has led many contemporary city planners, as Christine Boyer writes, to "myopically focus on improving a city's marketability" through enhancements of image, cultural offerings, and perceived "liveability." Indeed, in today's image-driven climate, marketing priorities can produce a rather distorted sequence of events. As Dennis R. Judd and Susan S. Fainstein write in their study *The Tourist City,* "The product must plausibly resemble the representation, and thus cities often remake themselves in conformity with their advertised image," noting that "the constant transformation of the urban landscape to accommodate tourists has become a permanent feature of the political economy of cities."[9]

Place marketers, of course, hope that the image they create and promote will become part of the civic reputation; they may in fact be working quite deliberately to overturn an earlier, less agreeable image. Likewise, staunchly devoted locals may be surprised or even offended that their sense of place differs widely from both the promoted image and the reputation, both of which may be far from their own experience. However, despite their close association, each of these factors is often discussed in isolation, although some recent historical scholarship has attempted to delve into the relationship between the promoted image and residential sense of place.[10]

Unlike these two components, civic reputation is not so easily defined or controlled. Most commonly applied to people, reputation is a sociological concept, a product of rampant public discussion rather than individual reflection or tightly focused market research. Everyone from high school to Hollywood understands the destructive potential of a bad reputation; while individual impressions wield little power for the most part, the overall pattern of impressions that emerges can become a formidable force with which to contend. In recognition of the economic value of reputation to the branding of consumer products, the field of marketing has generated the term "reputational capital," identified as one of the most important of a product's "intangible assets," as opposed to "cultural capital," the supply of cultural resources that a place can use for economic gain. Such formulations attempt to assign a specific market value to reputation, no easy task.[11] While a sense of place may be completely personal, just as a promoted image may be recognized by the marketing professional alone (although he/she would certainly hope not), a civic reputation is by definition an impression that is widely shared, perhaps not universally, but broadly enough to be recognized by a wide cross-section of society. Like a community's collective memories of the past, it is perpetuated communally and often incorporated into the broader culture.[12]

This does not necessarily make it accurate. Although a place's reputation may be founded on seemingly objective factors, including geographic features, economic climate, and aesthetic appearance, it is also dependent upon subjective assessments of those factors. The formulation of such impressions requires no forethought or knowledge and carries no responsibility. It can derive from informed opinion or sheer hearsay. It carries a moral dimension and implies a value judgment that is itself the product of the predominant beliefs and values shared by a culture at any given time. With respect to place, as cultural geographer Yi-Fu Tuan writes, "warm conversation between friends can make [a] place itself seem warm; by contrast, malicious speech has the power to destroy a place's reputation and thereby its visibility."[13] Indeed, a dominant reputation can wield immense power, providing the motivation for collective action, whether it be investment, visitation, disdain, or outright avoidance. For these reasons, a positive civic reputation is particularly valuable to a tourist destination that hopes to attract a continuous stream of visitors.

A city's reputation is not created at a single moment, and it does not remain fixed; rather, it continuously evolves due to a series of integrated processes. These may include changes in the place itself, shifting marketing strategies, and, most interestingly, shifting cultural values and broader consumer demands. Whatever their origins, as a critical mass of similar impressions cohere, they can gain a powerful momentum until the original reasons for those impressions may no longer even be traceable, and the reputation alone survives.

These three components of place identity—sense of place, promoted image, and civic reputation—can resemble each other closely or differ drastically, but all depend fundamentally upon the final factor in the matrix of place identity, the place itself. As the most tangible component in this equation, the physical place is ultimately prone to the most permanent alteration in the quest to improve a city's reputation. City leaders may attempt to control the shape of the urban landscape, hoping thereby to create an attractive environment with broad appeal and what Kevin Lynch defines as a visual "legibility" that identifies the place as a coherent whole. Such coherence is especially necessary for a tourist destination in order to create a distinctive place identity that potential visitors can recognize.[14]

Certain cities have long benefited from such visual coherence, even if manufactured, as with Santa Fe, a city whose harmonious appearance was legislated by a 1913 city ordinance creating a single architectural style intended to create, in the words of historian Chris Wilson, "a unifying vision of the city, its people, and their history." A distinctive natural setting can provide a clear identity for a waterfront city such as Seattle or the angular charm of San Francisco. Other places, by nature of their geography, politics, or other factors, are more fragmented, complicating the formation of a coherent reputation; urban sprawl is often the culprit. Los Angeles is the prime example of a place that, according to Mike Davis, has been "infinitely envisioned" amid an "anarchy of market forces," featuring a plethora of outward projections that have never cohered into a single, consistent image. In the marketing of such landscapes, the absence of unity and coherence can be a clear liability.[15]

Although it certainly cannot guarantee a universally positive response, visual appeal is, not surprisingly, one of the most important factors in establishing a positive reputation. Economic and aesthetic decline, when witnessed by visitors, can cause a city's reputation to plummet. A negative reputation, in turn, can affect investment and visitation, thereby contributing to the deterioration of the landscape, which is likely to damage the reputation further, and so on. In the worst-case scenario, this produces a vicious cycle whereby the battered landscape and reputation together spur an endless downward spiral.

For all of these reasons, Reno serves as an excellent subject to study this process. The city's reputation has played a determining role in its development from the very beginning. More than in most other American communities, Reno's leaders have been desperate to secure a positive reputation for their city, while at the same time strangely willing to make decisions likely to run counter to that goal. Although securing a positive reputation is critical to the success of any tourist destination, it has been especially important for Reno, a town that came into being with the already dubious distinction of being located in Nevada. Founded in 1868 as a tiny junction on the transcontinental railroad, on the so-called "barren" Nevada frontier near the California border, Reno appeared at first to have little future beyond that of a support community for the Comstock silver mining district, based in nearby Virginia City. Saddled with stereotypes related to its industrial base and austere landscape, city boosters found themselves on the defensive from day one, resentful of their community's poor reputation and determined to change collective impressions of it.

That need strengthened in the troubled economic climate of late nineteenth-century Nevada, prompting Reno's business community to consider even more drastic measures to attract new residents and visitors. While new mineral discoveries elsewhere provided economic security for the state, some of Reno's early entrepreneurs saw another gold mine in the instant economic gratification presented by the trafficking of vice. They were divorce lawyers and gamblers, politicians and boxing promoters, carnival barkers and saloonkeepers, and together they aimed to shape the city into what American culture craved: an escape from society's constraints, a departure from the everyday.

As many residents committed themselves to the gratification of American desires, others bemoaned the ensuing damage to Reno's reputation. Their determination to keep Reno respectable presented a difficult dilemma, borne of two seemingly opposed trajectories. Predictably, as with most profitable ventures, those in power hoped to cultivate additional capital by further developing the resources that had met with such success. The gradual dedication of the city center to visitors over residents began in the early decades of the twentieth century, and yet there was no sudden cataclysmic event or fatal moment when outsiders arrived in Reno to transform it into a tourist trap or even an identifiable moment when city leaders consciously decided to embrace tourism wholeheartedly. Rather, the downtown landscape simply edged out the residential, bit by bit.

In this respect, Reno's experience offers an alternative model to a popular contemporary paradigm governing the study of tourism in the American West, a paradigm that posits the unwelcome encroachment of outside interests on western places, pitting tourist town against hometown, sacrificing the cultural landscape to outsiders, and destroying a place's supposedly inherent qualities. In this declensionist narrative, the imposition of the tourism industry by outside investors inevitably leads to the destruction of a place's intrinsic nature, or "soul," defined variously as the local lifestyle, aesthetic appearance, independent business culture, and/or affordability. The rise of tourism is seen, in Hal Rothman's words, as a "devil's bargain" that initiates the rise of property values and renders a place less livable for its locals, by favoring marketing schemes over resident dreams. Overall, such accounts posit a mostly unidirectional process by which outside influences operate to the detriment of pristine local places, local residents are pushed aside, and sense of place is irretrievably lost.[16]

In somewhat less totalizing terms, some of these developments may indeed result from orienting communities to tourism. But the history of tourism in the American West is far more complex than this paradigm allows. While many western towns like Red Lodge, Montana, or Aspen, Colorado, were founded around extractive industries and only later turned to tourism, many others have been sites of tourism, to some degree, for most of their history; in fact, many, especially those that were not originally sites of industrial extraction but railroad junctions and early population hubs, have existed simultaneously as hometowns and tourist towns for more than a century, with civic leaders stumping for tourists nearly as long as they have boosted for residents.[17]

The polarization of tourism and residential sense of place—demonizing the former and bemoaning the loss of the latter—has limited utility in a West where tourist and residential landscapes have long coincided and where both will continue to expand and intersect in the years to come. The study of western tourism can only benefit from additional models that more clearly explain a wider range of experiences. By recognizing the interdependence of resident and tourist landscapes, as well as residents and tourism promoters, we can avoid the economic determinism of a paradigm that ultimately dismisses the agency of the very local populations it purports to value.

On the surface, Reno may seem a prime example of a place where consumer demand created a market for the prurient, favoring a tourist landscape that gradually expanded to the detriment of the residential community. But the study of Reno reveals a far less contentious, and far less simplistic, process. Faced with the opportunity to provide unique attractions to a nation thirsting for entertainment and release, Reno's promoters—significantly, residents themselves—eagerly complied. As they clearly recognized, a tourist town that could cater consistently to consumer demands could do quite well, and for a long time, Reno did.

The moment of crisis arrived, then, not with the introduction of tourism by outsiders or even with the corporatization of the tourist industry, but with the failure of civic leaders to recognize the balance of resident and tourist space, the overall aesthetic appeal, that had in the past ensured a reputation that worked, for the most part, in Reno's favor. The relationship between Reno's outward reputation and local response has been continuously reciprocal, with awareness of that image wielding a strong influence over decisions about policy and development, and those factors in turn inspiring fluctuations in the city's outward reputation, for better and for worse. As long as the landscape provided what the broader public desired, and the city's reputation captured the national imagination, Reno could continue its purveyance of vice undisturbed. But when just one of these components failed, when the landscape suffered, when business lagged, or when America's attention waned, city leaders and residents alike were forced to live down their carefree embrace of the unconventional. Their mistake was, perhaps, in growing accustomed to those shifts, in continuing to accommodate cultural desires so readily without maintaining a consistent vision of what the community should retain for itself. This, in essence, was Reno's big gamble: risking its reputation, along with its aesthetic appeal, time and time again, in the dogged pursuit of economic gain.

To study the relationship between a place and its reputation is to trace a process that has no clear beginning. It is the ultimate chicken-and-egg scenario. And yet, while a reputation's origin may be impossible to identify with any precision, its development over time may be traced and analyzed. Defined by public perceptions, a civic reputation is expressed, reflected, and debated through a diverse array of media, from magazine and newspaper articles to travel guides, novels, film, television, speeches, advertisements, photographs, postcards, media campaigns, and more. Such materials are disseminated for public consumption; by their very nature they are the expressions of an elite group, those possessing the power to command such public forums. Since Reno has long been a national destination, its most influential depictions have had a national audience; this study hopes to provide a representative, if not exhaustive, selection.

Reno's civic reputation has thrived, failed, and simply persisted within an ever-changing cultural context. Examining the relationship between Reno's reputation and that broader context is the task of this book. Throughout my study, I juxtapose the city's reputation with the two other components of place identity—the promoted image and the residential sense of place—to explore the dynamics among all three. My goal is to shed light not only on how a civic reputation is created and transformed, but also on the tangible consequences of that process. Reno is not just my subject; it has become my home. It is a fascinating place with a rich and often neglected history. It is, above all, a city of contradictions, but one should expect no less from a town best known as "The Biggest Little City in the World," a proud paradox all its own.

CHAPTER ONE

"In the Middle of a Frightful Plain":
The Quest for a Reputation

Reputation is an idle and most false imposition,
oft got without merit, and lost without deserving.
William Shakespeare, *Othello,* Act 2, scene 3

I had heard of such a place as Reno, but I had not been able to keep track of
the new towns that spring up along the line of the Pacific railroad, and really
could not say if Reno was in California or Utah. But here was a red-faced
man, sun-burnt and with sticking-plaster on his lips, who said he was
a citizen of Reno! Where was Reno? Was there any such place?
"The Gentleman from Reno," *Overland Monthly,* 1868

In the summer of 1868, an intrepid reporter for the *San Francisco Times*
boarded a passenger train in Sacramento and set out eastward to chronicle
the ongoing construction of the Central Pacific Railroad. The tracks, which
extended several more miles each day, had by that point stretched 250
miles from the California capital, ending somewhere in eastern Nevada,
with the last 60 miles accessible only by freight train. Leaving Sacramento,
his locomotive gained steadily in elevation until cresting the summit at
Donner Pass. As the train chugged through the stunning Sierra mountains,
he observed, "the beauty . . . is almost beyond description," and marveled at
the emerging vistas of "green meadows" and "beautiful cascades" where the
water "dashes sparkling over a rocky bed, breaking ever and anon in to
flashes of white foam." Truly this was an alpine dream, an enchanted, verdant paradise.[1]

After descending the eastern slope of the Sierra and entering Nevada,
however, enchantment gave way to metaphors of disease, sterility, gloom,
and wretchedness. The country, he reported, was becoming "drearier and
more depressing at every mile," and even the Truckee River, which hugged

13

the tracks, "has caught the tone of gloom which pervades the district, and moves sullenly between low and marshy banks" where "tall rushes . . . spot the banks like leprous blotches." The route winded through the canyon, as steep walls and lofty evergreens prevented any glimpse of what lay ahead. When the train finally emerged into the valley below, the panoramic view ahead revealed "no trace of vegetation other than the dusty blue sage brush, whose monotonous bunches alone hide the sterile sands." The meadows to the east and south stretched out, brown and low, and the curving sky overhead offered no cover. Clearly repelled, he continued, "through such a region we pass on, none too quickly, though the engineer should pile every available pound of fuel upon the engine fires, and arrive presently at Reno . . . situated in the middle of a frightful plain, destitute of any feature of beauty or picturesqueness."[2]

It was not the most auspicious introduction to the fledgling town of Reno, founded just three months earlier after an enterprising landowner, Myron C. Lake, persuaded the Central Pacific's owners to locate their "Virginia Station" on his land. Before that, Lake's Crossing, as it was called, had featured only an inn and a wooden toll bridge frequented regularly by groups traveling to Virginia City, 25 miles to the southeast. At the town's founding land auction on 9 May, the Central Pacific sold off 400 town lots carved of land Lake had deeded to the railroad, and settlement of the area began in earnest. By the time of the San Francisco reporter's visit, the churning roar and whistle of the locomotives punctuated the busy sounds of construction, as supply wagons steadily plodded to and from the booming silver district.[3]

By August, more than 200 wooden-frame storefronts and homes clustered around the tracks and trickled southward for four blocks to the shaggy banks of the Truckee River. A quick survey of its inhabitants did nothing to improve the reporter's initial impression. Upon disembarking, he disparagingly singled out a few recognizable western figures including "the suave and 'high toned' gambler," the "disreputable and hangdog looking sharper, beneath whose short and frayed coat tails the muzzle of a revolver protrudes threateningly," women "whose gay dresses are not needed to designate their shameful business," and "Piute Indians . . . [who] loaf about, accompanied by their heavy and degraded looking squaws." The surrounding environment appeared equally untamed, he noted, featuring "more than a fair proportion of groggeries, and dance-houses; and [driving] a very lively business in the gambling way." Overall, this reporter was

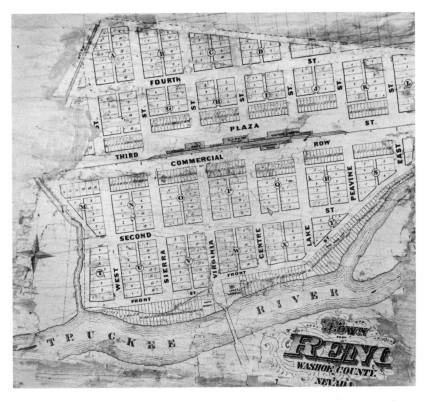

The original 1868 plat map of Reno identified 400 lots for sale by the Central Pacific Railroad, with narrower business lots running along either side of the railroad tracks. (Nevada Historical Society)

not impressed, writing dismissively, "It is one of those mushroom towns that seem to spring up in a single night, like Aladdin's Palace, and from the nature of its elements its sudden evanishment would be scarcely matter for surprise."[4]

In his description of Reno's coarse landscape and equally coarse inhabitants, the reporter likely would have confirmed his readers' expectations of one of the West's latest "mushroom towns"—that like the mining camps and other boomtowns that had been sprouting up throughout the region since the late 1840s, it was only "semi-civilized" and teeming with a rough assortment of transients and profiteers. To most outside eyes, Reno at its founding was less a place than a type made familiar through repeated accounts if not personal experience. By the 1860s, settlers had been making the trek to the Pacific coast via the Oregon and California trails for decades, and new factors like the Homestead Act were populating the West more quickly than ever. To a world-weary reporter from San Francisco (well established by then with a population approaching 150,000), it must have all seemed rather unremarkable.

If most Americans knew anything of Nevada at this point, it was that an immense silver lode had been discovered there a few years earlier, in an isolated mountain range east of the Sierras. Widely known as Washoe, after a local Indian tribe, the region encompassed the Comstock lode and its associated boomtowns of Virginia City and Gold Hill, which burst to life following the massive 1859 discovery. Approximately 10,000 prospective miners had flocked to the Comstock region from California between 1859 and 1860 alone.[5] Territorial status followed in 1861, and statehood three years later, bringing Nevada into the union as the "battle-born" state, largely to boost Lincoln's chances of reelection in 1864.

While little else in Nevada had received much attention by 1868, Reno's proximity to the Comstock lode did lend it a slightly higher profile than the other Nevada towns founded along the railroad line that year. To the public, Reno's status as the primary gateway to the "Big Bonanza" of the Comstock ensured its association with this colorful world, or perhaps more accurately, its absorption into it. Indeed, throughout the nineteenth century, Reno's reputation, or what there was of it, was inextricably linked to perceptions of Nevada's physical environment and mining industry. These opinions were disseminated through a number of nineteenth-century methods, including weekly and monthly magazines, newspapers, and travel guides directed toward both tourists and immigrants.

Since the onset of the California gold rush in 1849 through the 1860s, tales—factual, exaggerated, or even sometimes completely fabricated—about the Sierra region and its inhabitants had proliferated. Descriptions published in newspapers, in popular magazines like *Harper's Weekly,* and in any number of slender volumes promised inside information and eyewitness accounts of the ongoing activities there. Such publications had already endowed western mining towns in particular with a steadfastly unrefined image. As depicted in Bret Harte's short stories, such as "The Luck of Roaring Camp," published the year of Reno's founding, or in the detailed mining scenes of painter Charles Christian Nahl, the mining communities of the West were portrayed most commonly as volatile, male-dominated societies existing on the very fringes of society, governed by competitiveness and greed, although, as subsequent scholarship has revealed, the reality was far more complex.[6]

Associations of Reno with the rough mining societies of the Comstock appeared within months of its founding. A fictional piece appearing in the *Overland Monthly* in October 1868 presciently identified many of the factors governing Reno's emerging reputation in the nineteenth century—stereotypes that emerged independent of any firsthand knowledge of Reno's actual attributes or even its location. The *Overland Monthly* was itself new in 1868, having just commenced publication in San Francisco earlier that year under the editorial leadership of Bret Harte. In October, the magazine featured a story titled "The Gentleman from Reno," written by Noah Brooks, a journalist and future Lincoln biographer. In the story, a genteel physician's wife in San Francisco is visited unexpectedly one day by a "stout, dark-skinned man" in a new suit who claims to be from Reno and to know her husband, Henry, whom he familiarly calls "Hank." Fearful and suspicious, she judges the visitor to be both "rough" and "dreadful" while listening to his description of Reno, where, as he says, "we do things in a hurry, and you've got to look alive there, you jest bet yer life, now." She cringes as he brags about the previous week in his hometown, including "a right peart race, a ball at the El Dorado, four runaways, a tolerable lively shooting scrape, a new paper started, and four funerals!"

Such a description would no doubt prove jarring to a cultivated lady such as a physician's wife. Her reaction to the man's stated hometown, however, is curiously visceral, as though the name itself summoned up thoughts of criminals and con artists. This did not mean, however, that she had any idea where it was. Faced with such an uncouth figure, she muses,

> I had heard of such a place as Reno, but I had not been able to keep track of the new towns that spring up along the line of the Pacific railroad, and really could not say if Reno was in California or Utah. But here was a red-faced man, sun-burnt and with sticking-plaster on his lips, who said he was a citizen of Reno! Where was Reno? Was there any such place?

Her maid, Norah, is equally skeptical and equally lacking in the knowledge not only of Reno's location, but of its very existence: "'Rayno! Rayno!' she exclaimed indignantly, 'Does he think to play the likes of us for a Josh?

There's no such place as Rayno in all Californy, shure, unless its some dirthy hole that's lived in by the haythin Chinee.'" Shaped by their cosmopolitan California world, their personal geography does not even register Nevada as a potential home for any man, not even a rube like this one.

After reluctantly putting the man up for the night, the wife sends him on his way the following morning. However, when her husband returns and hears her breathless account, he smilingly informs her that he had indeed known the man "up in Brandy Canon in '50," and that "the gentleman from Reno *was* 'a gentleman, every inch of him—rough, to be sure, and as uncouth as any man gets to be knocking about the world and deprived of the society of women; but, nevertheless, a tender-hearted, whole-souled fellow.'" The Reno man, Bob Patchen, proves as much by sending the wife a delicate bouquet, which, she realizes, to her chagrin, "none but a refined taste could have selected."[7]

The response of the wife to the gentleman from Reno suggests that she possesses the same familiarity with, and disdain toward, western "types" as exhibited by the *San Francisco Times* reporter just a few months earlier. But in one important respect this story can be seen as a corrective to the earlier report; in fact, Brooks seems to conclude, things are not always what they seem. Indeed, Reno's peculiar situation with respect to Californian opinion seemed especially well encapsulated by the story. On the far reaches of a Californian's consciousness, the name resonated, but not necessarily in a good way. The story's actual impact on Reno's reputation was likely to be minimal—at the very most, bringing the town to the attention of readers who might otherwise have shared the characters' complete ignorance of it. That those same readers might themselves have been shamed into a greater appreciation of the town's potential for breeding gentlemen, however, is unlikely.

The general defensiveness of Reno's residents themselves over the next few years suggests that responses like that of the fictional physician's wife were fairly common. Throughout their town's infancy, Reno residents demonstrated a keen awareness of how outsiders perceived their community and, by extension, themselves. A typical local viewpoint was expressed by a writer for one of Reno's dailies, the *Nevada State Journal*, who announced in 1870, "We think this is a very quiet, nice place, notwithstanding some insist that it is the worst place on land, and that we are no more civilized than forty-niners or the aborigines."[8] A belief in the intrinsic connection between moral character and environment remained a fundamental

American premise in the nineteenth century; as J. Hector St. John de Crevecoeur had famously asserted in 1782, "Men are like plants; the goodness and flavour of the fruit proceeds from the peculiar soil and exposition in which they grow."[9] Such philosophies hardly worked in Nevada's favor. To a society increasingly familiar with Darwinian ideas about the formative influence of environment on development, descriptions of life on a barren and "frightful plain" would not tend to inspire thoughts of a cultivated population, or even of one likely to establish permanent roots.

In fact, more than anything else, it was the landscape that played the most dominant role in early perceptions of Nevada and, by extension, Reno. Nineteenth-century aesthetic standards did not accustom Americans to finding beauty in a high desert like the western Great Basin. To most eyes, it appeared unrelentingly bleak, forbidding, and exposed. As Nevada historian Wilbur Shepperson has written, "The aridity of the land and the absence of mementoes and man's handiwork deeply disturbed the middle-class visitors from east of the 100th meridian."[10] In a nation still espousing Thomas Jefferson's agrarian ideal—the perception that agricultural productivity was the defining point of a civilized society—barrenness was the most damaging stereotype imaginable. Immigrants in the nineteenth-century West sought both fertile land they could farm and beauty their eyes could register. To the majority of Americans, oceans of sagebrush hardly fit the bill. West of the so-called "Great American Desert," the name given to the Great Plains by mapmakers of the early 1800s, this was a region of which most national policy- and opinion-makers of the nineteenth century had only secondhand knowledge. To them, as well as to the thousands who had actually made the journey, Nevada was known above all as an obstacle. Migrants to the Pacific coast in the 1840s and 1850s had encountered the Great Basin on the last leg of their westward journey, leading to its "Book of Job" associations as a place of "thirst, sickness, despair."[11] It was the hardship of traversing the Great Basin, after all, along with the ill-fated choice of a "shortcut," that had delayed the Donner Party in 1846 so that by the time they arrived at the Sierra, the onset of an early blizzard season sealed their doom.

Impressions of Nevada's climate were not improved by the accounts of early Virginia City resident Samuel Clemens, otherwise known as Mark Twain, who accompanied his brother, Orion, to the territory in the early 1860s. His tales of life in Nevada's territorial period, published in 1872 in the volume *Roughing It*, both satirized and perpetuated many stereotypes of western figures and gave many Americans their first detailed descriptions of the region. Although Reno was not yet founded at the time of his stay, Twain expertly, albeit hyperbolically, conveyed how alien the region's climate appeared to an easterner. The most dramatic component, he explained, was the daily onset, in the summer months, of the "Washoe zephyr," a vigorous wind that "blows flimsy houses down, lifts shingle roofs occasionally, rolls up tin ones like sheet music, now and then blows a stage coach over and spills the passengers; and tradition says the reason there are so many bald people there, is, that the wind blows the hair off their heads while they are looking skyward after their hats." The description was satirical, but to those who had experienced it, not far from the truth.[12]

With the completion of the transcontinental railroad at Promontory Point, Utah, in 1869, growing numbers of cross-country travelers were now exposed to Reno, identified primarily as the transfer point to the Comstock. Most references to the town in the growing proliferation of travel and immigrant guides included brief lists of its businesses and amenities, but descriptions of any substantial length through the 1870s were dominated by comments about the weather. The wind, in particular, affected visitors traveling through, whether they disembarked or not, as alkali dust filtered through every available niche, coating the interiors of railroad cars and all who occupied them.[13] In her travel letters published in 1874, Chicagoan-turned-Californian author Caroline M. Churchill confirmed that any visitor to Reno experienced this phenomenon. "The Washoe zephyr," she wrote, "of which Mark Twain makes mention, keeps the streets with a fearfully swept appearance; these gusts of wind literally scattering the old boots and cast off paper collars to the four winds." Regular gales forced dust through Reno's unpaved streets and into buildings, clothing, and eyes already afflicted by the intense sunlight. The ultimate product, she reported, was "a dry, barren section of country, everything having a bleached appearance. The sidewalks are bleached and full of holes."[14]

By 1870, Reno's residential population barely surpassed 1,000, although its streets were filled with travelers conducting business with the area's livestock and mining interests. The town became the county seat in 1871, having wrested the title from nearby Washoe City, and its role as a junction expanded with the arrival of the regional Virginia & Truckee Railroad, which connected Reno to Virginia City by rail in 1872. By the end of the year, two freight trains and one passenger train left Reno daily for Virginia City, a journey of just over three hours each way. Churchill confirmed this

Reno's Virginia Street, seen here in 1882, remained for years a dusty wind-blown stretch with sidewalks that appeared "bleached and full of holes," according to early visitor Caroline M. Churchill. (Nevada Historical Society)

progress, too, stating "Reno forms quite a little metropolis for those towns and villages located some distance from the railroad. Fifteen or twenty 'prairie schooners' set sail each day for these various points, all loaded with some kind of merchandise."[15]

Still, the reputation of the entire state remained troubled. The completion of the railroad may have enabled more people to visit Nevada, but at the same time this also allowed them to compare the state more easily and directly to its neighbors. And in many minds, the contrast served only to accentuate the state's inferiority to them. Although just 12 miles to the west, California was a world away in national stature, having by the mid-nineteenth century achieved international acclaim as "El Dorado" or "Pacific Arcadia," a lush and blooming promised land. Utah had become its own promised land for the followers of the Church of Jesus Christ of Latter-Day Saints, who had irrigated the entire Salt Lake Valley in their determined quest to "make the desert bloom." Nevada was, accordingly, "East of Eden, West of Zion," a "vacuum between societies."[16] In a May 1869 article on how to travel on the new Pacific Railroad, the *Atlantic Monthly* advised travelers to cross the "cheerless and dreary" expanse of Nevada "as speedily as possible." In his 1883 account of travels across the country, British travel writer Phil Robinson candidly observed, "Nevada . . . lies under the disadvantage of having on one side of it the finest portion of California, on the other the finest portion of Utah, and sandwiched between two such Beauties, such a Beast naturally looks its worst."[17]

And so in its earliest years, Reno's reputation was subsumed by that of greater Nevada, with its primary industry of mining, its forbiddingly austere landscape, and its seeming inferiority to the abundance of its more fortunate neighbors. Aside from its profitable mining districts, there was little reason to take much notice of it, nothing particularly striking about it one way or another. This state of affairs might have proceeded indefinitely, as Reno grew into an ever more stable community, bolstered by the Comstock's perpetual need for supplies. But this was not to be. Beginning in the late 1870s, the state's fortunes took a dramatic turn, eventually sending Nevada's reputation into a nose-dive and forcing the residents of Reno to take more decisive action to distinguish their town from the larger whole.

The shift began as yet another economic slowdown, the likes of which the state's mining industry had suffered before. Beginning in the late 1870s, the Comstock mining district commenced a steady decline, ultimately leading to a final "borrasca," or bust, that sent the entire state into a severe economic depression for the remainder of the century. Many in the mining industry clung to hopes for the Comstock's revival, but substantial new veins of silver or gold failed to materialize, and the exodus of population began almost immediately. Earlier mining magnates like William Sharon, James Fair, and John Mackay had never settled in Nevada to begin with, instead toting their accumulated riches elsewhere, primarily to San Francisco, where these so-called "carpetbagger rich" constructed mansions, luxury hotels, and financial empires. The working miners, of course, like the storekeepers and saloonkeepers who had catered to them, quickly departed for more profitable ventures.[18] This was a striking, and all too literal, reversal of fortune for a state identified almost exclusively with its mines. At its peak, Virginia City had reached a population of approximately 25,000. Absent its primary purpose for existence, the formerly booming town disincorporated in 1881, and between 1880 and 1900 the population of Storey County, where Virginia City was located, plummeted from more than 16,000 to just 3,560. The population of the entire state similarly dropped from 62,266 in 1880 to 45,765 by 1890, making little gains through the rest of the century.[19]

As awareness of the situation spread quickly across the nation, opinions of Nevada changed from dismissive to downright hostile. The shrinking of an already sparse population prompted many to saddle Nevada with the derisive term "rotten borough," a phrase originating with English election districts that retained equal representation in Parliament following significant losses in population. To many in the political world, Nevada's shrinking populace resulted in an overrepresentation (even at two) in the U.S. Senate. And a reputation for rampant political corruption, in many ways deserved, made things even worse. Some commentators went so far as to assert that the federal government had erred in admitting Nevada into the Union in the first place. This was not an entirely new viewpoint; Nevada's rapid progress from territory to state had gained public support primarily for the riches its mines were thought to bring to the nation's coffers. Now everything had changed. The impression that Nevada had become literally worthless once stripped of its profitable mineral resources was echoed by many pundits, especially from the East, over the next several years. The *Chicago Tribune* asserted that Nevada was "a decaying State" whose "resources are exhausted." Tellingly, and with a wry defensiveness typical of the state's boosters, the Nevadan conveying this criticism commented, "Chicago papers usually display more intelligence."[20]

But Chicago's journalists were not alone. As a *New York Times* reporter predicted in 1878, "Nevada can have no population but the miners—the men who actually go down into the earth to bring up ores, and those who superintend their work and handle the product above ground." Nevada's value, they implied, had always been hidden deep below the surface, out of sight, and once depleted, left nothing but a worthless, crusty outer shell. Praising the then-territory of Utah for having "princely resources in comparison with Nevada," the *Times* reporter suggested a merger of the two, but admitted, "Possibly the consent of Nevada could not be secured, but it might be tried. In the end the union would be vastly beneficial to both." Three years later, another *Times* correspondent suggested that "the best thing that could be done would be to abolish the State and either return to a Territorial form of government or attach the Territory to California."[21] Not surprisingly, neither solution appealed to most of Nevada's residents.

Most residents of both of Nevada's neighbors remained unconvinced as well. In 1889, the *Salt Lake Herald* squelched any talk of annexation in a sympathetic but firm editorial that said of Nevada, "It is a matter for regret that she is so rapidly going to her grave, but we know of no rule of equity or charity which would suggest that Utah should be weighted down in order that the rotten borough may avoid death." The writer then attempted to volley the unfortunate state back in the other direction: "As California owns them, and also owns whatever is of value in the State, why not go to California for succor and ask to be attached to the great Commonwealth that is able to take care of them?"[22] This was also unlikely to occur. The idea of attaching Nevada to one or the other of its neighbors continued for decades but did not gain any greater traction through the years. Without the prospect of abundant riches, there was little incentive for its neighbors to redraw their boundaries, much less any provision in the U.S. Constitution for them to do so.

For better or worse, Nevada would be left to resurrect its own economy—and its reputation—but precisely how to accomplish this was unclear. Associations with mining had perpetuated many negative stereotypes of Nevada during the Comstock era, but to be considered completely worthless in the post-Comstock era was even worse, especially when new residents were needed to repopulate the state for purposes of political representation and tax revenue. Disdain for Nevada's arid climate and austere landscapes constituted the largest obstacle to generating positive views of Nevada's communities and, most importantly, attracting new settlers to them in this era. One of the most desirable demographics to attract was the farmer; miners might be transient but farmers were permanent, and as everyone knew, the most valued resource for prospective settlers of the West was land. Even before the discovery of the Comstock lode, farming communities had sprung up in western Nevada near the rivers and the foothills of the Sierra's eastern slopes. However, after the demise of the Comstock, and its built-in market for livestock and produce, the financial prospects of Nevada's agricultural industry admittedly appeared bleak.

Accordingly, the state's residents set out to assert the fruitfulness, aesthetic appeal, and limitless economic potential of Nevada's environment in the face of widespread opinion that it possessed none of these traits. Even as late as 1893, a guidebook published in Boston and promising "A Pictorial and Descriptive History of Our Country's Scenic Marvels" apparently did not include Nevada in its title category, unsympathetically describing the entire state as "the very nakedness of bleak desolation [which] stretches its cursed length through a distance of 600 miles."[23] Faced with such denigration, boosters in Nevada from the 1880s onward operated from a position of heightened defensiveness. The attempt to generate settlement along with sympathy was formalized with the creation of a State Bureau of Immigration in 1887. In an 88-page booklet published by the bureau in 1894, its editors lamented that Nevada "has long been the subject of adverse comment and hateful criticism" and its residents "have submitted with fortitude to the innuendoes showered upon us, scarcely raising a voice or touching a pen to change public sentiment." Like British critic Phil Robinson before them, they pointed out the handicap of comparison, protesting, "If Missouri or Virginia were located where Nevada is, with all their richness, they would find visitors making unfavorable comparisons, and it cannot be wondered at that Nevada has but few who understand or sympathize with her." They went on to laud Nevada's extensive pasturelands and fertile fields to "capitalists and homeseekers" across America.[24]

It was clear that reversing impressions of Nevada's barrenness would be no easy task, as opinions to the contrary were deep-set. Assuming responsibility for having identified the state so closely with mining in the first place, "one of the foremost men in Reno" told a reporter for the *San Francisco Call*, "We made a mistake thirty years ago when we insisted upon being known as producers of silver alone." Now, he argued, "we might more properly be called a cattle State, or a sheep State, or a dairy State, or a farming State than a silver State."[25]

In order to publicize these gains, concerned citizens formed Nevada's first Board of Trade, in 1889. That year, they endorsed a booklet for potential emigrants to Nevada, published by the *Reno Evening Gazette*. In it, they asserted, quite accurately, "Our lately barren hills and bench lands, hitherto regarded (often by our own people) as only good for stock ranges, are now being cultivated and covered with waving grain, flourishing orchards and vineyards." The potatoes grown by Irish immigrants became the area's best cash crop after alfalfa, exported in large quantities to northern California until Idaho came to dominate the trade after 1900. The state Bureau of Immigration was quick to promote the bounty of produce grown in Nevada; some Chinese and Italian farmers were said to experiment with "garden crops" including "cabbage, turnips, carrots, parsnips, beets, celery, in fact, the entire catalogue of garden vegetables" nearer the river. Strawberries grew well in greenhouses and fields, and even fruit trees flourished toward the foothills.[26]

In addition to such defensive rhetoric, Nevadans went on the offensive, parading their home-grown produce out of state at every opportunity. World's Fairs presented a particularly rich opportunity to reach a wide audience. Nevada contributed a number of exhibits to the famed Chicago World's Columbian Exposition of 1893. Alongside the expected exhibits featuring mined minerals and the hip bone of a giant mastodon, an agricultural booth overflowed with Nevada fruits and vegetables. An accompanying booklet drew attention to the impressive sight, raving, "Nevada's exhibit of her resources at the World's Fair is a surprise to all unacquainted with her resources."[27]

Unfortunately such exhibits were not always successful in producing the desired response. State boosters carefully prepared a similar exhibit for San Francisco's Midwinter International Exposition, held in Golden Gate Park in 1894. Nevada had the only state building on the site, a two-story structure with a rooftop café and a main floor brimming with agricultural products including fifty-eight varieties of apples, an array of potatoes, preserved fruits, alfalfa hay, honey, and flour from a Reno mill. After visiting the Nevada exhibits, a writer for the *Overland Monthly* seemed to confirm the exhibit's success, writing that although "To the public at large the name of Nevada brings to mind two things, and only two things,—sage brush desert and deep silver mines. . . . there is another Nevada, young, vigorous, growing." Regrettably, as the writer also noted, many visitors mistook the Nevada exhibit for a California exhibit—an honest mistake, it seemed, as "this lower floor in the Nevada Building is a revelation so unexpected that many people fail to apprehend it; for the attendant mournfully told me of many visitors that departed from the building saying, 'Pretty good for Nevada County!'"—a county that was, alas, located in California. Clearly Nevada's promoters had their work cut out for them.[28]

With the reputation of greater Nevada still so problematic, residents of Reno found it more critical than ever to distance their community from the rest of the state. It took the Comstock's decline for residents of Reno to become aware of what a liability an existing reputation could be and to recognize the importance of countering it with energetic promotion. Reno's fledgling business community in particular hoped to create new associations for their town, or risk suffering from a continued guilt-by-association. In just the second decade of its existence, then, efforts were under way to try, through whatever means possible, to create an identity for Reno distinct from that of Nevada.

These efforts were aided by the fact that, in many ways, Reno's environment, both physical and social, truly was different from much of the state. Its population growth bucked the statewide trend downward, albeit barely, at first gaining fewer than 300 residents between 1870 and 1880, but then picking up again over the next ten years, growing from 1,302 to just over 3,500 by 1890. By 1900 it would grow to just 4,500, but at least it was not in decline, like Virginia City and Carson City, which became the nation's smallest state capital in 1900, with only 2,100 citizens. With Virginia City's population shrinking from 8,511 in 1890 to just 2,695 in 1900, Reno ascended to the status of the state's largest town. As if to demonstrate the end of the Comstock era, the junction literally shifted its attention away from Virginia City in late December 1880, as construction began on the Reno hub of the Nevada-California-Oregon (then simply the Nevada & Oregon) Railroad, which connected the town to the productive mining, cattle, timber, and agricultural districts to the north.[29]

Some publications did begin to notice Reno's departure from the Nevada norm, with its many thriving businesses, the continued patronage of the transcontinental railroad, and an established residential and ranching community. In 1882, *McKenney's Business Directory,* published in Sacramento, gave Reno a much-needed boost by asserting that "no town in the State enjoys such a steady growth, or presents a more substantial and beautiful appearance to-day, architecturally." The surrounding environment boasted some natural advantages as well. Most of Nevada may have appeared brown and barren, but Reno, as its residents clarified to anyone who would listen, was located on the far western edge of the Great Basin, in the foothills of the impressive Sierra range. Quick to make this distinction were local reporters like one who wrote in 1879, "The hills east of the valley are like dozens of other ranges between Cheyenne and Reno, but the great western boundary rises in unapproachable majesty from the banks of the river to banks of everlasting snow above." At an elevation of 4,400 feet above sea level, Reno was just miles from those forested slopes and benefited from a generally mild climate, with moderate snow in the winters and sunshine year-round.[30]

As if in sharp rebuke to charges of desertlike barrenness, the Truckee River ran through the middle of Reno, providing enough water to irrigate hundreds of acres to the north and south. Crop production throughout the valley had skyrocketed thanks to a complex network of ditches established primarily in the 1860s and 1870s. Because of irrigation, the number of farms in Washoe County, in which the fertile lands stretched from just north of Reno south through the productive Washoe Valley, increased from 76 in 1870 to 235 in 1890, most comprising between 100 and 500 acres. Indeed, agriculture was the leading industry of Washoe County through this period, with alfalfa, used to feed the abundant number of livestock on area ranches, the leading crop. The number of those livestock, introduced to the area to support the Comstock miners, also increased dramatically in the later decades of the century, growing from just over 2,000 milk cows and other cattle in 1870 to nearly 30,000 twenty years later.[31]

As one Nevadan bragged to the *San Francisco Call* in 1898, "Reno is our natural metropolis," a phrase that surely represented yet another instance of exaggeration—"metropolis" was a term created by industrial urbanization and implied a conquered hinterland—and yet it was true that Reno had emerged as the focal point of the surrounding area, if not the state.[32] It was now not only the county seat, but the population center for a number of small surrounding communities including Huffaker's Station and Glendale. Like Reno, many a western town was labeled "a metropolis in miniature," and boosters of "mushrooming" railroad towns invariably pronounced themselves the inevitable regional "metropolis."[33] While the term was a bit disingenuous, the suggestion that its progress favored Reno's continuing dominance over the state did seem accurate to those who witnessed the diverse industries of the entire valley.

In their attempt to draw attention to these features, Reno's residents were not unlike the inhabitants of many other western towns, whose promoters swelled with unbridled optimism, inflated rhetoric, and often-exaggerated claims of climatic and economic superiority. To boost, after all, is not just to support, but to raise something higher than it is naturally capable of reaching, often straddling a fine line between description and deception. Those charged with promoting nineteenth-century western towns, no matter how obscure or unremarkable, regularly presented their communities as worthy of not just regional, but national attention. In this way, as David Wrobel has said, they functioned as "optimistic fortunetellers who told present and prospective residents what they wanted and needed to hear about western places." And Reno's location on the transcontinental railroad line had long given its boosters aspirations, if not outright delusions, of grandeur, hoping despite the Comstock's decline to imitate the size and independence of "instant cities" like San Francisco, Denver, or Salt Lake City.[34]

As the fundamental reason for Reno's existence, the railroad remained a major advantage to the area, but it was accompanied by some continuing problems. San Francisco increasingly attracted large numbers of visitors, most arriving via the Overland Limited, which passed directly through

Reno. Many individuals and families were also heading that direction to settle elsewhere in California. As a local paper noted in 1887, "We should keep up with other sections now making great efforts to attract the attention of home-seekers their way. Hundreds are passing through Reno daily for California." However, as the 1889 immigrant guide lamented, "The tourist or emigrant in passing through Nevada along the line of the Central Pacific Railroad only sees from the car window a desert waste and naturally forms his opinion from that vision that Nevada is a state only fit for lizards and blizzards to find comfort in, although he may have heard that the State has produced millions on millions in silver and gold."[35]

This tunnel vision presented a problem to Reno in particular, where the most immediate obstacle to changing travelers' impressions of the town was the limited vantage point available to railroad travelers from the tracks. A passing railroad traveler stopping briefly at the station in Reno would see a large rail yard, surrounded by corrals, warehouses, and the crowded storefronts, saloons, and hotels of Commercial Row. Even the route into and out of town revealed little of the surrounding fields and pastures, which lay mostly south of town.[36] If railroad passengers could be persuaded to spend some time in and around Reno, its residents reasoned, rather than simply passing through the center of it, they might gain a better impression of what the area had to offer. As the local *Nevada State Journal* stated, "It requires side excursions along the base of the Sierras to witness the grandeur of our scenic wealth." Observers were rewarded for venturing further away, according to a *San Francisco Call* reporter who confirmed, "If all you know of Nevada has been learned from a car window, it will surprise you to hear of the beauty and productiveness of the Truckee Valley, in whose heart the city of Reno is located."[37]

For those travelers who could not manage a side excursion, Reno's residents brought the fields to them in the form of exhibits presented in a space provided by the Southern Pacific railroad just across the street from the depot. After 1900, members of the newly-formed Chamber of Commerce erected a building there, where they continued the focus on the visual display of Nevada's resources that had been pursued at the various world's fairs. Its exhibits included mineral samples from each Nevada county, along with specimens of fruits and vegetables arranged on stands; apples, potatoes, and onions displayed in large preserving jars; and fresh flowers "in order that eastern visitors who pass through on the trains may see that Nevada can raise beautiful flowers as well as California."[38]

In addition to potential immigrants, this constant stream of travelers included another valuable demographic. In ever-increasing numbers, many of the railroad passengers breezing through town were traveling not for purposes of settlement, but for leisure. Many American tourists of the late nineteenth century were beginning to explore the United States to complement, if not entirely to replace, the so-called "grand tours" of Europe that had been popular among the American elite for decades. By the 1870s, tourism was emerging as a viable economic pursuit out west, providing an entirely new opportunity for the towns along the railroad line and throughout the region and prompting many of them to incorporate tourist-oriented pitches into their early promotional plans. California's promoters urged travelers to visit "America's Mediterranean Shores," with the state's evocation of exotic Spanish architecture and temperate climate. A number of California resorts soon drew travelers through Nevada, including San Francisco's Palace Hotel, built in 1875, and San Diego's 1888 Hotel del Coronado, which capitalized on their scenic surroundings to pull in an elite class of leisure travelers. By the end of the century, western cities were appearing on many tourist itineraries.[39]

Reno often appeared there as well, albeit almost exclusively as a brief stop along the way. Still, locals were determined to take advantage of the opportunity this provided, regularly noting the departures of the eastern elite for grand excursions out west and publicizing in the local papers the dates when they were expected to pass through town. The forty-six-day itinerary for one such group, departing in palace cars from New York in April 1882, included two days in St. Louis, a week in Colorado, two days "among the Mormons in Salt Lake City," a week in Yosemite, ten days in San Francisco, and visits to Monterey, the geysers, the giant redwoods (referred to as "the Big Trees"), and Lake Tahoe. As this schedule indicates, westbound tourists of the area were primarily in pursuit of sublime and awe-inspiring natural vistas or unusual cultural phenomena. Federal recognition of natural treasures like Yosemite's lush valley, waterfalls, soaring snow-capped peaks, and meadows—institutionalized in the Yosemite Act of 1864—or the crowning of Yellowstone as a national park in 1872, both steered and sanctioned such choices. Travelers swooned at the monumental grandeur of soaring peaks, curious geysers, and rushing waterfalls.[40]

Knowing full well that Nevada's landscape was unlikely to evoke similar raptures, the obvious answer for Reno's promoters was to hitch their wagon to another star. In the effort to forge new mental associations for

Reno, nature provided an invaluable asset in the form of nearby Lake Tahoe, a marvel recognized by the 1870s as one of America's great scenic wonders and described by Mark Twain as "the fairest picture the whole earth affords." Although partially shared by California, the pristine fresh-water lake became Nevada's most popular tourist destination through the nineteenth century, and it lay just over the mountains from Reno, approximately 40 miles to the southwest. The tourist industry was developing there in full force. By the late 1870s, sightseers could set sail across the lake on a number of steamers, including the *Niagara,* the *Meteor,* the *Truckee,* and the *Governor Stanford.* Over the next few decades, hiking, or "alpine climbing," also gained in popularity, and a growing number of hotels on the lake's shores offered lodging for the well-to-do.[41]

Linking Reno to Lake Tahoe opened up several economic opportunities, as Reno became a popular staging area for trips to the lake and the surrounding mountains. Hank Monk, the famous stagecoach driver immortalized by Twain in *Roughing It* for taking publisher Horace Greeley on the ride of his life, ran a six-horse coach daily from Carson City to Glenbrook, at Lake Tahoe. Advertising Reno as "the Place to Start for Lake Tahoe and Virginia City," his stage, which also carried the U.S. mail, connected at Glenbrook to a steamer that sailed the lake. By the early 1880s, a number of promoters offered round-trip excursions that set out by train from Reno to Truckee, linking there to stages bound for Tahoe City, on the lakeshore. Locals labored to construct a road just south of Reno over the Mt. Rose summit to create an even shorter route to the shores of Lake Tahoe. At the same time, travelers began to take the V&T Railroad southward from Reno to meet the Hawthorne stage, which then transported travelers to the mining town of Bodie, the peculiar Mono Lake, and onward to the awe-inspiring Yosemite valley.[42]

As the tourist industry matured, some travelers' guides began to acknowledge Reno as not just a junction, but a perfectly pleasant stopping place. Popular guidebooks like *Crofutt's New Overland Tourist and Pacific Coast Guide* at least attested to the town's recent improvements, drawing attention to Reno's five churches, two banks, courthouse, fire department, and two newspapers, the *Reno Evening Gazette* and *Nevada State Journal,* and especially its "very fine race track" and its "principal hotel," the Lake House.[43]

Reno's hotel proprietors, in particular, stood to profit from this new publicity. The town featured a number of lodging choices along Commer-

Just south of the Truckee River stood two of Reno's earliest landmarks: the Washoe County Courthouse, completed in 1873, and Myron Lake's newly improved inn, the Lake House. (Nevada Historical Society)

cial Row and nearby streets, some far more respectable than others. The Lake House, the original inn owned by Myron C. Lake, enjoyed the most scenic location, on the south bank of the Truckee River. After Lake's death in 1884, his stepdaughter's husband, William Thompson, gained ownership of the inn, and by 1888, had thoroughly renovated the structure, improved the grounds, and renamed it the Riverside Hotel. After a third story was added to the west wing in summer 1889, the *Reno Evening Gazette* named it "the finest family resort this side of the mountains," where patrons were encouraged to fish for trout just outside its doors. The Riverside became renowned for its luxurious touches; a free coach met all arriving passenger trains in order to transport guests from the station to the hotel, which, although just three blocks south of the tracks, was considered to be removed from the town's bustle. By 1896, new proprietor, H. J. Gosse, was justified in advertising the Riverside Hotel as "a popular stopping place for tourists."[44]

Reno's promoters were less successful in their attempts to establish the town as a tourist destination in itself. With such competition as Lake Tahoe and Yosemite, this would require more than a handful of attractive buildings, thriving farms, and some decent hotels. A successful tourist destination needed to offer something uniquely appealing. From the 1890s through the next several decades, a number of Reno promoters attempted to jump on a time-tested tourist bandwagon: the health resort. This was a common strategy for western towns from California to New Mexico situated in dry climates or possessing natural hot or mineral springs. Wealthy invalids had rushed to western resorts throughout Colorado, Wyoming, and Idaho in the 1870s and 1880s, seeking cures for tuberculosis and other complaints.[45]

Aspiring to similar success, Reno's boosters promoted the benefits of their climate and springs in combating an array of complaints including consumption, asthma, "phthisis" (pulmonary tuberculosis), bronchitis, rheumatism, skin disease, diphtheria, and bowel troubles. Some of the claims were, not surprisingly, hyperbolic. In 1889, C. C. Warner wrote, "No one can have asthma in Nevada. If people in the East only knew of our climate they would prefer it to Southern California." In 1891, William Thompson convinced *Journal* publisher C. C. Powning to promote the resort idea, and under the name of the newly formed Western Nevada Improvement Association, they published an attractive 34-page promotional brochure touting Reno as "Nature's Sanitarium" and "The Wonderland of the West." As the publication claimed, "Western Nevada has . . . that to offer the invalid, as an inducement to come within her borders, which is of greater value than were the gold and silver of her mines to the fortune seeker of past years, namely: the precious blessing of health." Other respectable names vouched for the superiority of Reno's "pure, dry atmosphere" in the fight against pulmonary disease. Writing in the local paper, Dr. H. Bergstein called Nevada "a veritable paradise for invalids," thanks to its dry air, moderate temperatures, and abundant ozone, as well as thermal mineral springs.[46]

As a sanitarium, however, Reno was a little late in its pursuit of those suffering, quite literally, from conspicuous consumption. By the turn of the century, communicable disease had begun to lose its social cachet, as standards of beauty no longer favored a consumptive pallor, and physicians began to advise against travel for the seriously ill. More successful was the more democratic promotion of the region's dry air and natural hot springs, so restorative for a host of afflictions. Two hot springs located within 12 miles of town became fairly popular: Steamboat Springs, 12 miles to the south of Reno, was open in the early 1860s and was visited by Mark Twain in 1863. Laughton's Springs was located 5 miles to the west.

These two "boiling cauldrons" were said to "contain all the properties in solution that have been found most efficacious in restoring rheumatic patients to their wonted health, and rival in virtue the far famed Hot Springs of Arkansas." Both would be fairly successful in the years to come as side excursions, but not primary tourist destinations in and of themselves.[47]

Reno may not yet have established much of a tourist trade, but the town was making some clear moves toward a stable future, the first step in combating perceptions of decline. Perhaps its most important accomplishment was the relocation in 1885 of the University of Nevada to Reno from far-flung Elko, the eastern Nevada town where it had been founded in 1874. Like other public institutions throughout the country, the university was a legacy of the federal Morrill Land Grant Act of 1862, which spurred the establishment of colleges devoted to instruction in agriculture and the mechanic arts. As Nevadans were quick to point out, the founding of a state university placed Nevada on a par with its western neighbor, where the University of California was formally established in Oakland (later moved to Berkeley) in 1868. The relocation of Nevada's institution to Reno, urged by residents for a decade, prompted many local predictions of cultural elevation for the community. An editorial in the *Reno Evening Gazette* pronounced the move "another victory for Reno," envisioning that its successful operation, along with that of two existing private academies, would make the town "the greatest educational center of the State."[48]

The university opened on a very modest scale, with just two instructors and, for years, a single building, constructed on ten acres of land purchased by the regents on the northern hillside. Morrill Hall, a brick French Second Empire–style building, opened in 1886, and the University of Nevada offered its first college-level instruction the following year. By 1889, the university had founded a Normal School for teachers, a Commercial Department, and Schools of Mining and Agriculture and enrolled over 100 students instructed by 10 faculty members. By 1900, the campus featured eleven buildings that overlooked the town, and, in the eyes of optimistic boosters, cast their influence as well as their shadows over it, with the imposing architecture of the new university buildings reflecting this civilizing impulse.[49]

Reno's standing rose even more with another addition to the landscape. In May 1889, the *Gazette* reported the arrival of Francis G. Newlands and revealed his plans to construct a "fine residence" on a bluff high above the south bank of the Truckee River. An architect and "New York landscape

Entrance to U. of N., Reno, Nev.

Just a few blocks north of Reno's business district, the main entrance to the University of Nevada offered a fine view of the campus's first building, Morrill Hall, in a picture postcard ca. 1903. (Special Collections Department, University of Nevada–Reno Library)

gardener" were already hard at work on plans of the house and grounds. As the article asserted, "Mr. Newlands will be a very valuable acquisition to Reno, as he is a man of wealth and influence and has come to stay." The words "valuable acquisition" could be taken quite literally. By the time of his arrival in Reno, Francis G. Newlands was already a nationally known figure. Born in Mississippi and educated at Yale, he had entered San Francisco society in 1870 after briefly practicing law in Washington, D.C. But it was his 1874 marriage to Clara Sharon, daughter of Comstock millionaire William Sharon, that brought him to national attention. Since striking it rich on the Comstock, "robber baron" Sharon had become one of the wealthiest men in the West, run the Bank of California, and even served for a term as a U.S. senator from Nevada without ever establishing permanent residency in the state. Newlands's wedding to Clara at the Sharon family mansion in San Francisco had been widely reported from coast to coast as the most extravagant event ever to take place in California.[50]

Following his marriage, Newlands managed many of his father-in-law's investments and businesses, including the Virginia & Truckee Railroad, which brought him periodically to Nevada. He also received mentions in the prominent national coverage of his father-in-law's romantic misadventures following the death of Sharon's wife in 1875, a testament to the rising level of interest in the romantic and economic escapades of the wealthy during the Gilded Age. After Clara and her father both died, in the early 1880s, Newlands ran an unsuccessful campaign for the U.S. Senate in California. Hoping for a fresh start, Newlands moved briefly to New York and then made the move to Nevada, ostensibly, many thought, to further his political career.[51]

Modest Reno might seem an odd choice for a man of such social stature, and yet the decision was a calculated one. After first considering Carson City, the expected destination for an aspiring politico, Newlands astutely noted the cultural progress of Reno, particularly the new university. Upon his arrival, Newlands claimed, "I have come here to stay and not for a political purpose. I find the Reno climate superior to any other; it's a nice town and a nice place to live, and there is no politics in it." With him were his three daughters and second wife, Edith McCallister, the daughter of another prominent San Francisco family.[52]

Newlands's choice of a homesite was also surprising but ultimately calculated: fifteen acres high on a brushy bluff formerly known as "Rattlesnake Point" overlooking the entire town of Reno. He was no stranger to real estate development, having previously devoted his energies to civic improvements and city planning in San Francisco, which he had hoped to transform into "the Paris of America." There, he had advocated the construction of sewer systems and new streets, boulevards, and parks as well as public funding for kindergartens. The location of his new home in Reno pioneered the establishment of the city's most elite residential district, as Newlands literally elevated the town's social aspirations, as well as its image. The stately two-and-a-half-story shingle-style, Queen Anne–influenced mansion became an instant landmark, and photographs of the home appeared in promotional materials for Reno well into the next century.[53]

Newlands's presence alone earned Reno national attention. And happily for the town, just as a convert can become the most fervent of proselytizers, Newlands became one of Reno's, and Nevada's, most avid boosters. Central to his stated mission was improving the reputation of his adopted city and state. His clear vision for Nevada's future, both in agricultural and civic terms, would have an enormous impact on the direction that Reno, and its boosters, would take. In recognition of his attempt to transform

Nevada into his vision of a "modern commonwealth," many Nevada historians have referred to the following decades as the "Newlands Era." Just over two decades old at his arrival, Reno was a town in the bud. But Newlands voiced the potential for much more, taking on Nevada as a project that he could help to shape and modernize.[54]

He got to work immediately, helping to organize the Reno Water, Land and Lights Company in 1889 and spreading word of Nevada's economic diversification throughout the country. He also had a hand in organizing the state's Board of Trade that year. At a Silver Party Convention in St. Louis in December, Newlands passionately defended the state against the "rotten borough" charge, forcefully arguing, "Nevada is not dead. She has within her the energies of a new life. When the low price of silver caused the closing of her mines, her industrious, restless, energetic people turned their attention to other enterprises."[55]

Newlands's civic-minded visions were shared by other leaders including University of Nevada president Joseph E. Stubbs, who served from 1894 to 1914. Newlands also became very close with Robert L. Fulton, publisher of the *Reno Evening Gazette*, which, by 1891, was fervently praising his work to improve the banks and open walks and drives alongside the river, as well as the construction of a street railway and general beautification of the town. Newlands's assistance in forming the Board of Trade was said to have "done much to advertise our advantages to the world and has changed the sentiment of the older States toward us," as the *Gazette* asserted that "a man of his social position and talent, his energy, wealth, and wit, is a valuable friend, and his work will begin to tell if kept up." Reno may not have produced Newlands, but they were determined to keep him.[56]

This desire intensified as his political stock began to rise. Despite Newlands's initial demurrals, it was unquestionably political aspirations that had brought him to Nevada. Wealthy and ambitious, and having inherited control of massive property holdings in the state, the eloquent and sophisticated Newlands entered Nevada politics with the benefit of national recognition and enormous financial resources. Taken under the wing of Nevada's U.S. senator William M. Stewart, he soon became involved in the Silver Party, and as early as 1890, speculation was on the rise that he was planning a run for the Senate. He ran successfully for the U.S. House of Representatives in 1892, and was elected again to the House in 1896. Elected to the U.S. Senate in 1903, he served in that capacity until his death in 1917.

At a time when Nevada was still judged by appearances, it was to the state's advantage that Newlands did not look like a Nevadan, or at least the way most expected a Nevadan to look. With his English-tailored checkered suits, he did not truly fit in, and although many longtime residents questioned his motives (and openly mocked his clothing), his visibility was hard to fault. He did not act like a typical Nevadan, either. National papers avidly followed Newlands's trips to Europe with his wife, and later, his family's involvement in the elite social circles of Washington, where they resided much of the year, and where his daughters made their debuts into society. By the mid-1890s, the Newlands owned a large home in Chevy Chase, Maryland, where they were reported to "live the life of landed proprietors in their big house."[57]

The style and social standing of the Newlands family reflected well on Reno's culture; however, it was the massive federal projects Newlands championed that made the most substantial impact on northern Nevada. Writing for *The Independent* in 1901, Newlands asserted that "the hostile attitude of the Eastern people and the Eastern press toward Nevada is not justified by the facts" and voiced his belief that "With the help of wise governmental action and a liberal railroad policy, Nevada will be, at some time in the future, the home of millions of people." In mentioning this "wise governmental action," he had something specific in mind. Large-scale irrigation was something Robert Fulton had been encouraging for years, knowing that it had the potential for transforming both Nevada's landscape and outside opinions of it. Aligning himself with advocates of reclamation, including Fulton and Senator Stewart, Newlands headed up the state's delegation to the first National Irrigation Congress in 1891. As a congressman, Newlands spearheaded the passage of the federal Reclamation Act of 1902, named after him and identified by some as the most important single piece of legislation in the history of the West.[58]

Backed by federal support, the Newlands Project became the first project of the U.S. Reclamation Service, a plan initially envisioned to irrigate approximately 450,000 acres of desert lands in the Truckee River and Carson River Basins through massive, federally sponsored irrigation projects. Although it ultimately irrigated only 87,500 acres, the project did permanently transform the region's landscape, creating the towns of Fernley and Fallon, around which fields of alfalfa, dairy farms, and diverse crops of fruits and vegetables quickly appeared. Thanks to this development, Nevada's agricultural resources as a whole were actually improving through physical transformation of the landscape into a form more generally recognizable as a fertile garden.[59]

Newlands's vision for an irrigated West was corroborated by William E. Smythe, whose book *The Conquest of Arid America,* published in 1900, offered a counter argument to Frederick Jackson Turner's melancholy assessment of the end of the frontier era in 1893. Instead, Smythe suggested that the new century would be the age of the West and that federally sponsored irrigation would make it happen. "No other State has been so bitterly derided as Nevada," Smythe acknowledged, countering, "Potentially, Nevada is one of the greatest States in the Union." Citing a state commission report issued under the auspices of the Irrigation Congress in 1893, he stated "at least six million acres of rich soil could be irrigated" and concluded "it is a climate fit to breed a robust and vigorous race." The reclamation projects went on to receive even more positive press in the first decade of the new century, from regional publications like *Sunset,* the *Overland Monthly,* the *Californian,* and *Land of Sunshine,* as well as national magazines including *Collier's, Harper's Weekly,* and *Leslie's Weekly.*[60]

Those who boasted of Nevada's potential soon struck another unexpected jackpot. After the state's boosters had expended so much effort in disassociating Nevada from mining, precious metals were discovered in the south-central Nevada mining districts of Tonopah and Goldfield, in 1900 and 1902, respectively. The establishment of Tonopah brought an enormous rush of new mining interest to the state, filling Reno's hotels with prospective miners. Further discoveries followed at sites with such colorful names as Bullfrog, Rhyolite, Searchlight, and Rawhide. Although these towns were located much farther from Reno than Virginia City had been—over 200 miles farther in some cases—the new boom brought an influx of capital to town. As these discoveries and federal projects flooded the state with new residents and new dollars, the state finally began to emerge from its twenty-year economic depression, and twenty years of accompanying derision.

Even better, as the young mining districts grew and prospered, many of the region's new mining magnates, unlike the Comstock millionaires who preceded them, invested their capital back into Nevada, and primarily into Reno. As a result, rather than functioning primarily as a junction, as it had in the days of the previous mining boom, Reno became both the headquarters and the beneficiary of the new Nevada riches. Reno, stated a reporter for *Sunset* magazine, the Southern Pacific's mouthpiece, "being to

Nevada what Salt Lake is to Utah, will necessarily reap the greatest advantage from this tendency. As the commercial center and metropolis of a reawakened state, its future seems to be assured."[61]

Others agreed. Touring the West in May of 1903, President Theodore Roosevelt took time out from stops in Yellowstone, Yosemite, and San Francisco to deliver a speech in Reno. A special "Roosevelt Edition" of the *Nevada State Journal* published that day laid out Reno's accomplishments as well as its residents' hopes that the president would "use his eyes and ears to good advantage while here in order that you may know of a certainty that Nevada is no rotten borough, no decadent commonwealth, no weakling in the sisterhood of States." They asked him to "Look about you to-day as your train is whirled through the foothills. Note the broad expanse of verdant fields, see the snow capped mountains clad in forest. As these valleys are so would many others in the State become if the flood waters were conserved."[62]

In his brief remarks, Roosevelt confirmed his faith in the state's new opportunities, telling his Reno audience, "Now here in Nevada, a new future opens to you." Of the town itself, he said, "It would be difficult to find in the United States a locality better fit to serve as an object lesson in the need of irrigation and the use of it than this particular locality." He continued, "Without in any way minimizing the importance of your mines, and of the mines from time to time discovered in the state, and without in any way minimizing what can be done in stock-raising, I yet feel that hereafter the most certain element of strength in the state will be the irrigated agriculture." The quote appeared in a newspaper story in Reno later that day and was reprinted in a brochure published by the Southern Pacific Railroad in 1903 and titled, appropriately enough, *The New Nevada.* The cover featured an illustration of a farmer following a plow rather than the more familiar Nevada miner. Through such publications, the Southern Pacific, having absorbed the Central Pacific in 1899, was doing its best to spread word of this transformation into an agricultural paradise. So-called colonist fares, cheaper one-way rates, were introduced in 1900. A 1904 article in *Sunset* rejoiced in the state's progress, having finally advanced from "a retrograde movement" to a course on "the up grade of advancement."[63]

Claims of cultural and social progress were ubiquitous among the state's promoters at the turn of the century. "Nevada is not on the 'frontier,'" reiterated the author of *The New Nevada*, boasting that "the railroad and the march of progress has pushed that old line into the Pacific." As another article in *Sunset* confidently asserted, Nevada was looking to the future: "The exponent of the red shirt, cowhide boots and ever ready hip arsenal, if he survives at all, does so at the expense of tourists. Romance still centers about him, but he is gone, like the prairie-schooner."[64] Such language was not unique to Nevada. Rhetorical distancing from the frontier was a deliberate strategy pursued throughout the nineteenth century in western locales from Pasadena to Denver. While historian Frederick Jackson Turner could wax nostalgic for the frontier, to many western boosters its demise was nothing to mourn. In the context of city building, the word itself had a negative connotation, and booster publications directed to potential residents began to stress the fact that the frontier was behind them. As Los Angeles promoter Charles Lummis wrote in 1903, cultivated tourists "naturally fear and shun the raw, unfinished civilization of most Western cities."[65]

Fortunately, regional observers were quick to note the signs of Reno's progress, praising the establishment of the university, the arrival of Newlands, and the infusion of money from the new mining districts. The *San Francisco Call* in 1901 acknowledged in Reno an "appearance of thrift and neatness that would attract the attention of the most casual observer," noting in particular the Newlands mansion, the well-kept streets and sidewalks, no longer punctuated with holes, the profusion of poplars and cork elms, as well as the university, whose buildings seemed to "equal in outward appearance the buildings of the State University of California that are situated at Berkeley." Another article in the same paper confirmed that Reno "has entered upon something like a new era in its history." Its residents certainly hoped so.[66]

Finally, it seemed, Nevada was securing positive coverage. A special "Nevada Number" of *Harper's Weekly,* published in July 1903, praised Reno's "modern buildings," "municipal improvements," "really excellent hotels" and "general bustle and activity of her markets," and a location that was "one of the most attractive in the whole mountain country." One writer predicted that the current wave of prosperity "if maintained will quickly transform Reno from a frontier town into a metropolitan city."[67] Such coverage would be expected to prompt great satisfaction among the local population. However, despite such flattering language, both Reno papers expressed extreme disappointment in the issue. Its praise may have appeared spontaneous, but in fact the entire "number" had been supported by approximately $2,000 contributed by Reno residents and endorsed in advance by the local Chamber of Commerce by arrangement with the *Harper's* representative.

The community felt cheated by the final product, and they were furious. As the *Gazette* complained, "the write-up is a very bum affair, being nothing more than a re-hash of what has from time to time appeared in nearly every paper in the State." The *Journal* concurred, calling the issue "big pay for very bad advertising" and "a literary fiasco." Financial contributors had been promised an entire issue featuring "fine half-tone engravings" reproduced from "good, late photographs" in order to "give to the outside world a correct and adequate idea of the resources of this wonderful state." In the final issue, only sixteen of the fifty-one pages were devoted to Nevada, and these were said to be full of "the cheapest kind of engravings" and "the poorest grade of hack writing."[68]

To the aggrieved community, such unflattering coverage, even when couched in words of praise, was worse than none at all. Since its founding, Reno had suffered from misconceptions and stereotypes, leaving its boosters desirous of nothing more than to be presented accurately. Discouraging *Harper's* from sending any more copies of the "misrepresentative write-up" to "this town or any other town," the *Journal* asserted, "All Nevada needs have told about her is the truth. When the people at large learn the truth about our resources they will come to us, but the truth must be presented to them in a different manner from this."[69]

As Reno turned the corner into a new century, it had certainly gained notice, although not yet a national reputation. Praised regionally and acknowledged kindly in a few morsels of national press, the little town's residents remained on the defensive, eager to boast of their successes and quick to bristle at any perceived slight. Reno may have achieved remarkable progress over the past three decades, but the inability of its promoters to control how others saw them remained a point of singular frustration. Their expectations were not especially high, but they adamantly demanded accuracy, believing that the facts would speak for themselves, if only they were properly conveyed.

CHAPTER TWO

"A Frontier Post of Civilization":
Chasing Modernity in the Progressive Era

The way to gain a good reputation
is to endeavor to be what you desire to appear.
Socrates

The population and social life of Reno, Nev., are undergoing a great change.
Where a year or so ago the optimistic mining promoter, in his corduroy or
khaki and his high russet shoes, was wont to disport himself, to-day may be
seen men of the East flashing by in high-powered automobiles.
"The New Divorce Centre," *New York Times,* 1909

On the seventeenth of May, 1903, a young motorcyclist named George A. Wyman powered his 1-cylinder, 1-1/2 horsepower machine out of San Francisco and headed east on an ambitious cross-country trek sponsored by *Motorcycling Magazine.* Already an established record-holder as the first to cross the Sierra on a motorcycle, Wyman was now attempting to become the first to complete a ride from coast to coast. Three days later, he reached Reno, where, according to the *Daily Nevada State Journal,* Wyman "didn't run around town much," probably, they posited, due to his exhaustion at having had to walk "forty miles through the Sierra snow." Wyman himself had a different explanation for his reclusiveness. Recounting the stop for the magazine, he later recalled, "I looked about for something to beguile the time away. I was in hard luck because I do not gamble, drink, smoke or chew. The old time picturesqueness of Reno has departed, but it is still a town of the West, western, and a man of no habits is at a discount in it."[1]

Wyman's disapproval demonstrated precisely what Reno's boosters did not want to hear from a visitor to their town, particularly from one whose impressions were being published in a nationally distributed magazine. His declaration that the town pandered only to the habitually unrefined was, to

Groups of loitering men were a common sight around the turn of the century along Gambler's Row, where the Palace, the Oberon, and other establishments offered food, rooms, and games of chance. (Nevada Historical Society)

them, an unfair characterization of the entire community. Yet it was admittedly true of some of the most visible neighborhoods at Reno's core, where gambling, legal in the state of Nevada since 1869, flourished, mostly as a secondary business for saloons. By February of 1902, Reno supported forty-eight saloons and sixteen licensed gambling games, concentrated primarily along the railroad tracks on Commercial Row. There, the Palace, the Oberon, the Louvre, and the Wine House offered drinks in busy front rooms and games of chance like poker, craps, and faro in smoke-filled back parlors, earning the entire stretch the nickname of "Gambler's Row."[2]

These establishments operated openly, running straightforward newspaper advertisements such as the Owl Café's boast of "First Class Saloon and Gaming Rooms, where pretty good drinks and cigars are sold, and square games are run for those who buck the Tiger," a euphemism for the popular game of faro.[3] They were gathering places, as well; most saloons served food, and many rented rooms upstairs. Other enticements were available nearby, from the brothels that clustered toward the river, to the opium dens of a small nearby Chinatown. As Wyman pointed out, these activities were not even mitigated by a rustic, frontier charm. With the era of wooden-frame buildings behind it, Reno seemed, to some, caught between the frontier and the modern era, not successfully embodying either one. To be "western" now, in Wyman's estimation, was to be socially stunted, a twentieth-century town trapped in a frontier mentality; the persistence of "wide-open" gambling was just the most visible indication.

The district had emerged naturally in the course of Reno's development into a busy crossroads. Throughout the late nineteenth century, with the state of Nevada in the throes of an economic depression, Reno had tolerated its "Tenderloin," although certainly not unanimously, due to fears that without it, those who frequented the town might take their dollars elsewhere. The mostly transient ranch hands, railroad crews, and miners with business in the region, as historian William Rowley explains, "saw Reno in the same light as sailors viewed a port city by the sea." These men demanded entertainment and indulgence of their "habits"—in saloons, clubs, and brothels—and many in Reno were happy to profit from their moral laxity.[4]

However, as the twentieth century approached, public pressure had prompted increasing regulation of gambling and other vices in the West as elsewhere in the country. This inspired a few opposing reactions among Reno's residents. To some, the national reform movement bolstered their own determination to become more like progressive communities across the country. To others, the reforms enacted in other states presented an incentive for Nevada to resist following their lead, as the increasing scarcity of commercialized vice increased its potential value wherever it remained. Gambling had a long and storied history in the West, ranging from the ragtag saloons of gold rush mining camps to the elegant gambling halls of San Francisco. But in the face of increasing national criticism and a desire to become more acceptable to easterners, California followed the line of reform by outlawing most banking games in 1860, and in 1885 by expanding its prohibition to criminalize not just the operation of, but participation in, prohibited games. Of course, as many had predicted, this ban proved to be a boon to Nevada; by continuing to offer legal gambling, the state's entrepreneurs had found a way to finally beat California, literally at its own game.[5]

Despite this development, Reno's residents at the turn of the century were divided over whether gambling remained critical to their economic survival. The operators of the targeted businesses were of course unwilling to relinquish their lucrative trade, but support extended beyond those who profited most directly from it. As a *Nevada State Journal* editorial argued in 1900, "In this western country the only moral communities are the cities of the dead. When there is faro playing there is money, enterprise, life. Where, under the peculiar conditions of the West, there are no gambling games, there is neither life, energy nor coin."[6]

For those determined to bring Reno firmly into the modern era, however, the town's saloons, gambling clubs, and brothels served as ugly remnants of a frontier past in dire need of burial, once and for all. To many residents, it was no longer Reno's physical environment, but its moral environment, that would determine its broader reputation. As a result, Reno's continuing tolerance of vice, etched on the streets and in the state's permissive legislation, became a growing concern for reformers and boosters who wanted their town to become known as a forward-thinking American community. Eager to maintain a steady influx of respectable residents, not just profligate transients, it was critical to be perceived as progressive and not regressive.

There was much progress to publicize already. Business and construction in Reno were booming, due primarily to the infusion of capital from the recent mining discoveries in central and southern Nevada. At the turn of the century, Reno had a population of just 4,500, but even at that modest size, it had become the beneficiary and imperial center of the entire state's rapidly diversifying economy. The county's agricultural and manufacturing industries were flourishing, as timber from greater Nevada was shipped to the lumberyards and planing mills of East Fourth Street, formerly limited to railroad shops and a foundry but now a bustling "hive of industry." Breweries, an ice and cold storage company, a brick works, a cheese factory, and other manufacturers thrived as well.[7]

Transportation and communication were also rapidly improving. New railroad lines were rendering all areas of the state more accessible, as three luxurious passenger trains crossed the state daily, with another running daily between Reno and San Francisco. Modern technology improved access to outlying areas, as power plants were installed along the line of the Truckee River, and the Nevada Transit Company laid down tracks for Nevada's first electric trolley line between Reno and neighboring Sparks in 1904. Since the turn of the century, the community had installed a telegraph fire alarm system, introduced free mail delivery, and established the use of electric power in factories and newspaper presses, promising soon to make it "a household utility."[8]

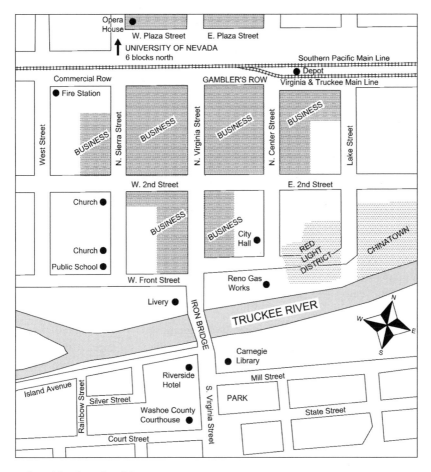

Selected landmarks of downtown Reno, 1904

The city limits continued to expand as well. Affluent families were beginning to construct some impressive homes in the new additions, including a neighborhood just south of the river, Lake's Addition, which featured so many "palatial homes" that it reportedly had earned the nickname "The White City." Later in 1903, Francis Newlands divided up some of the property adjoining his mansion on the bluff to form the "Riverside Heights" subdivision, advertised as the city's "Cream Residence Section." The civic infrastructure had progressed accordingly, as the town's full incorporation in 1903 marked a transition from administration by a board of county commissioners to a formal municipal government with a mayor and city council.[9]

All of these developments were admirable, and about as modern as could be expected in a small, rather secluded community out west. And yet still it seemed that Reno's promoters were always on the defensive, always anticipating negative responses to their town. In a letter explaining the need for a state Chamber of Commerce, to be based in Reno, newspaper publisher Robert Fulton wrote, "At present Reno is attracting a great deal of attention all over the country and the home seeker, the artisan, the capitalist, the miner and the leisure class as well, require correct information and fair treatment if a reaction is to be avoided." After the organization's founding, in 1902, the business community hoped to establish a degree of control over the nature of these "reactions." Based in Reno, the chamber's stated goal was to publicize the state's resources and promote immigration and investment in "the manufacturing, agricultural and mining possibilities of our town and State," acknowledging that Reno's favorable climate and abundant resources were useless without "money and men from elsewhere."[10]

In order to attract such long-term investment, many residents were convinced that the town needed to purge itself of its depravities. Just as Reno's farmers had irrigated the sagebrush to enhance the natural landscape, so did its reformers hope to flush out Reno's bad influences, to appeal to a more respectable element. In doing so, they were right in line with the Progressive reforms sweeping the country in the new century, most visibly in urban environments where vice seemed to be proliferating. Such communities were always quick to link material with moral progress, leading to the formation of movements to limit or ban activities including gambling, prostitution, prizefighting, and other pursuits widely deemed socially detrimental, unhealthy, or immoral. Nationwide, groups like the Anti-Saloon League, the Woman's Christian Temperance Union (WCTU), city vigilance leagues, and the American Purity Alliance targeted activities ranging from prostitution and political corruption to organized gambling and the Sunday sale of liquor.[11]

Reno's reformers similarly attacked a broad range of problems, some perpetuated by the town's status as a railroad junction, lamented by locals as "the natural dumping ground for a horde of undesirable characters daily." Short-term laborers spent their paychecks in Reno's saloons, then accosted pedestrians on the street after being thrown out, while others loitered in the railroad depot, "some of them asleep on the seats, others sprawled about on the floor, while the odor of the room is something unbearable." The pages of Reno's newspapers urged the county commissioners to rid the city of "this rubbish," complaining that transients constituted "an evil that does not speak well for a city the size of Reno."[12]

Such problems were always discussed publicly with an eye toward their effect on Reno's reputation. In the first years of the century, homeless men had constructed ramshackle shelters and "hideous cabins" on the south bank of the Truckee River, prompting one local reporter to complain, "the first impression of Reno gained by a traveler coming in over the V. & T. bridge is enough to cause him to invest his money in Carson." Having raised the specter of competition from the state capital, the writer pushed for public funding for parks and vegetation along the river. The need for attracting new residents was nearly always at the forefront of such calls to action. In 1906, after the city council passed a bond to fund city parks, a reporter affirmed, "Nothing that could be done in the way of municipal improvement will go further toward inducing desirable people to make their homes here than pleasant surroundings, beautiful driveways and walks."[13]

Other reformers focused on the brothels that spanned an entire block just north of the river, on the eastern edge of downtown. Reno's branch of the WCTU, organized in 1883 after a visit from national president Frances Willard, was joined by members of the Twentieth Century Club, another women's group, who called upon the city to move the red-light district at least 2 miles from the center of Reno, stating "A public park should be situated where the tenderloin now is, and we mean to use every power of persuasion with the city authorities and have those places purchased, razed, and trees and lawns planted on the site."[14] Inspired equally by principles of reform and the City Beautiful movement, they hoped literally to transform the landscape into cultivated ground.

But Reno's moral crusaders were perhaps most concerned about the town's wide-open policy toward gambling. If they could rid the town of this sordid activity, many reasoned, Reno's reputation would improve considerably. It had already been damaged by the experiences of travelers who fell victim to shady characters who loitered in the saloons. In June 1903, a "gang of card sharps and bunco men" was found to be swindling railroad passengers for large sums of money in a saloon near the depot. The six men had been ordered to leave town, but they returned a few days later. Reportedly, when the gang's alleged leader was brought before the sheriff and mayor, he "did not deny that he was 'doing' the traveling public, but said he was not injuring the town's people." Three of the gang members were arrested, but charges were not brought since "the complaining witnesses have all left town," thereafter, residents feared, encouraging all their friends and acquaintances to remain safely in their railroad berths should they ever pass through Reno.[15]

Faculty and administrators at the university, in particular, were concerned about the proximity of campus to the temptations of Gambler's Row, located just six blocks to the south. By 1900, the University of Nevada had expanded to eleven buildings and enrolled just over 300 students, but the administration hoped to attract many more—a goal which, like that of attracting respectable families to town, depended upon creating and promoting a healthy social environment. With Francis Newlands largely away in Washington after 1903 to conduct business in the U.S. Senate, other figures emerged to carry the banner of civic improvement at home. The university's president, Joseph Stubbs, was convinced that the stalled enrollment numbers were due to Reno's reputation as a town of loose morals. Determined to change this state of affairs, he emerged as a powerful voice of reform, dedicating himself, about a decade into his tenure, to fighting Reno's increasing proliferation of prostitution, gambling, and saloons.[16]

His campaign began slowly, and even Stubbs initially did not advocate the outright abolition of the gambling rooms, admitting that they seemed to be supported by "public sentiment." And yet, concerned for their impact on students, he did support restrictions on entry and the prohibition of music, in an attempt to keep the saloons from attracting minors. Measures did exist to curb the visibility and operation of gambling establishments, although they were not always enforced. An 1889 state law prohibited any businesses serving alcohol or offering games of chance from operating between the hours of midnight and 6 a.m. Some establishments, like the Monarch, had maintained back entrances that enabled ladies to come directly into the dining room without passing by the gaming tables.[17]

Stubbs initiated a move to keep the bad influences at a safe remove from the general populace with a petition to the legislature to confine gambling to the second floor of any operation. Citing student morality as his chief concern, he argued, "it is quite impossible to keep young men in check where gambling is done as openly as in Reno." That measure passed and went into effect in June 1903, immediately prompting at least three establishments to add an additional story to their buildings, providing local builders with a sudden flurry of business. Both local newspapers praised the measure's intent, with one editorializing, "no more will the tiger stalk in public gaze, but be allowed to have his lair in sequestered rooms above the street." In October, Stubbs brought in the mayor, the city attorney, and the chief of police to warn students about staying out of the saloons and gambling houses.[18]

The new second-story law made it harder for passersby to witness the gamblers in action, although many tourists did display an eagerness to try, a testament to the widespread notoriety of Reno's operations. When a California delegation of Native Sons and Daughters of the Golden West passed through town in September 1904, the group reportedly "alighted from their cars and went along Commercial Row peeping into the saloons and looking for the gambling rooms of which they had heard so much." Their efforts to witness gambling at the Palace and the Oberon, which they referred to as the "Monte Carlos of the West," were in vain, however, as "ladies were not allowed to climb the stairs." The very next week, another contingent of passing tourists missed their train as a result of "running along the streets of the city looking in the saloon doors and endeavoring to see the gambling rooms in operation."[19]

Clearly, the second-story measure was not enough. Estimating that the university was losing thirty to fifty possible students each year due to wide-open gambling, Stubbs campaigned heavily for the continuation of the second floor and closing time policies. Then, joined by other critics of gambling, including area ministers, the Young Men's Club, the Twentieth Century Club, and members of the university faculty, he backed an antigambling bill that was sent to the state legislature in February 1905. To the supporters' disappointment, it was defeated 23–10. As some legislators explained, while they did not necessarily favor gambling, they believed people had a right to choose whether or not to participate in it.[20]

Reformers' attempts to rein in gambling were made more difficult by the fact that the gambling and liquor interests were organizing as well. One hundred businessmen "identified with the saloon business" formed the Reno Lodge No. 32 of the Knights of the Royal Arch in June 1904. A list of officers included the owner of the Overland Hotel, C. J. Sadlier, who boasted the "finest bar in the state"; H. J. Thyes, a wholesale dealer in wines, liquors, and cigars; A. L. Mason, the proprietor of the Louvre, which specialized in "handling beer"; and Martin Evans, a bartender at Wieland's.[21]

The Royal Arch apparently had friends in high places. Just two weeks after the failure of the antigambling bill, the Nevada state assembly voted to repeal the restriction of gambling to the second floor, as well as the 12 o'clock closing law for saloons and gambling houses. The tiger was officially loose. Within days, the saloon owners of Gambler's Row were swiftly installing gaming tables and "nickel-in-the-slot" machines on their ground floors.[22] The *Daily Nevada State Journal* called it "the greatest victory the gambling men of Nevada have yet won." No longer would gambling operators need to build two-story establishments, one reporter wrote, as "a hovel is as good as a mansion so long as there is room for a gaming table and the people care to gamble."[23]

This was "wide-open" gambling at its most blatant, and to many reformers, at its most offensive. The development immediately inspired condemnation from expected quarters, locally and throughout the nation. The *Salt Lake Herald* intoned, "Where there are no laws against gambling the vice begets and breeds other crimes. Human life is never held more cheaply anywhere than it is in a State where there are no anti-gambling laws, or where they are loosely enforced."[24] For their part, Stubbs and his supporters seemed stunned. When asked for a response, Stubbs told the newspaper that he would rather see the city remove all gambling restrictions, as "with a free rein the people will soon learn that gambling is an injury to the best interests of the State. The reactions that will come will put a stop for all time to the traffic." His belief that the expected boost to the economy would not last was echoed by others who feared long-term damage to Nevada's reputation. Predicting the possible repercussions, prominent local real estate dealer Jerome A. Bonham asserted, "The wide open gambling and saloon policy is also a sad blow to Nevada and to Reno especially. This is the metropolis of the State and the university city." He added, "This wide open condition will result in damage to our future; home builders will fear coming to Nevada." As before, the reputation of a gambling town was feared unlikely to attract residents, still to many the state's most important task.[25]

At least not all outside assessments were entirely critical. Titled "Nevada Not a Hypocrite," an editorial in the *San Francisco Post* acknowledged that newspapers across the nation were castigating Nevada for "throwing herself wide open to the gambling element and the immorality that clusters about the speculative habit." And yet the writer claimed that, while "barbarous and elemental," Nevada was at least "open and above-board" in its social conditions, whereas other states, California included, were "smugly hypocritical," and that even California's morality was "a veneer to conceal the corruption that reeks within." Reprinted in Reno's papers, the story surely provided no consolation to dispirited reformers. To be called honestly barbarous was dubious praise, as prospective residents, like existing ones, were not likely to be impressed by that particular form of consistency.[26]

Although the passage of pro-gambling legislation presented a true challenge to the better angels of Reno's nature, its economic advantages were undeniable. Any operation offering games of chance had to pay a licensing fee every quarter, and in the case of the popular mechanical slot machines, invented in the 1890s, each individual machine was subject to its own licensing fee, resulting in more money for city coffers. In 1907, for instance, Reno made almost $50,000 from slot machine and gambling licenses alone, an understandable, if not altogether laudable, motivating force. However, at the same time, the legislation seemed sure to deliver a serious blow to the effort to establish Reno as a progressive, modern town. People passing through town would now be sure to see the games in action along Gambler's Row and, even worse, pass along their impressions of Reno's backwardness to others. Reno, many feared, would have regressed into that frontier town they had so hoped to leave behind.[27]

Then something completely unexpected occurred. Just a few months after gambling went "wide open," a visitor arrived in Reno, accompanied by more national press than the town had ever received. Like other travelers to Reno, she arrived on the train; unlike others, she did so in the private railroad car of steel magnate Charles Schwab. Upon arrival, she did not check into one of Reno's many hotels, but instead leased the furnished home of former *Reno Evening Gazette* publisher Robert Fulton, on First Street, for six whole months, "at a very high rent." As the *Gazette* reported in December 1905, she hired "a number of maids and servants" and was truly "living in luxury." On the same day, another report noted that her group "has an automobile, takes evening jaunts through the country and everyone in fact is living in luxury, though in a quiet manner."[28]

This was no gambler. Her name was Laura Corey, wife for twenty-two years to millionaire and U.S. Steel President William E. Corey. She had traveled to Reno from Pittsburgh along with Schwab's wife, and the sumptuousness of her lifestyle was new indeed to Reno. Locals were enraptured, and they were not alone. The millionaire's wife was pursued by reporters from across the country, all of whom breathlessly reported her every move and terse statements to the press. Most of these statements came in the form of denials—specifically, denials of the reported reason for her visit to Reno. Rumors circulated that she was there to secure a divorce, a claim that her husband had already acknowledged to be true. Neither one, however, had corroborated the accompanying reports that William Corey had taken up with an actress named Mabel Gilman, pushing his wife to this measure. To the papers, Mrs. Corey retorted, "There is no truth in that foolish story, and I am at a loss to understand how it gained currency. To even think that my husband is infatuated with an actress is ridiculous. I am not in Nevada to get a divorce, but came with my sister-in-law and her friend for the benefit of the latter's health."[29] Although the news that a prominent eastern socialite had traveled to Reno for its climate would have been music to the ears of its nineteenth-century boosters, her pursuit of a divorce set the stage for the town's biggest bonanza yet.

By filing for divorce in Reno, Corey took advantage of an 1861 law that provided for the conferral of Nevada territorial (and later, state) residency after just six months of continuous residence. Originally intended to hasten the ability of transient miners and other new arrivals to vote in territorial and, later, in state elections, the policy allowed newly minted Nevada residents to benefit from any of the state's laws, from casting votes to filing for divorce under looser grounds than in many other states. New York, for instance, provided only one ground for divorce, adultery. While many other jurisdictions had tightened their divorce policies over the years, Nevada had retained seven grounds for divorce: desertion, cruelty, nonsupport, drunkenness, impotency, imprisonment, and adultery. To make matters even easier, many of these grounds, like "cruelty," were quite open to interpretation; in addition, no evidence was required to prove any of these charges, sparing spouses the expense and embarrassment of having to reveal personal details of their marital troubles. Of course, this also allowed unhappy spouses to pursue a divorce without stating much of a reason at all.[30]

What the "quickie" divorce business would do for Reno's reputation was unclear, but the town was not new to marital legislation. Back in 1897, California had passed a law prohibiting remarriage within a year after receiving a divorce decree, prompting many elopements to Nevada, which had no such policy. An article published in the *San Francisco Call* in 1898 alluded to this "new industry . . . which is a source of amusement as well as of profit to Renoites." Noting that the Riverside Hotel had had to build a twenty-room addition just to accommodate the booming "marriage business," it continued, "Reno has become known as Cupid's town."[31] Such marriages were suspected to be legally invalid until 1902, when a decision of the California Supreme Court determined that all divorces in the state were absolute upon the occasion of the divorce decree, rendering any subsequent marriage legitimate.

Legal controversy aside, gaining renown for providing greater access to marriage was rather pleasant, like the association of Niagara Falls with honeymoons; a reputation for easing divorce seemed less so. The response to the other so-called divorce mills throughout the country had been mixed. New Yorkers had been crossing state lines in pursuit of more lenient policies since the eighteenth century, traveling first to Pennsylvania, followed soon thereafter by Ohio, Indiana, and Illinois. Shorter residency periods out west attracted divorce-seekers to Utah Territory for a brief period in the mid-1870s, and then to Dakota Territory. By 1889, after Dakota was divided in two, South Dakota, specifically Sioux Falls, emerged as the most notorious divorce mill, prompting national headlines with its short, three-month residency period. There, saloons, gambling houses, and houses of prostitution sprung up to entertain the idle divorce-seekers. Concerned for the town's moral environment, South Dakota's reformers managed to have that state's residency period extended to six months in 1893, paving the way for other states to gain a foothold. Englishman Earl Russell had moved to Glenbrook, Nevada, in 1900 to divorce his wife and marry another woman. However, he was found not to have established a true residency in Nevada, rendering his divorce illegal and subjecting him to charges of bigamy upon his remarriage.[32]

Corey did not make that mistake, settling into her luxurious digs for a full six months. For the purposes of her divorce, Corey claimed, as would legions of divorcées to follow, that she had traveled to Reno "for her health" with no intention of filing for divorce and that she sincerely expected to live in Reno for the foreseeable future. Her definition of "foreseeable" was soon proved to be quite shortsighted. Once establishing residency, Mrs. Corey immediately filed for divorce on the grounds of desertion. Her divorce decree hit the front page of the *New York Times* on July 31, 1906; by November the ex-Mrs. Corey had bid Reno farewell and taken up residence on a large farm in Chester County, Pennsylvania. As for William Corey, he married Mabel Gilman, who divorced him in 1923.[33]

Laura Corey may have left Reno, but the national spotlight did not. After her departure, other easterners turned their attention to Reno in order to put their own marriage vows asunder. According to local papers, by December 1906, Corey had "started the influx of the '400' to Nevada as a divorce center," referring to the legendary 400 top names in New York society, as identified by Mrs. William Astor in the 1890s. The names had changed, but the "400" still evoked the New York elite. Sources soon sighted Helen Bierce Ballard, daughter of writer Ambrose Bierce, who had reportedly just purchased a home in Carson City. It was Reno, however, that would become the favored site for a Nevada divorce, not just for its easy access to the railroad, but for other amenities including fine hotels and restaurants. The new industry was boosted even further in 1908 when, after additional pressure from religious leaders and concerned civic groups, South Dakota's residency period was increased from six months to a full year. Less than one year later, a *New York Times* reporter composed a report crowning Reno, whose residency period had remained six months, "The New Divorce Centre." *Munsey's Magazine* agreed that "the picturesque Nevada city" had become the "new divorce headquarters of the United States."[34]

Spurred on by the prospect of direct financial gain, a growing cadre of lawyers motivated by the search for well-heeled clients began to sing Reno's praises. One of the earliest to jump on the promotional bandwagon was New York attorney William H. Schnitzer, who moved to Reno in January 1907 to establish a law office catering to the divorce trade. In 1909, he published "Marriage and Divorce," a 24-page pamphlet describing the state's divorce procedures, which his firm claimed to have sent to "more than 2000 lawyers in New York and Canada." Schnitzer, as well as other attorneys, ran advertisements for the new divorce center in publications ranging from the *Brooklyn Daily Eagle* and *Washington Post* to theater programs in San Francisco.[35]

Wary locals were pleasantly surprised to find that these materials offered some of the best coverage of Reno they had seen yet. After examining Schnitzer's publication, the *Reno Evening Gazette* noted, "this booklet will do more good for the city than nearly any other pamphlet that has been sent out of the city for many years," commending its "glowing description" of the town. This made sense, as the new and established promoters all shared the common goal of making Reno as appealing as possible to prospective visitors. Divorce lawyers may have been interested in attracting lucrative clients rather than tourists or residents, but they were all in pursuit of the same outcome: increased exposure.[36] Schnitzer's methods certainly helped to achieve this, although they clearly did not enhance his own standing within the legal profession. Many members of Reno's legal community criticized such advertising as unethical, and in 1911, the Nevada Supreme Court went so far as to suspend Schnitzer's license temporarily. Other controversy arose after his booklet was discovered to be nearly identical in content to a speech delivered by a man named Channing Severance in Los Angeles in April 1910; when interrogated by the *Nevada State Journal,* Schnitzer said he "could not account for the similarity." He soon announced his intention to move to Goldfield, claiming that his divorce clients had been repeatedly "annoyed and swindled" in Reno.[37]

Other lawyers employed more direct methods. Brochures promoting Nevada divorces were directly mailed to households across the country, prompting domestic melodramas as the unsolicited booklets landed on the doorsteps of the unsuspecting. In August 1910, an article in the *Washington Post* headlined "Shock to Brooklyn Wives" reported "Wives in Brooklyn were tear stained today. Husbands were angry. Mothers-in-law were furious." The cause was "a little booklet with the title 'Divorce Laws of the State of Nevada'" that was delivered to "every home in Brooklyn possessing a telephone," supposedly prompting mistaken wives throughout the borough to burst into tears, demanding their husbands "Go to Reno right away. I always knew you only meant to treat me like this." For better or for worse, Reno was now literally a household name.[38]

As this article demonstrates, "going to Reno" and the "Reno cure" had quickly become nationally recognized euphemisms for seeking a divorce. In short order, the two phrases appeared in magazines, cartoons, and songs such as "I'm on My Way to Reno," in which popular crooner Billy Murray sang about a New Yorker about to take the journey west:

> I'm on my way to Reno, I'm leaving town today
> Give my regards to all the boys and girls along Broadway
> Once I get my liberty, no more wedding bells for me,
> Shouting the Battle Cry of Freedom.[39]

Headlines from coast to coast recognized Reno's new status. While most of the out-of-state coverage for Reno formerly had originated in neighboring northern California, now the small town was being recognized by the population and publication centers of America. To the *Los*

After Laura Corey's divorce, postcards affirmed that the "cure" for a troubled marriage could be found in Reno, where the chains of matrimony could easily be dissolved. (Special Collections Department, University of Nevada–Reno Library)

Angeles Times, Reno was the "Mecca of Broken Hearts," to the *New York Times*, the "Mecca of misplaced couples," and to the New York–based *Munsey's Magazine*, "The Refuge of Restless Hearts."[40]

Miraculously, to Reno's promoters, their town was suddenly a focus of national attention that they had not had to lift a finger to procure. Publicity was generated not by the Chamber of Commerce or local newspapers, but by large numbers of out-of-state press whose curiosity appeared insatiable. Everything about the town was subject to intense media scrutiny, as exemplified by a 1910 *Los Angeles Times* article that began with a barrage of

The words "I'm on my way to Reno" struck fear into the hearts of spouses everywhere, as the name of the small western town became synonymous with speedy divorces. (Special Collections Department, University of Nevada–Reno Library)

questions: "What about Reno? What kind of a place is it? What is the general atmosphere of the town? What is its social life? Is it an immoral Gehenna? Or can one live there without contamination? Why is it the most talked-of town in the West? Does it justify its reputation?"[41] In both volume and intensity, this new coverage presented a completely different picture of Reno to the outside world than had existed prior to 1905, if indeed any picture had existed at all.

In short order, the rising tide of divorce publicity was consumed by potential divorcées as well as by average readers drawn by the stories of society scandal. Divorce had feminized Reno's landscape, softening its rough edges. This new type of transient, the divorcée, was a much more broadly appealing figure than the miners, sharpers, and denizens of Gambler's Row. Rather than trying to steal a peek at gamblers trying their hand at bunco, visitors to Reno now hoped to catch a glimpse of a glamorous divorcée en route to the courthouse to receive her decree. The difficulty of identifying such elusive creatures added to the intrigue. Because they were not clearly distinguished by any obvious visual clues from the average female resident, accounts speculated at length about the number residing in Reno at any given time. The *New York Times* estimated that 350 individuals were establishing their residency in Reno in July 1909. *Munsey's Magazine* settled on 200, although referring to estimates of anywhere from 10 (from a local lawyer) to as high as 500.[42]

When *Collier's* correspondent Arthur Ruhl documented his first encounter with the Reno divorce colony, he began with an acknowledgment of this new notoriety, noting that, "In common with most of the world which reads newspapers, I had heard of 'The Colony.'" Of the divorcées, he wrote, "here they are, probably three hundred of them, and three hundred strangers, most of whom have comparatively expensive tastes and money to spend, make quite a stir in an isolated Western city of twelve thousand people." And while not all divorcées were rich, as most of the depictions would suggest, the required six-month period of residence did require either a certain level of financial independence or a willingness to find temporary work, which some did. Rather than rent rooms in fine hotels, some lived in boarding houses and rented rooms, securing jobs in order to support themselves during their residency. The majority of the literature, however, painted the whole town as one big playground for the well-to-do; it was tales of wealthy, glamorous divorcées that sold magazines, and publishers knew it.[43]

As such accounts revealed, there did seem to be a great many more women than men in the "divorce colony." Only one spouse needed to fulfill the residency requirement by living continuously in Nevada during the period, but this should not be interpreted to mean that more women than men initiated the separations. Scholars have hypothesized a number of reasons for the imbalance, ranging from sociological changes granting women greater agency, to gender divisions giving women the leisure time for the trip while men were more likely to have business obligations. Some have even posited chivalric motivations, suggesting the mutual decision by a married couple that any reason a woman might proclaim as grounds for divorce would be less damaging for both parties than what a man might say of his wife.[44]

Accounts identified the divorce-seekers when they could, although *Munsey's* preferred to keep them nameless, referring coyly to "the former wife of a well-known steel man," "an actress, whose name has lately been much in the newspapers," or "the wife of a New York stock-broker." Other reporters were not so discreet, although some divorcées drew attention to themselves deliberately, resulting in some colorful stories. A *Los Angeles*

Times story reporting on the antics of "striking brunette" Helen B. Tyler, a New York broker's wife who had filed for a divorce in Reno from her husband of just over a year, explained how the flaring crimson cape and hood she wore had earned her the nickname of the 'Little Red Riding Hood' of Reno.[45]

Many stories revealed their subjects' attempts to escape publicity and their obvious failure to do so in the face of an avid press. Actress Margaret Illington, who "joined the colony" in June 1909, reportedly "did not come with the usual flare that accompanies theatrical people," instead using her birth name and quietly settling in on "the fashionable Center street" for her six-month residency. Mrs. Gustave Luders, wife of a well-known musical composer, had attempted to evade reporters by taking the train to the next station and hiring an automobile to drive her back but made headlines anyway when the driver failed to appear, forcing her entourage to hitch a ride to Reno on a Southern Pacific switch engine.[46]

Within just a few years, some of the biggest names of the New York stage had graced the colony. Popular Shakespearean actor E. H. Sothern divorced his wife, actress Virginia Harned, in Reno, as did actor Nat Goodwin and his wife, actress Maxine Elliott. As the *Los Angeles Times* reported, "theatrical circles" were accustomed to "eagerly keep their eyes and ears on the Nevada divorce courts" for any news of their contemporaries. The theatrical nature of the town even inspired its own productions. Leslie Curtis, a young journalist and sometime actress, arrived in Reno in October 1909 to write about the colony. Apparently inspired by the dramatic environment, she wrote a "clever playlet" called "Housekeeping in Reno" for the Twentieth Century Club in December 1909 and another called "The Reno Divorce Mill," which was performed at Reno's own Majestic Theater in May 1910. The latter depicted a day in the life of a divorce lawyer who is trying to woo his stenographer (wittily named "Ima Peach"), while withstanding a series of interruptions by a collection of colorful divorcées ranging from a pretentious New York socialite to "an Indian squaw" named "Red Star" whose chief utterance is "Ugh!" Curtis herself played the roles of the divorcées in the production. The thought of divorcées watching divorcées earned a mention in the *Washington Post*, which reported, "The affair was a social event, the theater being filled with a fashionable audience of which the divorce colony formed a conspicuous part." The *San Francisco Call* printed the play in its entirety that July.[47]

The success of Curtis and her plays in Reno demonstrated broad local support for her humorous take on the situation, as many locals described her work as amusing and clever. Even so, Curtis made a deliberate effort to clarify that she was not herself a member of the colony, going so far as to assert her never-married status in the local paper. "It requires greater courage to be a spinster in Nevada than to be a collector of surnames," she wrote, in a paid advertisement. As a point of fact, the declaration was completely unnecessary, but as a publicity stunt, it worked like a charm; six days later, the *New York Times* repeated the tale for its readers.[48]

In addition to her plays, Curtis compiled a 33-page booklet called *Reno Reveries* later that year, advertising it heavily in the Reno papers with sensationalist lines like, "Don't forget to send Aunt Prudence a copy of 'Reno Reveries' . . . She will curl up and die of shock." Clearly entertained, the *Nevada State Journal* praised it as "eminently readable" and "much different from the ordinary treatise on the Reno situation because there are few hard knocks or slams." Curtis herself may have had ulterior motives in advertising her single status; while in Reno, she met an industrialist from Muncie, Indiana, who was in town to secure a divorce, and they married in 1911. Traveling to New York City that year, Curtis sent back word that New York's newspaper people

> expect her to be very hilarious after her residence in Reno, smoke a pipe, drink out of finger bowls, and other dainty stunts. She has found the word "Reno" to be an open sesame to a great many tightly barred doors, and thinks that this place ought to have an official information bureau . . . owing to the great many inquiries and the tremendous amount of misinformation that is being handed out.[49]

As Curtis indicated, hers was not the only fiction generated in the colony. In much of this coverage, it was clear that accuracy was not the point, so much as creating a good story. The correspondents often fabricated gossip, which their newspapers would then expand into larger generalizations about the divorce colony. While seated in "the Delmonico's of Reno," *Collier's* reporter Arthur Ruhl recalled speaking with a London correspondent who, "cheerfully regardless of the fact that the 'Saturday Review' would base on his report another withering attack on American depravity . . . hurried off to cable his paper that one's social position in Reno depended entirely on the number of times one had been divorced. You had to have at least one decree to be anybody at all, while to be really smart— 'well—ah—rather a happy idea I thought, wasn't it?' he observed next day with a complacent smile."[50]

Accurate or not, this national media attention had generated a level of publicity for Reno that generations of Chambers of Commerce and Commercial Leagues could never have achieved on their own. The advantages were many. This new industry had raised Reno's national profile and measurably increased visitation to the town. Most critical to local residents was that the coverage did not conflict with their own goal of promoting Reno as a modern and progressive community. In fact, many visiting reporters, glimpsing Reno for the first time, registered surprise that the town was not one big gambling den, but a charming, modern little town. The author of the *Munsey's* article was particularly pleased at this, having heard from a visitor—a U.S. senator from Pennsylvania, no less—that a day he spent in Reno was "the sorriest day [he] ever spent," where "the only place where [he] could get away from the rattle of dice and the click of faro-chips was in the Carnegie Library." In contrast, to the *Munsey's* reporter, "Reno disclosed itself as no town of gambling joints and a Carnegie Library, no rough-sawn mining camp, no 'jay burg on the left-hand side of the track.' It disclosed itself as probably the most beautiful small city in the United States."[51]

The unexpected modernity of the town was a common thread of many of these reports. An article appearing in the *New York Times* put this transformation in comic terms, satirizing Reno as well as its new industry. Transforming the town into a literal landscape of divorce, it read, in part, "This town was formerly rich from its mines—but no more. All the miners have now quit work and gone into the law-business. Reno is the only American municipality which is supported entirely by alimony. Principal business bldgs of this town are: Reno Co-respondents' School, Husband's Exchange Bank, Hotel Alimonia, Handy Witnesses' Employment Agency and Mrs. Trouble's Matrimonial Bureau."[52] In an accompanying cartoon, a prospector figure, consistently identified with Nevada, busily stamped divorce decrees for a row of fashionable women.

Other, more serious articles took the same line of argument, noting the surprising transformation of Reno "from a typical frontier mining town to a city that disports itself in eastern fashions and wealth." As one *New York Times* reporter observed:

Where a year or so ago the optimistic mining promoter, in his corduroy or khaki and his high russet shoes, was wont to disport himself, to-day may be seen men of the East flashing by in high-powered automobiles. Where Washoe squaws would a year ago sit and play cards at the corners of the public squares may be seen to-day handsome women in Paris gowns, sauntering in the afternoon sun.

Together, the divorce coverage and increased patronage had accomplished a remarkable transformation of Reno's streets in the collective imagination, if not entirely in reality, replacing miners and Indians with a fashionable eastern elite who loitered in "Paris gowns" and "high-powered automobiles." This "frontier post of civilization" had become a satellite of East Coast society in the midst of the western wild. The overall image conveyed was that of a colony of bored socialites creating, for their own amusement, an entire cosmopolitan scene in the little western town where sophisticated visitors "had the gossip of London, New York, Melbourne, at their finger-tips."[53]

Portrayals of this intriguing scene were not confined to generalizations about its characters. Most surprisingly, and to many residents, most gratifyingly, the articles provided more vivid description of a modern Reno than had appeared anywhere before. It was not Gambler's Row that was being described, but the various landmarks frequented by the divorcées. In previous years, any positive coverage had focused primarily on Reno's accomplishments in the realms of manufacturing and agriculture. Now, rather than a masculine landscape inhabited by miners and ranchers, Reno was presented as a more accessible space, centered on shopping and leisure activities. The new Reno landmarks, regularly featured in illustrations and photographic reproductions, were not the saloons of Gambler's Row, the hotels near the railroad tracks, or the brothels of the Tenderloin. Instead, they included the railroad depot where divorcées embarked from the Overland Limited; the apartment houses, cottages, and houses they rented; and the hotels, restaurants, cafés, clubs, and resorts they frequented to help while away the months. The focus had moved several blocks south from the railroad tracks to the county courthouse, site of divorce decrees, the Riverside Hotel, and the upscale residences near the river.

Not only did such views present a more cultivated side of Reno, but these visitors were actually helping to pull the town into the modern era with their sophisticated tastes and expectations. The increasing patronage of a more cosmopolitan, and more moneyed, crowd brought the latest modern innovations to town, and the press took note. By 1909, the *New York Times* estimated that the divorce colony had brought to Reno "over 100 motor cars," at a time when such purchases were confined to the wealthiest Americans. Some raced their Pope Toledòs and other models on the local race track, where the Nevada Jockey Club sponsored the community's first auto races in 1904.[54]

The press publicized upgrades in local lodging as well, more likely for the sake of reassuring prospective visitors than offering plaudits to the town. Yet there was much to praise. Harry J. Gosse of Virginia City, who had bought the wooden Riverside Hotel from William Thompson in 1896, completed construction of a new four-story brick hotel on the site of Myron Lake's original inn in 1907. The new Riverside featured 130 bedrooms with circular rooms in towers on the northeast and southeast corners, a veranda facing the Truckee River, a 120-seat dining room, and an elevator. Each room had a private telephone capable of calling long-distance. With its completion, the intersection of Virginia Street and the Truckee River gained an additional note of elegance. The Riverside Hotel, wrote *Collier's* correspondent Arthur Ruhl, "resembled a summer hotel whose summer girls were all about ten years older than they usually are—they would come sailing into the dining-room in twos and threes, chatelaines jangling, in a curious pseudo-girlish camaraderie."[55]

While many other divorcées rented rooms in houses or stayed in cottages, the colony also prompted the construction of modern apartment houses, part of a major building boom spanning the first decade of the new century. Partners Charlie Clough and George Crosby spared no expense in building their four-story Colonial Apartments, named not for the divorce colony but for its architectural style. Located on fashionable First Street, the building was said to be "strictly modern in every particular" and built "according to the plans of the modern apartment houses of Los Angeles." Luxurious features included hardwood floors in each of the thirty apartments, the "new wall-beds," a tiled entrance with marble paneled walls, marble steps and columns, and an elevator. Such a well-appointed residence earned the Colonial approving mentions in many articles.[56]

Reno's proprietors also won approval for opening up-to-date businesses that compared favorably to landmarks that readers of these articles would recognize. The Thomas, owned by Will Thomas, was arguably the most popular restaurant in town. After running an oyster house on Second Street, an intimate room with luxurious mission oak paneling, he opened his second restaurant on Center Street in November 1908. Sensitive to his patrons' desire for seclusion, the establishment featured private dining rooms on the second floor. As the *Los Angeles Times* reported, the Thomas was to Reno what Levy's was to Los Angeles, referring to Al Levy's Grill, a popular haunt for Los Angeles's actors, politicians, and other luminaries. The *New York Times* called the Thomas the "local Bohemian restaurant" where "New York's fast set" passed the time "in giving gay parties or in drinking cocktails," while *Collier's* generously labeled it the "Delmonico's of Reno."[57]

Such coverage certainly evoked a Reno that was endlessly entertaining, but when it came to Reno's reputation, the town's new identification with the actual practice of divorce was a bit more problematic. Located in one of the last states in the country to regulate human behaviors, Reno had already received widespread condemnation for the vices it allowed to flourish, especially after gambling had gone wide open in 1905. Now these accounts of decadent divorcées abandoning their spouses to drink cocktails in Reno threatened to group divorce along with those other civic transgressions. Like its tolerance of legalized gambling, the divorce laws might be seen as yet another indication that Reno, for all its titillation, lacked a fundamental respectability.

Such questions catapulted Reno into the center of a very modern debate about changing social mores around the turn of the century, when Americans were divided over the question of divorce. Many ministers and other concerned citizens decried the increasing prevalence of "the divorce evil." Their concerns prompted the formation of the National Divorce Reform League in the 1880s; under the leadership of a Congregationalist minister named Samuel W. Dike, the organization changed its name in 1898 to the National League for the Protection of the Family, suggesting a defensive stance against the rising threat of marital separations. To Dike, an increasingly individualistic and materialistic society was wrongly considering marriage a form of contract, among many other contracts, rather than a holy sacrament.[58]

Critics' concerns grew after 1900 with the increasing incidence of divorce, a trend that the media was quick to point out. As a *New York Times* reporter commented in 1909, "The married woman is still the type of respectability. But divorce for any cause or none grows commoner every day, and it is getting so that one hesitates politely to ask an acquaintance about the health of the wife one knows he had within the year." Impressions of a major escalation in the divorce rate were confirmed by a Bureau of the Census report issued in 1908. Studying available data on American divorces, it determined that over the forty-year period from 1867 to 1906, the rate of divorce had increased at a rate three times the rate of the nation's population increase. As the report stated, "The fact that divorces have increased more rapidly than the population means, of course, that they are more numerous in proportion to population than they were formerly, thus confirming the popular impression that divorce is becoming more common."[59]

After its publication, this study was frequently cited in stories about Reno's divorce colony, particularly because some had blamed the "divorce mills" in part for the rising divorce rate. But the same census report found that the number of people divorced in a different state from that in which they were married, around 20 percent, was nearly the same as the percentage of people living outside the state in which they were born. The statistic could, in other words, be explained not by the popularity of migratory divorce, but simply by "the general movement of the population." Still, some reformers believed that standardizing the country's divorce laws would decrease the number of migratory divorces, and hence, the number of divorces as a whole. Such standardization, however, would require a Constitutional amendment, something that was unlikely to happen.[60]

While some blamed the divorce colonies for contributing to the increase in divorces, a rising tide of social scientists claimed that the laws of any state were not to blame. In an article titled "Is the Freer Granting of Divorce an Evil?" sociologist George Elliott Howard pointed out that divorces had become more frequent even as laws became more stringent. In the search for an explanation, he noted that the "fundamental causes of divorce . . . are planted deeply in the imperfections of the social system—notably, in false sentiments regarding marriage and the family" and concluded "the great fountain head of divorce is bad marriage laws and bad marriages."[61]

Like others, Howard saw divorce patterns as a reflection of a changing society and changing values. Similarly, in his book *Divorce: A Study in Social Causation,* Dr. James P. Lichtenberger examined the census report data and agreed that divorce must be considered in its social context. "With the gradual emancipation of women and the attainment of greater equality," he wrote, "the right of women to divorce, to the same footing as men, must be conceded. As various coercive tendencies are removed and marriage becomes a matter of choice, equally free divorce will necessarily result."[62] Calling the rising divorce rate "an index of progress rather than a sign of social disintegration," Howard predicted that the trend would likely continue until "the new family finds its equilibrium in the changed economic, social, and religious environment" and asserted, "Progress cannot be won by clinging to the authority of ancient ideals in social questions."[63]

Sociologists were not alone in taking a less condemnatory view. To many Americans, the increasing availability and frequency of divorce was a sign of emancipation, not regression. Perhaps, they reasoned, it was more progressive and modern not to control behavior, but rather to free individuals, especially women, from the repressive grip of Victorian-era morals. In this view, the divorce mills were providing a needed service by countering the unjust laws that prohibited individuals from exiting destructive unions in their home states. As divorce attorney William Schnitzer argued, a marriage should not be a trap: "For a man or woman at the time of the marriage ceremony to promise to love each other until 'death do them part' is one of the greatest absurdities that prevails. Neither has any control over the attraction that drew them together." Justifying his professional specialty in terms of individual liberties, he argued, "Neither church, state, society or anyone else can know your real feelings; so, for any outside power to arbitrarily control your freedom to marry or to unreasonably prevent separation is wrong, vicious and indefensible."[64]

Not surprisingly, this perspective found common expression in Reno. "In the face of all the critics of divorce," a local editorial stated, "we say that the law which allows a mistake to be corrected, which permits sunlight to come again into a darkened, blighted life, is more charitable, more merciful, more just, than the steelclad statute which maintains that not until the man or woman is found guilty of adultery shall they be free of each other."[65] Whether rational argument or rationalization, framing divorce as a progressive sign of modern thinking allowed local residents to frame Nevada not just as a harbinger of modernity, but indeed, as one of the most modern places in the country.

However, as confident as this particular article may have sounded, it was written in direct response to the publication just over a week earlier of an article in the *New York Times* suggesting widespread anxiety among Reno's residents for their town's reputation. In that article, the *Times* had claimed that "the use of Reno as a temporary residence for men and women anxious to sever marriage bonds has become irksome to many of the permanent residents" who feel it "lowers the tone of the place and lends to it some sort of bad repute." It was this account in particular to which the *Gazette* took issue, countering:

All sorts of weird stories have been fed to an eager public regarding the "colony" and Reno. But for the sake of these papers and people who seem to be vastly concerned over Reno's welfare, apparently fearing that we who live here are apt to be contaminated by the presence of the divorce seekers we would simply say that we bid them take heart and abolish their forebodings. A more or less wide acquaintance with the make-up of different cities has shown us that the standard of morality in Reno is quite as high as it is in other places.[66]

Faced with such a public expression of sympathy for their community's supposed degradation, civic pride seemed to dictate a defense not just of the city's morality, but of the divorce industry itself, a position that local newspapers may have been unlikely to voice so directly otherwise.

Confident and defensive editorials aside, local opinion about the divorce industry remained mixed. Disagreement over whether to cultivate and exploit Reno's notoriety, or to attempt to eliminate the cause of it, pitted many residents against each other. The fact that Reno was becoming known, on such a massive scale, for an activity directly opposed to the maintenance of stable homes was indeed a travesty to those who had long tried to convince outsiders of Reno's stability and respectability. As one Reno attorney protested in the *Nevada State Journal*, "bad repute has been brought upon the name of the State. The Corey case was a glaring example."[67] In this view, to be nationally identified with divorce presented a substantial risk: would those who opposed divorce still want to live there, or even to visit?

The local *Gazette* expressed a general acceptance of the divorce trade in economic terms, explaining, "As the divorce mill is one of Reno's thriving industries, it would be very unpatriotic to argue against its operation." However, in a nod to maintaining appearances, the newspaper did urge Reno's divorcées to "be a little circumspect" before initiating a new romance while establishing residency. Noting that many divorcées "do not wait until they are freed from one tie to take on another," the paper acknowledged that "the six months of 'actual not constructive' residence may prove irksome to the members of the colony, but they should not parade the fact of their acquiring affinities with whom to while away the time, even if such is actually the case."[68] In a twist reflecting Reno's general ambivalence, the paper urged discretion in forming extramarital attachments, if not an actual end to the behavior itself.

Indeed, Reno's promoters found themselves in an unusual position, interested, as always, in attracting new business to the city, but hesitant to endorse outwardly a practice considered by some as immoral. The Nevada Commercial League considered taking a more active stance in promoting the divorce industry during a regular meeting in February 1908; however, according to one observer, "the members of the league did not seem to be enthusiastic over the plan to make Nevada as widely an advertised state in this regard as South Dakota." Instead, he noted, "the league put aside the tempting prospect and decided to allow Nevada's notoriety to grow without cultivation." In their refusal to officially endorse the lucrative divorce trade, the league implicitly revealed an awareness of the potential damage that could ensue from any official civic stamp of approval. To directly promote Reno as a divorce colony would be to open the city to charges that it was purely mercenary, willing to cast morality aside in the pursuit of money. The league's distinction was somewhat spurious, as even without official endorsement, this was already the governing interpretation of Reno's motives. As the *New York Times* observed of Reno, "the city is willing to sell easy divorce because the trade is profitable." Why else countenance such a questionable business?[69]

Leaving the advertising of the divorce trade to the attorneys, the league itself continued to produce brochures featuring the community's more mainstream attractions. One 40-page booklet highlighted the university, that most respectable of institutions. After perusing it, the *San Francisco Chronicle* remarked that such publications could, "if properly disseminated . . . go a long way toward removing the feeling entertained for a considerable period in the East, that a mistake was made in conferring statehood upon Nevada." It concluded, "Reno and Nevada are all right." Like so many other accounts, both positive and negative, this one was diligently quoted in local papers, reflecting a constant local awareness of Reno's national standing.[70]

Whether supportive of divorce for socially progressive or economic reasons, most residents, like the Commercial League, simply let it alone. Indeed, it would be difficult for the community, or the state legislature for that matter, to completely reject a new industry that was finally bringing people of gentility and style, the very best class of easterners, to Nevada. The advantages of this new industry were undeniable: a relatively affluent segment of the population had discovered an advantage buried in the state's permissive legislation, bringing to Reno copious amounts of disposable income and spurring the introduction of even more goods and services. Best of all, the people of Reno did not have to do anything to attract their patronage except retain a few statutes on the record books. At least for now, any community-wide moral qualms regarding the industry seemed vastly overshadowed by such a cascade of benefits.

At the same time, the discovery of an industry that could be so profitable to the community while simultaneously prompting improvements in the landscape, from the addition of new shops to modern apartments, only served to emphasize the vastly different impact made on the community by other industries. Some may have embraced divorce as an enlightened practice, but to the general public, businesses such as the "objectionable saloons" of Commercial Row and the tawdry "cribs" of the red-light district were neither modern nor progressive.

While differing in their assessments of its visibility, the divorce press almost unanimously dismissed Reno's gambling business as sordid and unpleasant. *Munsey's* reporter Allen Albert wrote that "the traveler sees practically all there is of it from the train. The people of Reno know almost as little of it, and care almost as little about it, as you and I know or care about its counterpart at home," referring to the illegal games still proceeding in New York, Baltimore, and Philadelphia. Unlike divorce, gambling was not considered glamorous or successful in attracting the "right sort" of people; rather, as Albert explained, "From three classes, and those three classes alone, come the patrons of these mountain gaming-tables. They are either miners, orientals, or bums." Dismissing the practice as "a relic of the early pioneer days," an article in the *Los Angeles Times* agreed that Reno's gamblers represented "the lowest social scale—dope fiends, drunkards, whoremasters, cattle thieves, thugs, ex-convicts . . . foul, shabby workingmen, miners, and narrow-faced clerks."[71]

Now that the town was getting national attention, the reform crowd had even more incentive to rid Reno of such ignominious elements and stepped up their actions accordingly. As the *San Francisco Call* reported in the summer of 1908, "The reform wave has struck Reno in earnest."[72] After the expansion of gambling in 1905, many of its critics had continued to oppose the practice, and their efforts received a renewed boost in January 1908 with the arrival in Reno of a renowned traveling evangelist named Reverend E. J. Bulgin. The minister and a companion, Professor Gates, were there to lead a series of revival meetings at the Methodist Church. Within a few days, Bulgin had begun to lace his sermons with an appeal to his audience to ban gambling from Reno. Encouraged by the response, about a week into his stay, Bulgin composed a petition to the Reno city council urging them to consider a citywide ban on gambling.

The petition proposed banning thirteen different types of gambling games: everything from "stud-horse poker" to something called "hokey pokey" (decades before the invention of a children's dance by that name). He also suggested fines of $100–$500 or imprisonment of up to six months for anyone who "deals, plays, carries on, opens, and causes to be opened or conducted, either as owner or employee, whether for hire or not, any of said prohibited games, and every person who plays or bets at or against any of said prohibited games." Making each of those activities a misdemeanor, his suggestions moved to criminalize behavior that had become everyday practice down on Gambler's Row.[73]

Clearly his efforts had struck a chord. A few days later, at his suggestion, several hundred of the "leading citizens of Reno," including five ministers, met in Wheelmen's Hall, a frequent site of amateur boxing matches, to form an Anti-Gambling League. They were headed by a Committee of Fifty. Their president was leading citizen R. L. Fulton, who had loaned his house to Laura Corey back in 1905. The group took charge of distributing petitions and passing resolutions, the first of which began with a clear statement of the league's position on gambling, which, they said, "destroys the habit of industry, causes idleness and crime, degrades character, destroys the home, deprives the helpless of support and comfort, brings disgrace and sorrow to the innocent, ruins those who would otherwise be useful and respectable citizens, keeps away those who would help build up the community, and attracts the vicious, dissolute and unworthy." At the end it was clear that their concerns extended to Reno's reputation as well as its moral decline. The resolution ended with a final assertion of the true cost of gambling, decrying the fact that "the city of Reno suffers the degradation of being known as a place in which vice is legalized and encouraged; and whereas, such evil reputation is founded upon fact and the shame and injury resulting therefrom reach home to all of us."[74]

The two sides quickly closed ranks. In the weeks after Bulgin's departure, the Anti-Gambling League called for a boycott of any merchants who did not support them. Their petition gained the endorsement of several parties, including the Women's Civic Reform League, the Twentieth Century Club, university president Joseph Stubbs and most of his faculty, the acting governor, a U.S. senator, and a Nevada Supreme Court justice. In the meantime, the supporters of the gambling community did not sit idle. Instead, they organized an alternate meeting at which thousands of dollars were raised to "fight the crusade." According to the *San Francisco Call,* which closely followed developments in Reno, "the gamblers say that if their games are driven out of town gambling resorts will be opened immediately at Moana Springs and other nearby places" just outside of city limits. The Royal Arch, the organization of saloon men, joined with the "gambling fraternity" and promised legal action against any attempts to shut them down. As these groups emphasized, it was not entirely clear how any antigambling ordinance, even if passed by the city, could supersede a state law under which gambling remained legal.[75]

The point became moot that October when the antigambling forces were defeated resoundingly in the city elections, but undaunted, they redirected their campaign toward the state legislature, where the influence of the Royal Arch and the "gambling fraternity" of Reno was not so strong. There, the movement intersected with statewide efforts to redeem Nevada's reputation, receiving an early endorsement from the legislature's "committee on public morals." To the delight and relief of the Anti-Gambling League and their supporters, as well as Progressive reformers throughout the state, Assembly Bill No. 74, outlawing the practice of gambling, passed by a vote of 27 to 20 in February of 1909. The state senate passed the bill unanimously a few weeks later, and the new law was signed by Governor Denver Dickerson on March 24. For logistical reasons, the statute would not go into effect for more than a year, but the reformers were content that victory was in sight.[76]

As they waited impatiently for the doors of the gambling dens to close forever, another door swung wide open for a different group of profiteers unconcerned with controversy. The roots of this activity also lay in the state's permissive legislation, introduced with an eye toward fulfilling the desires of an American public hungry for excitement. This was prizefighting, which, like both gambling and easy divorce, presented an opportunity for a handful of savvy business-minded Nevadans to profit from an activity increasingly regulated elsewhere. On a national level, interest in prizefighting had grown enormously in the late nineteenth century, due in large part to the astounding popularity of heavyweight John L. Sullivan, whose primal, bare-knuckled 75-round fight against Jake Kilrain in Richburg, Mississippi, in July 1889 generated fervent excitement from coast to coast.[77] This increasing popularity was a phenomenon that might seem antithetical to the national trend toward Progressive and moral reform. However, its appeal could be seen as cathartic. In a modern world increasingly characterized by the inhumanity of machine technology, many were attracted to the authenticity embodied by brutal and undeniably real events like prizefighting.[78]

Of course, that same brutality made prizefighting a major target of reformers, many of whom considered it immoral. The practice had been widely criticized and legislated against since the early nineteenth century, and the so-called purity crusade of the 1890s and early 1900s secured legislation banning prizefighting in many eastern states where it had previously been tolerated. When the practice was finally banned in New Orleans, its center for many years, promoters looked westward for additional venues.[79]

Motivated by the desire to stave off the state's economic depression, Nevada formally legalized public prizefighting in 1897. The purity crusade promptly labeled that move the "Nevada disgrace." A few months later, Carson City hosted the heavyweight championship between Bob Fitzsimmons and James J. "Gentleman Jim" Corbett. After that, promoters continued to stage fights throughout the state, despite a rising national tide of criticism. Concerned for the activity's impact on Nevada's reputation, the state's Republican party campaigned against prizefighting in 1900, calling its legal status "a stigma upon the fair name of our State." Although its economic recovery was under way, Nevada, they reasoned, should remain concerned for its image and its subsequent standing in the minds of others. However to many, as with gambling, the economic potential of the fights far outweighed any moral qualms felt by its promoters or broader society.[80]

Many in Reno's business community were eager to jump on the bandwagon. In 1905, the newly formed Reno Athletic Club arranged a match between heavyweights Jack Root and Marvin Hart. Promoting it as the national heavyweight championship, a fact that was later disputed due to confusion over proper title succession, the club clearly anticipated an enormous crowd. Both Reno newspapers enthusiastically promoted preparations for the bout, closely following the fighters' training regimes and the construction of a 6,500-seat, open-air boxing arena on the east side of town. As the highlight of a five-day Reno Carnival, the fight ultimately drew approximately 4,000 spectators, many of whom had traveled from San Francisco on a chartered train. Apparently bettors who expected to find gambling on the fight in "wide open" Reno were disappointed, however. Reno's gamblers weren't taking bets, fearing a fix, but the promoters were delighted by the outcome, reporting an estimated take of $12,000, a clear indication that people would make the journey for an event they deemed worthy of the trip.[81]

The long-term advantages of this industry, however, were questionable. As might be expected, this further bucking of mainstream social trends earned Nevada opprobrium nationwide. By 1907, boxing contests proceeded in just five major cities—Baltimore, Philadelphia, Denver, Los Angeles, and Indianapolis—and there only with limited rounds. As a writer for the *Washington Post* reported that year, "Nevada alone is open to the pugilists to go it to a 'finish.' And it's wholly and solely for advertising reasons that prize fighting flourishes there." He ended with the assessment that Nevada was the exception solely "because there are new lands to advertise and because the trend of civilization has not made much progress." Obviously, this dismissal of the state as a frontier backwater was not what many modern-minded residents wanted to hear.[82]

However, even they could not completely condemn the enormous tide of publicity accompanying the news that Reno would be hosting a heavyweight championship between Jack Johnson and Jim Jeffries on the Fourth of July, 1910. The bout was promoted in advance as the "Fight of the Century," a rather brash claim, considering the century was just a decade old. But the import of the fight was undeniable. Jack Johnson, a black fighter, had ascended to the top of the sport. Charismatic, confident, and wealthy, Johnson flouted social convention, openly consorting with, and even marrying, white women and spending his money on a luxurious, flamboyant lifestyle. For his combination of raw talent and arrogant swagger, he was both widely admired and widely loathed, especially by a prejudiced public resentful of his success. His competitor, Jim Jeffries, had retired as the heavyweight champion of the world six years earlier, and some said that since he had never been defeated before retiring, he still was the champion. Promoters eager to find a "great white hope" to defeat Johnson convinced Jeffries to come out of retirement in order to reclaim the heavyweight title for white America.

Reno was not originally slated to be the site of this landmark event; that dubious honor went to San Francisco, where boxing promoter Tex Rickard, who had won the bidding for the fight, originally intended to hold the bout. An arena was already under construction there when California's governor was informed pointedly that hosting the fight could jeopardize San Francisco's chances of securing the Panama-Pacific Exposition in 1915. Af-

All eyes were on Reno for the intensely promoted heavyweight championship fight between Jack Johnson and Jim Jeffries on 4 July 1910. (Nevada Historical Society)

ter weighing the potential advantages of both events, he canceled the bout, just two weeks before it was to take place. Over the protests of local clergy who feared that Reno would be flooded by "riffraff" and "the offscouring of the country," a powerful group including Reno mayor Arthur Britt (a former saloon owner and beer distributor) and Governor Dickerson immediately invited Rickard to bring the fight to Reno. Although promoters in Goldfield, Nevada, also cast their hat into the ring, Rickard determined that Reno was a better location, and workers quickly set to work on the construction of a new 20,000-seat wooden amphitheater at the same location where the Root-Hart bout had taken place, just a few years earlier.[83]

As the fight approached, Mayor Britt received letters and telegrams from across the country urging him to prevent the fight from happening.

Because it was technically taking place outside of city limits, the mayor protested, rather disingenuously, that he had no power over it. He did, however, make arrangements with the chief of police for a uniformed officer to guard the ticket office where the tickets were being sold. The national and even international press convergence on Reno for the fight was staggering. The purse was $100,000, at that time the largest ever for a prizefight. It seemed that every major newspaper (and many minor ones) along with every nationally distributed magazine had sent a correspondent. These writers included Jack London, already an established writer with a national audience, whose coverage of the fight appeared in the *New York Herald, Los Angeles Times,* and *San Francisco Chronicle.* And the press did not just appear for the fight itself, but settled into Reno for the entire week-long training period that preceded it. Reporters watched closely as the competitors arrived in Reno on June 27 (Jeffries) and 28 (Johnson), covering subsequent developments at their training camps, located respectively at Moana Springs and Rick's Resort.[84]

As the date of the fight approached, Reno's carnival atmosphere intensified. The *Los Angeles Times* published a detailed itinerary and driving directions for those taking their motorcars to Reno for the fight. The Riverside Hotel and other hotels were booked to capacity, and some even rented cots to visitors who did not mind sleeping in their lobbies, gaming rooms, or hallways. Most locals were thrilled; thanks to the fight, thousands would experience Reno in person for the first time, and unprecedented numbers of reporters would be filing reports across the country. Although it was the target of much criticism, prizefighting was by far more acceptable to the American public than gambling. While the practice itself generated criticism for its violence, the staging of prizefights attracted a wider array of spectators, including many women and children, who regarded it simply as a form of entertainment. The fights also brought in dollars not just for individual business owners, but for the community as well, in the form of other services, including but not limited to hotels and restaurants to service the visiting crowds.[85]

If anything, locals seemed most concerned that the publicity generated by the fight, the most publicized sporting event in American history to that date, would present only one side of Reno rather than a complete view of the entire community. Frank M. Lee, vice president of Reno's Nixon National Bank and a prominent member of the Reno Commercial Club, when interviewed for the *New York Times* the day before the fight, voiced his wish that Reno would get equal attention for its university and other civic accomplishments. "Reno has suffered somewhat from the stories emanating from the divorce colony," he stated, "and now comes the fight that will send her name resounding to the uttermost parts of the earth. The name of Reno is now pretty well associated in people's minds with divorces and prizefights. It is not generally known that we have churches of every denomination in the city, also the State University and Mining School." Lee concluded, "I would much rather see Reno bask in the limelight of publicity over the new $125,000 Y.M.C.A. building which is to be erected there." No doubt pleased by his statement, Lee replicated the claim in Reno's city directory, placing the Y.M.C.A. construction on a par with the Johnson-Jeffries fight and saying, "That Reno should have done both of these things is typical of her western spirit and the indomitable pluck and energy of her people."[86]

A new Y.M.C.A. was all very well and good, but it was hardly national news, especially when there were so many other aspects of Reno to attract the attention of reporters in town for the fight. As Lee had anticipated, many focused on Reno's more unconventional features, but in a way that seemed more entertained than shocked. Gambling remained legal during the summer of 1910, and the knowledge that it was on its last legs inspired many to try their luck at the tables while they still had the chance. They were aided by the decision of many gambling houses, saloons, hotels, and even the resorts where the fighters were training to install additional games and roulette wheels in the days before the fight. Women and others who would never have dared enter a saloon tried their hand at the roulette wheels, now that they could do so in more respectable surroundings.[87]

When the day of the fight finally arrived, attendance in the arena reached 18,000. For all fifteen rounds, the world was riveted live, keeping track of the action via telegraph. Many cities, including San Francisco, presented a play-by-play of the action in front of enormous crowds, enacted in real time by stand-ins dressed as the fighters. Nine cameramen from Essanay, Selig, and Vitagraph filmed the entire fight from a number of angles. What they captured quickly escalated from a few tentative thrusts into a brutal beating of the former heavyweight champion by the much stronger and faster Johnson, who was crowned the undisputed heavyweight champion of the world when Rickard recognized that Jeffries was about to collapse and called the bout. The news of Jeffries's defeat prompted violence, riots, and random targeting of blacks from New York City to Omaha to

Pueblo, Colorado, although not in Reno. Because of the violence, many towns across the country banned the film when it later became available, but others showed footage not just of the fight, but of the training camps, as well as shots of the lively downtown streets in the days leading up to it. Viewers saw a thriving business district inhabited by enormous crowds of well-dressed men, women, and children, all in buoyant good spirits. In the end, the fight was an incredible success for Reno, surpassing all existing records for attendance at a sporting activity and demonstrating the economic potential of staging massive events.[88]

The approaching demise of legalized gambling earned national coverage for Reno that summer and fall, as well. With the approach of October 1, most spectators saw this as a very positive development, proof that Reno had finally progressed to a point of mainstream American cultivation, putting the Wild West period behind it at last. The *San Francisco Post* agreed that the occasion was momentous, signifying long-awaited progress for their neighboring state. As one of their reporters wrote,

> With the closing of the gambling houses in Nevada, one of the worst remaining relics of the "wild and wooly" west has passed out. . . . The gambler does not belong to the newly established city and town; the open gambling house does not belong beside the schoolroom and the home; the rattle of the poker chips and the whir of the roulette wheel have no place amid the sounds of a thriving municipality. The spirit of chance in the west must disappear, like other phantoms of a wild and lawless region and wraiths of wild and lawless days. Nevada was the last place of refuge for these phantoms. They must now pass down into history as unsavory memories.[89]

Such reform brought Reno in line with other modern communities; still, the *San Francisco Sun,* although ostensibly pleased with the legislation, waxed strangely nostalgic about the demise of legalized gambling, reflecting,

> So it is that all the glorious, wicked, picturesque, ruinous, adventurous life must pass. There is nothing picturesque or adventurous about collars and store clothes and barber shops and consolidated mining companies. Nevada is to be just like all the rest of us. She is taking her place in the line. There is something decidedly pathetic about breaking a

young colt to harness, or in seeing an adventurous youth cramped into commercial pursuits.

Still, the reporter clarified,

there is nothing to be deplored or regretted in the ending of gambling in Nevada. Those little white ivory balls have clicked off murder and suicide, and despair and endless misery have issued in fateful eloquence from that polished nickel faro box. Let the dealers and the cappers and the lookouts and the casekeepers and the bouncers and the bosses and all the rest of the crew go out and get a job, or several jobs, and go to work.[90]

The *Los Angeles Express* satirized the old frontier mentality in a poem written from the perspective of a fictional Nevadan and quoted in the *Reno Evening Gazette:*

Why, th' gang is plumb disgusted at the way th' law is run;
Purty soon they'll be declarin' that a man can't pack a gun;
I don't savvy how it happened, but they's somethin' wrong, you bet;
When they try to separate us from our poker and roulette.

In truth, most Nevadans saw the legislation as a sign of great progress. Demonstrating their concern for ensuring their community's high moral standards, for instance, the Reno Commercial Club publicized their central role in the antigambling campaign in the next city directory. A cartoon published in the paper showed a roulette wheel being relocated to the Nevada Historical Society, signifying the demise of the industry and its relegation to the history books.[91]

As the *Reno Evening Gazette* reported, with the exception of those who would have to find new work, "everybody else seemed satisfied, even glad, that the era of lawful gaming is at an end." The paper described the final night of open gambling as "more in the nature of a frolic than a funeral," explaining, "When a rotten structure is razed it is the part of progress to rear a better building in its stead. This is what Nevada must do . . . this city must now stand upon its own bottom and must progress through development of legitimate industry." By the first week of October, the Palace, Oberon, Louvre, and Casino were closed for renovations, as their owners retooled their business for a nongambling Reno. Some raised concern that

Commercial Row, the stretch that offered the first glimpse of Reno to in-
coming visitors, now appeared dark and desolate. One club owner said he
was going to board up his building to make the street look as deserted as
possible, presumably out of protest or bitterness, but the city council announced that they would deny licenses to any businesses that stayed closed
for more than thirty days.[92]

Like observers from across the country, most Reno residents regarded
this development as a turning point for Nevada. In November 1910, Jeanne
Wier, an instructor at the University of Nevada and founder of the Nevada
Historical Society back in 1904, spoke in California to the Pacific Coast
branch of the American Historical Association. Decrying the continued
criticism of the state of Nevada, she placed the end of gambling alongside
other of the state's Progressive reforms, proudly stating, "The political
progress [Nevada] has made with respect to anti-gambling laws, primary
election, referendum and recall, etc., would indicate that social consciousness is rapidly being developed in spite of isolation." Backward no longer,
the entire state seemed well on the way to increased acceptance by the rest
of the country.[93]

Local and state officials had considered the repercussions of every legislative decision of the past decade, not just to the state's economy, but to
its broader reputation. The success of the divorce industry and the Johnson-Jeffries fight had revealed the economic potential accompanying the
promotion of activities banned elsewhere. And as long as the activity in
question could be perceived more widely as a promotion of freedom rather
than vice, many officials and residents believed they could live with it. Although there was still major disagreement over the morality of both, divorce and prizefighting seemed at least capable of making this leap in the
national consciousness; gambling did not.

Perhaps predictably, the national attention, not to mention income,
generated by the first two industries made many Reno residents eager to
expand their visibility on the national, and even global, stage. This desire
was demonstrated quite literally in a new promotional booklet produced
by the Commercial Club and the Reno Business Men's Association in 1910.
On its cover, an image of a globe turned to display North and South America brandished the bold headline, "Reno, The Biggest Little City on the
Map." An editorial in the *Gazette* published a few weeks after the big fight
reported that visiting journalists had picked up the phrase "Biggest Little
City in the World," while in town. The editorial continued, "Isn't that

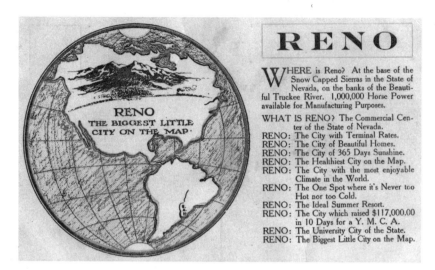

RENO

WHERE is Reno? At the base of the Snow Capped Sierras in the State of Nevada, on the banks of the Beautiful Truckee River. 1,000,000 Horse Power available for Manufacturing Purposes.

WHAT IS RENO? The Commercial Center of the State of Nevada.
RENO: The City with Terminal Rates.
RENO: The City of Beautiful Homes.
RENO: The City of 365 Days Sunshine.
RENO: The Healthiest City on the Map.
RENO: The City with the most enjoyable Climate in the World.
RENO: The One Spot where it's Never too Hot nor too Cold.
RENO: The Ideal Summer Resort.
RENO: The City which raised $117,000.00 in 10 Days for a Y. M. C. A.
RENO: The University City of the State.
RENO: The Biggest Little City on the Map.

In 1910, a promotional campaign naming Reno the "Biggest Little City on the Map" touted the town's university, diverse businesses, and superior climate, among other features. (Special Collections Department, University of Nevada–Reno Library)

something to be proud of? It is a merited title, to a certain extent, but should be earned in its entirety. It is the duty of every public spirited citizen . . . to make the title true." Little in size but big in stature, the city finally had tasted fame, and it was sweet indeed. Urging residents to dedicate themselves to beautifying the city, building its industries, and attracting both summer and winter tourists, the writer laid out a clear agenda: global dominance.[94]

To embrace the new slogan was to accept that agenda and to commit to the continued pursuit of international acclaim. In just a decade, Reno had been transformed—in image and, incipiently, in its built environment, through efforts both deliberate and unintentional—from an obscure railroad junction into an increasingly modern and cosmopolitan society seemingly capable of untold profit and publicity. Nevada's liberal legislation had directed more national attention than ever anticipated to its largest town, a development all agreed was positive and long deserved. Reno's residents now needed only to agree upon how best to parlay that brilliant flicker of attention into a permanent spotlight.

CHAPTER THREE

Selling Reno in the Consumer Age

Indeed the Idols I have loved so long
Have done my credit in this World much wrong:
Have drown'd my Glory in a shallow Cup,
And sold my Reputation for a Song.
Omar Khayyam, *The Rubaiyat*, 1120 C.E.

The role of sinner among the cities of America should be profitable.
Henry Pringle, *Outlook Magazine*, 1931

Leslie Curtis launched a robust defense of Reno in an article written for the *New York Herald* and published nationally in the summer of 1911. "The general opinion of Nevada and its divorce law is far from right," she complained. "People think of Reno as a wide open, immoral, debauched community, the abode of crime and duplicity, with reverence for nothing but money. This is not true!" On the contrary, she declared, "Reno is nothing more than a progressive little country town surrounding a peculiar nucleus of human puzzles." Such a rousing denial of Reno's financial motives might have seemed just a bit disingenuous coming from a writer who had gained fame and profit from writing "Housekeeping in Reno," "The Reno Divorce Mill," and *Reno Reveries*—two "playlets" and a short book satirizing the Reno divorce colony. But as Curtis knew, perhaps more than anyone, it was important not to appear to be in it for the money alone.[1]

A reputation for valuing profit over principles was not the most desirable image for a small town with big aspirations. Nevertheless, even with its recent ban on wide-open gambling, the state of Nevada was best known for tolerating, and even encouraging, morally questionable behaviors and activities. From six-month divorces to the "Fight of the Century," Reno had become a source of endless tales of excess, scandal, and excitement. That reputation only grew through extensive coverage of the divorce colony in magazines and daily newspapers from coast to coast. Looking back at the

Laura Corey divorce from a vantage point six years later, Arthur Ruhl summed up Reno's rapid ascension for *Collier's* magazine. Immediately after her visit, he recounted, "Lawyers, coached in the latest 'modern methods,' including that of advertising in the newspapers, hastened westward; picturesque despatches began to appear in Eastern newspapers, and Reno's reputation—to which, it is only fair to say, the more conservative citizens of this most agreeable little city decidedly object—was made." In just a few short years, Reno had achieved an astonishing level of fame, but the precise nature, and ultimate repercussions, of that new status remained uncertain.[2]

Although many of these dispatches described Reno as surprisingly conventional, still more favored the decadent and outrageous side of life in the divorce colony. For instance, a typical article in the *Los Angeles Times* described a "secret ball" organized in Reno by "thirty of the prominent women of the colony from New York" where, reportedly, "Each divorcon vied with her fellow colony members in gorgeous display of gown and figure, and the importations in costumes and jewels are said to have represented at least $75,000." Reno appeared as a town of extremes in everything from society columns to literary fiction. In Edith Wharton's brilliant satire of divorce, *The Custom of the Country*, published in 1913, the much-married, continually aspiring New York socialite Undine Spragg travels first to Dakota and then to Reno for two of her many divorces. After the Reno divorce from a French marquise, of which, it is reported, "no case has ever been railroaded through the divorce courts of this State at a higher rate of speed," Undine takes advantage of Reno's legislative flexibility by remarrying her first husband fifteen minutes later. Wharton came by her interest in the subject honestly, having herself secured a divorce the year of the novel's publication.[3]

As Reno's profile grew, such accounts earned money for their authors, just as the industries they described provided income for the town itself. Whatever the motivations of both, it was clear that selling Reno had become good business. To the community, the divorce industry was potentially more lucrative than any other tourist attraction they had presented thus far. Even the Johnson-Jeffries fight, which had generated staggering numbers of visitors and money in 1910, did so only for a discrete period. In contrast, divorcées arrived in a steady, overlapping stream, consistently bringing to Reno both income and attention. Staying for six months at a time, each divorce-seeker functioned as an extended tourist, and a broad spectrum of residents stood to benefit from their presence. Lawyers and lodging operators profited most directly, but the ripple effect spread to clothing stores, restaurants, salons, pharmacies, and other businesses that provided services to them as well as to the permanent population.

Like it or not, Reno had gained a clear notoriety, an image neither promoted nor endorsed by the Chamber of Commerce or Commercial Club. For years, those organizations had worked to convey the impression that Reno was just the same as other communities across America, but now uniqueness seemed to hold more promise than conformity. Nevada had stumbled upon a valuable commodity in the form of its permissive legislation in a variety of areas. As a result, the Reno experience was taking shape as a readily identifiable commodity, a product that could be described, advertised, and purchased like any other goods and services.

This commodification of Reno fit right in with the new landscape of consumption emerging in the early twentieth century. As standardized products became available to a wider swath of the population, America's mass culture took shape. The increasing affordability of travel produced a market for mass tourism, now accessible to the elite and non-elite alike. At the same time, advertising was becoming more sophisticated, through the use of psychological pitches intended to inspire emotional responses. Product manufacturers of all kinds became aware of the need to generate a broad appeal to the masses in order to attract the demanding consumer.

Communities were as aware as any manufacturer of the competitive nature of the modern marketplace. Civic promoters from San Francisco to New York recognized the importance of conveying a distinct "urban personality," an amalgamation of physical and social characteristics, to promote and distinguish their cities. Yet while most cities, as historian Catherine Cocks writes, strove to emphasize their "unique yet conventionally appealing . . . people-pleasing traits," Reno was making a name for itself along other, more controversial lines.[4] Many were afraid that a bad reputation, once gained, would be impossible for Reno to shake. As Delos F. Wilcox wrote in 1910, "Cities, like men, have careers, which to a great extent are determined by environment and to a great extent by the innate energy and the habitual ethical standards of their inhabitants. The city can no more escape from the penalties of early heedlessness than a man can remove from his life the scars left by recklessness and wickedness in his youth." Many in Reno agreed, and through the next decades, would find themselves engaging in emotional debates over the consequences of past civic decisions as they tried to determine the best career path for their maturing city.[5]

Its promoters did hope to create a positive impression with their new civic slogan, "The Biggest Little City on the Map," although labeling Reno a "city" at this point was rather generous. The town had more than doubled in the first decade of the new century, but even so, its population in 1910 hovered around 11,000. The physical size was not the point, however; the slogan reflected a cosmopolitanism that belied its actual numbers, and Reno's boosters wore it with pride. "Reno has been justly christened the 'Biggest Little City on the Map,'" boasted C. T. Stevenson of the Reno Commercial Club, "and it has received more advertising, probably, than any city of its size in the Union." As a result, some thought, the attention Reno received from divorce could serve as a vehicle for promoting Reno's other civic accomplishments.[6]

Debates over whether—and if so, how—to capitalize on this attention intensified over the next few decades, as city leaders and residents publicly weighed the costs and benefits of fastening Reno's reputation to consumer desires. The appeal of the national spotlight, even for such controversial activities as divorce or more unsavory activities, proved difficult for some in Reno's business community to resist. To others, it was a clear liability, leading to concerns that the state's legislators and city officials were motivated purely by economics. Projected outward as crassness or greed, this threatened to become a permanent component of Reno's reputation, too.

The contradictory nature of much outside press coverage did not make the decision any easier. Indeed, the *New York Times,* centered in the city from which many of the early divorcées originated, expressed a typically paradoxical response to Reno. Beginning in 1913 and continuing on a regular basis through the next two decades, the *Times* published the names of prominent divorce-seekers, often on the front page and itemized by location. At the same time, while breathlessly reporting every new arrival to the Reno divorce colony, the paper's editorial pages regularly criticized the colony, stating at one point, "The divorce mill itself is a scandal. Reno has made itself a reproach and a shame." At other times the paper's criticism was more measured, acknowledging that while economically profitable, divorce was hardly conducive to the formation of a stable community. As one editorial read, "To nobody, however, is a 'divorce colony' exactly a pleasing spectacle, and it is more than doubtful if the real interests of any town are advanced by the possession of one widely notorious."[7]

Of course, to locals concerned more for Reno's residents than tourists, the town's "real interests" would be best advanced by creating a stable, moral environment. This was clearly on the mind of University of Nevada president Joseph Stubbs during a visit to Southern California in December 1910. Speaking to a local reporter, he protested, "Reno isn't half as bad as it's made out," continuing, "Like all things of this character, its vices have been far more widely heralded than its virtues." Pleased at the recent ban on gambling, Stubbs voiced his hope to see further reforms in the community. Next, he promised, "we are going right after the divorce problem," which he knew would be a "hard fight" in the next legislative session. "In another six months," he predicted, "you may hear that this little city in Nevada has suddenly lost all its attractions for the men and women who are tired of their other halves."[8]

In the quest to turn his hopes into reality, Stubbs had some prominent allies. When former president Theodore Roosevelt visited Reno in April 1911, he was said to have "hammered the Nevada divorce colony, declaring that no city or State could long exist by harboring divorce and building up a colony of married people who sought to be rid of their mates." As the city had earlier outlawed the "gambling evil," Roosevelt encouraged them to drive out divorce. By the following year, support for this new crusade had grown considerably. *Nevada State Journal* editor George D. Kilborn summed up his perception of community sentiment, arguing, "People at Reno and in the remainder of the state, for that matter, do not like the notoriety that we have gained through the numerous divorce proceedings brought into the state by persons from other commonwealths." Although admitting that some in Reno continued to "profit financially by this evil," he was quick to place them in a minority, claiming that "the citizenship of the state generally are tired of it and are demanding such amendment of the laws as shall put an end to it."[9]

The growing criticism was not due solely to moral concerns. Others objected to inconsistent enforcement of the residency requirement for divorce when so many applicants clearly had no intention of remaining in the state. The theatrical crowd in particular was often charged with failing to reside within the state for a full six months. Attorney William Schnitzer had openly informed potential clients that the requirement could be easily evaded, "So, if a party comes to Nevada, and, in good faith, takes up a residence, the party may leave the State at any time after establishing residence, may go and travel when and wherever the party chooses, and may return to

the State whenever inclination prompts."[10] Other couples reportedly col-
luded to evade the residency requirement through a loophole that allowed
a quicker divorce if the proceedings were said to have been instigated by
events occurring within the state of Nevada, or if the defendant, the other
spouse, happened to be "found" and served within the state.[11]

Whatever their specific motivations, a diverse array of citizens gathered
at the state capital of Carson City in 1913 to encourage the state legislature
to extend the residency period to a full year. Members of the Y.M.C.A.,
Twentieth Century Club, St. Margaret's Society, and other church and
women's groups were supported by Governor Tasker L. Oddie who, in his
opening remarks to the legislative session that year, criticized the inconsis-
tencies of the state's migratory divorce trade, arguing, "the adverse advertising which Nevada is receiving therefrom is retarding the state's healthful
development."[12]

These groups were overjoyed when the legislature agreed, extending the
residence requirement to twelve months for parties with only one spouse
residing in Nevada, effective 1 January 1914. The public response was immediate, and the national media soon demonstrated how fickle it was; just
as quickly as it showered attention on a place, it could take the spotlight
away. With the implementation of the new law, the *New York Times* bid
"Farewell to Reno's Supremacy as a Divorce Centre," proclaiming, "the
Nevada Metropolis Is No Longer a Paradise for the Matrimonially Dissatis-
fied." California journalist George Wharton James, writing for *Out West,*
declaimed, "No longer can the ill-mated from other states flaunt their domestic infelicities or marital unfaithfulnesses before the unwilling eyes of
the pure men, women, youths, maidens, and children of Nevada. . . . They
must thereafter cease from making Reno the wash-house of the nation, and
cleanse their soiled linen in the washtubs provided by their own respective
states."[13]

However, it also became clear that the notoriety and the money went
together. The legislation might have pleased moralists, but the damage to
city coffers was palpable. Tourist Effie Price Gladding, arriving in Reno in
1915, noted the preoccupation of residents with the widespread loss of
business since the recent legislation. While visiting a local hairdresser for a
shampoo, she was told that the recent extension of the residency period
from six months to one year was unpopular among Reno residents, "as formerly the town was full of boarders and lodgers 'doing time.'" Wrote
Gladding, "I confess I was somewhat shocked by such a sordid point of

view. I found myself looking quietly around the Riverside dining room to see whether I could pick out in the well filled room any candidates for divorce, and then I reflected that they were probably looking at me with the same query in their minds."[14]

The slump in Reno's economy following the 1913 act was more than hearsay. To the members of the Reno Business Men's Association, the city's economy needed the divorce trade, even at the risk of national censure. Along with other supporters, they began to campaign for the reinstatement of the six-month residency period, and in 1915, with the help of many new faces in the legislature, as well as a new governor, they succeeded. In a statement immediately following the decision, Governor Emmet Boyle acknowledged fears that the statute would "lead to abuses tending to a lowering of moral standards in the state, and especially within the town of Reno" and encouraged Nevada's women, who had won the franchise in 1914, to help enact "more stringent regulations along moral lines" to maintain public decency in the divorce colony. As far as outside opinion was concerned, Boyle said, "If I am correct in assuming that public sentiment in Nevada favors the six-months law it is not my function to concur in any hypocrisy tending to give the outside world a mistaken impression of our ideals."[15]

That same legislature continued the liberalizing trend by allowing perimutuel betting at the racetrack. Previous legislatures had already eased restrictions on gambling since the 1910 ban by allowing social games like whist and bridge, as well as "nickel-in-the-slot" machines as long as they paid out in cigars, drinks, or sums less than $2. Even when not licensed, gambling continued in many tightly controlled clubs along Center and Virginia Streets and Commercial Row, in basements and behind closed doors. The practice had become an established part of life in the Great Basin, capitalizing on the same psychological urges that had led so many to seek their fortune in the state's mines decades earlier, and was simply too popular to disappear. The public response to these developments was predictably divided. While the press in many other states reflected condemnation, the *Oakland Tribune* had a measured response to both statutes. Accustomed by now to Nevada's pattern of legalizing practices made illegal by California, a *Tribune* writer reflected, "The more virtuous we are the greater the prosperity of our wicked neighbors."[16]

Although permanent residents could certainly take advantage of both gambling and streamlined divorces, both industries were primarily intended to capture business from the outside. In a flurry of legislation, the state's representatives had expressed their commitment to the tourist dollar. The business community was the first to voice the need to translate the attendant publicity into broader visitation. In a 1916 address at the Nevada State Business Men's Convention, held at the Reno Commercial Club, one member stated, "All the talk about Nevada has simply made people curious to see the country and the people. We have nothing to be ashamed of in our laws or in our courts." He concluded that "we should have a comprehensive plan to encourage tourist travel. Everyone who comes should be received cordially, and be given pleasant memories to carry away." In saying so, he voiced a common hope that the city could both exploit people's curiosity and at the same time control Reno's subsequent reputation by providing positive experiences for those who visited for themselves.[17]

In their increasing awareness of the enormous potential of tourism, previewed for them by the pseudo-tourists of the divorce trade, Reno's business leaders recognized the new opportunities stemming not only from their unconventional laws, but also from the introduction of the automobile. Just as earlier residents had been highly attuned to the railroad travelers passing through town, so they now were acutely aware of the arrival of motor tourists in search of scenic vistas. With automobiles still something of a novelty, local papers reported on the arrival of "the first ocean-to-ocean tourists" of 1913, a group of "prominent and wealthy business men" who were driving across the country from their home in Los Angeles to the Atlantic coast and staying overnight at the Riverside Hotel.[18]

The rise of popular automobile tourism opened a new market of visitation to Reno, as well as to towns across America. Although a relatively new technology not available to everyone, the automobile was already becoming a presence on the national landscape. With the introduction of more affordable cars and paved highways, the number of vehicles registered nationwide skyrocketed from 458,000 in 1910 to 8 million by 1920. In this decade, Americans were increasingly taking to the road for independent travels, representing what historian Earl Pomeroy called the "new democratization of vacation travel." Mobile and liberated, motor tourists would no longer have their experiences dictated by the railroad's fixed tracks, itineraries, or picture windows.[19]

The construction of an improved road extending from Reno toward San Francisco would be critical in order to effectively capture these new mobile tourists. Without such a route, local residents feared, drivers might detour south at Salt Lake City toward Los Angeles, which continued to grow and prosper. Just as early entrepreneurs like Myron C. Lake had campaigned energetically for the establishment of a railroad junction, members of Reno's business community intently monitored plans for the proposed Lincoln Highway and were thrilled in September 1913 when the Lincoln Highway Association officially announced that the highway's route would pass through Reno. The organization's funds were matched by money from the Federal Highway Act of 1916; however, the highway took more than ten years to complete. In the meantime, work also began on a competing highway, the Victory Highway (U.S. 40), which ran through Nevada on a route north of the Lincoln Highway, along the route of the current Interstate 80.

This project was definitely deemed worthy of local investment. In 1917, Reno Commercial Club Secretary George A. Raymer reported that Washoe County would contribute $15,000 toward improving the Lincoln Highway from Reno to Lake Tahoe in hopes of attracting additional tourists. Interviewing Raymer that year for her master's thesis at the University of Nevada, Annie Estelle Prouty maintained, "Many tourists look forward both coming and going from California to a rest and stopping place for side trips in Reno. Much money is to be spent in improving the Highway. . . . It is Reno's opportunity to improve all the advantages and advertise these in a practical way in order that people may find rest and recreation of the highest order."[20]

Reno found itself in an interesting position with respect to these new tourists. The vast majority, to be sure, would hold preconceptions about Reno, impressions that might dissuade them from stopping to rest and recreate there. This necessitated making a clear distinction in the public eye between the two sides of Reno. True, the state's permissive legislation had enabled the growth of the divorce colony and a certain amount of gambling, but the "real Reno," boosters asserted, was the respectable university town, a typical American landscape inhabited by families who went about their business just like everyone else. At the same time, the idea of the "real Reno" helped residents to justify the existence of certain businesses in their midst by asserting to themselves, as to outsiders, that the true and authentic town was clearly distinct from the commodified image so widely propagated by the media.

A number of publications reinforced this notion of a "real Reno"— most prominently, the *Nevada Newsletter*, a weekly paper published by a newspaperman, artist, and writer named Boyd Moore, beginning in 1914 and continuing through the 1920s. Commencing publication "for no other purpose than to assist in promoting the welfare of Reno and Nevada," he wrote in his first issue, "we are going to try mighty hard to help out in the way of good, wholesome publicity." Each issue featured articles about Lake Tahoe, local irrigation projects, updates on highway construction, the university and public school system, and, occasionally, full-page halftone photographs of local residences, businesses, and landscapes. Advertisements for the newsletter in the local newspapers urged residents to "Mail a copy to a friend or acquaintance abroad and through that single effort you may reach the eyes of a hundred or more persons in a campaign to picture the 'Real Reno' and the 'Real Nevada,' this that false notions regarding our make-up may be wiped out and the true picture of our beauty and attractiveness and greatness pictured instead."[21]

In a special 20-page promotional magazine published in 1920, Moore clarified, "It is the 'Real Reno' that we are here to discuss. This for the reason that in all this broad land of ours there is probably not another city, even of considerably larger size, that is so widely spoken of but so little known in a real, true light." The "Real Reno," he argued, was the "Commercial and Banking Center of Nevada," a respectable, cosmopolitan city— "modern, progressive, thrifty and thoroughly up to the mark." The booklet defended this assertion through a series of attractive photographs of street scenes and professional buildings.[22]

It was a lovely picture, but that was not the image of Reno that captured the national imagination. As Reno's residents continued to present their version of the "real Reno," a number of new guidebooks to the city began to appear, selling their version of the town to a completely different audience. George Bond's *Six Months in Reno* and Lilyan Stratton's *Reno: A Book of Short Stories and Information* came out in 1921, both published by eastern presses, both directed toward divorce-seekers planning a trip to Reno. Highly descriptive, they functioned much like other tourist guides, containing all the usual features of mainstream guidebooks, from local history to transportation schedules, hotel descriptions, climate information, and business profiles, with the additional feature of legal guidelines for divorce proceedings and, in Stratton's case, short tales of the "romance, tragedy, and humor of the divorce colony." Their descriptions clearly targeted the easterner skeptical of her (or his) ability to survive six months out west. The arrival of such books represented two significant developments: first, the existence of enough potential divorce-seekers to justify the production

of full volumes targeted specifically to them; and second, a growing convergence of migratory divorce and mass tourism. Both trends confirmed
the value of the divorce trade to the outside, indicating that it was in no
danger of slowing down.[23]

Indeed, the state's divorce industry received a renewed boost in 1920
with the decision of Hollywood actress Mary Pickford, "America's Sweet-
heart," to divorce her husband, actor Owen Moore, in order to marry even
more famous actor Douglas Fairbanks. Although her divorce did not tran-
spire in Reno, but in the small ranching town of Minden, approximately 50
miles to the south, it drew further attention to the state and helped to establish a connection between northern Nevada and the young Hollywood
crowd. Pickford's appearance also prompted renewed discussion of the
value of divorce to the state and the great potential for abuse of its statutes.
The controversy arose when Pickford received a divorce after residing just
seventeen days in the state, having taken advantage of the legal loophole
that negated the six-month residency requirement if the other spouse happened to be located in the state as well. As Pickford explained in court,
Owen Moore had coincidentally arrived in the state during her own stay,
ostensibly scouting out a coal mine for one of his pictures, in Virginia City.
When the judge asked if she meant gold mines, she immediately corrected
herself, but skeptics rightly suspected fraud.[24]

The legal matter was ultimately settled in Pickford's favor, but a writer
for the *Carson [City] Appeal* reflected strong local opinion when asking,

> of what lasting benefit is Mary Pickford to the state? She came for a stay
> of less than a month, spent a few thousand dollars and left. As a result
> Nevada has added to her already unenviable reputation as a state of easy
> divorce laws. One man or woman coming to make a home in the state is
> worth more . . . than a hundred divorcees, such as Mary Pickford.

A few years later new legislation was signed that did away with the legal
loophole allowing "'short time' cases of the Mary Pickford type," and the
industry continued, unabated.[25]

For those still supportive of the trade, Pickford's value lay in bringing a
renewed sense of glamour to the practice. The most popular movie star of
her era, Pickford often played strong characters who asserted their own
personal liberties and economic independence. Beloved for her screen persona as well as for her fascinating personal life, Pickford's divorce demon-

strated to many devoted fans that marriage need not be permanent and that divorce was often essential to the pursuit of true love. Like Pickford, the "new woman" of the 1920s was liberated, active, and independent. With ratification of the Nineteenth Amendment in August of 1920, all American women finally had achieved the equal suffrage for which they had labored so long. Other recent developments pointed to a new spirit of liberation, from the opening of the first birth control clinic, by Margaret Sanger in Brooklyn in 1916, to the election of the first woman, Jeannette Rankin of Montana, to the U.S. Congress that same year. For men and women alike, the Jazz Age represented a growing spirit of unconventionality, freedom, and individualism.[26]

That spirit was manifested in criticisms of the standardized society that was emerging from a culture increasingly characterized by mass production, assembly lines, and materialism. Author Sinclair Lewis was one of the most famous figures to satirize the conformist landscape of the average American town in his extremely popular novels *Main Street* (1920) and *Babbitt* (1922). Both struck a chord in exploring the deadening impact of materialistic and socially conservative communities on the individual desire for self-expression. Considered in this context, Reno could be interpreted in one of two ways: as a materialistic community concerned only with financial gain, or as an individualistic town bravely transcending the strictures of a conservative society. Sinclair Lewis's own wife, in Reno to divorce the novelist in 1928, chose to see the latter. A writer and former editor for *Vogue*, Grace Hegger Lewis judged Reno to be a place with its own unique spirit, not a standardized or morally corrupt town at all. Lewis wrote that the spectator "begins to take heart—this is a place with character, with color, and, you are suddenly conscious, with air to make you hungry." Published in *Scribner's* magazine, the account earned praise from locals for being both "different and truer to facts than many that have appeared heretofore."[27]

Her positive impressions were shared by another literary chronicler of the average American community, Sherwood Anderson. The author of *Winesburg, Ohio* (1919), a portrait of one man's struggles in a repressive and narrow-minded small town, Anderson secured his own Reno divorce in April 1924. While in town, he contributed a piece to Boyd Moore's *Nevada Newsletter,* expressing his delight with Reno's distinctiveness. "Everyone speaks of Reno and everyone has something to say about it," he wrote, continuing,

It is one of the places in America. Larger cities, Detroit, Cincinnati, St. Louis and even that huge Chicago in some way get lost. One forgets just what is made in them—is it Fords or shoes or sealing wax? There are other towns about which folklore grows—Boston, New York, Baltimore, San Francisco, New Orleans, Reno. . . . I fancy it is because all of these have been the scene of real human adventures. Reno is the center, the metropolis of Nevada, and Nevada is something, and perhaps always will be something special.

Undoubtedly, Moore was thrilled at this confirmation of Reno's unique character, something he had been asserting through his paper's pages all along.[28]

As many agreed, one had to accept Reno on its own terms to truly appreciate it. Essayist and short story writer Katharine Fullerton Gerould, reporting on Reno for *Harper's* in 1925, was apparently unable to do so. Her assessment that Reno was both "very dull" and even "sinister" could be explained, at least in part, by her frequent comparisons of Reno to another prominent divorce colony for the well-bred, known by some as the "European Reno." As Gerould put it, "the people with money and imagination go to Paris." The divorce colony there, she noted approvingly, "has resources of entertainment, distraction, civilization; and Reno has none." And yet, she admitted, thanks to the constant stream of divorcées, "something cosmopolitan has washed off on the Nevada metropolis," thereby saving Reno "from being Gopher Prairie," the name of the oppressive town in Sinclair Lewis's novel *Main Street.* Faint praise at best, it seemed all she was willing to impart.[29]

As a growing cadre of writers began to declare, Reno's appeal was not just confined to its divorce statutes but extended to the entire atmosphere of the town. Like it or not, it was the descriptions provided by those who were covering the divorce industry in Reno that truly helped to perpetuate the impression of Reno as a cosmopolitan place worthy of the title "Biggest Little City on the Map" or "The Biggest Little City in the World," as it had come to be known. To any lingering apprehensions that Reno was nothing but a cow town, these outside accounts offered concrete evidence to the contrary. Like Boyd Moore's newsletter, many claimed to be revealing the "Real Reno." A primary task assumed by these authors, the vast majority from the East Coast themselves, was to reassure eastern readers accustomed to a life of luxurious dining and nights at the theater that Reno was up to their standards of cosmopolitanism. In doing so, they often utilized not only photographs, but also facts and even direct phrases employed by the city's own publicity machine. Stratton, for instance, referred to Reno as the "big little city on the Truckee River," suggesting her familiarity with the city's favored slogan.[30]

In their attempt to demystify this western divorce mill, such writers often corroborated local boosters' claims of cultivation, finally confirming what Nevada press and boosters and officials had been saying for decades: that Reno's frontier period was over. In a consumer era, the product needed above all to match its description, and in this respect, the literary community continued to act as energetic marketers. Claiming that "a great deal of more or less exaggerated information has been dispensed" about the "un-hitching post," or the "mecca of the marriage-lorn," a writer for *Travel* magazine confirmed in 1922 that "Reno's evolution from the very roughest and toughest of pioneer towns into a little modern city has been remarkable."[31]

In his guidebook, *Six Months in Reno,* George Bond confirmed that this transformation had been accomplished, although perhaps not yet in the eyes of all those who regarded Reno from afar. "When, in the course of conversation round tea-tables, in the theatre, or elsewhere, one hears the statement that Mrs. So and So has gone to Reno," he wrote, "nobody ever asks why she went there, because poor little Reno is only known in the East as being a place one goes to for divorce." But according to Bond, "poor little Reno" deserved more praise than pity. He continued, "Most Eastern people who talk of Reno, seem to think it is a little town composed of cowboys, wooden shacks and wild Indians" and noted with apparent surprise, "After a night's ride from San Francisco I arrived at Reno about eight o'clock in the morning, to find myself not in a town of cowboys, wooden shacks and Indians, but in a real up-to-date progressive little City of some fifteen thousand inhabitants." In asserting how impressively the town had surpassed Bond's expectations, his own words seemed sure to raise the expectations of those who followed.[32]

Lilyan Stratton's *Reno,* promoted in Reno newspapers as the "Greatest Book of the year just off the press," corroborated Bond's impressions. "The Easterners somehow have an idea that Nevada has made very little progress since pre-historic days" and "that the West is still wild and wooly and consists of cow-boys, cattle ranches and rattlesnakes; but this impression is very erroneous," she wrote. On the contrary, she assured her readers, "All traces of the 'wild and woolly' Western town have disappeared. The people of Reno are very docile indeed . . . there are no cowboy yells nor Indian whoops, which some of our Eastern and Southern friends imagine still to exist." In seeking to correct such false impressions, Stratton voiced her desire "to change the world's opinion of Reno and its laws from ridicule to admiration." Even her language aligned with that of local boosters.[33]

At the same time, while defending the town against charges of frontier backwardness, these writers demonstrated a fascination with Reno's western qualities. With the frontier period clearly over, the American public felt free to romanticize the period and to classify any remnants of it as picturesque. An awareness of cultural fascination with the West, as well as traditions borne from the ranching heritage of the area, prompted the community to found its own rodeo in 1919. Planned by the Commercial Club, the "Nevada Round-Up" was intended to be a wholesome tourist attraction. It also served as a sign that in the modern era, celebrating a frontier past no longer carried a stigma.[34]

Symbolic of organizers' perceptions of how far Reno had come since its frontier days was their construction, for the rodeo's duration, of an imitation Wild West mining camp, named Stingaree Gulch, in the very center of town, at the intersection of Commercial Row and Virginia Street. Due to Prohibition, reluctantly enacted in Reno in November 1918 under national wartime pressure, the "town" featured no saloons, but did feature mock storefronts, stables, dance halls, dancing girls, and singers. An initial plan to offer gambling tables, using tokens rather than cash, was cancelled when the town sheriff contended that even such games violated the current Anti-Gambling Act. This was, then, a controlled Wild West, with no gambling, no prostitution, no drinking, and cowboys who galloped tamely within the limits of the rodeo arena. It was a version of the West suitable to the cultivated town that Reno had ostensibly become, celebrating a frontier heritage planted firmly in the realm of nostalgia. The rodeo was an enormous success, attracting over 10,000 people and convincing its promoters to make the celebration annual.[35]

To the easterners and urbanites who devoured the divorce literature, Reno's western flavor was an integral aspect of the town's unique character, reflected in everything from the natural landscape to the personalities of its residents. Commercial Reno, wrote Tom Gilbert, offered "a bit of 'Western,'" with the "true Western spirit" evident in the friendly demeanor of the town's proprietors, who "come right back at you with that famous Western

Smile, and ask you to come back any time."[36] As William Greene wrote for *Travel* in 1922, "Good-natured and open-hearted, happy-go-lucky, free and easy, worldly-minded and superficial, living supremely and sublimely in the present hour, Reno is to-day one of the last towns where the true western spirit still exists in much of its pristine vigor." And yet it was also "indeed cosmopolitan with its flotsam and jetsam of divorce-seekers from various walks of life, to say nothing of the interesting heterogeneity of Indians, Chinese, Japanese, French, Italians, Mexicans, Basques, negroes and many a half-breed and hybrid." As writer Ramona Park Brockliss wrote in a letter to *Sunset* magazine, Reno "has a personality all its own. . . . Cosmopolitan in its outlook, and with a certain degree of sophistication, there is, nevertheless, a spirit of true western friendliness that warmly actuates those who live there."[37]

The presence of Native Americans on Reno's streets added to the exotic appeal as perceived by easterners. The city had founded an "Indian colony," a small reservation outside city limits, for members of the area's Washoe, Paiute, and Shoshone tribes in 1917. They were now commodified too, treated by many tourists as part of the scenery, the objects of a "tourist gaze" that often exemplified a racist infantilization. This brand of ethnic tourism already was operating in full force in New Mexico, where "Indian Detours" sponsored by the Fred Harvey company and the railroad brought tourists directly to sites of native dances and rituals. As Greene reported,

> The Indians of Nevada . . . are always in evidence on the streets of Reno, often sitting on the edge of the sidewalk or on the bare ground, remaining thus in perfect contentment for hours at a time. . . . They present to visitors an unusual sight, with their bright-colored clothing and gaudy blankets, the women wearing silk kerchiefs around their heads and carrying little papooses upon their backs, securely laced up in their wicker carriers like diminutive mummies.

Unlike the native inhabitants of Santa Fe, Reno's Native Americans were primarily depicted as static components of the picturesque landscape rather than performers with whom visitors regularly interacted.[38]

In 1929, *Pictorial Review*'s Genevieve Parkhurst was similarly intrigued by the scene produced by such an array of characters:

> Miners in dungarees or dressed up in their store clothes, ready to spend their dollars earned with pick and shovel beneath the ground, cowboys

in full regalia, "desert rats" there for a glimpse of a peopled world. Painted women, ready to feed on the loneliness and the generosity of the men from the mines and lumber-camps and cattle-ranches, form their gay parade by day as well as by night. Indians in bright blankets, or ancient squaws in tattered garments, walk the streets, or, squatting at corners, beg pennies from the passers-by or seek to sell their wares of moccasins, basketry, or beadwork.

Oddly reminiscent of the first outside perceptions of Reno, back in 1868, this scene was now considered not threatening or coarse but lively and picturesque. Clearly it was not the simple presence of the western types that intrigued the observers, but the juxtaposition of such figures with "modern" people like themselves. Mixed with the cosmopolitanism of a little city, this western flavor produced the intoxicating cocktail that these writers tried to convey to their readers.[39]

Scribner's Grace Hegger Lewis described the mix in vivid detail: "A lordly Rolls-Royce, driven by a foreign chauffeur, is parked by a muddy Ford, held together by faith and a piece of string, out of which steps a cowboy in overalls, high-heeled boots, and a two-gallon hat. A fat Indian woman, in wide pink gingham skirt and a purple plaid shawl, with a papoose strapped to her back, stands giggling at the nile-green 'braziers' and brief panties" in a window display. To such observers, Reno exemplified both the urban and the primitive, all the comforts of home as well as an appealing exoticism, making it different enough to be unique without being frightening. This, it seemed, was Reno's peculiar niche.[40]

Through repetition, such features of the landscape became commodified as part of the "Reno experience." By including them again and again in word and image, the burgeoning divorce literature elevated buildings into landmarks, constructing a tourist landscape that revolved around divorce-seekers and their escapades. For the prominent role they played in the divorce trade, the Washoe County Courthouse and the Riverside Hotel were consistently pictured in coverage of the colony. Images and descriptions of the courthouse appeared in nearly every story about Reno from this period, as chroniclers treated the neoclassical building, which resembled so many other courthouses across the country, as one of a kind. In their eyes it was Reno's most significant architectural landmark, without which, as Stratton pronounced, "Reno would not be Reno." William Greene, from *Travel,* agreed that the courthouse was the focal point for the visiting divorcées, the structure "in which the interest of some two thousand members of that rare exotic class of Reno's population is chiefly centered."[41]

The building's centrality to the divorce narrative prompted many reflections on its larger significance. In 1921, Stratton moved quickly from description to metaphor when describing the structure as "a very imposing building with its big golden dome, numerous marble pillars and broad steps" and continuing, "These steps might truly be called the 'great divide,' as many thousands have tripped up united and returned divided." She continued, "As one looks at this palace of Justice one cannot help conjuring up mental pictures of famous beauties and prominent men, whose stories have furnished headlines for the leading newspapers of our big cities in years gone by."[42] In addition to "The House of Divide," Tom Gilbert offered a number of popular nicknames for the "famed marble and plaster Mansion," including "The Castle of Lady Luck" and "The Separator." Grace Hegger Lewis found the structure symbolic of doom, writing that to a new guest staying on the courthouse side of the Riverside Hotel, "it seems like living in death-row with your eyes always on the death-chamber. You learn that those two whitely opaque windows on the second floor hide the two judges on their separate benches, and that one of them will eventually pass sentence upon you."[43]

References to these and other divorce landmarks enhanced their mythic status. Legends had already spread about traditions of the newly divorced in Reno, stories that alert observers recognized as manufactured fictions. In her travelogue, *The Macadam Trail: Ten Thousand Miles by Motor Coach,* Mary Day Winn wrote of "humorous stories about these buildings, which are handed down from one . . . generation to the next." In one such story, divorcées were supposedly led by their lawyers to the six courthouse columns, which they kissed in succession at the end of every month to mark time served, leaving "a pink lip-stick glow." In his 1927 brochure, Tom Gilbert also claimed that women kissed the courthouse upon receipt of their divorce degree, and that "impressions of a million kisses" on the building's columns had distorted the appearance of the marble from a distance. This peculiar practice itself, or at least the frequent depictions of it, reinforced the lighthearted treatment given to the Reno divorce. As a final step before leaving town, the columnar kiss was framed as a joyful gesture of gratitude bestowed upon the symbol of the long-awaited decree. It also brought a marriage to a close with a perverted inversion of the first kiss of a bride and groom, turning the groom into a pillar of stone, and allowing

A postcard by cartoonist Lew Hymers helped to popularize the legend that newly minted Reno divorcées flung their unwanted wedding rings off the Virginia Street Bridge into the rushing Truckee River below. (Special Collections Department, University of Nevada–Reno Library)

the newly divorced ex-bride to continue down the courthouse stairs alone and free.[44]

By the end of the decade, writers were relating another ritual supposedly practiced by newly minted divorcées who threw their obsolete wedding rings off the Virginia Street Bridge and into the Truckee River. Calling the bridge the "Arc of Sighs," Gilbert waxed poetic about a "charming little Divorcette" who paused on the bridge after getting her divorce decree, and "removing the wedding ring from her finger accompanied by a declaration of 'never again' . . . started the little orange blossom circle of gold on its journey to its last resting place—the bosom of the River Truckee." Possibly apocryphal, the colorful story was taken up by the press and reportedly practiced by a number of divorcées who continued to perpetuate the story.[45]

A survey of the literature reveals that it was images of wealthy divorce-seekers, especially divorcées, that held the greatest mass appeal. Just as the advertising of an increasingly consumer-oriented age emphasized depictions of attractive customers over utilitarian images of products, most outside accounts of Reno focused on the glamorous divorcées and their experiences rather than the "product"—the divorce itself. In doing so, they helped to promote what Roland Marchand has called the "pleasure-minded consumption ethic" of a nascent tourist destination. The divorcées turned Reno's downtown into a landscape of consumption, where shoppers could buy all sorts of appealing goods, stay in fancy hotels, and live out a little adventure in a safe western setting. Those who did not actually make the journey could simply consume the stories of those who did, further contributing to the commodification of the town.[46]

Interpreting Reno's built environment through the lenses of their own experience, such writers elevated the landscape by relating it to the world they knew. Tom Gilbert praised Virginia Street, the "mile of a million moods," for its impressive collection of shops:

> Looks like a bird's-eye view of some Eastern city, doesn't it? I may add in passing that if your imagination is good you may say to yourself, a mammoth eagle as strong as the giant Atlas, has swooped upon the heart of New York City, then arising in the firmament and traveling 3,000 miles, he deposits his little city half and half across the River Truckee. . . .

With a keen awareness of his audience's points of reference, Gilbert related many of the key businesses on Reno's landscape to eastern standards, including the Monarch Café (the "Ritz of Reno"), Burke and Short clothiers ("Man, oh, Man! You've been to the style centers of New York, London and Paris when you pause at these windows"), and the Gray, Reid, Wright Co. department store ("The store would be a credit to a city of one hundred thousand people or more"). He also created a few divorce landmarks of his own, for instance labeling the Colonial Club "the Mistake-Makers rendezvous."[47]

As described, this consumer landscape contributed to the positive responses of a certain class of observers, literally selling the city to its visitors. And those who reported it through the media "sold" it to their readership, further enhancing Reno's reputation. The town's shops were regularly cited for their high caliber. Bond, for instance, wrote that Reno's main street "reminds me very much of Thirty-fourth Street in New York," reassuring his readers, "I was instantly struck by the exceedingly high class of merchandise exhibited in the store windows and any one imagining that the stores of Reno have a lot of last year's fashions, will receive a very severe shock to this impression after he or she walks up Virginia Street." Some of the shops, Bond noted, were even staffed by easterners, as many upscale divorcées found employment in the shops, and as a result, "in place of the very ordinary and usually obnoxious person that one finds in the Eastern retail stores one finds here in the dry goods stores, the grocery stores, the restaurants and other shops, a very high class and genteel force of store people." Western spirit was fine, apparently, but sometimes one needed the reassurance of a social peer.[48]

Stratton, writing in her guidebook, confirmed the quality of Reno's merchandise, writing, "The shops do the city credit; they are up-to-date and well kept, and you will find almost every kind of shop. . . . These places employ hundreds of people and the department stores send their buyers to New York and Paris." *Pictorial Review* reporter Genevieve Parkhurst confirmed in 1929 that "Virginia Street, with its smart hotel, its chic women, its exclusive shops, its high-powered motor-cars, is a bit of a metropolis. In the large department-store the latest jazz rings out the day long." And *Outlook* editor Henry Pringle admired Reno's "little shops where the ultra-fashionable could obtain ultra-fashionable clothes."[49]

The retailers in turn embraced this elite clientele, aspiring to fulfill their every desire. Many wisely geared their advertising toward the divorce crowd; in guidebooks and magazines, the Grand Cafe advertised itself as "Headquarters for the Colony." In a blatant appeal to the recently divorced and their now-surplus wedding sets, jeweler R. Herz & Bro., Inc., announced, "Visitors to Reno can have their old jewelry reset in Gold or Platinum in the very latest up-to-date styles." The Silk and Linen Shop claimed to be "continually supplying Silks, Linens and real Laces to Eastern customers who originally made their purchases here," and Madame Schick advertised "the very latest styles in Sport Specialties and Gowns of all kinds from London, New York and Paris."[50]

Visitors could buy experiences too, of course. Bond himself priced nearly everything for his readers, from renting a horse for $60 per month to buying a secondhand five-seated touring car for about $900. Many accounts mentioned the racetrack as a popular activity, although only in the warm weather. It could be a lucrative pastime, or an expensive one; as James Bolin wrote, in his self-published guidebook of 1924, "The fleetest thoroughbred animals from all sections of the country are brought to Reno to compete for the liberal cash purses that are offered." The disdainful Katharine Gerould,

The

GRAND

Cafe

The best known Cafe in the State. Known from
Coast to Coast for its Excellent Service and
High-class Entertainment

HEADQUARTERS FOR THE COLONY

Located in the Heart of the Business District
33 East Second St., Reno, Nev.

Reno's upscale Grand Cafe claims the title of "Headquarters for the Colony," the popular term for Reno's divorce crowd, in an advertisement appearing in George Bond's 1921 divorce handbook, Six Months in Reno.

of *Harper's*, stated that although "the racing is not first-class," the racetrack was "the most exciting feature of Reno social life" and that except for the racing season there was, in fact, "nothing whatever to do in Reno." To see the spectators alone was worth the price, a mix of "collarless farmers and their tightlipped wives, divorcées painted and unpainted, children in arms, drifting males of every type, a few squaws with papooses on their backs, spectacled Chinamen," and as Gerould noted, "everyone, male and female—except the squaws and the infants in arms—is betting."[51]

Reno's nightlife was another lively subject in these accounts. An elegant dinner house and speakeasy called the Silver Slipper operated out on East Fourth Street. The Willows, located on the Old Verdi Road, later Mayberry

Patrons of the swanky Willows resort play roulette in evening gowns and tuxedos. (Special Collections Department, University of Nevada–Reno Library)

Road, several miles west of downtown, was universally considered "the most fashionable night club in town," and patronized by divorcées and residents in dress suits and evening gowns. Known formerly as Rick's Resort, where Jack Johnson had trained for the 1910 "Fight of the Century," the resort was purchased in 1922 by James C. "Jimmy the Cinch" McKay and William J. "Curly Bill" Graham, two shady characters who purchased a number of Reno clubs and other properties, many of them disreputable, in the 1920s. After spending large sums on its opulent décor, they operated the club as a speakeasy and gambling resort, complete with a dining area and dancing. The Willows' "famous Blue Room" featured a "silver-voiced entertainer" who crooned to those entering, incorporating their names into his songs, describing their ensembles and prompting spontaneous applause. As writer Basil Woon informed his readers, "You must be introduced or bear good credentials to enter 'The Willows.'"[52]

Thanks to a series of legislative decisions, many forms of gambling were now completely legal, and others, while illegal, flourished anyway. Visitors outlined the two-tiered system of gambling in Reno. An upscale, exclusive environment could be found in resorts like the Willows, where the elite indulged in roulette and faro. Downtown, card games of all types ran in back or basement rooms of Reno's many clubs, a fact of which city officials were not unaware. Graham and McKay, owners of the Willows, controlled a large percentage of the operations as well, including the Bank Club, where games of all types were run in a basement clubroom. The Owl Club had been open since 1917 and offered poker games. As *Travel* magazine reported in 1922, the "shifting crowds" of downtown gamblers included "transient players," "hundreds of professional gamblers," "old-timers from the ranches," and "the derelicts of town," but their haunts were quite confined and easily avoided.[53]

It all added up to a bustling environment, populated by a diverse and ever-shifting crowd whose patronage bolstered the confidence of city officials. By 1920, Reno's population had just surpassed 12,000, but promoters still asserted their town's rising prominence as "the biggest little city on the map." As *Travel* writer William Greene reported in 1922, this ambition was part of Reno's character as well. "Reno is very proud of itself," he wrote, "standing out on the edge of the desert with its metaphorical hands in its pockets and feet apart, like a small boy who thinks he is a man." At the same time, many chroniclers expressed the opinion that Reno's ambitions were clearly monetary as well. Its residents were not naturally degenerate, some thought—just calculating. Greene estimated that each divorcée brought to Reno "an average income of $100 a month per capita, at a conservative estimate, or a total of $2,500,000 a year." A writer for *Collier's* in 1923 labeled Reno "intelligently commercial," predicting that it could yet become "one of the most moral towns in the United States," and explaining, "I see no reason why she should not become godly as soon as the Chamber of Commerce learns that godliness is profitable."[54]

That was not likely, particularly with the ascension within Reno's business community of some powerful figures whose pursuit of profit was no secret. Partners in the Goldfield Consolidated Mining Company, which ultimately produced more than $50 million worth of ore, George Wingfield and George Nixon had earned their fortunes in the central Nevada town of Goldfield, and together established the Nixon National Bank of Reno in 1906. Both moved into large mansions in Reno after Nixon was elected to the U.S. Senate. After Nixon died, in 1912, Wingfield became the president of the Nixon National Bank and later renamed it the Reno National Bank. Eventually he became the owner of a chain of twelve banks, giving him unparalleled financial power, political influence, and capital to direct events in Reno and throughout the state.[55]

Wingfield invested in a great deal of real estate throughout the state and gradually bought a number of properties in Reno, one of the earliest of which was the Golden Hotel, on Center Street, in 1907, a purchase that indicated his rising interest in the tourist trade. A momentously powerful figure, Wingfield became known to many as the political head of Nevada, although he never held a political office. His profit-driven strategies influenced some of the most pivotal governmental decisions made in Nevada over the next few decades. Divorced, with proclivities for gambling and drink, no one could accuse George Wingfield of being a reformer.[56]

Located on the second floor of the Reno National Bank, on Virginia Street, Wingfield's office, known as "the cave," became Reno's political and economic fulcrum. His consolidation of power was reflected in the relocation of the city's Chamber of Commerce from the Odd Fellows' Building to his bank. The newly improved and expanded chamber, with more than 1,000 members, occupied offices spanning the building's entire fourth floor, complete with a spacious carpeted reception room, comfortable upholstered sofas and chairs, reading lights, and large vases of flowers.[57]

Wingfield's priorities became clear when local ministers continued to push for the reinstatement of the twelve-month residency period, which came up for a public vote in fall 1922. In advance of the vote, and cognizant of the need to appeal to the female franchise, the Nevada Business Men's Association took out a large ad in the *Nevada State Journal*. Headlined "A Final Word to the Women Voters of Nevada," the advertisement cited the words of female leaders including Alice Paul, Carrie Chapman Catt, Ida M. Tarbell, and other famed figures who supported easier access to divorce for women. "A majority of these same great intellectual women," the ad declared, "recognize Nevada as a woman's refuge—a refuge from domestic unhappiness, cruelty, barbarism." At the bottom of the advertisement was an open admission of the group's motives: "While we, as an association, admit frankly that the primary motive behind our activity in this campaign is the protection of our investments in Nevada's present and future, we have no apologies to offer for the cause we espouse. On the contrary, we take a pardonable pride in the altruistic merits of our case." The ad also included the text of a letter written to the association by Wingfield, who pledged his support for their efforts to retain the six-month residency period and reminded voters of the drop in property values and general business slump that had accompanied the fifteen-month period in 1914 and 1915, when the residency requirement had been extended to twelve months. Apparently such arguments were persuasive, as voters rejected the residency extension by a margin of three to one.[58]

In light of decisions like this, some feared that financial motives were beginning to dominate local politics, to the detriment of the community. These tensions came to a head in the mayoral election of 1923, a turning point that single-handedly may have determined the course of Reno's future growth and development and established the lasting nature of its national reputation. The incumbent, Harry E. Stewart, had been mayor of Reno since 1919. Stewart shared the Progressive impulses of Francis Newlands, who died in 1917, and devoted much energy to civic improvement initiatives like street paving and the construction of schools and parks. His major effort was backing the "Redlight Abatement Movement" to permanently abolish Reno's "restricted," "regulated," or red-light district.[59] Reintroduced after a brief ban during World War I, prostitution was becoming an increased concern to some residents. Demand remained high due to the continuing numbers of potential customers who kept passing through, men involved in the railroad, mining, livestock, or other trades. After the war, prostitution was scattered throughout the east side of downtown, in hotels and clubs on East First and Second Streets, and in Chinatown's remaining wooden shacks. In 1922, the League of Women Voters and various reform-minded civic groups campaigned against prostitution, and Mayor Stewart finally declared the red-light district closed through an executive order that was backed by the city council in January 1923.[60]

To Stewart, Reno's fame had done nothing to improve life in the little town. Reflecting on the priorities that had driven him during his previous term as mayor—moral uplift and beautification—Stewart told his constituents, "I knew that a City Attractive was bound to grow far faster and longer than a City Notorious." His agenda brimmed with civic improvement measures including street paving, the establishment of city parks, and banning vice from the downtown area. He was also very aware of what outsiders were saying about Reno. Referring to a recent article in *Collier's* that had lauded his ban of the red-light district, Stewart was emphatic that it not be reinstated.[61]

In his reelection campaign of 1923, Stewart made his philosophy clear, asserting his belief "that it is the desire of the majority of the people that Reno continue to progress in civic betterments, both physical and moral."[62] He faced competition from two parties: Frank J. Byington, who had served as Reno's mayor from 1914–1919, and Edwin E. Roberts, a colorful divorce lawyer who had served as the Republican U.S. congressman from Nevada from 1911 to 1919. With his experience in the position, Byington was a serious contender, but Roberts was not considered a factor in the election by most. Two days before the election, the *Nevada State Journal* dismissively editorialized, "Roberts as a candidate was invented to take enough votes from Byington to elect Stewart."[63]

The election prompted the largest voter turnout in Reno history, and to the surprise of many, ended with Roberts "smothering his opponents in an avalanche of votes," three times more than either competitor. After his victory, Roberts told an audience in an impromptu speech at a Kiwanis Club luncheon, "We must . . . pull together and do something to make Reno a bigger city, a more hospitable city, and a place where people will long to come and hate to leave." Like many others, he favored growth and finding new ways to put Reno "on the map"; unlike many, Stewart in particular, he opposed legislating reform. That August, speaking to the Sparks Lions Club, he clarified his position on the subject, telling his audience, "A minority of paid reformers in the United States are trying to legislate morals into the people. I am not in favor of such an attempt. You can't make a man good by law. . . . If you will use your influence for common sense and bring up your children with common sense training there will be less disrespect for law and less fool laws passed."[64] For his part, Roberts continued to practice divorce law from his office in city hall, the walls of which were decorated with "pack upon pack of playing-cards," as *Pictorial Review*'s Genevieve Parkhurst noted. The national press delighted in the western demeanor and pithy comments of such a colorful and outspoken character, but the reform community was not amused.[65]

In supporting Roberts, the voters of Reno had moved decisively away from Newlands's Progressive philosophies to the more profit-driven vision shared by George Wingfield, Roberts, and others. Reno was already notorious for bucking convention, and it was about to go much further. After Roberts won the 1923 mayoral election, the new city council passed Bill No. 893, an amendment to the new antiprostitution law, permitting brothels to operate "at a distance of 250 feet or more distant from any public street or alley in the City of Reno, now being actually used as a public thoroughfare." With this new requirement, brothel operators were required to relocate, but could remain in business. As a result, most brothels moved further east from downtown, but not very far.[66]

In fact, a few new houses of prostitution were built, with names like the

Green Lantern and the Cottage, but the best known and longest running in Reno history was the "Crib," built off Second Street in 1923. The principal operators of the Riverside Securities Company, which constructed it, were "Jimmy the Cinch" McKay and "Curly Bill" Graham, owners of the Willows. Nicknamed the "Stockade" for the tall wooden fence at its entrance, the compound featured two rows of "cribs," twenty-five on each side, with a dance hall, the Pastime Club, at the end. Up to three shifts of women per day rented the cribs, registered with the police, and were tested regularly for venereal disease. Mayor Roberts voiced his approval of the arrangement, claiming that it kept prostitutes off the streets.[67]

Roberts was reelected in 1927, in a campaign openly backed by George Wingfield, and embarked upon a term in which some of the most decisive and far-reaching decisions about Reno were made. In a divorce guidebook published in Reno after Roberts's initial victory, James H. Bolin praised the mayor as a kind of "Moses" who had made Reno "the widest open town in the United States" by encouraging licensed poker games, public dance halls, book-making and even "an occasional Chinese lottery."[68] His impatience with national Prohibition echoed that of many of Nevada's leaders, a rebellious perspective that made national headlines. In 1926, a *New York Times* special correspondent reported that "Of the States west of the Rocky Mountains, Nevada alone has the hardihood to take a positive stand on prohibition. She is 'agin' it without equivocation or compromise, and is not only willing but eager that the world shall know it." Reflecting latent national support for repeal, he continued, "At a time when pretty much everybody else is singing low on prohibition, Nevada's attitude brings a certain sense of moral refreshment." A few months later, the same reporter described Roberts himself as "a rip-roaring wet" with the "character of a 'helluva feller'" who, as Reno's mayor, had "advocated and sustained the wide-open principle, illustrating in his own character and practice a fairly complete exemplification of his publicly declared views."[69]

In addition to his liberal views on these other social issues, Mayor Roberts, along with George Wingfield, was among a group of politicians who conspired to have the required residency period for divorce shortened from six months to three, legislation that passed in March of 1927. A few years later, Roberts told a reporter from *Pictorial Review* how it was done. The original bill introduced to legislators was purportedly intended only to amend the standing divorce law by adding "insanity" to the accepted grounds for divorce. However, an amendment to the law required that the law first be repealed and then resubmitted with the new language. After receiving a copy of the bill, which mentioned the six-month residency requirement twice, Roberts and a group of lawyers replaced each "six" with a "three" and then took their version to George Wingfield, who arranged to have it taken to the floor by a collaborating legislator. The amendment passed just before dawn, surprising sleepy legislators once they were informed of precisely what they had signed. "I had no compunctions about it," Roberts asserted, after the fact.[70]

Those who did have compunctions were seemingly in the minority. The day after the bill passed, H. R. Cooke, the president of the State Bar Association, criticized both the method and the result. He said, "I regard the enactment of this three months bill as nothing more nor less than a cold-blooded bid for the dollars of the divorcées of other states," a motivation that many others were perfectly willing to admit. The president of the Washoe County Bar Association approved of the move, reasoning, "It seems to me that if people are to be divorced there is no moral question in whether the divorce be granted in Reno or Paris." He continued, "Economically I believe it is to the advantage of Reno to have the residential period for divorce three months. I am not touchy over the adverse criticism of Reno which arises from some sources. In my travels I have found more favorable comment than unfavorable." A political cartoon appearing in New York's *Herald Tribune* the following month translated public opinion of Nevada into a single image. In it, a miner figure labeled "Reno" emerged from a hole in the ground, lifting up a large prospecting pan dripping with gold coins; next to him, a sign read "New Divorce Law, Quicker and Easier" while a "Legislative Badger" exclaimed, "I found it for him!" From one jackpot to another, Nevada's motives seemed clear.[71]

The legislative change made the front page of the *New York Times*, as more people than ever before started traveling to Reno for the new ninety-day divorce. Five days later the *Times* reported a "divorce suit every hour," or forty-eight suits filed in the past forty-eight hours, remarking that "Even when Reno, under the advantages of the six months' residence law, was famous as a divorce centre, the filing of separation suits never reached such numbers as now." Indeed, the number of divorces granted in Nevada courts nearly doubled that year, from 1,021 in 1926 to 1,953 in 1927 and 2,595 in 1928. They included high-profile socialites like heir and writer Cornelius Vanderbilt, Jr., who headed to Reno just four months after the new legislation passed to pursue a heavily publicized divorce.[72]

ANOTHER GOLD STRIKE IN THE WEST
—Brown in the New York *Herald Tribune*

A political cartoon depicts a gleeful Reno celebrating the passage of a new three-month divorce law in 1927. Use of the prospector figure, traditionally employed to represent Nevada, paints the burgeoning divorce trade as the state's next big bonanza. (New York Herald Tribune, *April 1927*)

The association of Reno with celebrities like Vanderbilt, as well as intrigue with the legislative shenanigans of such a brazen state, kept Reno in the public eye. Gustavus Swift Paine, a professor of English at the University of Nevada who wrote for the *North American Review* in 1930, argued that celebrity patronage had granted Reno enough social cachet that its residents need not be ashamed of its reputation. Comparing 1930s Reno to the heady days of the Comstock Lode, when Nevada contributed to the fortunes of the Comstock silver barons, he wrote,

> Now Nevada has been of vital service to such other splendid names as Vanderbilt, Morgan, Gould, Rhinelander, DuPont, and Whitney. Three of the foremost American writers of the present time have been divorced in Reno—Sherwood Anderson, Sinclair Lewis, and Eugene O'Neill. Names that are household words, such as Church (soda, not seats), Colgate (soap), Durant (automobiles), Hoover (vacuum cleaners), Pratt (Standard Oil), Fargo (express), and Clark (both thread and copper) have all appeared in the Reno news within the last few months.[73]

In a new consumer age, it seemed, what better way to assert the stature of a town than through association with consumer royalty? In a strange twist on Thorstein Veblen's theory of "conspicuous consumption," the manufacturers of consumer goods were functioning here both as "conspicuous consumers" who purchased for themselves what Reno had to offer, as well as commodities invoked to market the product that was Reno.[74]

Businessman George Wingfield was prepared to benefit personally from the new legislation and specifically from the new consumers it would attract. After a disastrous fire burned down the Riverside Hotel in March 1922, owner Harry Gosse was unable to secure the funds to rebuild. In 1924, Wingfield bought the property and soon began to construct a new and improved Riverside Hotel on the same site, designed specifically with the divorce trade in mind. The new six-story red brick structure opened in May 1927, just two months after the new legislation passed, with sixty luxurious hotel rooms and forty corner suites suitable for extended stays, each with a combination living room/bedroom, dining room, and kitchen complete with tile-lined refrigerators and electric ranges. The lobby floor was made of Tennessee marble, and the lounge floor and all other woodwork of mahogany. In constructing the massive building, Wingfield obviously shared the opinion held by the *New York Times* that "Reno expects to come back under the new law and attract the divorce seekers of America."[75]

Wingfield's plan worked like a charm; travel writer Mary Day Winn reported in 1931 that the Riverside was "patronized almost one hundred per cent by divorce-seekers." Official city-sponsored publications did not mention divorce in relation to the Riverside, although they praised the hotel for its elegance and style. Residents were said to understand the unspoken references, however. Henry Pringle wrote that "The Riverside Hotel in Reno, Nevada, is invariably described as 'smart' or 'swanky' or 'ultra-fashionable' in the local newspapers; which means that the elite of the divorce trade register there."[76]

Indeed, the new, even more lavish Riverside Hotel became the centerpiece of stories about the divorce colony. Writer Basil Woon called it "a pocket edition of the Ritz." Grace Hegger Lewis praised the Riverside's one-room apartments, where stowaway beds were hidden behind "silk-curtained French doors." With enthusiastic approval of the hotel's provision of china, cocktail glasses, silver, and linens changed daily, she raved, "This arrangement is not only adequate but rather fun, like playing house, especially for the lone woman who heretofore has had the responsibility of a large ménage." That anyone could describe the securing of a divorce as in any way "fun" was a testament to the successful adult "playground" that Reno had ostensibly become.[77]

With the completion of the Victory and Lincoln Highways, many locals saw the potential for even more tourist dollars. City officials predicted that "with the completion of improved transcontinental highways and the improvement of highways tributary to the main arteries in Nevada in 1926, there will pass across this state a flow of tourist travel from the East alone, that will be unprecedented in the history of modern methods of transportation."[78] To celebrate the momentous occasion, Reno hosted a Transcontinental Highways Exposition in June 1927 on the grounds of Idlewild Park, a 49-acre expanse on the south bank of the Truckee River, just west of downtown. For purposes of publicity and celebration, city officials constructed a metal arch that spanned Virginia Street near Commercial Row and brandished the word "RENO" with electrified torches above and lines below announcing the dates of the Exposition. The arch remained in place after the event ended and gained new wording in 1929, when hundreds of light bulbs set aglow the phrase that had now become the city's permanent slogan: "The Biggest Little City in the World."

With the coming of the Highways Exposition, increasing numbers of motor tourists, and the rise of auto camps in and around Reno, the Chamber of Commerce embarked on a new kind of outdoor-oriented civic promotion, specifically emphasizing the area's recreational opportunities and directing people to "Invite your Friends to spend their Vacation in Nevada's Wonderland." That wonderland had expanded from the shores of Lake Tahoe, the focal point of nineteenth-century recreationists, to sites closer

"The Biggest Little City in the World" became the town's official slogan once affixed to the existing Reno arch in 1929. (Special Collections Department, University of Nevada–Reno Library)

to home. In the city's directories, the Chamber of Commerce wrote, "Nevada, vast state of mystery and dormant natural wealth, is rich in a history to be revealed to the hordes of visitors from every clime who will respond to the attractions of our Wonderland." An advertisement appearing in subsequent directories labeled Reno "The Recreational Center of America" and depicted a man in golf clothes, a woman in riding jodhpurs, and a ranger standing beside a sleek convertible. Men and women alike, it seemed, could find a plethora of outdoor activities to fit their interests in and around Reno.[79]

Promotion of these attractions targeted mainstream tourists as well as members of the divorce colony eager for a change of scenery. The requirement that they remain within the state for the duration of their residency period increased the appeal of nearby attractions accessible by automobile. George Bond's divorce guidebook encouraged motor trips to Pyramid Lake and area hot springs. A brochure called "Ramblings through the Pines and Sage," published by the Nevada State Automobile Association in 1928 outlined a series of one-day motor tours out of Reno. Directed to "Mr. and Mrs. Average Visitor," it included detailed motor trips around the town it-

Through the 1920s and early 1930s, advertisements hyping Reno as "The Recreational Center of America," with easy access to activities from golf to horseback riding, regularly appeared in Reno's city directories. (R. L. Polk & Co.'s Reno City Directory, 1927)

self; heading west to Lake Tahoe; "Following the Trail of Romance" to the Comstock; sampling four of the area's hot springs; exploring the so-called "Canyon-Land" area irrigated by the Newlands project; and even a northward visit to the "Vacation Land" of Lassen Volcanic National Park and northern California. For those unwilling or unable to drive themselves, arrangements could be made through the local branch of Pickwick Stages, a national company advertising itself as "the world's greatest stage line."[80]

The automobile was not the only mode of transportation available to travelers. By the late 1920s, Reno's Hubbard Field, opened by Boeing in 1928, introduced passenger flights, and by 1929, air travel to and from Reno was common. As the Boeing company reported, the "great majority" of travelers flying between Reno and San Francisco were divorce-seekers interested in shopping trips that would not force them to violate the requirement that they not be absent from the state for longer than twenty-four hours. The flight leaving Reno at 1:30 a.m. and arriving at Oakland by 4:30, as well as the flight leaving Oakland at 8:00 p.m., became known in-

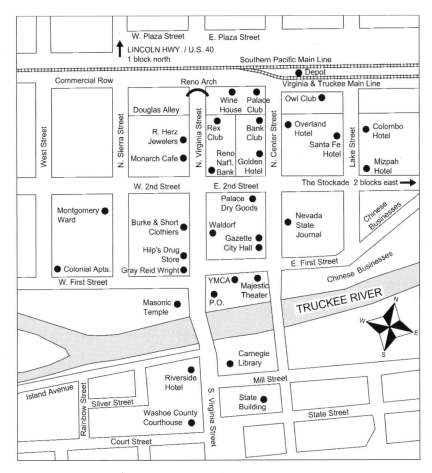

Selected landmarks of downtown Reno, 1930

formally as the "Divorce Special." The flights were reportedly very popular for wedding parties, too.[81]

But the claim that the town valued income over all was never far from the thoughts of its chroniclers. A 1930 article in *American Magazine* stated that "The town has been made beautiful, largely as a bait for divorce seekers. They spend three to four million dollars a year in Reno." The author blamed Reno, at least in part, for the country's rising divorce rate, "because Reno has done its best to make divorce-getting as easy, as cheap, and as agreeable as possible." Of Reno's residents, she said "The people are delightful. But—they have given up a good deal in exchange for the divorce revenue which makes possible their boast of being 'The Biggest Little City in the World.' They think they have made a good bargain. But I wonder."[82] Others would wonder, too, as the state legislature took a number of rather shocking steps that oriented Reno's landscape even more toward the transient, tourist population.

Numerous strategies to channel more money into the state were proposed after the stock market crash of October 1929, although Nevada did not suffer major financial repercussions right away. Nationally, the onset of the Depression brought a decrease in both weddings and divorces, as both cost money. In 1930, of forty states measured, thirty-three recorded fewer marriages than the previous year, and thirty recorded fewer divorces. Nevada was one of the few exceptions, reporting slight increases in both.[83] However, it was not long before the uncertainties of the incipient Depression, a major statewide drought in 1930–1931, and the imminent collapse of the city's banking institutions, including those of the formerly untouchable George Wingfield, all combined to increase anxiety about the state's future. Nevada's political leaders recognized the need for additional measures to ensure the state's financial health and to maintain Reno's hold on the lucrative divorce industry.

That hold seemed even more precarious once Idaho and Arkansas each reduced their state residency requirements to three months in early 1931. Upon hearing of the new competition, humorist Will Rogers voiced his satiric version of the Reno perspective on divorce, vowing "we will give you one in six weeks, and if any other State goes under that time, we will give you a divorce, marriage, and another divorce all for the same time and price" and concluding "we are the State that will divorce you even if we have to do it by telegraph." Newspapers across the country reported on the subsequent "War for the Divorce Capital of America" between Reno and the Arkansas resort of Hot Springs; an estimated 2,000 divorcées per year hung in the balance. Hot Springs offered "swell night clubs," "famous baths," and "a plan to legalize horse racing," while Reno was said to offer horse racing, "gay night life," and "swanky gambling casinos."[84]

This last advantage was the subject of another bill intended to sweeten Reno's appeal to divorcées and bring more money to the state. The proposed legalization of gambling met with strong disapproval from a handful of citizens, including a philosophy professor from the University of Nevada, R. C. Thompson, one of those who had taken up the reform mantle of president Joseph Stubbs after his sudden death, reportedly of heart failure, in 1914. As Thompson declared, "Gambling, as a business, has no standing-ground whatsoever. It represents a parasitic business which preys upon the welfare of society."[85] However, most residents seemed accepting of the full legalization of a practice they well knew to have been continuing for years in various forms, some legally sanctioned, some not.

The announcement in March 1931 that Nevada governor Fred Balzar had signed legislation that not only reduced the state's residency period to six weeks but also fully legalized gambling prompted a national uproar. Although other states permitted some casino gaming, Nevada was the only one to legalize "full-scale, public casino gambling," and no other state would match the forty-two-day divorce. As the largest city in Nevada, Reno would be the primary beneficiary of both new pieces of legislation.[86]

As the national response suggested, the two bills were in many ways intertwined. Up to that point, divorce had been the bigger business by far, and many observers saw the legalization of gambling as the means by which Reno hoped to save it. As the *San Antonio Light* wrote, "Nevadans are old hands at gambling and when their big divorce trade stake was threatened, they did not hesitate to throw enough chips into the pot to scare the other fellows out." With these new laws, they wrote, Nevada would "probably keep the bulk of the very profitable Eastern divorce business."[87] As Carol W. Cross, a Central Press correspondent, reported, "Divorce is recognized as a social necessity in Reno, but it also is recognized as a profitable business and for that reason Nevada's key city welcomes the unhappily wed with 'open arms.'" She continued, "'Come here,' Reno seems to say, 'Come here for your divorce, but don't forget to spend your money.'"[88] The American public had been familiar with Reno's "quickie" divorces for decades now, and with the increasing acceptability of divorce, even the passage of such a short residency period provoked more satire than outrage.

The new divorce law would not grant any six-week divorces until the first week of May, but the gambling law became effective immediately. Among the legal games now were roulette, keno, faro, monte, blackjack, twenty-one, craps, draw poker, and more. With reporters already on the scene, the *New York Times* announced, "In the flush of wide-open gambling the new forty-two-day divorce law virtually was forgotten." Many gambling clubs had already been in operation, openly or not, but immediately upon legalization, as the *Times* reported of one establishment, "The hum and hubbub of gambling, the click-clack of machines and the clatter of poker chips were partly drowned by the staccato noise of a compressed air drill operated by a construction crew engaged in cutting through massive walls to enlarge the gaming room."[89] Mayor Roberts triumphantly stated, "For eight years I've been trying to make Reno a place where everybody can do what they please, just so they don't interfere with other people's rights. Now we can do lawfully what Nevada has always done under cover."[90] It was this spirit, this brash confidence in the value of what Reno had to offer, that later inspired historian Daniel Boorstin to characterize the town as a community of "Go-Getters"—American entrepreneurs who "exploited the federal commodity" with a competitive spirit that characterized the age.[91]

Within days, twenty-one clubs applied for their gaming licenses, at a monthly cost of $25 per social game (such as bridge, whist, and poker), $50 per mercantile game (such as faro or craps), and $10 per slot machine.[92] Located on Commercial Row, the Owl Club had already offered poker games and now was licensed for casino games including roulette, craps, 21, and slot machines. The operations of the Bank Club now moved to the ground floor and it quickly expanded to become the largest and most profitable casino in the state. A new façade and marquis drew the attention of passersby, while inside, an expensive electric keno board featuring 1,000 light bulbs dominated a gaming floor offering roulette, craps, 21, faro, hazard, keno, stud poker, pan, and one slot machine.[93] Other clubs flinging their doors open to the public included the Rex Club, also owned by Graham and McKay; the Wine House, a former site of cockfighting battles among other activities; and the Waldorf Club, on North Virginia. The Rex Club, Bank Club, and several others fronted Douglas Alley, located between Commercial Row and Second Street, which became a center of gambling in Reno.

As was true for the divorce trade, national publicity for the new attractions arose without any local effort. With no competition anywhere in the country, the casinos did not need to advertise; the press accomplished that for them, and the novelty alone drew enormous crowds to Reno. On the first national holiday following legalization, Memorial Day weekend, a local reporter wrote, "The crowds were the largest Reno has seen since the recent gambling and six-weeks' divorce law secured widespread 'free' publicity." He estimated that 5,000 visitors had descended on Reno and observed, "thousands of holiday visitors swarmed the streets to see for themselves the

In the mid-1930s, the Bank Club's crowded and smoky no-frills gambling atmosphere catered to a mostly male clientele. (Special Collections Department, University of Nevada–Reno Library)

things which they have been told about Nevada's gay metropolis." Hotel rooms were booked to overflowing, and buildings in local parks and local residences were temporarily turned into hotels for the weekend, reminiscent of the 1910 "Fight of the Century." Men and women alike tried their luck at the tables, and "a carnival spirit prevailed," noted one writer, with the crowds undeterred by a Salvation Army preacher who reportedly stood on a downtown corner warning casino patrons to seek salvation. Two downtown casinos were still in the process of enlarging their gaming floors, and new neon lights glowed on the city streets.[94]

This was not to say that these casinos were all immediately appealing. For the most part, the newly legalized downtown clubs remained neither impressive nor glamorous. Contemporary observers described most of them as dark and uncomfortable. The Bank Club, wrote Henry Pringle in *Outlook,* "is a really enormous establishment, quite devoid of style, wholly drab and businesslike." He continued, "Miraculously, they all seem to be busy, and, inside, their appearance is very much the same. The air is thick with smoke, and insufferably warm."[95] As the *San Antonio Light* explained, "Easterners are not encouraged to patronize these promiscuous resorts.

They are steered to the 'country clubs' in the outskirts of Reno, which specialize in running respectable fortunes down to thin dimes." Such resorts, such as the Willows, were said to "approach the magnificence of Monte Carlo and other Continental casinos."[96] The *New York Times* agreed that "Dozens of the so-called 'speakeasy' establishments, where divorcées and others play in an atmosphere of seclusion, enjoyed generous patronage."[97]

Every paper from California to New York, it seemed, had something to say about the new legalized gambling. Many, like Ohio's *Portsmouth Times,* clearly recognized the financial motive, which was generally disparaged: "Unable to pull itself out of the doldrums by enterprise, the state has resorted to a common device—cheapening itself for the sake of money to be gained. It is fortunate, indeed, that there is only a handful of native Nevada citizens to share in the shame the state should feel."[98] Even criticism, from predictable quarters, provided publicity. Not surprisingly, religious leaders nationwide criticized Reno for its immorality, but supporting the old adage that no publicity is bad publicity, *Outlook*'s Henry Pringle wrote that

> Reno is well satisfied. Publicity such as has not come to her in decades has resulted from the new liberalism. Every knock, every denunciation, makes her that much better known. A few more divorce suits will be filed. A score of tin-can tourists, making their way across the continent to golden California, will plan their journey to allow for several days of sin. The role of sinner among the cities of America should be profitable.[99]

The new "wide open" policy took some of the more conservative observers aback. One visitor that summer noted disapprovingly that "there is no attempt to cover up Reno's open vice"; in fact, it was quite the opposite, as "certain features of it are blazoned to all the passing world. Center street, for example, after dark is a shrieking jungle of neon tube signs—those blazing reds and blues and greens that are so much more strident than any other form of outdoor signs—and practically all are advertising gambling 'clubs.'" And upon entering, he reported, "the scene inside these clubs is anything but glamorous. It is, in truth, almost unrelievedly sordid."[100]

His criticisms were not solely aesthetic, however. The author of this last account, Paul Hutchinson, was a former Protestant minister and missionary and the managing editor of the *Christian Century,* "An Undenominational Journal of Religion." In a series of four articles about Nevada,

Hutchinson criticized the "wide-open town" for contributing to a number of social evils. Generalizing, as many did, about the entire state, he concluded that "it is the belief of Nevada that the nation is full of people who, in the secret of their own hearts, are eager to escape from the social regulations of their own communities in order to indulge in forms of relaxation there taboo. And Nevada is out to cash in on this supposed desire of virtue for vice."[101] Indeed, Nevada had been banking on the public's desire for escape, and if the Memorial Day crowds were any indication, that desire was shared by a great many people.

But Hutchinson was not through. Painting Reno's residents as ambivalent toward their outward image, he wrote, "As long as the town's reputation is bringing in money, what of it? And besides, what business is it of the rest of the nation what Reno, or Nevada, does in a matter of this kind?" Labeling Nevada a "prostitute state," Hutchinson anticipated "Her citizens will, of course, resent such a designation. One finds them, in conversation, rather bristlingly defensive of their state's 'good name.'"[102] That defense was made a bit more difficult as Reno's actual prostitution business began to expand. As Henry Pringle noticed that July, "The 'Crib' is prospering. In the daytime, the sound of carpenters' hammers can be heard, for an addition is being rushed to completion. The number of girls is now approximately double that of the pre-boom, non-gambling days, and more will be added shortly."[103]

Those who disapproved of prostitution, gambling, divorce, prizefighting, and the like could now single out Reno as the repository of all that was immoral and reprehensible in society. The city therefore became an immediate target for other ministers and moralizers. The leaders of the International Christian Endeavor Society convention in San Francisco that summer called Reno "a blot on civilization" and "a distinct menace to the American home." One minister announced, "The State is a disgrace to the nation, both in its divorce and gambling phases," and another agreed, "Reno and what it is doing presents a distinct menace to the ideals and concepts for which this country has always stood." Reverend Clarence True Wilson, head of the Methodist Church's board of temperance, prohibition, and public morals, promptly charged Nevada with advertising the state as "a three-fold compound of Sodom, Gomorrah and Perdition," to which the *Kansas City Star* confirmed, "it fits."[104]

Mayor Roberts defended Reno from the Methodist leader's charges in a speech to the Reno Lion's Club on March 26. Claiming that Nevada's motives had been misunderstood, Roberts stated his firm belief that morals should be instilled through education, not prohibition. Quoted in pieces and out of context by the national press, his words would be used for decades to come as an endorsement of drunkenness, debauchery, and the pursuit of vice. In its original form, however, his proposed solution, radical as it sounded, combined a libertarian belief in loose governmental regulation with a call for individual responsibility. To bring an end to bootlegging, he stated, "I would have the city of Reno go to the expense of manufacturing 1,000 gallons of good corn whisky at $2.50 per gallon and would place a barrel on every street corner in the city of Reno with a dipper attached labeled: 'Good corn whisky. Help yourself, but don't carry any away. Drink all you want, but do so openly and above-board.'"[105]

The result, he stated, would be to "take the profit out of the stuff," thereby removing any incentive for criminal activity. But this was not all. "I believe in letting every man do just what he wants to do so long as he does not interfere with the rights of others," Roberts continued, referring to the legislation of gambling as "tearing off the mask of hypocrisy and doing in the open what we know is going on all over our nation today behind closed doors." Roberts repeated these points a few days later to a packed house in a speech for "men's night" at Reno's Methodist Church, where he professed his support for temperance but repeated his claim that Prohibition was unenforceable. The combination of such liberal views delivered in a house of worship earned the speech national headlines along the lines of "Reno Defender Goes It Alone" and "Wants Free Whisky."[106]

Up for reelection that spring, Roberts repeated his philosophy again in interviews with correspondents from across the country. To the *Kansas City Star*, he stated, "I would repeal all blue laws. I would make Reno the playground of the world. . . . I would have gambling legalized, as it is here, because close contact with gambling will show any man with a lick of sense that he can't win, and in that way open gambling will kill itself."[107] Putting the onus of responsibility for self-regulation on the individual gambler and drinker, Roberts presented a vision of Reno not as greedy or mercenary, but tolerant and above all, realistic. The majority of locals apparently liked what they heard, reelecting him as their mayor, a position he held until his death in December 1933.

Although in the minority, at least publicly, a handful of commentators acknowledged that Nevada, although worthy of rebuke, was only tapping into a common, all-too-human impulse manifested in various forms throughout American society. While acknowledging that gambling was clearly a "fruitless, time wasting and evil influence," the *Helena Independent* reflected, "gambling on the spin of an ivory ball on a roulette wheel is no worse than gambling on the trend of the stock market," no worse than "going to any one of ten thousand places in the United States and buying race-track tickets or participating in baseball pools." In fact, the editorial continued, "We all gamble in a way, in our business, in our lives, but most of us gamble on our ability."[108] We might criticize Reno, the writer seemed to suggest, but perhaps we might question our own hypocrisy before doing so. Nevada's leaders had taken a radical step, staking Reno's economic future on Americans' willingness to follow their own natural impulses. It remained to be seen whether, and how far, the general public would buy into those impulses and what the ensuing consequences for Reno's reputation might be.

CHAPTER FOUR

"City of Sinful Fun":
Reno Hits the Mainstream

Time, which alone makes the reputation of men,
ends by making their defects respectable.
Voltaire, "On Tragedy," 1732

Wide open as Reno is, there is nothing vicious about the night life of the city.
There is a gayety and friendliness about Reno and about the people who go
to Reno to enjoy themselves but there is no viciousness nor ugliness about it.
Tolerance, not license, governs Reno.
Quentin Reynolds, *Collier's,* 1935

When executives in the motion picture industry adopted the Hays Office's Motion Picture Production Code in March 1930, their primary goal was to crack down on the sex and violence creeping into the new "talkies." Of particular concern to those behind the measure were the emerging gangster films, a genre that continued into the 1930s with such titles as *Little Caesar* (1930), *Public Enemy* (1931), and *Scarface* (1932). Morality, the code asserted, must be recognized as the chief responsibility of filmmakers and be maintained through restrictions of ingredients including detailed portrayal of "brutal killings" and "excessive and lustful kissing."[1]

The code relied upon studio self-censorship until 1934, but even before its restrictions were enforced, filmmakers were anxious to find subjects that would conform to the new standards while still fulfilling audiences' desire for drama and titillation. In May 1931, a story in the *Los Angeles Times* identified one potential solution. "Searching feverishly about to find something sensational to take the place of the forbidden gangland stories," it announced, "producers have hit upon the happy idea of making Reno and the new Nevada divorce laws a subject for sizzling drama." Reportedly in the development or production stages were three such films, *The Road to Reno, Merry Wives of Reno,* and *Six Weeks in Reno,* all featuring divorce-related storylines and set in the increasingly notorious Nevada town.[2]

Labeling this apparent new trend "the Reno cycle," another Hollywood reporter mused,

> Perhaps it is considered that the growing mind will be in less danger of contamination from a good all-around divorce education than from an expose of how to run beer and use a 'rod.' For them as considers Reno the focal point of romance in America, there is a swell time ahead. After the release of the initial three already scheduled it is very likely that gangsters will give way to American-made divorcees.

She continued, "A boom town already, all Reno needed to complete its fame and fortune was recognition by the movies. It is about to have that, will probably continue to enjoy it for some time to come and must surely be the happiest little community ever to be included in a cycle."[3]

Many in the community were happy indeed, although the choice of subject matter for this new "cycle" seems at first counterintuitive. How could the "new Nevada divorce laws" constitute an appealing premise for "sensational" treatment and "sizzling drama," while also conforming to the Hays Code, which warned, among other things, that "the sanctity of the institution of marriage and the home shall be upheld"? How could a little western town known for divorce, gambling, and prostitution also be presented as the "focal point of romance in America"? The answer lay in the evolving nature of media depictions of Reno from the 1930s through the 1950s. Cultural fascination with Reno continued through mid-century, with movies now added to the usual array of newspaper and magazine articles, short stories, novels, and breathless exposés about the town. And yet, although the attention persisted, its overall tone changed. Whether as a result of changing American values, familiarity breeding acceptance for Reno's unconventional laws and culture, or a combination of the two, the majority of observers gradually ceased their moral outrage and began to accept Reno as a landscape of entertainment rather than scandal. At last, Reno was going mainstream.

A number of cultural trends, both regional and national, helped to make many of Reno's well-publicized vices seem somewhat less transgressive in this era. As the 1933 repeal of national Prohibition indicated, Americans were growing increasingly tolerant of activities previously condemned or even criminalized during the Progressive era. In this new climate, Reno could be recognized as a more publicly acceptable destination, to be more readily explored and enjoyed by the media and tourists alike. Its absorption into the mainstream was eased by a number of additional developments, including but not limited to the birth of a celebrity culture associated with the Hollywood star system, the continued expansion of mass tourism, and the increasing popularity of the American West.

At the same time, the passage of Nevada's two most notorious laws—the legalization of gambling and the six-week divorce—not only provided Nevada with a surge of attention and profit, but also provided the country with a distraction from the intensifying effects of the Great Depression. Just as the early nickelodeons had provided the working classes a form of escape during the early 1900s, now people from all walks of life turned to entertainment during the Depression years. And if the country needed an escape from the workaday world, Reno certainly fit the bill, as the media transformed the little western town into a landscape of decadent fun that extended the Roaring Twenties into the new decade. As Henry Pringle of *Outlook* magazine wrote in July 1931, "Reno gladly takes the place of short skirts, of rouge, of drinking, of flappers, of rolled stockings."[4] As he described it, Reno might be wicked, but in the most charming way possible. Mayor Edwin E. Roberts had wanted Reno to become the playground of the world, and it seemed that his wish had finally come true.

The town was hitting its stride as many downtown entertainment districts in large American cities were beginning to decline, reaching the end of the often sentimentalized "golden age" of movie palaces, amusement parks, sports stadiums, and other sites of public leisure that spanned the first three decades of the new century. Still a small town of around 20,000, Reno in the 1930s profited from both divorce and legalized gambling, although in different ways. Although immensely lucrative for its operators, gambling was not yet a major source of revenue for the city; the licensing fees levied on table games and slot machines were split among state, city, and county coffers. In 1933, for instance, licensing fees raked in a total of around $69,000, approximately $50,000 of which went to Reno. The government did not yet share in gaming revenues.[5]

Of its two renowned industries, divorce was by far the bigger business. By 1931, Reno's divorce mill had operated for more than two decades, and the new six-week residency requirement only solidified its dominance.

With the new legislation, the number of Nevada divorces jumped from 2,609 in 1930 to 5,260 in 1931. As statistics from 1931 demonstrate, Nevada had the highest divorce rate in the country that year; compared to the national ratio of 173 divorces per 1,000 marriages, Nevada's ratio was 689 divorces per 1,000 marriages—four times the national average.[6] Although it is difficult to determine with any precision, the divorce industry brought anywhere from $1 million to $5 million per year to Nevada, mostly to Reno, through the 1930s, even if the shorter residency period translated into fewer contributions by each individual divorce-seeker to the community's treasure chest.[7] As Harry Carr of the *Los Angeles Times* glibly pointed out, "In providing the nickel-in-the-shot divorce [Nevada] overlooked the fact that the divorcee would not stay long enough to shop. A sensible way out would be to require a passport from the Reno department stores." Nevertheless, what it lost in individual spending, the state hoped to gain in sheer numbers of visitors.[8]

As demonstrated by such lighthearted commentary, divorce, although still a source of drama and controversy, was increasingly less scandalous in the eyes of America. Whether because of its growing visibility or despite it, the practice simply did not carry the stigma it used to. As one *New York Times* reporter stated in 1931, "in this trend the Far West is the pace-maker, the Middle West goes faster than the East and everywhere the rising rate is matched by a corresponding change in the social temperature. In a generation divorce has become not only fashionable but respectable, and not only respectable but the custom of the country, as common as the two-car garage."[9] Hyperbole aside, the crux of the observation rang true enough, as the frequency of divorce nationwide increased steadily through the end of World War II.

Reno's increasingly popular divorce mill was, in this respect, reflective of a changing society. Across the country, Americans were growing to accept divorce as, in certain cases, the best possible option for a failing marriage. George A. Bartlett, one of Reno's most experienced district judges, gained fame in 1931 for stating this perspective in a widely publicized book called *Men, Women, and Conflict: An Intimate Study of Love, Marriage & Divorce.* An acknowledged authority on his final two topics, eventually officiating at nearly 20,000 divorce cases, he argued that the institution of marriage was changing, increasingly failing to fulfill its purpose, and should, as a man-made institution, perhaps be reevaluated.[10] Increasingly, many seemed to share this opinion, in Hollywood and elsewhere.

Depictions of Reno may not only have reflected the fading stigma of divorce, but may in fact have contributed to this increasing acceptability by publicizing high-profile divorces by celebrities whose lives were closely monitored by an eager public. Reports of the first divorcées to take advantage of the six-week law reinforced the glamorous image of Reno's divorce colony. Spotted among those awaiting their turn with the judge on 2 May 1931 was up-and-coming New York interior decorator Dorothy Draper, who had just completed designing the lobby of Manhattan's Carlyle Hotel. That day, both the *Los Angeles Times* and *New York Times* contained nearly identical front-page reports of a new trend witnessed among Reno's divorce-seekers. As the *Los Angeles Times* noted, "the fad of wearing colored glasses to prevent newspaper photographers from procuring good pictures" was apparently all the rage. In fact, he wrote, "They mark one as belonging to the divorce colony and no woman happily married will have a pair around the house." The accessory was even called "a badge of admittance to all the local speakeasies."[11] With sunglasses having been introduced on the Atlantic City boardwalk just two years earlier by Sam Foster (founder of the Foster Grant company), Reno was now revealed to be on the cutting edge of the fashion world, as well as a feeding ground for the 1930s-era paparazzi.

More and more celebrities would develop a need for the new accessory as the route between Hollywood and Nevada, traveled so famously by Mary Pickford in 1920, became an ever more popular pilgrimage. With the ascendance of increasing numbers of movie stars to national fame, the explosion of gossip surrounding their romantic lives and the all-too-frequent disintegration of their marriages led to increased references to Reno as a popular—and to Hollywood, a conveniently located—divorce site. Accordingly, the decade brought a surge of divorce-related stories about Reno, all purporting to tell the truth about this notorious town. However many were traveling there for a divorce, that number was far overshadowed by the number of people reading about them in newspapers and magazines and watching their celluloid counterparts on movie screens across America. For these consumers, the Reno fantasy provided a more figurative than a literal escape, but an escape all the same.

National correspondents assigned to the "divorce beat" added to the conflation of divorce and entertainment, at least for those who voraciously read the gossip sheets. These reporters, in turn, were determined to establish their credibility as people-in-the-know. Bill Berry worked for the *New*

York News as a stringer, primarily a divorce reporter, from the 1930s through 1950s. Celebrity gossip columnist Walter Winchell, credited with inventing the modern gossip column in the mid-1920s, as well as the slang term "Reno-vation" for getting a divorce, kept Reno in the spotlight with his tales of celebrity breakups, both on the printed page and in his weekly radio show.[12] Designated columnists discussed the "latest studio and theater gossip" in newspapers, intertwining the personal lives of stars with stories about their latest productions. In an article discussing the filming of *Charlie Chan in Reno,* in 1939, one *Los Angeles Times* reporter mentioned that the cast was "singularly free from 'renovations,'" with not a divorce among them, proceeding to delineate each star's marital status.[13] Such gossip humanized the celebrities, as tales of their divorces, romances, parties, and various escapades brought them down to a level to which average people felt they could better relate. Winchell, especially, played a large role in the formation of a new "mass culture of celebrity" that brought consumers together through their shared interest in the figures they idolized.[14]

Reno figured prominently in most of these stories as shorthand for marital trouble. Indeed, the frequency of references to Reno in the gossip columns may have made divorce seem more commonplace than it actually was. As *Los Angeles Times* columnist Mollie Merrick wrote, just after the passage of Nevada's newest legislation, "Those six-week Reno divorces have set the correspondents of Hollywood all agog. Every star who doesn't show up at luncheon is under suspicion. Every notable who goes into the good old Hollywood hide-out for a brief rest is suspected of a Reno vacation." In an article called "Why Hollywood Can't Stay Married" in March 1931, gossip queen Hedda Hopper surmised that the percentage of divorces in Hollywood was probably the same as in the rest of the country, "only ours are so much better advertised."[15]

Others saw in Hollywood's many breakups a rising trend that pointed to an industry-wide disillusionment with the institution of marriage. Reporting that there were thirty-seven divorces "in film circles" in 1930, the *Los Angeles Times*'s Alma Whitaker wrote that for the most part, "these short-lived and easily forgotten romances no longer inspire the sentimental excitement they once did. People can feel enormously romantic about the marriages of royal princesses, because they know they are 'forever,' till death do them part. We used to feel that way about our film princesses, but now there is almost always some cynic to remark, 'I wonder how long it will last?'"[16] It seemed only natural, then, to ask, if celebrity spouses had become expendable commodities, why should average men and women put up with loveless marriages?

As in the realms of fashion and hairstyles, celebrity worship may even have led to imitation. During the 1920s, studies showed that middle-class city-dwellers were increasingly basing their purchasing decisions on models found in the movies. They also looked to the silver screen for standards of behavior, values, and social ideals.[17] And it was becoming clear to many that divorce was starting to become fashionable. This fact was sometimes acknowledged in the films themselves. In *The Road to Reno* (1931), a grown son says of his mother, Jackie, "Divorce is pretty fashionable and Jackie would do almost anything to be in style."[18]

Reno divorces had inspired a handful of motion pictures in the 1920s, generally silent, melodramatic domestic dramas, including *Wedding Bells* (1921), *The Primitive Lover* (1922), *Reno* (1923), *Forbidden Waters* (1926), *A Reno Divorce* (1927), and *On to Reno* (1928). These were primarily dramatic tales, full of tragedy, suffering, and lessons learned. In *Wedding Bells,* a young couple marries, divorces, and after a series of obstacles is finally reunited after rediscovering their love for one another. In *Forbidden Waters,* a Reno divorce leads to arrests, plots, and dissimulations, culminating again in remarriage of the former spouses. The 1923 film simply titled *Reno* features a man whose many divorces and marriages in various jurisdictions have led to confusion over his true marital status. Continuing animosity between the scheming husband, his ex-wives, and their new paramours culminates in his death when an erupting geyser flings him onto the rocks at Yellowstone. A *Variety* review deemed the film more successful as social commentary than entertainment, calling it "Goldwyn propaganda against the conflicting divorce laws of the United States," while a *New York Times* reviewer suggested it "would have made a side-splitting farce," but "as a drama it is as flat as the proverbial pancake."[19]

Other Reno films of the 1920s had more simple ambitions. *A Reno Divorce* features socialites (including one played by Hedda Hopper) competing for the heart of a disguised heir, with false accusations temporarily separating the star-crossed lovers. One review, although critical of the film, indicated the high expectations accompanying use of Reno as a setting; the story, it said, had "no connection with the title which seems to indicate a spicy theme entirely lacking in the picture." A similar criticism was later lodged against *The Road to Reno* (1931), described by one reviewer as "not as glamorous as the title may indicate."[20]

This changed in the 1930s, as Hollywood's increased interest in Reno strengthened the perceived link between the two communities, rivaling a longstanding association of Reno divorces with moneyed easterners. The increasing association of Reno not with staid conservative representatives of old money, but with charismatic members of the entertainment world, led to a transformation in the nature of representations of the town. Most Reno films of the 1930s seemed to take it all a lot less seriously, providing the glamour and spiciness reviewers had seen lacking in the previous decade. Reno's unique culture lent itself well to various genres of fiction and film, from melodrama to slapstick. Many of its features, introduced to the American public through the magazine and newspaper coverage of the previous two decades, were instantly recognizable when incorporated into the new feature films, very few of which, it should be stated, merited stellar reviews. Although often acknowledging the appeal of certain actors and scenes, most reviewers criticized the typically shallow characterization and formulaic aspects of the genre.

One of these formulaic ingredients was the ubiquitous montage of assorted neon signs and recognizable buildings to establish the Reno setting—often, these were the only segments actually filmed on location. Director Richard Wallace filmed such a montage for *The Road to Reno* in 1931, including all the expected landmarks: the famous Reno arch (which went neon in 1934, an appropriately glitzy touch); the Washoe County Courthouse; an array of clubs including the Wine House and the Waldorf Club; and a woman flinging her ring into the Truckee River (and startling a fish), all to the tune of the "Wedding March." After returning to Los Angeles, Wallace told Los Angeles reporter Grace Kingsley that he had witnessed this last tradition personally. "I watched this bridge for more than an hour," he reported, "during which time no less than ten new divorcees observed the custom. Several of them were crying, others had set expressions, one was accompanied by a new boy friend and laughed uproariously, while another stood there ten minutes before she put her ring in her hand bag and hurried away." A *Life* magazine cover from 1937 winked at another well-known divorce ritual with a photograph of a courthouse column–kissing divorcée, an incident admittedly staged by photographer Alfred Eisenstaedt and labeled in small print below as the "Reno Divorce Myth."[21]

In the 1930 film *Reno*, a tour guide literally turns the entire town into a landscape of divorce, pointing out "the heart of Reno's business section— five blocks and a hundred lawyers"; the courthouse ("where every Monday

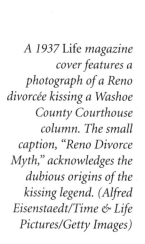

A 1937 Life *magazine cover features a photograph of a Reno divorcée kissing a Washoe County Courthouse column. The small caption, "Reno Divorce Myth," acknowledges the dubious origins of the kissing legend. (Alfred Eisenstaedt/Time & Life Pictures/Getty Images)*

is Independence Day"), "Alimony Park," and the Truckee River, accompanied by the line "Just as the Ganges is supposed to wash away the sins of the Hindus . . . so the Truckee is said to wash away the mistakes of the past," presumably by carrying discarded wedding rings downriver, out of sight, and presumably, out of mind. Films often featured the Riverside Hotel, either playing itself or thinly disguised, as the "Riverview Hotel," for instance, in *The Road to Reno*. That film also nodded to the Willows resort with the inclusion of a "Pussy Willow Café." In a gushingly melodramatic 1931 short story by Charles J. McGuirk called "Betrayal," the resort appeared as "The Oaks," and according to the author, existed "for the pleasure of people comfortably situated, for divorcees who are rich—or who are able to imagine themselves rich for a night. And it is almost as important a landmark of Reno's restless divorce colony as is the Washoe county courthouse."[22]

Familiar landmarks and rituals like these, specific to Reno, offered a variety of colorful ingredients for filmmakers and writers to incorporate into

A postcard by cartoonist Lew Hymers depicts a cast of characters commonly associated with Reno, including the divorcée, her attorney, the judge, and the cowboy, all glimpsed outside the Washoe County Courthouse. (Special Collections Department, University of Nevada–Reno Library)

their work. The city's cinematic appeal entered into the description of author/journalist Mary Day Winn when taking note of Reno's collection of cattlemen, prospectors, Indians, and sophisticated New Yorkers for a 1931 travelogue. "One can almost imagine some super-producer sitting down and deliberately planning Reno," she wrote, "throwing in humor, pathos, brutality, beauty, naiveté, greed, and tenderness, like a barman striving for the perfect cocktail."[23]

As Winn had found, the diversity of those populating Reno's landscape, from cowboys to movie stars, provided great intrigue. Stock characters, like the divorce attorney, the judge, and the local cowboy who helped the divorcée pass the time, further scripted the entertainment fantasy in such depictions, as an expected series of transactions and stock elements added to the familiarity. A new figure, the witness, also emerged, having become a pivotal part of the action once the 1931 legislation required a sworn witness to testify that the divorce-seeker had been sighted in the state each and every day for six weeks. Intended to reduce the potential for no-residency divorces, the addition only added to the cast of characters inhabiting the Reno landscape.

Fact and fiction intertwined as writers for print and screen enhanced Reno's reputation as a ripe location for scandalous fun. Many observers seemed downright titillated, and their reports helped propagate Reno's reputation for raciness. Placing the town in the best (or, depending on one's interpretation, the worst) company, Mary Day Winn wrote,

> Reno possesses more sex appeal than any town between New York and Hollywood. Sex appeal, often thwarted, walks the streets; it coquettes in the smart little shops, so different from those in other cities on the fringes of the desert; spends hours of patient effort at the many beauty parlors; and keeps the courthouse, one of the most imposing west of the Rockies, aflutter with well-dressed men, good-looking women, brisk lawyers, curious reporters, congratulations, flowers, and Black Narcissus.[24]

Descriptions like these raised the possibility of experiencing a romantic interlude around every corner, and the press reinforced that perception through tales of real folks who ended one marriage only to immediately embark upon a new one before leaving Reno together. The films generally presented these ebbs and flows as one steady stream. In the film *Reno* (1930), when a man is asked what he is doing at the Reno railroad station, he responds, "Watching the tied come in and the untied go out."

Seen as a playground for adult amusement, Reno was subject to much less moral condemnation than before. According to a new generation of writers, the town simply had to be considered on its own terms. A reporter for *American Magazine* agreed in 1938 that Reno "has a character and a state of mind definitely its own, with a history that could be simulated only if a wild West show, a swanky New York night club, the Salvation Army, and a spendthrift Indian maharajah on a spree in Paris were all stirred together in one pot." Limited only by the viewer's imagination, he continued, "it is pious and wicked, beautiful and ugly, rich and poor, exciting and dull, cultured and vulgar. Depending upon your point of view, it is a boil that's giving America a pain in the neck, or the last stand of individualism and right thinking." The magazine's own position could be inferred by the main photograph illustrating the article: a beaming man and woman, stylishly dressed and jitterbugging with joyful abandon. Writing in a similar vein for

Collier's in 1935, Quentin Reynolds assured his readers, "Wide open as Reno is, there is nothing vicious about the night life of the city. There is a gayety and friendliness about Reno and about the people who go to Reno to enjoy themselves but there is no viciousness nor ugliness about it. Tolerance, not license, governs Reno."[25] Described in such a way, this was a sanitized, urbanized frontier, untamed in many ways and yet regulated enough to satisfy the most civilized sensibilities.

This did not mean that Reno had developed overnight the reputation of a family resort. While female writers emphasized the town's sex appeal, romance, and intrigue, some male writers were more likely to emphasize sex itself, describing not only the availability of lonely divorcées, but also the prostitution that Reno had long tolerated, if not formally legalized. Divorce lawyer Kendrick Johnson confirmed Reno's overt sensuality in his *Rabelaisian Reminiscences of Reno by a Bachelor Lawyer* in 1934, a racy collection of twenty-seven vignettes, each titled with the name of a woman and her hair color—blonde, brunette, or redhead. In it, he catalogued his experiences, most sexual or at least sensual, with his clients and other divorcées. A male reporter for *Real Detective* in 1936 deemed Reno "The City That Sex Built," beginning his story with a conversation with bare-breasted "New York Betty," one of the prostitutes in the Stockade. The writer then related a perfectly casual and informative conversation with Betty about the specific legislation governing the Nevada prostitution business and the divorce industry, as they smoked cigarettes together on her bed.[26]

Such stories were quickly becoming the minority, however, as the films and fiction of this new era tended to distance Reno from impressions of licentiousness or vulgarity. Although the majority of their storylines revolved around Reno's divorce colony, most of the plots incorporated the threat of divorce as a precipitating factor for the ensuing action rather than the main attraction itself. This in itself rendered the stories less morally problematic and softened the treatment of divorce to create the effect of drama but not devastation. Like other divorce-related movies of the 1930s and beyond, the Reno films did not feature realistic depictions of the divorce process. Indeed, the majority of the films, whether in order to conform to the Hays Code or simply to provide a more satisfying conclusion, ultimately affirmed marriage, employing the threat of divorce as a reason for visiting the lively little town, which provided such possibilities for drama and comedy alike. Much of the Reno-based fiction of the era, as had Leslie Curtis's satiric plays two decades earlier, followed a similar pattern.[27]

Indeed, in most of these films, characters who have experienced serial divorces are often punished, like Jackie, the heroine of *The Road to Reno,* whose callous indifference to her children's disapproval leads to her son's suicide. Others are portrayed as victims of poor judgment, like the comical Countess de Lave in *The Women* (1939), a wildly successful film based on a play by writer and editor Clare Boothe Luce, herself the recipient of a Reno divorce in 1929. At one point in the film, nearly the entire cast of New York socialites takes the train to Reno to divorce their society husbands; while in transit, the Countess tells her fellow travelers of her marital misadventures following the death of her first husband, including her attempted murder by her third and fourth husbands, who respectively pushed her down a mountain and tried to poison her. Ever the optimist, the Countess waves it off with a glass of champagne and the repeated sigh, "L'amour, l'amour!"[28]

If the heroine of these tales files for divorce, the action is generally presented as justified, as her husband is either cheating on her, is planning to cheat on her, or through some misunderstanding *appears* to have cheated on her. In *Night Life in Reno* (1931), Joan leaves her Los Angeles home for Reno after finding her husband in another woman's apartment. In *Merry Wives of Reno* (1934), based on a story by Robert Lord, Madge hears through the grapevine that her husband, Frank, has left his missing over-coat at another woman's house. While the coat in question was really left behind as an innocent Frank fled the woman's advances, the misunder-standing sends him following a furious Madge to Reno all the same. Norma Shearer's virtuous character, Mary Haines, on the other hand, is clearly justified in seeking a divorce in *The Women,* after her husband initi-ates a public affair with shop girl Crystal Allen, played with reptilian glee by Joan Crawford.

In fact, many of the cinematic divorces are initiated but never finalized. The six-week delay between the statement of intent to divorce and the con-ferral of a final decree offered abundant opportunities for reconciliation. The comedy *Merry Wives of Reno* eventually reconciles its feuding couples, as does a second film with the title *The Road to Reno* (1938), a 1939 *Reno,* and many others. After a penitent John, the husband in *Night Life in Reno,* finds his wife in the divorce colony, she flirts with another man to make him jealous. When that man, Roy, is found dead, she is charged with mur-der, prompting her loyal husband to confess to the crime in order to save her. All ends well once Roy's jealous wife confesses to the deed, allowing a reconciled Joan and John to depart Reno together. Even Mary, the heroine of *The Women,* although reluctantly following through with a divorce from her philandering husband, is eventually reunited with him back in New York once he realizes his mistake (and she hers, to the everlasting disappointment of later generations of feminist critics).

Although tragic storylines continued, they were less frequent, and often incorporated comedic elements as well. Occasionally the attempt to achieve both simultaneously earned the derision of reviewers. To one, writing for the *Los Angeles Times,* this problem was found in *The Road to Reno* (1931), which he stated "never comes through either as comedy or melodrama, although both extremes meet."[29] *Merry Wives of Reno,* in contrast, took a madcap approach to the topic, producing what one contemporary viewer described as "a comedy based on the marital mix-ups of the celebrated divorce center," with two main characters who "are reunited in Reno, which, like the man who bit the dog, is news." And yet even though presented as a harmless "parlor, bedroom and bath farce," as another reviewer described it, including a running visual gag about a sheep named Eloise, the film still earned a place on the Catholic Church's annual list of "immoral and indecent films" for its divorce component.[30]

Given Reno's rising popularity, even some established serial movie characters had to have an adventure in Reno. The comedy team of Bert Wheeler and Robert Woolsey starred in the RKO comedy *Peach o' Reno,* originally known as *Six Weeks in Reno,* one of the three films marking the beginning of the "Reno cycle," in 1931. Featuring the duo as a team of Reno divorce lawyers whose office transformed into a gambling club by night, the slapstick comedy featured cross-dressing, musical gags, and bulletproof lawyers. After watching the "pictorial burlesque of the divorce mart" with an enthusiastic audience, one reviewer deemed it "a good deal of rowdy fun."[31] With the release of *Charlie Chan in Reno* in 1939, one reviewer remarked, "It was inevitable that Charlie Chan would get to Reno. Not, of course, to seek a divorce for the Oriental sleuth is probably the happiest husband and father in filmdom, but to solve a mysterious murder."[32] A comic-action approach was taken in *Maisie Goes to Reno* (1944), the eighth in a series of comedies featuring Ann Sothern as a Brooklyn-born, wise-cracking showgirl. In this installment, she heads to Reno, "not for the usual reason," as two separate reviewers clarified, but simply to rest her nerves, and lands in the middle of a scheme involving divorce, gambling, and a hapless young soldier she saves from a group of conniving criminals.[33] Significantly, the stars of such series were never placed in Reno in order for their characters to pursue their own divorces; this might have been too much for their fans to take.

On film, Reno was becoming a destination for a broader cross-section of divorcées than ever before, not just the well-to-do. The same was true for the real Reno, thanks in large part to the legalization of gambling, which had legitimized, at least in name, an activity formerly associated with shady characters and professional sharpers. That it was now completely "wide open," no longer operating under cover, lent the practice the veneer of respectability. Slowly but surely, in person as on screen, gambling was moving toward broader acceptance as mainstream entertainment. Its increasingly democratic appeal could be witnessed in downtown Reno, where a broad array of socioeconomic classes frequented the established clubs. More and more women patronized these establishments, too, in a way most would never have dared prior to legalization. In 1933, a delighted British visitor named William Teeling recalled gambling downtown with a "real Western crowd" of "farmers and their wives in for the evening," as well as "Canadians, foreigners and people from all the States of the Union." Teeling did note, however, that the "smarter people" still gambled primarily in "river-side clubs" a few miles outside of town.[34]

But this self-imposed segregation of social classes was about to change. The famous Willows resort burned down in just two hours while under renovation in 1932 and was never rebuilt. Filling the void were a host of popular downtown hotels, both old and new, that adapted to the new economy by offering licensed gambling in a more rarified atmosphere than the established clubs. In 1930, a Syrian immigrant named Abe Zetooney began construction of the six-story art deco El Cortez Hotel on West Second Street in order to capitalize on the divorce trade. The hotel opened the following spring, and within a few years, offered a number of gaming tables, as did the California Club, located in the lobby of the Overland Hotel. The luxurious Riverside Hotel offered a roulette wheel, 21, and hazard in its new Riverside Buffet. With these new additions to the landscape, the smarter set became more inclined to take their chances downtown. Nearly every Reno film after 1931, and some before, contained scenes of gambling, mostly in elegant lobbies and in full dress, which although not the typical attire for a Reno gambler, certainly looked chic.[35]

As Reno became a playground for amateur gamblers of all backgrounds, visitors and audiences alike were exposed to even more of what the town had to offer. Like the stories of the divorce colony from the

1920s, the images, articles, and guidebooks of subsequent decades continued to function as an indirect form of tourist promotion. Previous generations had read of divorcées enjoying Reno's racetrack, shops, and resorts,
and this new generation witnessed divorce-seekers and others engaging in
an even wider range of recreational activities. It was a landscape that
seemed tailor-made for leisure. As *Life* magazine noted in its June 1937
cover story, "Reno divorce seekers on pleasure bent can find plenty to do.
They may gamble, drink, dine, dance, and watch entertainment ranging
from striptease acts to female impersonations." Calling Reno the "city of
sinful fun," the writer balanced references to the Stockade and racy nightclubs with descriptions of the town's more respectable elements, including
the state university and several churches. This was a city of sinful fun, certainly, but heavier on the fun than the sin. That same year, the *Saturday
Evening Post* presented a "Day of a Divorcee" with large color photographs
of one of the "fashionable" divorcées frequenting the Fortune, the Bank
Club, the Tavern, and the Cal-Neva, riding on a dude ranch, boating on
Lake Tahoe, and visiting Virginia City—a menu of activities that could
not possibly all be accomplished in one day. But it sure looked like some
vacation.[36]

Indeed, from the media coverage, both factual and fictional, it seemed
that divorcées could pursue so many fun activities in Reno that their divorces became something of an afterthought. When the city built a new
horse racing track in the summer of 1931, one reporter wrote, "Reno divorces will hereafter have to be hustled through during the brief morning
hours. In the afternoon the divorcées have to go to bet on the races and
can't be bothered."[37] In the film *Merry Wives of Reno,* a newly arrived divorcée disembarking from the train in Reno is overheard saying, "I hope it
takes at least a month for my divorce. I want to stay here long enough to
improve my backhand." In subsequent years, outside observers increasingly
portrayed divorce as a recreational activity in itself. As one reporter wrote,
presumably tongue-in-cheek, "Nevada handles its divorces with such neatness and dispatch that even happy husbands and wives might be tempted
to go out and take a ride through the mill, just for the fun of it. For most
divorces you spend six merry weeks in Nevada, six minutes in the court-
room, and it's all over."[38]

In such depictions, the "Reno divorce" seemed to stand not for the moment of the actual divorce decree—which generally received very little attention, if it occurred at all—but for the six weeks that preceded it. More

and more, the "Reno divorce" came to resemble an enjoyable western vacation. This growing conflation of divorcée and tourist served to increase the perception of Reno as a unique destination where visitors could escape the conventions of mainstream society and have a good time, whatever their motives or marital status.

Perhaps the most striking illustration of the divorce-as-vacation could be found at the divorce ranch, Nevada's distinctive version of the popular dude ranch. Such ranches started appearing around Reno in the late 1920s and soon became a regular component of features written about the colony. Culturally, the appearance of the dude ranch, where tourists played cowboy, as opposed to a working ranch, where cowboys raised livestock, demonstrated an important shift in attitudes toward the American West as well as changing attitudes towards outdoor recreation. As suggested by the noble title character of Owen Wister's popular 1902 novel, *The Virginian*, the image of the western cowboy transformed in the early twentieth century from a social outcast to a romanticized figure worthy of the notice, and even the imitation, of the wealthy easterner. The patronage of the dusty dude ranch by well-to-do tourists represented a remarkable shift on the part of a population who had attempted in previous generations to avoid such rustic locations as much as possible. The first national dude ranch trade association was formed in 1924, and these resorts began to attract visitors of all classes over the next few decades.[39]

In Reno, the terms "dude ranch" and "divorce ranch" were largely interchangeable, as such resorts were known to have been constructed around Reno specifically for the entertainment of visiting divorcées. Depending on their degree of luxury and celebrity patronage, dude ranches cost the visitor anywhere from $100 to $160 or more per month.[40] They were, to a large extent, feminized spaces, providing goods and services known to appeal to women, from organized shopping trips to male ranch hands. In an article entitled "Reno the Naughty," appearing in *American Memory* in 1936, Anthony Turano wrote that the dude ranches were created in response to eastern divorcées' insistence on "going Western," which he considered completely egregious, "as enterprising natives have provided dude ranches where the jaded divorcee may enjoy the primitive life, dressed as a cowpuncher."[41] With the growing popularity of these sites, "going Reno" became a new euphemism for dressing western, allowing the visiting city dweller to purchase a slice of the supposedly "authentic" Wild West during his or her stay.[42]

Socialite and heir Cornelius Vanderbilt, Jr., took advantage of this new consumer demand by going into the local dude ranch business after moving to Reno for his divorce in 1927. A wealthy and savvy businessman, Vanderbilt bridged the affluent eastern socialites and Hollywood, becoming the subject of intense interest amid both populations. The novel he wrote, based on his own experience and titled simply *Reno*, was published in 1929 and turned into the 1930 film by the same name. Vanderbilt's first ranch, the TH Ranch, was 45 miles northeast of Reno, and his second, the Lazy Me, was located just south of town. Vanderbilt admitted to advertising exclusively in two publications known for their "snob appeal": New York's *Town Topics* and *The Beverly Hills Script*. Modest advertisements listing "high class saddle horses" also appeared in the local newspaper. On his Lazy Me Ranch (known locally to some as the "Lay Me Easy"), Vanderbilt hosted celebrities like Amelia Earhart as well as friends including Charlie Chaplin, Will Rogers, Gary Cooper, Tom Mix, and Clark Gable and produced private rodeos for them to watch and sometimes to participate in.[43]

Realizing the desire of his guests to mix glamour with the frontier, Vanderbilt would often "dress up a couple of wranglers in ten-gallon hats" and send them in Rolls-Royces and Packards to meet the Southern Pacific trains at the station, and later at the airport. Other dude ranches in the area followed his lead, albeit on a slightly less luxurious level; one even utilized an old stagecoach. Vanderbilt advertised a "package ranch divorce," including "six weeks' room and board, a horse to ride, a trip to Reno twice a week in our station wagon, a free package of cigarettes per diem, and a free bottle of any liquor they asked for once a week." As he later reported, the package was so popular that the ranch was flooded with reservations from across the country, forcing him to build twenty additional cottages and expand the existing main house, thereby increasing the resort's capacity to fifty or sixty guests.[44] By the mid-1930s, nine area dude ranches belonged to the Nevada Dude Ranch Association. They ranged from the Flying N Ranch, just 4 miles south of town, with room for six guests, to the Olinghouse Dude Ranch, housing up to twenty guests, 38 miles east. The Pyramid Lake Dude Ranch, 34 miles north, with a capacity for sixty guests, was widely considered the most luxurious.[45]

Divorce ranches profited from the rising popularity of Western films, as Reno's landscape contained many of the characteristics consumers recognized from such movies. Icons of cowboy masculinity such as Tom Mix, Tex Ritter, and Gene Autry populated the films of the 1930s, and the Reno films included their own casts of cowboys and women "going Reno." Quentin Reynolds, writing for *Collier's,* painted the entire divorce experience as one big western adventure, describing for his readers the life of the lucky divorcée: "You have, if you live as most do while waiting for freedom, spent perhaps $500 during your six weeks residence and in addition to your divorce you've gotten a nice tan, you've learned to ride a horse and you've gone into the hills on horseback-riding picnics, and you've eaten barbecued chicken and thrilled to the soft-voiced cowboys singing."[46] A local club called the Town House even used the image of the cowboy flirtation on its outdoor sign, advertising itself as "the most intimate bar and dancing rendezvous in Reno" with a cartoon of a cowboy standing between two stylish women at a bar. As one article explained, "Unescorted ladies are no rare sight at bars where cowboy pick-ups may supply relaxation after a hard day's riding."[47]

In the film *The Road to Reno* (1931), the heroine stays at the "Eternal Triangle Ranch," where the hubbub of activity includes a woman practicing her archery by shooting arrows at her husband's picture while others drink "lemon squash," and still more ride horses in the background. When a single man approaches, they all swarm around him like eager, famished puppies. The ranch in *Vacation in Reno* (1946) is suggestively titled the Bar Nothing, while the divorce ranch in *Reno* (1930), the film based on Cornelius Vanderbilt's novel, is called the McKelvey's Dude Ranch. There, a band with a lead singer dressed as an Indian chief plays a song called "Reno, the Land of the Free"; its lyrics describe Reno as a mythical land where "Cowboys ride on horses, and even drugstores sell divorces." It sure looked like one big party.

Many of the divorcées in *The Women* "go Reno" with some fairly elaborate western outfits. At the Double Bar T Ranch, clearly located not outside Reno but on a Hollywood stage set, the wealthy Countess de Lave wears ropes of pearls and elaborate necklaces with her rolled up trousers and plaid shirt, while Miriam Aarons sports a cowboy hat dangling from a string around her neck, wrist cuffs, flared shorts, and pristine cowboy boots. The film also presents another aspect of the western fantasy, the rustic ranch romance. Divorcées fell into the arms of local cowboys in Reno stories from the 1920s short fiction published in *Collier's* to the 1960 film *The Misfits.* In *The Women,* it is the Countess de Lave who takes up with the ranch's resident cowboy, Buck Winston, vows to make him a radio star, and eventually marries him, taking a sizeable souvenir of her western vacation home with her.

Folksinger Woody Guthrie immortalized the phenomenon in a song he wrote in 1937 called the "Reno Blues," also known as "The Philadelphia Lawyer." Reportedly based on a newspaper clipping Guthrie had read, and on an older folk ballad called "The Jealous Lover," the song told of a tragic love triangle involving a "gun-totin'" Reno cowboy named Wild Bill, a Philadelphia lawyer, and the woman they both adored. "Way out in Reno, Nevada," it began, "Where romance blooms and fades / A great Philadelphia lawyer / Was in love with a Hollywood maid." The story turns on Wild Bill's untimely discovery of the lawyer and his love locked in an embrace, as the lawyer urges her to "leave this wild cowboy behind" and return with him to the city. The result is perhaps all too predictable, as the final lines reveal, "Now back in old Pennsylvania / Among those beautiful pines / There's one less Philadelphia lawyer / In old Philadelphia tonight."[48]

While the women swooned, most male observers were more dismissive of these allegedly rough-hewn Reno natives. As Basil Woon wryly noted, "The cowboy-gigolo is Reno's own special product." In terms that could easily have described one of Hollywood's B-Western singing cowboys, Woon wrote, "He is usually a dandified puncher who leans toward brightly colored scarves, polished spurs, silk shirts and brass-studded chaperajos. Ah, they're a handsome, swashbuckling lot—and can they handle the women!" Anthony Turano griped, "such cowboys are usually synthetic; their chaps and bandannas are more redolent of cheap perfume than the realistic scent of the corral. Very few of them know the difference between a saddle horn and an automobile siren. But they are all competent gigolos, respectful listeners, and reliable consolers of unhappy bitter-halves." As both comments suggest, the intended audience for these cowboys and ranches alike was primarily female.[49]

Kendrick Johnson, author of *Rabelaisian Reminiscences of Reno*, agreed in 1934 that most of the "ranch bums who are politely called 'cowboys' . . . could not tell a cow from a bull or a steer from either, but nevertheless they are cowboys in Reno, anyhow they dress the part and don't bathe so they MUST be cowboys."[50] The sarcasm practically drips from the page. But to many women, the divorce ranches were a central component of the Reno story, in which the ranching pedigree of a handsome cowboy was not considered half as important as his appearance and charm. If he looked the part, that was good enough, and the point after all was to have a good time. And the image apparently sold itself. In a scholarly article on migratory divorce written in 1937, a legal scholar commented on the ability of such imagery to influence actual behavior among its viewers:

An illustration depicts a bevy of divorcées "going Reno" in their fashionable western regalia while cozying up at the bar to a "cowboy-gigolo," presumably from a local dude ranch. (Basil Woon, Incredible Land, *1933).*

The cowboy-gigolo is Reno's own special product

Not long ago, a photograph was taken at a Nevada "dude ranch," of a group of paying guests who were awaiting their divorces. This picture, with an informative caption, was widely published in the newspapers. A guest at the ranch told me that subsequently the ranch owner, a woman, was flooded with letters from women in all parts of the country, inquiring how they might secure divorces in Nevada.[51]

In a way, the divorce ranch had come to represent an alternate reality, providing an opportunity for the divorce-seeker to escape into a new identity, to inhabit another persona and lifestyle for a brief period while transitioning to the new identity of a single person.

Local clothing stores satisfied visitors' desires to complete their western

adventure by purchasing all the necessary accoutrements to "go cowboy." A
J. C. Penney ad in a local Dude Ranch Association brochure urged readers
to "Equip yourself with western apparel if you would enjoy to the fullest
those happy, carefree days on the Nevada Range." A popular family-owned
store, Parker's Western Wear, asserted, "You will find a complete assortment of ideal western togs from boots to Stetsons to fit your needs as well
as your purse."[52] With such shops at her disposal, a liberated woman could
don her newly purchased western togs to ride around the ranch all day,
dress to the nines to flirt with the cowboys over drinks at the Town House
or the Trocadero Room, and gamble all night at the Riverside Hotel.

Many local nightclubs capitalized on the popularity of the West
through the use of often exaggerated western motifs. The Dog House, a
popular club on North Center Street long known as "The Divorcee's
Haven," was remodeled in 1939 with an elaborate Old West interior, which
it maintained until 1944. The staff even wore cowboy and cowgirl outfits.
Cedars, a popular nightclub and dinner house located just out of town on
South Virginia Street, featured a rodeo and riding stable motif in the
1930s. The Comstock Club offered an elaborate underground Virginia City
mining theme complete with a mine tunnel entrance. Belle Livingston, a
notorious nightclub hostess who had fled New York City in July 1931 after
a series of run-ins with Prohibition agents, opened her own short-lived
nightclub, known as "Belle Livingston's Cowshed," or more colloquially,
"Belle's Barn," on the Hall Ranch, 1 mile south of downtown, to the dismay
of neighboring ranchers. But these shared equal space with clubs displaying more sophisticated themes such as the Bonanza Club's Gay Nineties
design, the moderne décor of the palatial Club Fortune, and the ornate
French resort–inspired ornamentation of Deauville.[53]

Reno profited from the popularity of the West in other respects as well,
as depictions of the divorcées and their Reno adventures provided an avalanche of publicity that served to promote Reno as a tourist destination for
everyone. The Reno Rodeo, after taking a financially motivated hiatus
through most of the 1920s, reappeared in 1932, bigger than ever, as "Pony
Express Days." The parade that year was more than a mile long and included representatives from area dude ranches, state and city officials,
celebrities, and "Indians clad in tribal regalia." Hollywood luminaries including Rex Bell, Roscoe Turner, and Harry Carr joined in, and a motion
picture crew from Hollywood even popped up to film the proceedings for
broadcast in movie theaters across the country.[54]

Upon its reinstatement, the rodeo quickly became one of Reno's biggest tourist events of the year. In its honor, local businesses decorated downtown with banners and special window displays and established a "Kangaroo Court" to enforce a "Go Western" rule requiring everyone found on the city streets to dress accordingly. Local society women would "go western" in rodeo-themed annual luncheons that were structured, and reported, like fashion shows. In 1935, the Reno Rodeo and Livestock Association was founded and began to solicit local businesses to subsidize the rodeo, a move that finally secured its continuity. That year, organizers built an enormous grandstand, with corrals and chutes, north of town. Through the next two decades, the Chamber of Commerce gave a Silver Spur Award each year at the rodeo to the celebrity "who best kept the Western spirit alive," recognizing actors including John Wayne, Gregory Peck, James Stewart, and Gary Cooper. The connection to Tinseltown produced a number of exciting events in the heyday of the Western film; in March 1940, a chartered train of celebrities direct from Hollywood arrived in Reno to celebrate the world premiere of the film *Virginia City*. Among the many famous visitors were the film's star, Errol Flynn, Western film stars Tom Mix and Bill Boyd, who played "Hopalong Cassidy," Humphrey Bogart, and Jane Wyman, accompanied by her new husband, Ronald Reagan. A series of parades, premieres, and special appearances drew thousands to Reno's streets and theaters.[55] By the 1960s, with the decline of Western films, the Silver Spur award shifted focus to television, awarding Dan Blocker, Lorne Greene, and Michael Landon, among others.[56]

However, despite all these efforts, some thought that the city did not take its westernness nearly far enough. Writing in June 1939, a former Nevada mining man complained to a local paper,

> You [Reno] "go western" for a few rodeo days—and spend the rest of the year bending over backwards to prove Reno is just like every other small city. This is a young state, one of the last outposts of the old West. You'd never guess it to look around Reno. Why not play it up? There's tremendous appeal in the pioneer stuff—do you flaunt it? You do not.[57]

Given the popularity of the West in American culture, it was perhaps a good question. And yet, the unwillingness of city officials to completely "westernize" the town revealed a refusal to turn Reno into a themed resort for tourists. To its promoters, the "real Reno" had much more to offer both tourists and residents than a replication of Virginia City, by now a growing tourist attraction for those interested in experiencing a glimpse of life on the Comstock.

Reno's promoters wanted their city to be seen for much more, including the beauty of its natural setting, which gained increasing praise with the further development of a number of outdoor sports and activities like golf and snowshoeing. In the early 1930s, the Reno Chamber of Commerce produced a pamphlet called *Reno, Land of Charm,* featuring the tagline "Where Nature's Playground Smiles for Miles and Miles." A far cry from former Mayor Roberts's campaign to make Reno the "playground of the world" through legalized vice, this campaign described the city's setting as "one of nature's most entrancing playgrounds" and emphasized Reno's status as not only Nevada's commercial and banking center, but also a center of recreation. By 1940, the city had replaced its long-running slogan advertising Reno as "The Recreational Center of America" with another calling Reno a "Year 'Round Playground" with "1000 square miles of superb ski terrain" as well as "summer, spring and fall fishing, hunting, boating, swimming, riding, camping, and all sports in season." Recreational travelers began to take note; as *Cosmopolitan* magazine reported in 1937, "Reno's growing resort reputation brings two types of visitors—those out for all-night gambling and sightseeing, and those seeking a regimen of rest, riding, hunting and fishing."[58]

Despite the promotion of these other activities, the most visible tourist attraction on Reno's landscape was gambling. The appearance of the downtown district had begun to change following its legalization, as many clubs added bright neon signs and others opened for business throughout the commercial district. But as the appellation of "club" indicates, these ventures were not large enterprises. Many changed hands repeatedly, with some suffering from the financial, and political, difficulties of their management or untimely disasters. Although the Willows burned in 1932, the Bank Club, Reno's largest club, continued to prosper, spending more than $20,000 to install a new bar, said to be "the classiest bar this side of the Waldorf-Astoria," in 1937.[59]

These expanding clubs were interspersed among traditional businesses, creating a terrain trafficked consistently by residents and tourists alike. Locals uninvolved with the gambling or divorce industries continued to work and shop downtown, where jewelry and stationery stores, banks, and hardware stores shared space with the clubs, cafés, and restaurants patronized heavily by locals, as well as divorcées and other tourists. At the same time, local residents often rented out apartments, rooms, and adjoining cottages to the divorce-seeking crowd, integrating them into the town's primarily residential areas.[60]

This juxtaposition of the residential and the tourist-oriented lent the town a general appearance of normality that belied its occasional flashes of neon and ubiquitous slot machines, a fact that never failed to strike many visitors. Still, the notion that there were "two Renos" continued, as some asserted that the divorce colony functioned entirely separately from the residential community. Basil Woon, for instance, reported that the divorce colony "lives its own life, and a pretty hectic one it generally is." But more often than not, writers acknowledged that there was just one Reno, and that it was mostly typical, partially idiosyncratic, and largely misunderstood. As one visitor proclaimed in one of the local papers, "Many people out East have an entirely wrong idea of Reno. . . . Well, of course one can get plentiful good liquor, and gambling is very far from being forbidden. But this talk of Reno as a town of reckless gaiety is all hooey. It has many charming homes. It offers quiet to the student. The neighboring ranches are places of simple beauty."[61] Such reassurances had long peppered firsthand accounts of Reno, but as defensive statements like this one revealed, expectations of Reno were now more likely to be filled with images of exuberant decadence than coarse vulgarity.

New divorce guidebooks continued to reassure their readers that they had nothing to fear in a six-week sojourn to Reno. In his 1934 manual, attorney Philip Siggers explained, "Reno's vices have been over-publicized by the American Press anxious to please a sensation-loving public. It does not have a hard-drinking population and drunkards are at least as scarce as in other American home cities. Nor is the gambling a pre-dominant feature of Reno life." His continuing description was worthy of a Chamber of Commerce publication: "Reno is not merely a pleasure city: it is after all, a residence city, with thousands of modest, well-cared-for cottages; a city to which families with small children may come to live in beautiful, inspiring surroundings, with assurance that the little ones will have every opportunity and good influence to become well-educated and self-reliant citizens."[62]

And yet in their depictions of Reno's separate worlds, some observers did extend blame toward the residents who tolerated industries many considered antithetical to a stable home life. *American Magazine*'s Mary Mullett called Reno a "City of Strange Contrasts," a "thriving community with lovely homes and delightful people" that was "built on broken homes and shattered hopes," following with the observation that "the citizens despise the goose which lays this golden egg; but apparently they have no idea of killing it off."[63] Although this perception granted residents a degree of moral discernment, it still criticized their mercenary nature. This pointed to a clear and continuing paradox in the defensive responses of many residents. As a community, they wanted the attention and the money, but not the criticism.

Residents became most defensive at the suggestion that the divorce and gambling industries dominated Reno life, and anyone who painted such a picture of the community was subject to derision and outrage. After Cornelius Vanderbilt, Jr., published his book *Reno* in 1929, he met protests from the Chamber of Commerce and members of the Reno 20-30 Club, who denounced his book as exaggerated and contemptible.[64] One of the most verbal defendants of Reno's reputation was resident Gladys Rowley, who penned a regular column, "Reno Revue," for the *Nevada State Journal* in the 1930s and 1940s. Like many other local residents, she was highly cognizant of Reno's outward reputation, as well as any perceived slight to it, but she usually approached the topic with a sense of humor. In one column, she sighed, "This Reno—scarlet woman to her sister cities—and nice little suburban town to her residents. A reversed case of sheep in wolf's clothing. If this isn't a case of aproned housewife pictured in harlot's robe! Oh well, she can take it. Valiant little city!"[65] Often, Rowley relayed bits and pieces of her recent conversations with visitors who voiced their surprise at encountering Reno's many charms, and their comments frequently peppered her column. As one woman recounted her initial encounter with Reno, Rowley reported her saying, "But this is perfectly beautiful! I'd heard it was just desert country!" and "You actually have concerts and amateur theatricals? Astounding!" Five months later, Rowley published another visitor's surprised comments: "Why this is really living—this Reno! City? This is God's country made for man—where you do as you wish and no one cares naught! But it's Grand—this land of freedom—feels as though the fresh air and sunshine are free."[66]

Rowley seemed to have designated herself the arbiter of media coverage about the city. Impressed by Leslie Ford's short story "Reno Rendezvous," which appeared in *American Magazine* in 1939, Rowley noted approvingly that the author "evidently spent a little time here—then painted an accurate picture, fiction notwithstanding. Unlike most of our visiting firemen—who make a thorough round of the local bars and depart—producing, thereafter, 'authentic' articles on the divorce capital."[67] At other times, Rowley lost patience with what she saw as bad publicity. Recognizing that new arrivals would be reading her column, she was quick to assert that Reno was as respectable as any other hometown. For some time, she wrote, she "had been lamenting the adverse publicity given Reno, by publications outside the state, complaining that they didn't see Reno as Reno really is. It had to be a lurid picture—or no go."[68] Her attempts to set the record straight were not confined to commentary alone. In September 1938, Rowley met with a group of local women at the Riverside Hotel to discuss promoting Nevada at the upcoming World's Fair in New York. The group was more concerned about establishing a presence there than at the 1939 fair in San Francisco, since they believed the western states were more familiar with each other, but "to the majority of the millions who will see the New York Fair, Nevada is a divorce center." They proposed a motion picture to highlight all the positive attributes, asserting, "those of us who live here resent that Reno as a divorce center is all Nevada means to the outside world."[69]

A reporter for the *American Magazine* in 1938 seemed to hit the mark when he observed,

> The only discordant note in Nevada these days is opposition to *publicity* about gambling and divorce. Some of the older folks, who have no thought of stopping the roulette wheels or changing the divorce laws, are becoming staid and conservative and a bit ashamed of the state that gave them their fortunes. When they go out of Nevada and say they're from Reno, people make jokes about them and they don't like it.[70]

A reporter for *Collier's* found this to be the case when interviewing the retired Judge Bartlett, of divorce fame, in 1938. To the reporter's surprise, Bartlett chastised him for focusing his attention on Reno's less respectable attractions, complaining,

> You drop off a plane and head for Club Fortune or The Palace or The Town House. You go to the courthouse and listen to some divorce cases. Then you tell the world about the gambling and the hell-raising

that goes on in Reno. Not just you, my dear sir, but all of your craft. . . . Dammit, not one of you ever sees the decent side of Reno.

After being similarly chastised by several of Reno's other leading figures, including George Wingfield, Riverside Hotel manager Charlie Sadlier, and even Governor Dick Kirman, the bewildered reporter asked a colleague, "we've been up here before and nobody gave a tinker's damn what we thought about the divorcées and the gambling joints and the hotcha side of Reno. Now everybody's harping on Nevada's respectability. What's come over these people all of a sudden?" His friend responded, "One sound state. It's the new religion up here."[71]

As a promotional strategy, the "One Sound State" campaign reflected local concern that the only Reno most Americans knew was the image purveyed by the media. But residents' motivations for correcting that image went far beyond Gladys Rowley's desire to correct the impressions of Reno held by mainstream America. This campaign, in contrast, was an attempt to change actual behavior, to attract rich new residents to Nevada. The strategy was to convince the very wealthy of the state's economic "soundness" by stressing Nevada's lack of numerous taxes including, most significantly, state income tax. One article claimed that the idea for promoting Nevada as a tax haven began in 1928, when a man named James Langford died in Los Angeles, but had legally resided in Nevada, where he had a summer home at Lake Tahoe, and therefore his estate was not accountable for estate taxes.[72] Although perhaps apocryphal, the story suggested that like the divorce trade, the discovery of Nevada's advantages in this respect had been unplanned.

In 1936, the First National Bank of Reno, in conjunction with the *Nevada State Journal,* published a pamphlet that it sent to a select list of 10,000 wealthy prospects, outlining a series of fiscal advantages to establishing residency in Nevada. It also dropped the names of a number of wealthy individuals who had already made the move, including yeast mogul Max C. Fleischmann.[73]

Knowing that a liberal Nevada was the familiar Nevada, the One Sound State campaign emphasized the state's conservative side. As the *Collier's* reporter observed, "the Nevadans aren't going to play up this gay, devil-may-care side of life in their state anymore. They're going to put the emphasis on civic respectability." The campaign's promoters also emphasized the state's proven economic stability, pointing out how well Nevada had weathered the Great Depression. Although George Wingfield's chain of twelve banks had failed in 1932, sending the former civic leader into a bankruptcy from which he eventually rebounded (although he would never regain his former political dominance), the city had unquestionably benefited from the legalization of gambling, the shortened residency period, and the state's distance from eastern financial centers. Subsequently, a group of businessmen in Reno, led by Jack Cartwright (pronounced a "human dynamo" by Gladys Rowley), formed a group called Nevada Unlimited, in order to "sell Nevada short on hellraising and long on economic stability" and promote Nevada as "the cyclone cellar for the tax-weary." The group also wrote letters encouraging wealthy individuals to move to Nevada.[74]

The pamphlet published by the First National Bank incorporated testimonies from appropriate sources in order to target the specific needs of the wealthy. Such contributors testified to Reno's status as a hub of entertainment, clear proof that even Nevada's most conservative contingent recognized the value of its booming nightlife. In one of its articles titled "Why I Chose Nevada," Christian Arthur Wellesley, identified as "Fourth Earl Cowley," mentioned both of these complementary traits. After first calling Reno the "City of Moderation" and emphasizing its natural beauty and outdoor pursuits, he proclaimed, "when the bright lights beckon, there's a little city called Reno, which can supply the wants of the restless with all the amusement obtainable in the entertainment capitals of the world: I have had as much fun in Reno as I ever have had in New York, Paris or London."[75]

This pamphlet demonstrated an important shift in the state's own promotional machinery, as local leaders realized the need to acknowledge all of Reno's "amusements" and present them in positive terms. Like the creators of the One Sound State campaign, the Chamber of Commerce began to assume this approach in its publications, casting the gambling industry as emblematic of freedom and tolerance, just as Mayor Roberts had asserted a decade before. In *Nevada, the Last Frontier,* published in 1939, the Nevada Information Division of the Reno Chamber of Commerce announced,

> With an understanding of human nature that scorns hypocrisy Reno has chosen to bring its games out into the open instead, as in other cities, of permitting them to exist sub rosa under "protection." They are duly police inspected and regulated and definitely kept beyond the

reach of adolescents. . . . All in all, Reno is primarily an intelligent city, intelligently administered, and a city which appeals irresistibly to those individuals seeking health and enjoyment, relaxed living and subsistence under the happiest conditions of personal freedom.

In promoting this angle, the Chamber of Commerce happily reprinted an article from *Barron's* that primarily discussed Nevada as a "haven for the tax weary" but also explained the city's controversial industries sympathetically as part of a tradition of supporting personal freedoms:

> Since Nevada became a state . . . it has hewed closely to the line that those who are governed least are best governed. Settled by rough cattlemen and raw miners, the State authorities would have found it impossible in the early days to enforce anything but a simple statutory fabric. Thus laws were framed to fit what would be obeyed and not to accord to an ideal. Now, on top of that, Nevada has found that there are dividends in liberal laws, which makes tightening them highly improbable.

The article continued, "There is no better illustration of this, perhaps, than the state's attitude toward divorce," framing the six-week residence period and the creation of the "mental cruelty" ground as a "common sense" move "to correct the evil of illegal desertions." Likewise, it argued, the state's policies toward "gambling and what is usually called 'vice'" have been brought into the open "on the theory that people are going to do it anyway and hence they should be allowed to do it legally—and pay for the privilege." By reprinting an article, rather than making these claims for itself, the pamphlet secured an endorsement that established a credible outside perspective, perhaps recognizing that it was other outsiders who could most effectively influence a place's reputation; it could not be improved by promoters' words alone, no matter how eloquent.[76]

Nevertheless, it was an inside operation that made the greatest strides toward democratizing the image of Reno's gambling operations. Through an unprecedented level of promotion, it helped to transition the perception of gambling from vice to mainstream entertainment. At the same time, its national publicity campaign fully incorporated gambling, for the first time, into Reno's larger identity. Founded in 1935, the casino known as Harolds Club quickly became one of the most powerful image-makers in Reno's history and its most widely recognized gambling operation. Its

Promoting itself as "The Friendly Club," Harolds Club departed radically from Reno's other gambling establishments in the mid-1930s with cartoonish images of cowboys and Indians, mountain men, trains, and pioneer wagons on its front facade. (Special Collections Department, University of Nevada–Reno Library)

owners openly dedicated themselves to establishing the respectability of gambling as they fully embraced mainstream advertising as a business tool.

Large-scale advertising was a foreign concept to most gambling clubs, since many of the early operators, having begun as disreputable or even illegal establishments, were accustomed to running businesses that did not wish to attract too much notice. Harolds did not suffer from this handicap, having opened on a very small scale, with only a single penny roulette wheel, in February 1935, well after the 1931 legalization of gambling. A true family operation, Harolds Club was run by the Smith family, whose members had previously worked on the carnival circuit in California. Harold Smith, Sr., and his brother Raymond A. Smith opened the club with a $500 investment from their father, Raymond I. "Pappy" Smith, who later joined the operation as well.[77]

In the first few years after opening, Harolds added new games and in 1941, leased the property next door and took over the Rex Club. Their advertising was initially very subtle, at first providing only the club's name and the line "Games of Every Description."[78] In 1941, Harold Smith announced that he had initiated a $25,000 advertising campaign to advertise both Harolds Club and Reno throughout the nation. The inclusion of the city of Reno was significant. As the club succeeded, the walls between gambling and the town's other businesses came down not only figuratively, but literally. Through the mid-1940s, Harolds Club financed the production of advertising material that functioned as promotion for the entire city, while the city itself had shied away from promoting casinos, considering them too controversial. According to Thomas Cave Wilson, who founded the Wilson Advertising Agency in Reno in 1939 and began to handle advertising for Harolds after World War II,

> Sometimes in those days, it was impossible to draw a line and say, "on this side is the Reno Chamber of Commerce" and "on this side is Harolds Club." Because if we felt there needed to be a brochure to encourage people to stay in Reno another day, it would look and appear much like a typical chamber of commerce brochure, but it carried the Harolds Club name and was paid for by Harolds Club. . . . it was a straight chamber of commerce-type pitch on all the things that the people [wanted]—maybe the children and the wife didn't want to gamble.[79]

As for the club's own promotional strategies, of chief importance was targeting the broadest audience possible; in that effort, Wilson and Raymond I. Smith agreed that they should take a shamelessly lighthearted approach. Early advertisements featured the tagline "The Friendly Club," along with cartoon characters such as a man wearing only a barrel, presumably having lost everything including the shirt off his back, at Harolds. The use of cartoon characters was a deliberately unsophisticated strategy, Wilson recalled,

> because . . . the minute we treated gambling as the serious business, we became tangled with all kinds of things, and seriousness was just a bad approach. But if we treated it as *not* being serious, that it was a form of recreation, that it was *fun,* it was simple, it was not going to make or break civilization, and it was a thing that was optional, we were on reasonably sound ground.

Their new, catchy slogan, based on the standard motto of the westward migration, was "Harolds Club or Bust." Other advertisements pictured covered wagons emblazoned with the "Harolds Club or Bust" slogan, pulled by a team of laughing oxen.[80]

The club's strategy seemed almost too simple: the casino would make gambling respectable by *deeming* it as respectable as any other activities tourists might be pursuing out west, during the same vacation. In order to do so, Wilson chose an "old western" theme, since gambling fit right into the Old West. That way, even if visitors weren't familiar with gambling, Harolds could demonstrate to them that it had always been a natural component of western communities like Reno and was therefore nothing to fear. A subsequent print advertising campaign reinforced this link by featuring short vignettes about Nevada history, with a new ad every week for all the Nevada newspapers. In addition to print advertisements, the casino directly targeted auto tourists, increasingly the majority of Reno's visitors, by affixing the slogan to outdoor signs. Placed along high-traffic roads nationwide, like the famous Burma-Shave ads of the 1920s through 1960s, the Harolds billboards eventually numbered in the thousands. Some of those billboards were so large, said Wilson, that "there was no name in the industry for the size that we bought." As the slogan caught on, members of the public began to distribute them voluntarily, and Harolds even sent party kits to members of the military to create their own miniature "Harolds Clubs" while stationed overseas.[81]

In addition to their advertising strategies, the owners of Harolds Club linked the casino to the community in a number of concrete ways. They joined the Chamber of Commerce, although represented by their bookkeeper, Guy Lent, as it was "unthinkable" to many that a gambler would sit on the Chamber's board, recalled Wilson. The club entered a float in the annual Labor Day parade and, along with other clubs including Club Fortune and the Bank Club, offered trophies for the competitors at amateur boxing tournaments.[82]

As Harolds worked to improve the image of gambling in the public eye, the entire city was forced to deal with another challenge to Reno's standing. Around 1940, the tremors of a momentous shift began to rumble through Nevada. It was well encapsulated by a description found in a 1940 guide to the state, sponsored by the Work Projects Administration, which read, "The town is particularly lively at night. Neon lights call attention to the bars, gambling and night clubs, in which Hollywood celebrities, miners, prospectors, divorcées, corporation presidents, cowboys, and little old maids bent on seeing life at last, add to the stacks of silver dollars and watch the whirl of roulette wheels, or splash ink over the horse keno slips. Some restaurants are crowded till dawn."[83]

Such descriptions had long been applied to Reno, reflecting the town's unique character and its distinctive blend of cosmopolitanism and small-town western charm. This, however, was not a description of Reno, but of Las Vegas, located 445 miles to the south.

Up until the late 1930s, nearly all of the attention given to Nevada, from derision to delight, had focused on Reno. Divorce and Reno had been interchangeable for decades, and the legalization of gambling had led immediately, and almost exclusively, to articles about how Reno had done it again. But now, the southern Nevada town of Las Vegas, improbably located in the middle of the desert, was gaining the country's attention. Officially founded in 1905 as a sleepy railroad town, Las Vegas was growing steadily in the early 1940s, due to the construction of nearby Boulder (Hoover) Dam and the more recent construction of a federally sponsored magnesium plant and military gunnery range nearby. Its proximity to Los Angeles—a 275-mile drive through the desert—allowed Vegas promoters to tap into a culture already oriented towards entertainment. In fact, by the end of the 1930s, the Las Vegas Chamber of Commerce had begun to advertise the town's connections to Hollywood celebrities, encouraging potential visitors to fraternize around its gaming tables with "writers, movie stars, directors, and other vacationists."[84]

The Las Vegas bid for Reno's business was not new. As early as 1911, eager residents of the southern town had announced their intentions to establish a rival divorce colony there, particularly to attract the "winter divorce trade." Upon hearing of these plans, the *New York Times* had commented, "The demand for divorces increases yearly, and if the Las Vegas people keep up their courage, advertise freely, and deliver the goods according to advertisement, there is no doubt that they will soon place their city on a thriving basis."[85] It took a few decades, but by the late 1930s, Las Vegas, with its proximity to Hollywood's disaffected marital scene, had become a serious contender. Many identified an important turning point as 1939, when Clark Gable's second wife, Ria Langham, chose Vegas over Reno when establishing her residency for a divorce.[86]

While Reno still granted more than twice the number of divorces as Las Vegas through the 1940s, Langham's visit drew substantial media attention to the clubs and resorts of Las Vegas, which by the early 1940s was beginning to encroach on Reno's gambling market as well.[87] Nearly ten years earlier, Paul Hutchinson, the managing editor of the *Christian Century*, had been prescient, although certainly not complimentary, when he predicted, "There is open gambling going on in places like Carson City and Las Vegas, and before the Hoover dam is completed the latter city may manage to attach to itself almost as unenviable a name as is Reno's." By 1940, the main thoroughfare of downtown Las Vegas, Fremont Street, featured its "big four" clubs, the Las Vegas Club, Apache Club, Northern Club, and Boulder Club, all similar to the early western-style clubs of downtown Reno. But it was the clubs venturing beyond Las Vegas city limits that brought the competition to a new level. Entrepreneurs from outside Nevada began their first tentative forays along dusty Highway 91, the road leading toward Los Angeles. With the appearance of the El Rancho Vegas and the Hotel Last Frontier, not to mention the new El Cortez on Fremont Street, Las Vegas had entered the age of the resort hotel. In 1942 a *Saturday Evening Post* article marked the emergence of the southern city on the national scene by deeming Las Vegas "Nevada's New Reno."[88]

As the new sinners on the block, promoters of Las Vegas had their work cut out for them, and they were determined to live up to that designation. Although Las Vegas could boast a population of just 10,000 in 1940, its Chamber of Commerce was already embarking upon innovative tourist promotions, often remaining open late into the hours of the night in order to assist visitors in finding places to stay. In an effort to keep the name of Las Vegas in the public eye, the chamber collaborated with the town's casino owners from the war years through the early 1950s to create a series of sophisticated and expensive promotional campaigns. These took a variety of approaches to selling the city, stressing everything from Old West appeal to family vacation opportunities to Hollywood connections.[89]

Reno's economy had by now come to rely upon tourist dollars, and with the dawn of real competition for its gambling and divorce business, Reno's promotional machine revved up its engines. The primary concern was to distinguish the city's reputation from that of Las Vegas in order to attract out-of-staters who might be equally willing to visit either city. If Las Vegas won the popularity contest, Reno's economy would be in serious trouble. As journalist Max Miller wrote in 1941, "Reno lives on getting talked about. It is Reno's reputation that packs the cars into the city's parking spaces, their license plates calling the roll of the Union."[90] It would be no longer sufficient to rely on the media to cover the Reno beat whenever they felt inclined to do so.

In the years just preceding World War II, Reno's promotional efforts first began to benefit from the expertise of advertising professionals, who directed their attention to maximizing media coverage of the city. After establishing his advertising agency in 1939, Thomas C. Wilson served on the publicity committee of the Chamber of Commerce, without charge, in what he later described as a "labor of love." At this point, the chamber had very little money for such campaigns. In this capacity, Wilson helped to perpetuate some of the longstanding Reno divorce legends, including the stories that newly divorced women kissed the columns of the courthouse and threw their wedding rings off the Virginia Street Bridge into the Truckee River. Occasionally manufacturing what Daniel Boorstin would later refer to as "pseudo-events," Wilson would sometimes buy "a few dollars worth of dime store wedding rings" from Woolworth's "and then when nobody was lookin', toss 'em in the river off the bridge." Then, he said, young kids who were playing or fishing in the river in the summer would occasionally find a ring and make a big scene, attracting the attention of tourists and therefore perpetuating the popular story. He was not above smearing lipstick on the courthouse columns, either.[91]

As Wilson later recalled, "We had a continual series of stories running in national magazines. Gambling was still new. It was easy to get feature stories. I didn't overdo it, but I could hit the *Saturday Evening Post,* six to eight months later, hit *Time* magazine. I would get story ideas, and write them to editors. And it didn't require any great thinking." Demonstrating the continued appeal of western iconography, he often staged photographs featuring Native Americans and stagecoaches, and as he recalled, "strangely enough, the pictures would get used, although it was pretty corny." However, in addition to the lighthearted features, Wilson was also concerned with promoting Reno as an elegant destination and gambling as a classy activity. In covering the 1941 opening of the Trocadero, an elegant nightclub, cocktail lounge, and gaming room in the lobby of the El Cortez Hotel, Wilson orchestrated a black tie opening with elegant décor and entertainment and even secured newsreel footage. As he later recalled, "We hit everything in the country with it. And it did more for Reno's image than, I think, anything else that we managed to get on at that time. I think Reno could have kept this image. It was a replay from the twenties."[92]

With the advantages of population and established institutions, Reno's promoters often focused on the city's cultural superiority to Las Vegas and its ability to host such elegant events as the Trocadero opening, hoping to

recapture an earlier glamour. The two Nevada cities ran competing promotions in 1945, as Las Vegas hired the J. Walter Thompson Advertising
Agency for an $85,000 campaign, and Wilson headed up a $100,000 advertising campaign for Reno. The Reno campaign was a true media blitz, comprising publicity, stationery, and literature for the travel bureau; advertisements on Nevada's tax policy, designed to appear in financial magazines;
and more general advertisements in Western airline publications and other
national magazines. For his part, Thompson advertised Las Vegas as a
"desert paradise," perfect for a fantasy getaway.[93]

Occasionally, one of the cities' casinos would stage a dramatic media
event, as in 1945, when the El Rancho Vegas chartered a plane to Reno in
order to "rescue" a Hollywood actress, in town to seek a divorce, from what
she had found to be "inappropriate surroundings" there and fly her to Las
Vegas. The stunt was a success, as the event was picked up by *Business Week*.
Staged events involving movie stars were extraordinarily successful in attracting the national press. In one of his nationally circulated "In Hollywood" columns, Erskine Johnson described the celebration following the
1947 divorce of starlet and pin-up girl Marie "The Body" McDonald, who
had spent her six weeks' residence in luxury at the Strip's "swank Flamingo
Hotel." As part of a parade for Helldorado, Las Vegas' annual celebration of
the Wild West, Johnson reported, McDonald rode a "big floral flamingo"
down Fremont Street, "as Chamber of Commerce officials, 18 press agents,
and 50,000 Helldorado Week celebrators cheered."[94] The lavish Flamingo
Hotel was just a year old at the time, but already well on its way to fulfilling
the intentions of its visionary, *Hollywood Reporter* founder Billy Wilkerson,
and its primary investor, Los Angeles mobster Ben "Bugsy" Siegel, to bring
an elite slice of Beverly Hills to the southern Nevada desert.[95]

Despite, or perhaps because of, all this hoopla, Reno's Chamber of
Commerce continued to assert that the most important draws for Reno's
tourists were the city's conventions, year-round sports, fashionable dude
ranches, and the "sheer love of nature," as reported by the *San Francisco
Chronicle*.[96] Those promoters were likely gratified by a documentary trave-
logue called "Romantic Nevada," produced in 1943 as part of the popular
James A. Fitzpatrick "Traveltalk" series. Created under the auspices of
MGM, these short ten-minute features aired in movie theaters nationwide
before the main attractions. This installment featured Lake Tahoe, Virginia
City, Pyramid Lake, and Reno, with no mention whatsoever of Las Vegas.
Quirky and highly selective, with a soundtrack that prominently featured

the "Wedding March," the film asserted that "The main theme of Reno life revolves around marriage or divorce." After identifying the Washoe County Courthouse as the center of all this activity, Fitzpatrick proclaimed, "Up and down the steps of this famous court house go the feet of disillusioned divorcees along with the feet of romantic couples, seeking the happiness that the divorcees lost." Accompanying this description was an odd reenactment of these feet in action, never showing the upper bodies of the figures it described. Cognizant, no doubt, of its mainstream audience, the film focused in on the strange anomalies of Reno life—including demonstrations of column kissing and ring tossing—while clarifying that Reno was the site of far more marriages than divorces, and only showing, but never describing, the gambling clubs that lined its main street. As much as anything, the production of this short feature sanctioned Reno as a respectable destination for Americans everywhere.[97]

This perception was corroborated by Reno's most famous literary figure and longtime resident, Walter Van Tilburg Clark, author of *The Ox-Bow Incident* (1940) and *The Track of the Cat* (1949). Clark, whose father, Walter E. Clark, served as president of the University of Nevada from 1918 to 1938, made Reno the setting for his nostalgic second novel, *The City of Trembling Leaves* (1945). The story of Tim Hazard, a young musician who, like Clark, grew up in Reno, the novel posed the residential Reno against what Clark critically labeled "the ersatz jungle, where the human animals, uneasy in the light, dart from cave to cave under steel and neon branches, where the voice of the croupier halloos in the secret glades, and high and far, like light among the top leaves, gleam the names of lawyers and hairdressers on upstairs windows."[98]

This dazzling neon landscape, he wrote, although the most instantly recognizable, "is the region about which the world already knows or imagines more, in a Sunday-supplement way, than is true." Like columnist Gladys Rowley before him, Clark devoted the rest of his novel to describing the Reno he knew best, a close community characterized by peaceful tree-lined streets, churches, schools, parks, and wistful romance. In a nonfiction piece written a few years later, Clark repeated this distinction, claiming that "the average Renoite moves in a different world than that of the downtown casinos, and that "he is essentially a small-town person still." This "dual nature" of Reno, he wrote, was epitomized by its local newspapers: cosmopolitan on the surface, but on the inside, reflective of a small town that prided itself on its civic improvements and local sporting events.[99]

That small town grew considerably during and after World War II, with the establishment of the Reno Army Air Base (later known as the Stead Air Force Base) north of town and the Naval Ammunitions Depot in Hawthorne, just over 100 miles to the southeast. Through the 1940s, Reno's population grew from 21,317 to 32,497. Although still not a big city, resident Clarence Jones later recalled that Reno changed significantly in this period, as the military installations "brought lots and lots of people to Reno, which really began to set the wheels in motion economically. It also changed the character of the town, because we had a lot of outside people coming in here. Reno went from being an old country town, as we called it, to one where you know very, very few people."[100]

The introduction of a nearby military presence prompted another dramatic development that promised to boost Reno's reputation considerably. In January 1942, citing the proximity of active servicemen, the Federal Security Agency ordered the closing of Reno's houses of prostitution, including the notorious Stockade. They did not go quietly or quickly. Two months after the initial order, at least two of the brothels remained open, and by way of explanation, Reno's chief of police stated that there were no existing laws on city books directing him to suppress their operation. Since prostitution was technically not illegal, the notorious Stockade brazenly reopened in April with a posted sign prohibiting servicemen from entering; however, renewed federal, county, and city orders finally forced it and the other "vice houses" to close their doors by the end of May.[101]

The ban on brothels within Reno city limits survived a flurry of challenges in the late 1940s. The first was brought by Mae Cunningham, who opened a brothel called the Willows on Reno's Commercial Row in the summer of 1948. When Cunningham ignored an order by the Washoe County Commission to cease operation, the district attorney ordered the brothel closed as a public nuisance. Cunningham's attorney appealed up to the level of the state supreme court, which ruled in 1949 that brothels could indeed be closed as a public nuisance, even though prostitution was not itself technically illegal in the state of Nevada. Unhappy with the ruling, state legislators immediately introduced a bill to the Nevada legislature that would exempt brothels from the public nuisance law and make prostitution legal, subject to local jurisdictions. Although that bill passed both legislative houses, it was vetoed by Governor Vail Pittman, who cited concerns for the state's reputation, stating that such a law "would result in sensational and sordid publicity throughout the nation and the world to the inestimable damage of the good name of our state and its citizens." Reno's city council rejected an attempt by Cunningham's lawyer to hold a special election on the brothel issue, and in subsequent years, city ordinances from Reno to Las Vegas outlawed brothels within city limits by declaring them public nuisances.[102]

This development did not go unnoticed. In the aftermath of the 1942 ruling, the United Press ran a story that was picked up in newspapers from New York to Tennessee; it began, "This city, with a reputation for easy divorce and wide-open gambling, is becoming as pure as the snow on the mountains behind it." With divorces on the decline and marriages on the rise, the reporter labeled the occasion the "re-birth of Reno." As for the city's remaining vices, identified as gambling and liquor, the reporter indicated that due to their long legacy stemming from the early-day mining camps, the city's "gaudy gambling houses" were not likely to go "without a good, healthy fight."[103]

Indeed, they were not likely to go at all. Abolition of gambling became even more unlikely once the state adopted legislation that finally gave it a share of the profits and established much-needed regulation of the industry. In 1945, the state introduced a 1 percent tax on the gross earnings of all gambling operations, a number that was raised to 2 percent in 1947. The introduction of table fees generated further income, in amounts that exceeded $1 million per year by the end of the decade. Also beginning in 1945, any new gambling operation was required to apply for a license through the State Tax Commission, a body that consisted of representatives of the livestock, mining, agriculture, business, and banking industries. This step removed regulatory power from the hands of city and county officials, and attempted to forestall the influence of organized crime, known to be infiltrating the gambling scene in Las Vegas.[104]

Through all these changes, family operations like Harolds Club provided some stability to Reno's downtown landscape through sole, continuous ownership. Another family legacy began when William Harrah, who had opened his first bingo parlor in Reno in 1937, opened Harrah's Club with his father, John, on Virginia Street in 1946. Advertising their family-friendly qualities, both establishments attempted to make gambling seem compatible with conservative, family-oriented postwar values. Both the Smith and Harrah families pursued this image by submitting to lengthy profiles by national magazines that highlighted their reputation for fair play. A lengthy profile of Harolds Club, written for *Life* magazine by

Douglas Alley became a hive of activity in the 1940s, boasting entrances to several clubs including Harrah's, Harolds, and the Palace, as well as a number of cafés. (Special Collections Department, University of Nevada– Reno Library)

Thomas Wilson's friend Roger Butterfield in 1945, presented the image of a fair and honest family business run with an eye toward civic responsibility. The Smith family, Butterfield wrote, "are pillars of civic enterprise and good works," contributing to the Boy Scouts, area churches, servicemen's clubs, the Reno Day Home, and even a "rest camp for wounded veterans."[105]

Harrah's Club gained similar press. In 1947, a profile of the club in the *Saturday Evening Post* asserted, "In the land of honky-tonk, elderly John Harrah operates a dignified gambling house on strictly business principles." Contributing to the Red Cross, the Reno Chamber of Commerce, and local charities, John and William Harrah were described as conservative, traditional, and fervently American, with a lineage stretching back to the Revolutionary War. Orchestrated by advertising men like Thomas Wil-

*Completed in 1947,
the elegant Mapes
Hotel-Casino featured
art deco stylings and
the glamorous Sky
Room, which boasted
unsurpassed views
of the entire city.
(Nevada Historical
Society)*

son, such puff pieces can hardly be said to present objective views of Reno's
establishments. And yet they did reflect changing attitudes toward the
practice of gambling, increasingly accepted by an ever-widening swath of
the American population.[106]

Another Reno dynasty entered the casino business as the Mapes family,
longtime Reno residents, prominent ranchers, and rodeo supporters,
opened their Mapes Hotel-Casino on the riverfront site of the old post office in 1947. The logical solution to the space limitations of downtown
Reno was to build upward, and at twelve stories high, the Mapes upon its
completion became the tallest building not only in Reno, but the entire
state of Nevada, earning the status of the first high-rise hotel casino in the
country. Although Las Vegas already featured the sprawling ranchlike com-
pounds of the El Rancho Vegas and the Hotel Last Frontier, the Mapes was
the first building to combine gaming, dining, and restaurants in a three-
part vertical structure and therefore became the "prototype of modern, ur-

ban, vertical casino design." Towering over the city's skyline, the Mapes complemented its neighboring stone and brick buildings; even at just twelve stories, its dominance accentuated the small scale of Reno's existing downtown. With 300 hotel rooms, the building boasted a glamorous lobby, a casino, several restaurants, and a Turkish bath. But the top floor was literally the Mapes's crowning glory, housing the "Sky Room," an elevated oasis dominated by floor-to-ceiling windows overlooking Virginia Street and the Truckee River, a sizable bar, dance floor, stage, full kitchen, seating for 400, and another casino area. The Sky Room was literally built for entertainment, and it showed.[107]

An array of promotional postcards celebrated this latest addition to the city, which gestured, through both its architecture and advertising, to Reno's western heritage, but in a subtler manner than the cartoony kitsch of Harolds Club. Its official brochure advertised the Mapes as "a unique family-owned hotel and casino that still specializes in personalized Western Hospitality." The logo, appearing on the outside of the building as well as on promotional materials and hotel key chains, featured two cowboys standing side by side with legs akimbo, forming the "M" for Mapes. Local journalist Rollan Melton remembered the Mapes as a "national hit from Day One," a democratic space "where Somebodies and Nobodies collided in harmony, where East met real cowboys, without turning up its Eastern nose." The Mapes family encouraged this perception, announcing their "policy" in an opening night advertisement: "The hotel is informal in keeping with the western tradition which makes Reno so hospitable. Come in full dress if you want any time . . . or come in cowboy boots. You will feel equally at home."[108]

Outside observers found the juxtaposition of elegance and informality slightly confusing but ultimately appealing. Upon its opening, Herb Caen of the *San Francisco Chronicle* wrote that the dignified exterior of the Mapes belied the rows of slot machines located just inside the doorway. "But," he wrote, recognizing Reno's ongoing quest for respectability, "I guess that's to be expected in a giddy little city that's still trying to prove, for its own benefit, that gambling can be a legitimate enterprise run by legitimate people." He continued, "Aside from the social implications, however, the Mapes is a beautiful hotel that any city in the country could point to with pride." The *Nevada State Journal* certainly did so, stating in an editorial the day after the hotel's opening day that the Mapes was "an asset to Reno and the state of Nevada and a monument to the courage and civic pride of the Mapes family," noting in particular the hotel's connection to "a pioneer family which played a highly important part in the general development of Reno and western Nevada." As the article concluded, "Reno's continued growth will aid the hotel and the hotel certainly will aid Reno."[109]

While the Mapes strove to infuse the western heritage with a strain of luxury, Harolds Club continued to take the opposite approach. In 1946, a businessman named Raymond Stagg moved to Reno with what may have been the largest collection of western memorabilia in the country and opened a combination museum of the West, club, and bar that he called Roaring Camp. The attraction became an immediate hit among tourists, prompting Raymond I. Smith to buy the club in 1949. After running the establishment at its existing location for several months, he moved the memorabilia up to the third floor of Harolds where it became the foundation of the Roaring Camp Room. In 1949, the Smiths commissioned an enormous mural of a pioneer scene for the front of the casino. Once installed, the two-story mural, composed of hundreds of separate porcelain tiles and dedicated "in all humility to those who blazed the trail," dominated Virginia Street. In 1957, historian Earl Pomeroy described Harolds as the centerpiece of a downtown landscape where, even more than in downtown Las Vegas, "the Western theme reached a kind of zenith."[110]

The approach resonated with tourists bent on having fun, and Harolds expanded rapidly. In 1947, the casino took over a property to the north as well as Harrah's Bingo, and in 1949, expanded its second floor after demolishing the Virginia Hotel. In 1950 and 1951, Harolds bought the Ritz Hotel on Commercial Row, and another building on North Virginia formerly leased by the Reno Club. In 1954 the company began construction of a seven-floor addition and opened its own parking garage. By the mid-1950s, Harolds was advertising "More than 5,000 visitors daily—4 out of 5 from outside Nevada."[111]

Gilman Ostrander has claimed that Harolds Club, through its national promotions, affordable amusements, and kitschy décor, "succeeded in democratizing gambling 'as Henry Ford had democratized the automobile.'" In effect, wrote Daniel Boorstin, "by lowering the stakes and so enlarging his clientele, [Raymond Smith] aimed to produce a Woolworth's of the gambling business. Harolds Club was as different from the old gambling casino as the five-and-ten-cent store was different from the elite specialty shop." Thomas Wilson agreed that in its advertising, Harolds deliberately appealed to a customer base that was "largely uneducated, lower and middle income. They gambled because they thought it was fun. They were treated to all kinds of wisecracks and jokes in the club, which was fun. So we made that the general theme of the advertising. . . . The signs reflected the cartoon approach."[112] A *Life* magazine reporter in 1954 had harsher words for the casino's strategy; Harolds, he said, was characterized by "strictly assembly-line gaming. . . . There's nothing fancy about Harolds. Indeed Harolds is as garish and nakedly ugly as an unshaded light bulb hanging from the ceiling in a flophouse dormitory."[113]

Gambling in Reno had come a long way from the dark basements of Gambler's Row or the discreet roulette wheels of the Willows. In fact, through a number of strategies, Reno's gambling establishments were attracting a more diverse crowd than ever, an effect that was not appreciated by everyone in the local business community. Many grew increasingly concerned by the gradual creep southward of the gambling district from its origins along Commercial Row and Douglas Alley toward the primary retail area along Virginia Street south of Second Street. As a *Nevada State Journal* editorial stated in 1946, "City and county officials should recognize the fact that it is detrimental to the general welfare and future growth of the community to permit further expansion of gambling or saloons." Reno's citizens, the column asserted, "do not want Reno converted, even on the surface, into a honky-tonk."[114]

The city council agreed, voting just over a week later to suspend the granting of any additional gaming licenses for the time being. This move precipitated an intense debate in the coming years over whether gambling should be formally restricted to a specific area of town, in order to insulate mainstream businesses and their customers from the gambling environment. By the early 1950s, the city council was pursuing an informal policy along those lines, but in September 1951, the Reno Chamber of Commerce and Nevada Retail Merchants Association urged the city council to go further by adopting a formal ordinance to ban any gambling establishments or saloons on the west side of Virginia Street or anywhere south of Second Street. The council determined that the power to deny permits lay firmly within its jurisdiction without a formal ordinance.[115]

The matter came to a head when a man named Ernest J. Primm applied for a gambling permit for his new property on the west side of Virginia Street in late 1951. Denied by the city council, Primm took the case all the way to the state supreme court, which upheld the city's decision. However, in 1954, a newly elected city council reversed their predecessors' decision, enabling Primm to open the Primadonna Hotel and Casino across the street from Harolds Club and pioneering the migration of the casinos' neon lights to a new downtown block formerly confined to traditional businesses. The expansion of the gambling district remained limited to that single block for the moment, but a precedent had been set, and the boundary would not remain in place for long.[116]

Increased leisure time for many Americans in the postwar era also worked in favor of casino expansion, supporting the construction of ever-larger temples to every individual's desire to make it big. As a result, some of Reno's most successful clubs continued to expand and consolidate their domination of downtown. Selling the Golden Hotel allowed George Wing-field, who had regained his financial footing after his disastrous Depression-era bank failures, to commence a $1.5 million expansion of the Riverside Hotel. This was completed in 1950 and included eighty-four new rooms, a dance floor, theater-restaurant, banquet area, and Reno's first swimming pool located inside a hotel. Four years later, a three-story addition doubled the number of the hotel's rooms. In December 1955, Wingfield ended his long association with the landmark when he sold the building for just over $4 million to a group of investors, and the hotel changed hands repeatedly over the next few decades. The Mapes expanded when the neighboring Y.M.C.A., source of such civic pride a few decades earlier, was torn down due to a boiler room explosion. In addition, Harrah's Club nearly doubled in size when it bought the Frontier Club next door in 1956 and knocked down the wall between them.[117] Other entrepreneurs added to Reno's gaming landscape, in some cases replacing former homes. In 1956, Norman Biltz, one of the masterminds behind the One Sound State campaign, opened the modern, eight-story Holiday Hotel, on the south bank of the river.[118]

As these clubs transformed into full-fledged casinos, they each constructed large showrooms like the Mapes's Sky Room and the El Cortez Hotel's elegant Trocadero Room where audiences could dine as they took in a glittery performance. In the 1950s, entertainment became a central component of the most successful casinos. The Riverside, Golden, and Mapes all competed in this arena at a time when, as publicist Mark Curtis later recalled, "Nevada casinos went through entertainers like cocktail napkins." Curtis had begun in 1957 to work on publicity for Harrah's, with two goals in mind: to distinguish the casino from Harolds and to promote its reputation as a classy entertainment destination. In his memoir *It Was*

Great While It Lasted, Curtis argued that the 1950s brought an opportune climate for the gaming industry as the country embraced rock-and-roll, a thriving economy, and showy cars. In those decades, as Curtis remembered, Nevada "had all the elements that made Nevada the center of the universe for entertainment." Frank Sinatra, Liberace, Jimmy Durante, and other national entertainers were regularly booked in Reno's casino nightclubs. Over the next few decades, the Mapes's top-floor Sky Room housed some of the biggest names in show business, including Judy Garland, Mae West, Sammy Davis, Jr., Nelson Eddy, the Marx Brothers, Liberace, Rudy Vallee, and Milton Berle. Occasionally, the Mapes even ran live feeds on the Ed Sullivan show from its Sky Room.[119]

Unfortunately, Reno's entertainment industry was not immune from the racial prejudices of the era. Black performers were allowed to entertain but not to sleep, eat, or gamble in most of Nevada's hotel casinos. By the 1950s, this practice, along with a record of discrimination and segregation more severe than most other states in the region, had earned the state the nickname of the "Mississippi of the West" among some civil rights advocates. Integration of all public places in Reno would not follow until the advent of state and federal legislation in the 1960s. In the meantime, members of Reno's small minority population ran their own casinos and nightclubs, some integrated, like the rowdy Harlem Club, located on the eastern, or what was known as the "skid row" side of downtown, through the 1950s and 1960s.[120]

Reno kept singing and swinging even after federal investigations of Mafia links to the gambling industry began to challenge the contention that it was all in good fun. In 1950, investigational hearings by Estes Kefauver's Senate Committee on Organized Crime questioned a number of figures active in the gambling circles of Las Vegas, as well as New Orleans, Cincinnati, and other cities. Reno's reputation suffered less from these accusations of mafia influence than that of Las Vegas, where gangster figures like Bugsy Siegel, Moe Sedway, and Moe Dalitz had been operating since the late 1930s. For once in its history, and perhaps for the last time, it was preferable to fly under the radar. In response to continued concerns about the mob and other undue influences, the state formed a Gaming Control Board in 1955 and a state Gaming Commission independent of the tax commission in 1959.[121] The titles of these bodies reinforced the longstanding distinction made between the individual activity of "gambling" and the industry of "gaming." These added regulatory measures finally helped to curb the charge that gambling operations in Nevada were "wide open," the derogatory term that had been applied to them for so long.

As the 1950s came to a close, big changes on the horizon prompted optimism among Reno's promoters. The town's tourist trade had long suffered in the winter months due to the often treacherous nature of the two-lane highway over Donner Summit, the highest point on the road between Sacramento and Reno. Profits dropped whenever the mountains experienced inclement weather, leading some casinos to close their doors in the deep of winter, a practice that was prohibited by the city council in 1952. The selection of the nearby Lake Tahoe resort of Squaw Valley as the venue for the 1960 Olympic winter games prompted the Reno Promotions Committee to advertise Reno as "The Gateway to the Winter Olympics," highlighting the area's outdoor attractions. With the help of the National Defense Highway Act of 1956, U.S. 40 was finally expanded into a four-lane freeway over the Sierra. Concerned that initial plans called for widening the highway only as far east as Truckee, California, by the time of the Olympics, Raymond I. "Pappy" Smith of Harolds Club embarked on a crusade to secure its expansion all the way to Reno. Through a combination of political negotiation and the construction of billboards encouraging citizens to petition their representatives, the campaign succeeded. The four-lane freeway was nearly complete by 1959, the same year that Reno's new municipal airport opened for business. With the Olympic Games just around the corner, Reno seemed poised on the brink of an exciting new era of increased visibility and visitation.[122]

To help ensure this, the city hired Jud Allen, a professional public relations executive who had most recently headed up the Chamber of Commerce in Redwood City, California, after years as a college publicity director and Hollywood press agent. In a measure approved in 1959 by the thirty-three voting members of the chamber, including the owners of the city's largest hotels and casinos, Allen was charged with maintaining the city's competitive edge. As one of his first acts, he announced plans to promote a "New Reno," a four-season town "with far more to offer than Las Vegas." He then engaged a San Francisco public relations firm to promote Reno in the Bay Area, while select Reno businessmen fanned out to host groups of travel agents and media representatives at "luncheon get-togethers" throughout the West.[123]

When Johnny Cash rumbled, "I shot a man in Reno just to watch him die" in his 1956 hit, "Folsom Prison Blues," his chosen crime scene placed

Reno right where its boosters wanted it to be—smack in the middle of a popular song, repeated again and again on turntables throughout the country. And if the reference itself was a little shady, a little dark, no matter. A combination of legal legitimacy, increased familiarity, and changing cultural values had finally brought Reno into the light. Its brothels had been abolished, the divorce trade had become a respectable business, and as the success of Las Vegas demonstrated, the country clearly was ready to gamble. George Wingfield, the last of Reno's old-time movers and shakers, died in 1959; in his time, he had seen Reno grow from an elite divorce capital with a dark underbelly to a popular tourist destination for the masses. Now, as the sixties approached, the nation demanded entertainment, and the citizens of the "Biggest Little City" were happy to oblige. Casting a wary eye to Las Vegas, they turned resolutely toward the future.

CHAPTER FIVE

Big City Struggles in the Biggest Little City

At every word, a reputation dies.
Alexander Pope, *The Rape of the Lock,* 1714

Las Vegas has the glitz and Reno is the pits.
Forbes Magazine, November 1984

In July 1960, some of Hollywood's biggest names, including Clark Gable, Marilyn Monroe, Montgomery Clift, Arthur Miller, and John Huston held a press conference in the Sky Room of the Mapes Hotel. This convergence of major star power attracted the attention of an impressive flock of media including renowned French photojournalist Henri Cartier-Bresson. But it wasn't just the celebrities' arrival that drew the flashbulbs. For the next several months, the hotel served as home base for the filming of *The Misfits,* written by Miller for Monroe, then his wife, and directed by Huston. Over the course of the summer, the group brought a tidal wave of glamour and excitement to town as locals caught glimpses of the cast and crew in moments of leisure, watched the filming in a number of Reno's streets and clubs, and even joined the action as extras.

The Misfits, which had first appeared in 1957 as a story in *Esquire* magazine, was inspired by people Miller had met while securing a Reno divorce the previous year. The film starred Gable as an aging cowboy and womanizer named Gay who is tamed by Monroe's character, a beautiful but lonely divorcée named Roslyn. Filmed in black and white, the movie hearkened back to an earlier era, yet without the romanticism that suffused the traditional Western film. Populated by characters unable to find a comfortable niche in the modern world, it captured the uneasy tension between the Old and the New West.

Like the melancholy plot, the production also took a dark turn. Monroe, chronically late for her daily shoots, ultimately required an extended break due to exhaustion. By the end of production, Monroe and Miller

175

were barely speaking, and they divorced soon after. Clark Gable, taxed severely by physical stunts in the summer heat, died of a heart attack just twelve days after shooting ended. Upon its release in 1961, the film received decidedly mixed reviews and became best known as the final completed project for both of its stars, after Monroe was found dead in August 1962. The ill-fated film ultimately served as an elegy not just to Gable and Monroe, but also to Hollywood's "Reno cycle." According to longtime Reno publicist Mark Curtis, "*The Misfits* was based on Reno's story, when the image of the small town with its wide-open, almost frontier atmosphere, was about to fade from the landscape," overcome by the unstoppable forces of growth and urbanization. For the duration of the film, however, Curtis added, "The town was open-faced, enjoying the last of its frontier personality, unsophisticated and unashamed of it."[1]

In truth, *The Misfits* had little to do with Reno, which functioned more as a symbol than a setting; according to one reviewer, Miller had chosen Reno for his screenplay "because it is the city most connected with separation and emotional failures."[2] Like many of the earlier Reno movies, the film included a marital confrontation on the steps of the county courthouse, a short discussion of tossing wedding rings into the river, and a scene in a gambling club—in this case, the jangly slot machine ruckus of Harrah's. Unlike those other films, however, this one used the setting solely as a means for introducing its characters to each other before catapulting them into the open spaces of rural Nevada. By the sixties, the attention of Hollywood, like that of these modern-day nomads, had moved on.

Some of that attention had moved on to Las Vegas, the playground for a new generation of celebrities. Reno may have had Clark Gable, but Vegas had Elvis. The connections between Las Vegas and Hollywood, initiated in the 1940s by Bugsy Siegel and an array of Tinseltown divorcées, was solidified in the 1960s by the patronage and performances of such popular icons as Presley, Frank Sinatra, and Dean Martin. The films in which they starred, *Ocean's 11*, released in 1960, and *Viva Las Vegas*, in 1964, brought an avalanche of attention to the Strip. The characters in these films were obviously having a fantastic time, immersed in an energetic swirl of music, dancing, rock-and-roll, and razzle-dazzle, an all-around entertainment experience.

By 1960, thanks to such exposure and some canny decision making on the part of its business community, Las Vegas was developing its own distinct identity. In the 1940s and 1950s, the main streets of Las Vegas and

Reno had looked remarkably similar, blending residential and commercial in a quirky mélange of brick and neon. Many casinos in both towns favored old western themes, from Reno's Harolds Club, Dog House, and Frontier Club to the Pioneer Club, Western, and Golden Nugget of downtown Vegas's Glitter Gulch. Even the two earliest resorts on the Las Vegas Strip, the El Rancho Vegas and the Last Frontier, incorporated the popular western style in everything from décor to staff uniforms.

However, by the 1960s, entrepreneurs in Las Vegas were creating resorts with a very different flair. As historian Carl Abbott writes, Las Vegas "was trying to define itself as a universal and generic resort rather than simply a Western gambling den." The frontier-tinged clubs of Fremont Street had been superseded in the public eye by the new exotic resorts of the Strip.[3] The Last Frontier became the "Hotel New Frontier" in 1955 and adopted an entirely new, modern facade, and many of the other new resorts along the Strip blazed their way onto the big screen. Sinatra and his *Ocean's 11* Rat Pack ran all over the Sands, also their favored performance venue, which opened in 1952. In *Viva Las Vegas,* Elvis Presley and Ann-Margret flirted their way through a variety of Vegas locations including the Sahara (1952) and the Tropicana (1957). Also bursting onto the Strip in this era were the Desert Inn (1950), the Dunes (1955), the Riviera (1955), and the Stardust (1958). These oasis resorts were unlike anything anyone had seen before, and their signs towered ever higher, beckoning drivers in from the desert heat.[4]

By 1960, the population of Las Vegas boasted 64,405 to Reno's 51,470, but it was not just the size of Vegas that was increasing; so were the ambitions of its promoters.[5] With the fierce determination of an underdog, the Las Vegas Chamber of Commerce had continued to promote the southern city's attractions, even invading Reno's traditional territory of the San Francisco area and violating what Reno promoter Jud Allen called an "unwritten rule that Las Vegas would promote itself in Los Angeles, while Reno and Lake Tahoe would have a monopoly in San Francisco." By 1960, tourism was bringing 10 million visitors to Las Vegas annually.[6]

This escalating competition radically changed Reno's situation. Throughout the first half of the twentieth century, Reno had reigned as the country's undisputed divorce and gaming capital, without expending much promotional effort; the state's permissive legislation had created the draw and press coverage had followed naturally. With its unique blend of legalized vice, cosmopolitanism, and small-town charm, touched with a hint of celebrity scandal, the Biggest Little City in the World had attracted reporters, movie producers, gossip columnists, and curious visitors from across the country. However, in the 1960s, the country's attention increasingly was diverted by competing recreational attractions, from Disneyland to ski resorts like Sun Valley and Aspen. Whether as a result of familiarity or competition, Reno did not inspire the same easy fascination as in the past, and for the first time in decades, its promoters had to work for attention. This turn of events made the type of publicity Reno received even more critical. In the past, it truly had seemed that any publicity was good publicity, as only Reno could offer its peculiar blend of attractions. But in this new context, bad publicity could damage Reno's reputation and, worse yet, steer visitors toward Las Vegas or some other destination entirely.

Competition with its southern neighbor was not the only challenge confronting Reno in the 1960s. Federal investigations of Nevada gaming continued throughout the decade, with the 1962 investigation by U.S. Attorney General Robert Kennedy of links between organized crime and Nevada casinos, and further investigations by the FBI and IRS of Mafia involvement and skimming. The level of national publicity for these scandals was immense and, to some, devastating. In a 1966 *Atlantic Monthly* article linking the gaming industry to political scandal, criminal activity, and economic decline, Edward F. Sherman, a former legal aide to Nevada governor Grant Sawyer, went so far as to announce "The End of the Casino Era."[7]

Although, as with the Kefauver hearings, Las Vegas received more scrutiny for its mob connections, some of Reno's casino operators did encounter both economic and legal difficulties in this period. Although gaming remained a growing industry, with statewide revenues of nearly $200 million in 1960 and over $300 million in 1965, its rate of growth slowed considerably in the early 1960s. The Riverside Hotel, Reno's grand old lady, was especially struggling, passing through several hands before closing on December 20, 1962, when its owner filed for bankruptcy. In January 1963, a short article in *Newsweek* reported that "the Riverside . . . was silent and dark as a deep rock mine," but predicted "it was 3 to 2 and take your choice that the Riverside will soon be booking the high rollers again." The reporter was right; the Riverside reopened in July 1963 under new ownership. However, in 1967 it was shut down again by the Nevada Gaming Commission for harboring fixed games. A *Saturday Review* article soon afterward noted Reno's desire to rise above such controversies, reporting, "Although its gaming-table operators have been getting into the papers with some frequency lately for practicing sleight of hand, Reno would like to think it is not just a watering hole where both the customers and the dice are likely to be loaded."[8] As if competition and controversy weren't enough, Reno's tourist industry also suffered from a few logistical liabilities. Even with the advantage of the new four-lane highway over the Sierra, Reno still experienced a very slow winter season, compounded by poor air service. Citing these factors as well as the city's shortage of hotel rooms, many travel agents were actually discouraging their clients from visiting Reno.[9]

With so much at stake, Reno's Chamber of Commerce decided to overhaul the city's promotional machinery. Harolds Club and Mark Curtis's advertising agency had spearheaded most of Reno's publicity campaigns through the 1940s and 1950s. While Harolds had embarked upon its own unique roadside advertising and print strategies, the city's official publicity efforts had been limited—by financial resources, as well as by an apparent lack of need—to such small-scale strategies as staging occasional photo opportunities for visiting media and pitching stories to magazines. But now it was clear that the simple availability of legalized gambling was not enough to guarantee a continuing stream of visitors from across the country when Las Vegas casinos offered the same attractions as did Reno, and on a larger, even more impressive scale.

More sophisticated promotion of Reno, then, began in the 1960s, steered by a small community of enthusiastic advertising professionals who worked for the Chamber of Commerce and the larger hotel casinos. At times, their desire to preserve Reno's reputation called for drastic measures; Chamber of Commerce manager Jud Allen later recalled that when the Riverside closed in 1962, it was only the efforts of community leaders that kept *Time* and *Newsweek* from writing obituaries for the city. Allen and his associates convinced them that "Reno may be wounded but it was far from dead," although he acknowledged that "had the stories been printed as originally planned it would have been such a psychological setback to Reno's future that our recovery would have been delayed by many years."[10]

Such emergency measures took initiative and creativity, but a full-fledged promotional campaign would take a lot of money, and the Chamber of Commerce had very little in its budget to implement new strategies. Even Harolds Club, the casino most accustomed to promoting the entire community, was still contributing just $700 to the chamber per year. When

Allen and the chamber president approached Guy Lent, general manager of Harolds, for an increased contribution, Lent suggested a method whereby Harrah's, Harolds, and the city's three major hotels would each contribute a percentage of their payrolls to the chamber, quickly calculating that under such an arrangement, Harolds would be willing to contribute $52,000 per year. An astounded Allen was even more surprised when the heads of Harrah's Club and the Holiday, Mapes, and Riverside Hotels all agreed to contribute the same percentage to the Chamber of Commerce, evidently recognizing the need to pool their resources.[11]

Suddenly the organization had the funds to support elaborate promotions involving partnerships with travel agencies and airlines. After opening a Reno reservation office in San Francisco, Allen chartered a Southern Pacific train, dubbed the "Fun Train," to run from Oakland to Reno during the winter, when potential tourists might hesitate to drive over the summit. Working with Vernon Durkee, Sr., who had opened Reno's first travel agency in 1946, Allen also initiated a "Reno Fun Flight" package to fly in tourists from California and the Pacific Northwest. The Fun Flight promotion in the 1960s became the most popular tourist package anywhere for United Airlines. The city also promoted special events, like the popular Reno Rodeo. In 1960, at the urging of Reno businessmen, the rodeo was moved from the Fourth of July to mid-June, in order to spread out major events and hopefully increase total visitation to the city. Through such promotions, Allen claimed, "Reno's reputation was going from negative to positive," but that direction was not entirely clear to all.[12]

In the midst of this changing context, one of the pillars of Reno's tourist economy began to crumble. Nevada's divorce trade, that industry that had first established Reno as a glamorous and cosmopolitan destination, was finally losing currency. The primary reason was purely practical: other states relaxed their divorce laws significantly in the postwar decades, reducing the demand for migratory divorce. For example, after a 1968 change in the laws of New York state, the number of divorces there increased dramatically, from 4,073 in 1966–1967 to 18,180 in 1968–1969. As experts explained, New York's residents could now stay in the state to secure their divorces rather than traveling to permissive sites like Reno. Having experienced a large spike during and after World War II, divorce had become increasingly common throughout the United States.[13]

Some Reno-area guest ranches still clung to their reputation as divorce ranches, including the Donner Trail Ranch, where Mary Rockefeller stayed in 1963 while awaiting her divorce from New York governor Nelson Rocke-feller. After a profile of Donner Trail appeared in the *Saturday Evening Post* in 1965 under the title of "The Last of the Divorce Ranches," three other lo-cal guest ranches took exception to that designation. The owners of the Lazy A Ranch, Whitney Guest Ranch, and Sierra Gables all asserted that their own divorce business was thriving. To many observers, however, the glamour was gone. By 1968, a *New York Times* article announced that Reno was "Divorcing Itself from Divorce." In that article, Jud Allen voiced his pleasure that "the divorce spotlight has been toned down," continuing, "Di-vorce is not a happy image. It does not present the fun-and-relaxation pic-ture so important to sound tourism. Let's face it. Someone back in Iowa is not going to tell his wife: 'Load the kids in the car. We're going to Reno to see all those divorcees.'"[14] Although many tourists in the past had done just that, the climate had now changed; divorce was no longer exotic or scintil-lating, and besides, Reno now had other demographics in its sights.

One of those target audiences was made clear in the illustrations ac-companying the *Times* article; below the familiar image of the Washoe County Courthouse was a photograph of a young couple contemplating the façade of the Park Wedding Chapel, constructed across the street from the courthouse in 1957. Reno's wedding industry was picking up, with small chapels specifically catering to visitors in town to capitalize on Nevada's instant marriage licenses. By the end of the 1960s, Reno had thir-teen independent wedding chapels: five conveniently located on the right side of U.S. 40 when entering town from California, and five others in close proximity to the courthouse. Those not located within walking distance of-fered free limousine service there. In 1970, one study estimated that each individual getting married in Reno spent approximately $185 in town, in-cluding fees for the license and ceremony, flowers, lodging, and other ex-penditures. Although not a large amount in itself, individual expenditures added up as the practice became more popular.[15] Even the Chamber of Commerce got in on the promotion in a 1969–1970 business development profile of the Greater Reno area. Acknowledging the city's longstanding reputation as a "divorce and gambling center," the profile was quick to as-sert that the number of marriages in Reno far outweighed the number of divorces per year. The industry had the added advantage of corresponding with the attempt to promote Reno as fun, along the lines of the "Fun Flights" and the "Fun Train." A wedding was much more likely to be per-ceived as fun than a divorce—even a Reno divorce.[16]

The Park Wedding Chapel opened across the street from the Washoe County Courthouse in 1957 and catered to Reno's wedding trade for fifty years. (Photograph by the author)

Despite the popularity of this growing industry, many were convinced that the future lay in Reno's casinos. Visually, they were attracting more attention than ever. The largest remained Harrah's and Harolds Clubs, while the Riverside, Mapes, and Holiday hotels offered slots and table games on their ground floors. All employed increasingly larger and more visually arresting street-side advertising. The Harolds sign towered high above the club's giant pioneer mural. Beginning in 1964, the eye-catching marquee of the Primadonna Club featured five statues of showgirls, at an average height of 20 feet. Their large neon signs hovered over a new $100,000 arch that was installed above Virginia Street in 1964, with chunky letters spelling out "RENO" on octagonal orange and yellow blocks, a sparkly stylized star spinning above, and, of course, "The Biggest Little City in the World" slogan below, all set off by over a thousand twinkling lights.[17]

To casino owners, the solution to economic competition was clear: expansion. However, the Reno City Council was still prohibiting the further encroachment of gaming into the business district, having established a boundary, or "red line" across the center of Second Street that confined gambling establishments to the area north of the line and south of the railroad tracks, from Virginia Street eastward past Lake Street. Outside the

A new Reno arch, erected in 1964, presided over a downtown visually dominated by the bright lights of the casinos. (Special Collections Department, University of Nevada–Reno Library)

line, gaming was restricted to just twenty slot machines and three gaming tables. The line pushed further west in December 1961 when the council granted Ernest Primm permission to expand his Primadonna casino all the way to Sierra Street. Despite this slight concession, the red line still confined gaming to a limited portion of downtown, presenting more restrictions in Reno than for the new casinos springing up along the Las Vegas Strip. Far distant from any residential area or existing commercial buildings, those were limited only by their owners' imaginations and the market, something that made Vegas a much more appealing investment location for aspiring casino operators.[18]

Exempt from Reno's restrictions were casinos accompanied by a hotel of 100 rooms or more, a caveat established in 1961 with the express intention of encouraging the establishment of more luxury hotels in downtown Reno. In hopes of remaining competitive, many existing casinos undertook major expansions, knocking down walls and moving into neighboring

storefronts as they became available. Such a growth pattern did not result
from planning, but from quickly jumping on opportunities as they presented themselves, as when smaller clubs went out of business. Having
doubled in size in 1956 when it bought out the adjacent Frontier Club and
knocked down the wall between them, Harrah's continued to expand
through the 1960s. The casino took over the locations of the former Grand
Hotel and Golden Hotel and the Petronovich family's Grand Cafe, of divorce colony fame, in order to open a showroom and a number of restaurants and bars. Harolds Club followed the same pattern, buying the Colony
Club in 1964 and transforming the space into a new entertainment lounge
and offices.[19]

As the casinos installed ever more slot machines, table games, and other
amenities, the familiar streetscape of Reno's business district was defini-
tively changing. The earlier generation of Reno's clubs had matched the
scale of the existing landscape, but many of the new casinos did not, and
not everyone liked the increasing dedication of downtown Reno to
tourism. Some of these concerns were articulated in April 1965 by a Reno
architect named Graham Erskine in a series of four pointed lectures at the
University of Nevada in Reno under the provocative title, "Reno, Haven or
Hovel?" To Erskine, the city was at a crossing point, both literally and figuratively, between remaining a friendly little city or becoming a frenzied
tourist town.

The effect of the unchecked commercial aspects, Erskine argued,
ranged from overwhelming to outright hostile. Nearly every approach to
town was lined by rows of motels, their neon signs jostling for drivers' attention. "From the very beginning," he said, "Route 40 or Fourth Street and
Route 395 or Virginia Street took the aspect of commercial gauntlets. Passing through these gauntlets, the citizen has to escape the clutches or the
tentacles reaching out toward him from both sides of the street consisting
of a riot of unrelated color, mass, design, neon lights, signs, sign posts,
stoplights, etc." As a result, he complained, "The four ways a visitor usually
enters our city are so cluttered up with manufacturing and commercial de-
bris that he immediately has a negative impression of the town before he
gets into it." Erskine was not alone in his criticism. As a reporter for *Holiday* magazine admitted in 1965, "the clutter of motels and hot-dog stands
that mars the approaches to Reno, and the jumble of convoluted neon that
assaults the eye on Virginia Street are not always a pleasure and a comfort
to see."[20]

According to Erskine, the time had come to create a concerted vision for the downtown area; otherwise, he feared, "The sum total of all this will be the eventual allocation of Reno's old core entirely to amusement and gambling and those novelty stores which feed on the gambling winners and cater to the tourists." As a design professional, he feared the repercussions of such haphazard development, warning, "If the design of this center is allowed to continue along the standards set by the gamblers on Virginia Street from the railroad tracks to Second Street, this area within the next decade or so will really be ripe for an urban renewal project."[21] Knowing that, to casino owners, bigger casinos meant more money, Erskine framed "the upgrading of aesthetics in our city" as an investment in the future. "This goal," he asserted, "will in no way damage the economy, but rather will provide our best advertisement as a tourist center both within our own country and abroad." He concluded, "If we are bold enough to bend our full efforts to becoming the 'most beautiful little city in the world' instead of just the 'biggest little city in the world,' we'd all have to spend our time helping the various banks build better and better branches to hold the money that comes in."[22]

Erskine's points were articulated well, but whether those in power would listen was not clear. Making the biggest little city even bigger had long been the priority of city government and local businessmen alike. In his lecture, Erskine put his finger on an issue that would dominate civic discussion for the next several decades: if and how to manage growth, particularly with respect to the casinos. As they expanded, their operators not only gained greater control over downtown property, but also increased their political power within the community. And clearly, they did not have much incentive to limit themselves. In the decades to come, Reno's gaming community continued to embrace growth enthusiastically, prompted by an ever more desperate desire to remain competitive with Las Vegas, and putting more and more of Reno's eggs in one basket.

That basket became even larger in 1970, when Harolds Club was purchased for an estimated $11 million by billionaire Howard Hughes. The sale was prompted by the death in 1967 of Raymond I. "Pappy" Smith, the patriarch of the Smith family, after which his son Harold Smith, Sr., said, "My Pappy and I were partners, and when I lost my Daddy, I couldn't run Harolds Club." By then a recluse known widely as the "phantom billionaire," Hughes had been living in the Desert Inn Hotel-Casino on the Las Vegas Strip since 1966 and went on to buy the Sands, the Frontier, the

Landmark, and many more gaming and nongaming properties throughout the state of Nevada.[23]

Despite his own personal eccentricities, many believed that Hughes's investment in gaming helped to remove much of the industry's remaining stigma, saving the industry from the taint of mob ownership.[24] However, although he may have given gambling a new face, not everyone shared the perception that Hughes had "saved" casino gambling with his respectable name. Many in Reno's casino industry in particular were dismissive of his influence. As Palace Club owner Silvio Petricciani later complained, "they say [that] Howard Hughes cleaned up the state of Nevada. Well, the state of Nevada wasn't dirty! What'd they clean up? . . . What image did he put on the state of Nevada that we didn't have before? . . . All he did was buy something from somebody else that was supposed to be dirty, made it successful, and created a lot of money and taxes for the state of Nevada."[25] Though insiders may have scoffed, Nevada gaming certainly could not suffer from an association with a figure so widely known for his high-profile innovations in film, aircraft, and other industries.

But Hughes's entry into the casino business was just one of two developments that moved the gaming industry further into the mainstream. The second was the passage of the Corporate Gaming Act of 1969, which permitted corporations to invest in gaming operations, thereby allowing the scale of gaming to get even larger. Harrah's Club was the first Reno casino to go public, in 1971. Public ownership further legitimated the gaming industry by making it appear as less of an insider's club, and more of a traditional business.[26] Previously, every owner of a Nevada casino needed to apply for a gaming license; now, a corporation could apply for a license without individual licensing of all stockholders, leaving some possibility for partial ownership by unsavory characters. Still, the combination of these new policies, in addition to improved regulation of gaming on the state level, boosted confidence that the industry was on the up and up. As a government-sponsored Commission on the Review of the National Policy toward Gambling concluded in 1976, "Nevada has used its 45 years of experience in the gaming field to develop a regulatory system that is sophisticated, efficient, and on the whole, capable of maintaining the integrity of the gaming industry at an acceptable level."[27]

The advent of big business brought further changes to the atmosphere of Reno's casinos. The city's gaming community had always been composed of familiar figures with a very public face, like Pappy Smith and Bill

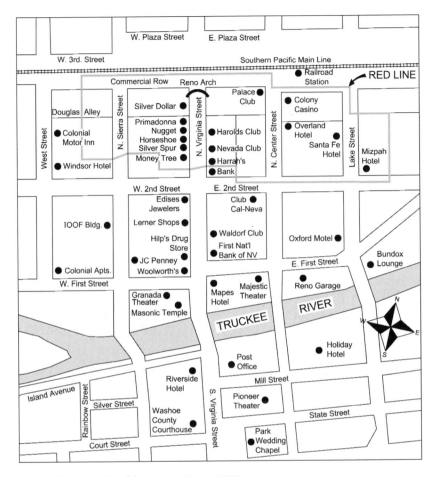

Selected landmarks of downtown Reno, 1970

Harrah, whose visibility lent their establishments an intimate, personal quality. Ownership changes in the 1960s made this less common. Harolds Club was no longer run by the Smiths, while the Riverside Hotel was sold again, opened without gambling in 1969, was closed again by the IRS, sold again two more times, and then sold finally to Jessie Beck, a longtime employee of Harolds Club, who reopened it in 1971. Bucking the trend, William Harrah remained in charge of Harrah's Club, adding a 326-room, $6 million, 24-story hotel to his casino in 1969, making the new 28-story structure the city's tallest building.[28]

Gaming had clearly become the big moneymaker for Nevada, with gross statewide revenues topping $550 million in 1970.[29] With casinos going corporate throughout Nevada and their revenues increasing, Reno's political and business communities focused on creating a friendly climate for the industry. In the late 1960s, Reno businessmen organized a group called Reno Unlimited, dedicated among other things to beautification of the riverfront area and the "orderly development" of downtown. One of the most common phrases in the discourse of professional planning, "orderly development" could suggest any number of things, from a measured rate of growth to the coordinated zoning of entire districts. In Reno's case, it seemed to refer directly to the provision of expansion opportunities for casinos. According to Harrah's executive Robert Ring, a board member of Reno Unlimited, the group's mission was "to keep the downtown area stimulated and upgrade the downtown area" and "to make the tourists and our convention people feel at home when they arrive in Reno." As Ring's words suggest, casino executives had become aware that even tourists needed to see Reno as a comfortable community rather than an alienating, haphazard collection of tourist attractions.[30]

Members of Reno Unlimited also were involved with Project RENOvation, which raised $137,000 in March 1969 for an initial study of the downtown situation, including a survey of downtown visitors. The city contributed $40,000 in order to hire a San Francisco firm to continue the study. The resulting report included a number of recommendations intended to benefit the gaming industry. Perhaps most important to casino owners, it concluded that "a new program is essential to increase the supply of land available for casino operations," found the existing "red line" regulation that limited gaming to a confined area downtown to be too constrictive, and encouraged further expansion and construction, concluding that Reno needed to gain at least 485 new hotel rooms each year to remain "competitive."[31]

The political community responded immediately. In May 1970, the Reno City Council voted to retract the red line restrictions. A new ordinance, effective 1 January 1971, abolished the red line but retained a policy of issuing unlimited gaming licenses only to businesses that included 100 or more hotel rooms, even in the downtown area. A restricted license would still allow a business to offer a limited number of slot machines and table games without operating hotel rooms; nevertheless, smaller operators objected to the room requirement, arguing, quite accurately, that it favored the bigger, more moneyed clubs. The Greater Reno Chamber of Commerce defended the new requirement, arguing, "It is obvious that our tourism jumps with the opening of hotels. . . . Our tourism mail never asks how many gaming establishments we have. Almost all requests for information ask, 'What's playing?' Entertainment is the name of the game and big hotels are the only facilities that can support a theatre-restaurant year-round."[32]

As the industry continued to grow in the 1970s, public discussions about the impact of growth proliferated, not just within the casino industry but throughout Reno. Concern intensified as the city's population nearly doubled in just two decades, rising from 51,470 in 1960 to 72,863 in 1970 and to 100,756 in 1980.[33] One of Reno's primary assets, besides its unique attractions, had always been its visual charm, now even more important to maintain with the steep competition from Las Vegas. With the increasing cultural acceptance of gambling, legal for four decades now, a positive reputation now depended largely upon eliminating aesthetic dissonance of the kind previously identified by Graham Erskine.

Unfortunately, Reno's center was beginning to experience some typical urban problems as the city's population increased. Reno did not experience the onset of widespread blight, entire neighborhoods of slums, white flight, or urban riots as did many larger cities at mid-century. Prompted by some or all of these developments, western cities including Tucson, Denver, Seattle, and San Antonio began urban renewal programs in the 1960s.[34] Reno's urban challenges were on a much smaller scale, but it did experience some problems with crime and homelessness, particularly on the eastern side of downtown, where commercial businesses shifted to light industrial and where the red-light district had always been located. By now, indigent populations were living in the cribs of the Stockade, which still stood in the center of one of the least respectable parts of town, the site of the old Chinatown and still the center of illegal prostitution, although the closest brothels, like Joe Conforte's Mustang Ranch, were now in nearby Storey County, which legalized prostitution in 1971.

As one observer wrote in 1970, "The Lake Street-Commercial Row section of Reno is essentially a carbon copy of a thousand streets in a thousand other cities in the United States. It is a skid row." He continued, "Starting from the casino area of Virginia Street and moving east along Commercial Row, the bright lights and garish atmosphere fades into a line of pawnshops, low class White and Indian bars, and then Lake Street."[35] Also contributing to a dispirited air in parts of downtown were a number of vacant buildings, attributable to the incipient exodus of businesses to new outlying shopping centers, to their purchase by casinos to retain for future expansions once other properties could be secured, or, in the competitive environment, simply to prevent others from purchasing them.[36] As Mark Curtis argued in his memoirs, the notion of aesthetics became much more important in this period, as Reno "wanted to present a very clean image, conveying stability."[37] When Jerry Garcia of the Grateful Dead sang, "I lit out from Reno, I was trailed by twenty hounds" in the band's 1970 hit "Friend of the Devil," city officials must have hoped potential tourists would not follow his lead.

Even as its casino district grew, the Chamber of Commerce still drew visitors' attention to what they continued to identify as the "real Reno" where residents lived, worked, and played. This effort met with some success, as outside writers occasionally mentioned the "other Reno," the respectable, even conservative town beyond the neon lights. A 1971 article in *Travel* magazine called "Finding the Real Reno" directed readers that "to savor the essence of gentle, gracious Reno, have a look at the campus of the University of Nevada." It was the existence of this Reno that local residents emphasized in distinguishing their town from Las Vegas. As another reporter wrote in 1967, "It is popular in Reno to glance down the proboscis at Las Vegas. The prime industry in Reno may be gambling and tourism, but Reno is a city, whereas Las Vegas is a resort," a distinction that Reno boosters including casino executives believed that most visitors shared. In 1973, after years of interactions with tourists, Robert Ring claimed, "Many of them say that southern Nevada is more or less a lot of glitter, of honky-tonk-type operations (and they have some fabulous hotels, as you know). But they feel that Reno, with the beautiful Truckee River, it feels more of a city, and they're quite impressed." Lucius Beebe referred to such boosters of respectability as the "see-our-schools-and-churches group," but they had a point. With its gaming core firmly situated in the city's commercial center, Reno's primary tourist and residential landscapes still coexisted, and often coincided, while the schools and churches of Las Vegas, including a southern division of the University of Nevada, founded in 1957, operated a sizeable distance from the Strip.[38]

However, this promoted image of a charming small city could not take hold unless Reno still possessed a landscape to match. Its downtown was dominated more and more by casinos, and the city was getting bigger. Such concerns sent Reno in search of ways to maintain the city's strengths while

trying to accommodate a growing population. In the process, Reno's leaders became intimately familiar with studies and surveys, if not definitive action, regarding the issue of urban growth. On a county level, members of
the Washoe County Board of Commissioners and Regional Planning Commission attended a HUD-sponsored conference on growth in Portland in
1972 and decided the following spring to initiate a "citizen input program"
dedicated to the study of growth-related problems in Reno. The Regional
Planning Commission and the Area Council of Governments sponsored a
Blue Ribbon Task Force Program on Growth and Development, dividing
the study into ten areas. Each was addressed by a different task force of approximately ten experts and interested nonexperts appointed by the study's
sponsors. The comprehensive study was broken down into categories of
water, air pollution, housing, codes, design, physical constraints, economics
of growth, public finance, optimum size, and plan relationships. Overall, its
goals were "to determine what local problems of growth existed, if any;
what possible solutions might be pursued; and what the timing and cost requirements of such solutions might total."[39]

When completed in 1974, the ten-volume report was unprecedented in
size and scope for any government-sponsored study of the Reno area.
What it revealed most markedly was widespread community concern
about the problems of potential urban growth. Put simply, most residents
did not welcome it. According to the study's findings, a local survey of
Washoe County in 1969 revealed that 72 percent of respondents "felt that
the size of Reno should be kept the same or would be even better if it were
smaller." In 1973, another survey indicated that 85 percent of the sample
"would prefer that the population of the Reno-Sparks area be either what it
is today or smaller."[40] The conclusion was as clear as it was paradoxical: the
larger Reno became, the smaller Reno residents wanted it to be.

The firm opinions held by the residential population were reflected in
strong, and in some cases, conflicting, attitudes among the study's own authors. The Committee on Economic Growth experienced such dissension
that its members finally submitted two separate and completely contradictory reports. The first to be filed was headed by University of Nevada economics professor William Eadington. Among its findings, the report maintained, "Current rates of population and economic growth in Washoe
County are excessive and must be slowed, if problems like those in California's urban areas are to be avoided" and that "Washoe County should attempt to achieve an 'optimal' population growth rate of 3% or less per

year." The group also concluded that "the only effective means of slowing the rate of population in a community such as Washoe County is to restrict the rate of growth of jobs in the area's basic industries, which are gambling, warehousing, and manufacturing." They cited concerns for the ability of the city to plan for "necessary public services" and to manage community development and general quality of life factors including traffic congestion, air quality, and water consumption if growth continued at the current rate of more than 5 percent.[41]

This was not what the advocates of unrestrained growth wanted to hear. One month after Eadington turned in his report, a second contingent of committee members headed by Reno businessman Wayne Dennis filed a second report stating that they were "in no way in agreement and concurrence with the Final Report as submitted by Bill Eadington," a report they pointedly referred to as the "minority" report, although the Task Force itself made no such distinction. This second group asserted that the influx of population, growth in gaming revenues, and increase in the city's industrial and commercial base over the past few decades "has brought about a greater financial and economic stability to our community that we . . . feel must be encouraged." They appealed to a rhetoric of patriotism, liberty, and free enterprise, arguing the following:

> To restrict, slow or in any way attempt to manipulate the natural economic forces that are at work in our community, as well as our country, will encourage chaos and disaster. . . . We believe in the free enterprise system, and we believe in the mechanics of the economic system as they have evolved for the last 250 years. We support, without qualification, the opportunity for everyone to live where he may so desire, [and] work where he might be able to obtain the financial security, the level and the quality of life that he feels is within his capability.

In order to reinforce their position, the authors of the second report included twenty-one letters of endorsement from an array of representatives of organizations including the Nevada Chapters of the Associated General Contractors of America and the National Electrical Contractors Association, the Builders Association of Northern Nevada, the Sierra Pacific Power Company, and several area banking institutions, all of whose support for further development was hardly surprising.[42]

As was true in planning circles throughout the country, the supporters of unrestricted growth interpreted Eadington's calls for restraint as a desire to prevent growth entirely, an interpretation clearly voiced by the chair of the second report, Wayne Dennis, who later claimed that "Eadington wanted to go to the people and totally shut off growth and our group was in favor of a strong planning commission doing planning work, not compliance zoning work."[43] Despite the objections of Dennis and his coterie, the final comprehensive report recommended that "The governing bodies of Reno, Sparks, and Washoe County, in cooperation with all residents of the area, should make every effort to slow our rate of growth." The report also found that while studies were helpful, the city needed action, stating, "A transformation must take place in the existing planning process from a process which basically attempts to obtain more rational decision making to a planning process which is also dedicated to improving the responsiveness and quality of plan implementation." As the local newspaper noted, "Some elected officials display a dismaying belief that 'things will take care of themselves.'" According to a later editorial, "The Blue Ribbon Task Force reports probably stirred more hope, enthusiasm and concern than any such proposal for improvement in Washoe County history."[44]

Upon completion, the ten reports were reviewed by the Reno City Council, but many residents feared that the study's recommendations would simply be ignored. This was no idle concern. A group of outside experts arriving on the scene in September 1975 agreed that Reno's most pressing planning-related problem was implementation. That month, a ten-member team of architects from the American Institute of Architects' Regional/Urban Design Assistance Team (RUDAT) spent five days studying the cities of Reno and Sparks in order to devise potential solutions to improve their design and appearance. Such teams had been sent to twenty-nine other American cities, but this was the first to visit Nevada. The team observed that the city had lost control of the expansion of the city core, due to its "liberal zoning code," and encouraged future development to take better advantage of the Truckee River. A $2 million bond issue approved by Reno voters to improve the area around the river would help with that goal. In observing such plans as well as Reno's past discussions about growth and revitalization, team member Ron Straka, an architect and design specialist from Colorado, noted that "the area has an overabundance of committees and study groups" and yet "few of the recommendations of studies and committees had been implemented."[45] An editorial in the *Nevada State Journal* enthusiastically supported the RUDAT actions and ruefully acknowledged the inaction of past officials in saying "Reno citizens with imagination and creative ideas may find the design team members will listen to ideas with enthusiasm which may have been dismissed by persons with less vision." The editors wrote, "It is to be hoped that the design assistance team will offer a fresh look at this stalemated condition and make suggestions to resolve problems."[46]

The situation may have called for design assistance, but money talked. Statewide, gambling was bringing in unprecedented amounts of money, and consumer demand seemed only likely to increase. By 1975, statewide gambling revenues rose to just over $1 billion, and Las Vegas clearly had the edge over Reno, with Clark County bringing in approximately $729 million and Washoe County approximately $180 million. The numbers were sufficient to convince residents of Atlantic City to vote in 1976 for legalization of gambling as part of a plan to revitalize that city.[47]

New competition brought new calls for growth within the gaming industry. But even after the red-line ordinance was lifted, it was hard for any casino downtown to grow very far. The first hotel casino north of the railroad tracks appeared in 1973, when Reno natives Don Carano, Jerry Poncia, and four other partners opened the eleven-story Eldorado Hotel-Casino, Spanish-themed in hues of gold, brown, and black. In order to build the Eldorado, the entire 300 block of North Virginia street was razed, including the buildings formerly housing the Little Waldorf, the Reno Hotel, Leo's Den, Silver State Camera, Ace Coin Shop, and Welsh's Bakery. Acquisition of so many properties proved difficult as well as controversial.[48]

Aware of such obstacles, and desirous of more square footage, some casino executives chose to avoid the downtown area entirely. In the fall of 1975, the MGM company, which had erected the massive MGM Grand Hotel on the Las Vegas Strip in 1973, announced its plan to construct a similar project in Reno. As Mark Curtis later recalled, "The real change in public opinion began with the arrival of companies such as MGM and Hilton. After all, they weren't really gamblers. They were public companies in the movie and hotel business. Gaming was just a sideline to which they added their expertise and reputation." After what its attendees described as a "luncheon" and many later complained had been a "secret meeting" between seven members of the Reno City Council and the Board of Directors of MGM, a group that included actor Cary Grant, the company announced its intentions and eventually arranged a land exchange with the city that secured the site of the Nevada Aggregates gravel pit, close to the airport and nearly two miles due east of downtown, next to the Reno-Sparks Indian Colony.[49]

The scale and distinctive architecture of the Eldorado Hotel-Casino helped to inaugurate an era in which the appearance of Reno's casinos stood in stark contrast to the traditional pedestrian-oriented streetscape of earlier years. (Nevada Historical Society)

Construction of the twenty-six-story MGM Grand Hotel-Reno began in summer 1976. Over the next several years, the looming project inspired an unprecedented public discussion about the repercussions of growth. Major concerns included the potential impact on traffic congestion, air pollution, rising crime, school overcrowding, available social services, and the supply of affordable housing for the projected thousands of new employees and their families who would be moving to Reno to work there. Reflective of municipal lack of planning for the huge project was the city's mishandling of plans to expand the Reno-Sparks Joint Sewage Treatment Plant. After the plant's completion in 1966, contemporary rates of growth dictated a need for expansion by 1973. Yet the city council did not even begin discussions of expansion until 1972 or hire a consultant to study expansion requirements until 1974. A $6 million bond for expansion of the sewage plant was not approved until November 1976 and did not begin until summer 1978. That year, city councilman Ed Spoon blamed the 1971 city council for failing to follow through on the project.[50]

After the approval of the MGM Grand, a number of other local casino projects announced their plans for construction or expansion. The *New*

York Times took a particular interest in this process. An interview with William Harrah before the completion of the MGM Grand revealed the magnate's plans to construct a downtown tower even higher than the twenty-six stories of the MGM, "whatever that takes," as well as a new "self-contained" resort called "Harrah's World," west of downtown, if the MGM "shows the climate is right." By March 1978, the *Times* reported a "billion dollars' worth of construction" centering on twelve new "Las Vegas–style, hotel-casino-resorts," along with a 1.6 million-square-foot J. C. Penney distribution warehouse. The repercussions, the reporter noted, ranged from "overcrowded schools and streets" to "a severe housing shortage and other big-city ills that Reno used to pride itself in avoiding."[51]

Even the most enthusiastic advocates of growth acknowledged that it would come with a price. In July 1977, the director of MGM, Art Linkletter, predicted, "Like every place else, Reno is going to lose something and gain something. It will no longer be the quaint, cute little town it is now, but it's going to be a very busy place." MGM's Fred Benninger agreed, "In five years you won't even recognize Reno. . . . Las Vegas grew steadily for 25 years, but this town is going to explode."[52]

The momentum for growth was clearly building as, beginning in the mid-1970s, downtown Reno underwent a blitz of construction. The *Nevada State Journal* reported that "according to former Councilwoman [Pat] Lewis and Councilman [Clyde] Biglieri, there was no way the city council could reject the projects because the areas were properly zoned and no special use permit procedure was in the city ordinance." It also reported that "Reno Mayor Bruno Menicucci has on several occasions expressed the fear that the city could be sued if it prevented developers from building on properly zoned land."[53] With the lack of obstacles, developers went right ahead, transforming the downtown landscape forever.

The casinos also benefited from other planning decisions. In 1974, nineteen years after its initial approval, Interstate 80 was finally completed through Reno. Five different routes had been considered for the highway's path through the center of town. The Regional Planning Commission and Reno City Council initially chose Third Street, which would have allowed them simultaneously to lower the railroad tracks and thereby eliminate a major traffic problem on Virginia Street. But criticism from Congressman Walter Baring, who favored keeping the downtown area intact, led to the highway's final location along Seventh Street.[54] The completion of the interstate, sunk beneath street level, kept the casino district intact but made formal the existing division between the casino district and the university, just a few blocks further up the road. Virginia Street and the other primary streets bridged the highway via overpasses. The division created another barrier isolating the other parts of town from the gaming district. Additionally, in July 1975 a plan was approved to construct a large shopping mall, the Meadowood Shopping Center, on South Virginia Street, in close proximity to the Centennial Coliseum, the convention center constructed far from the city center in the mid-1960s. This would pull shoppers away from downtown just as the traditional downtown retail district was being edged out by the expanding casinos.

Such developments greatly contributed to the ongoing transformation of Reno's city center into the tourist-oriented landscape that Graham Erskine had feared, as any remaining nongaming businesses became dwarfed by the casinos' soaring hotel towers, brilliant lights, and accompanying noise. The most radical changes yet to Reno's downtown landscape accompanied the arrival of massive high-rise casino-hotels in the mid-to-late 1970s. Their construction made a bold statement of faith not only that the appeal of gambling would continue, but that the city would be able to attract enough people to fill all the new hotel rooms. The resulting building boom permanently changed both the skyline and the character of Reno's downtown, as commercial establishments frequented by locals for years, even decades, were bulldozed and replaced by block-size windowless casinos, just as cities elsewhere had earlier replaced older and smaller downtown buildings with massive malls, convention centers, and movie theaters.

Unlike the urban renewal projects that transformed so many other cities in the postwar era, however, the expansion of Reno's downtown casinos was not a matter of clearing perceived slums, but viable businesses, and other casinos soon continued along the trail that the Eldorado had blazed before them.[55] In May 1976, Lincoln Fitzgerald, who had run the Nevada Club since 1956, demolished the Blue Bird Hotel, Cannan's Drug Store, the Stag Inn, and the Silver Dollar Club in order to open the sixteen-story Fitzgerald's Casino-Hotel on a half-block of North Virginia. In 1977, Harrah's leased and then closed the Overland Hotel-Casino, on the corner of Commercial Row and Center Street. Three months later, the Overland's owner, Pick Hobson, demolished the building. Harrah's then bought the Riverside Hotel from Jessie Beck in 1978, and traded it to Pick Hobson for the Overland property site, where he constructed a parking garage for Harrah's. One year after gaming pioneer William Harrah died, in June 1978,

Harrah's merged with Holiday Inn, a mainstream hotelier, and the following year, the company bought the legendary Palace Club, which immediately closed, and was soon demolished.[56] Commentary was quick to follow. In April 1978, one month before the projected opening of the $131 million MGM Grand Hotel, the *Nevada State Journal* and the *Reno Evening Gazette* ran an extended series of investigative articles analyzing growth in the area, prefaced by a near-complete reprinting of the 1974 Blue Ribbon Task Force Report. The two lead journalists of the series, Jack McFarren and Burton Swope, took a clear stand on the issue, claiming,

> Local elected and appointed government officials, particularly in Reno, have been and continue to be short-sighted in their views of the needs of the community and its people. All too often, professional planners' advice has been lost amid the clamor of special interest groups who equate any mention of growth management as destructive to the free enterprise system.

Their charges seemed supported not only by the position voiced by Wayne Dennis five years earlier, but also by the composition of city agencies. Of the seven city council members serving in Reno in spring 1978, three were in insurance, real estate, or both; another was the president of a construction company; and another a banker with interests in development.[57]

As McFarren and Swope indicated, many community members were concerned not only with the physical problems of growth, but also with the more intangible collateral damage—specifically, Reno's reputation for small-town friendliness. In 1975, the Chamber of Commerce put a positive spin on the city's replacement of the old with the new, explaining, "The skyline of Reno's burgeoning downtown area assumes new patterns as multistoried buildings replace old structures to provide modern hotels, office space and apartments" and quickly reassured readers that "the atmosphere of the city . . . remains cordial and friendly as rapid growth continues."[58]

Others were not so sure; one local official predicted that Reno would experience a "personality metamorphosis" within the next few years. Three days before the MGM opening, a "task force" composed of twenty-eight Reno gaming representatives, businessmen, and city officials including Mayor Menicucci visited Minneapolis/St. Paul to observe downtown development there and to consider hiring a Minneapolis firm to initiate a program specifically aimed at "keeping Reno friendly," including the development of a "friendliness factor index" incorporating perceptions of Reno's cordiality by residents and tourists.[59] Some outside observers suggested that the new project acted in direct opposition to this goal. As one *Newsweek* reporter wrote of the MGM, "The colossus stands like a beanstalk among the weeds in the friendly little antlers-over-the-bar gaming town." He concluded, "Reno might choke on its own success; at least six other casinos are now in the works and the 'biggest little city in the world' is already plagued by housing shortages, water problems and traffic jams."[60]

Some residents also saw Reno's charm disappearing along with what they saw as the careless demolition of the community's heritage by the enormous construction projects occurring downtown. In December 1977, an editorial in the *Reno Evening Gazette* observed, "It seems that almost daily magnificent structures from Reno's past are leveled with barely a word of protest or a note of regret." At that point, according to Reno resident Walt Mulcahy, only 21 historic buildings remained of 113 that had been standing just a year and a half earlier. Those demolished included structures from the town's original founding in the 1860s and its second major building boom at the turn of the century. These included the Reno Steam Laundry and an entire row of buildings on Commercial Row east of Virginia Street. In the past five years, the McKissick Opera House (later the Plaza Hotel) and the China Club had also been demolished. The cribs of the Stockade, the city's most famous brothel, were finally demolished in July 1977, after decades of serving as an apartment complex and an unsuccessful attempt by an arts group to purchase the entire structure for a cultural center.[61]

Whether considering it an avatar of progress or imminent disaster, no one could deny that the new MGM Grand Hotel upon completion was unlike anything Reno had seen before. The opening of the massive 145-acre structure in May 1978 was covered by all three national television networks, prompting one local reporter to rave, "Reno probably hasn't received this much national news media attention since Jack Johnson, the world's first black boxing champ, knocked out Jim Jeffries in 15 rounds in an outdoor arena by the railroad tracks east of town in 1910." Most gratifying, he wrote, was the positive image the new hotel was spreading: "For a change, Reno is receiving national and world-wide notoriety for something besides 'Divorce Capital of the World' or home of the nation's largest brothel." The hotel contained more than 1,000 hotel rooms, a 100,000-

Located over a mile east of the downtown casino district, the MGM Grand Hotel-Reno upon its completion in 1978 towered over the surrounding neighborhoods. (Nevada Historical Society)

square foot gaming floor, seven restaurants, 19 bars, a 50-lane bowling center, an Olympic-size swimming pool, a movie theater, and an underground, 43-store shopping mall.[62]

Some believed that the arrival of the MGM finally put Reno back in competition with its downstate neighbor. As one reporter raved of the lavish casino, "One moment you were in Reno, the next in Las Vegas." In an article entitled, "Good-bye Las Vegas . . . Reno, Hello?" a reporter for *Forbes* agreed that Las Vegas should feel threatened by Reno which, with nearby Lake Tahoe and Virginia City, "has the natural tourist attractions Las Vegas lacks. As a gambling mecca, Reno is far less sophisticated than Las Vegas—for now. But for the future? Las Vegas, look out!" Such statements thrilled local promoters. Marlene Olsen of the Reno Chamber of Commerce later reflected, "No one was willing to take Reno seriously" until MGM decided to build its massive hotel, and that "suddenly . . . it was okay for everyone else to bet on Reno." United Airlines certainly did so, tripling its service to Reno, since, in the words of the airline's western marketing head, "Las Vegas has gambling, shows and a little golf, but Reno will have all that plus skiing, Lake Tahoe, and the Old West." As a tourist destination, Reno would seem to have it all.[63]

New York Times reporter Les Ledbetter participated in the massive press junket sponsored by the city for the MGM's opening. To that group, Chamber of Commerce manager Jud Allen announced that Reno had finally overcome two major obstacles: its reputation as a "cow town" and "divorce capital" and the lack of "that top hotel" that the MGM now provided. No mention was made, Ledbetter noted, of the "enormous problems facing this area because of its unrestrained growth in the 1970s." However, he concluded, despite the protests of some, "In the boom-town atmosphere pervading this area, everyone appears to expect the boom money to trickle down to even the poorest and to solve many of the problems."[64]

Indeed, Jud Allen urged the city not to overreact to some of the problems by discouraging further investment in Reno. In a local newspaper commentary, Allen voiced his continuing support for growth, claiming:

> Because of the immediacy of these announcements, we are no longer thinking clearly about the economic future of Reno. Our first impulse is to put the lid on and discourage investors from looking at our area. We seem to have learned nothing from the past. The economic faucet cannot be turned on and off with a whim or through panic.

Referring to the city's continuing planning discussions, he echoed the rhetoric of the dissenting growth report, years earlier, by asserting "this is where our local government has failed and continues without direction. To continue to tamper with the free market is inviting future economic disaster." Finally, he said, "If we desire a high degree of quality of life for our community, it starts with full employment. There is no quality of life for the unemployed. Let's stop belittling our success and meet the challenge of today."[65]

While Allen's enthusiasm remained undiluted, other local leaders voiced their ambivalence about the arrival of the MGM. State Attorney General Bob List, campaigning for the Republican nomination for governor, said at the opening, "It's an awesome place. . . . But we have a tremendous challenge here to blend this type of growth into the community and maintain the quality of life in Northern Nevada." He continued, "For better or for worse, we're at the beginning of a new era for the northern part of the state. Only time will tell whether we did the right thing." Reno city councilman Bill Wallace commented, "It's a little like *A Star is Born*. . . . For years we tried to get this town moving. Now suddenly everything is here, and we aren't sure we want it."[66] And while Bill Raggio, a state senator, remarked that the MGM was a symbol that would take Reno's image from that of a second-class city to one possessing "first class, exciting" attractions, an editorial in the *Nevada State Journal* countered, "MGM is a symbol. It is in part a symbol of an upsurge in the economy of the Truckee Meadows. . . . But MGM is also a symbol of problems that could more than offset the benefits it brings to the Truckee Meadows. And it has brought to light planning problems in the area."[67]

For several years construction continued to boom as the repercussions of some of these planning problems had yet to play out. The owners of the Saviers and Osborn building, which sold electrical appliances, at the intersection of West Second and West Streets, decided to build a hotel casino, forming the Comstock Land and Development Company. The partners of the Cal-Neva ran the gaming as the Fiesta Corporation, with both parties owning 47 percent of the stock. The Comstock opened in May 1978 with a nine-story hotel, 160 rooms, and a Comstock mining–era Virginia City street theme. In 1984 the building expanded further, adding seven stories to create a sixteen-story tower. Its decor summoned a more specific mining heritage than most with its direct reference to the silver boom of Virginia City, a prospector-pick logo, and the decorative scheme of a rollicking mining boomtown. Life-size Disney-like animatronic characters, including "Lulubelle and Slim," a burlesque singer and piano player, and the "Pick and Shovel Gang," a ragtag band of musical miners, sprang to life above the casino floor every fifteen minutes. Continuing the theme were restaurants and shops including the Miner's Café, Silver King Saloon, General Mercantile Emporium, and Prospector Club, as well as a change counter labeled the "Cashier and Assay Office." The overall effect was that of a raucous, cartoonish Wild West.[68]

In addition to the Comstock, so much construction was under way in the summer of 1978 that three major downtown attractions opened on the same day: July first. The Del Webb Corporation had begun construction of the twenty-story Sahara Reno on North Sierra Street in April 1977. At the same time, Charles Mapes began an expansion of his Money Tree casino, in order to add a show lounge, disco, and three restaurants. To do so, Mapes authorized the demolition of the Crest Theatre, the Carlton Hotel, Hamilton Opticians, and the Baby Doll Topless Lounge. And the Circus Circus Corporation, which had opened its first casino on the Las Vegas Strip in 1968, opened Reno's Circus Circus on the former site of the Gray Reid Department store, a Reno institution since 1901, and the Nevada National

Bank, using both buildings as the core of its 102-room hotel structure. The new casino combined midway carnival and circus attractions with gambling attractions, in order to create a tourist destination for the entire family. The pink bigtop and an enormous sign with the casino's mascot, Topsy the Clown, quickly dominated the street.[69]

While the construction proceeded apace, the unease many residents felt about this so-called "progress" came to a head in the 1979 mayoral election. In what was widely considered an upset, political neophyte Barbara Bennett, an outspoken advocate of limiting growth, handily won the election against incumbent Bruno Menicucci. Several years earlier, the retired Bennett had begun her move toward political activism by founding the Northern Nevada Mobile Homeowners Association, in response to large increases in rent in the mobile home park in which she lived. That project only enhanced her desire to be an advocate for the unheard.

According to Bennett, who served as mayor until leaving for another position in 1983, the city's elected representatives only talked with people who thought as they did, and as a result "it was very difficult for the elected officials to believe that not everyone was perfectly happy to have an MGM hotel in this city." In her opinion, the concerns of many local residents had not been acknowledged. Echoing economics professor Bill Eadington's earlier concerns, she later stated, "There are many people like myself who have felt very strongly that we should monitor and limit—not completely *prevent*—area growth, because of the problems attendant with the growth-related experience." Of particular concern to Bennett was the city's lack of housing at a time when thousands of people were moving to town to work for the MGM and the newly expanded Harrah's.[70]

Like other advocates of managed growth before her, Bennett ran into a great deal of opposition by many who interpreted her position as anti-growth. Many of the casino owners seemed to support growth without reservation, sharing the position of Palace Club owner Silvio Petricciani who believed "the more people that come into the town and the more businesses and hotels that grow in the town, the better it's going to be for everybody because they're just going to bring more people into the town." Such circular reasoning made sense only to those who believed that growth was inherently good.[71]

And many in Reno believed precisely that. The expansions that were already under way at the time of Bennett's election continued into the early 1980s, most involving the addition of large numbers of hotel rooms. The

Sands added a thirteen-story hotel addition and an expanded casino in 1979. The Eldorado expanded in 1978 and then spent $30 million on another major expansion in 1985. The Cal-Neva bought enough neighboring properties to complete a $10 million expansion by 1980. Having bought out a pawn and jewelry shop, the Western Union office, and Armanko's stationery store, among other businesses, the Cal-Neva now owned the entire block with the exception of the First National Bank high-rise and one other holdout property that eventually became the Virginian Hotel-Casino. The Sundowner Hotel-Casino on North Arlington and West Fourth Street also added a tower to its existing eleven-story hotel in the early 1980s. Together, the construction of these new buildings, with their enormous half-block and even block-long facades, took out scores of older buildings and independent businesses.[72]

Such growth might have continued unabated, unaffected by growing community concerns, if not for the onset of a deep national recession in the early 1980s that put a serious damper on American tourism in general and Reno's increasingly tourism-based economy in particular. Even the Mustang Ranch, the notorious brothel located east of city limits, off Interstate 80, went on the market in 1984. The rate of growth of Nevada's gaming revenue decreased significantly between 1980 and 1983, although total revenues continued to top $2 billion per year. Downtown Reno suffered the most, and it soon became clear that the massive casino-building boom of the late 1970s and early 1980s had produced too much competition for not enough visitors. Reno was overbuilt, and all too soon, its casinos began to close.[73]

Most at risk due to the combination of the national economic downturn and local overbuilding were Reno's smaller, family-owned casinos. According to the Nevada Gaming Control Board, the twenty-seven smaller casinos in the Reno area lost a total of $8.8 million between July 1978 and July 1979. The Mapes family in particular experienced serious financial difficulties after an ill-advised expansion of their second casino, the Money Tree, in 1978. The property simply could not survive the intense competition of all the new development, and its new wing closed in January 1980. The Mapes organization filed for bankruptcy that December, but the family's financial struggles did not end there. In an effort to turn the Mapes Hotel's vintage appearance into an asset, a $1.3 million renovation completed in June 1981 added $800,000 of antique furnishings, renovated restaurants and hotel rooms, an expanded casino, and big band entertainment.[74]

But all these changes could not compensate for poor financial planning. The failure of the Money Tree placed the Mapes in jeopardy, as it served as collateral for a loan for the other property. As the building's new owner, the First Interstate Bank of Nevada hired a new management team for the Mapes, but it was too late. The Mapes family could not regain their financial stability after filing bankruptcy, and the building closed, as did the Money Tree, in December 1982, a little over two decades after it had sparkled as the focal point of Reno glamour for the cast of *The Misfits*.[75] The Gold Dust, on West Second Street, also closed, standing vacant for the next five years. The sight of such large, deserted properties quickly became a liability for those that managed to keep their doors open. The operators of the Comstock, in clear view of both the closed Money Tree and Gold Dust, were especially worried about the repercussions for their property. As Comstock co-owner Jack Douglass recalled, "from the Comstock as you looked down Second Street towards Virginia there were two dead proper-ties—a real barrier to any foot traffic that we might have had."[76]

Many Reno residents were critical of the casinos that remained open. As Thomas C. Wilson said in 1982, "They're dirty, they're sleazy, they're rundown, and as a result, our town lost some of the quality which was built for it during the '20s by the fashionable divorcées who came out here with lots of money. It will be a very difficult market to recover." Wilson identi-fied a key demographic shift in the patrons of these newer establishments; the bus packages introduced in the 1960s, according to Wilson, had had the inadvertent effect of cheapening the Reno market, with the result that "Reno has become a motel—[a] cheap, carnival-type gambling town" as the buses brought to town lower economic levels of people who mingled with the other patrons. According to Wilson, Harrah's was careful to time the buses so they did not arrive at the same hours as normal play, but other casinos, in adopting the practice, were not so careful. "It's significant the hotels we're getting now are really 'vertical motels,'" he wrote. "Some of 'em are better quality than others. But they're mostly aimed at low-income groups in which there is not going to be significant gambling revenue or high-rollers."[77]

In his memoir, *It Was Great While It Lasted*, Mark Curtis was similarly critical of the direction Reno's casinos had taken. "Somewhere things started going to hell," he wrote:

> As star salaries grew more and more preposterous, all those elegancies and civilities, all the things that made gaming more than a grind, were diminished or eliminated. The chorus lines and house bands went out the door. The menus got smaller, the food portions got smaller (but

looked bigger because the plates were smaller); the prices were bigger; the showrooms became enormous and service was minimal. You were elbow-to-elbow with strangers in jeans and T-shirts.

Such strategies were employed as many of Reno's establishments made a conscious effort to focus on gambling rather than other amenities like din-ner shows and entertainment. In 1983, banker Jim Mort concurred with Wilson and Curtis: "Right now we are drawing the lowest form of gam-bling business, the bus-tour slot pullers. We are rapidly watching our downtown area deteriorate into a dirty little hole." He did not place the blame on the casinos alone. Like others before him, Mort blamed munici-pal passivity, complaining "The city fathers commission thousands of dol-lars for studies and plans. They neither accept them nor implement them when submitted. Instead, they merely study the problem to death."[78]

Many of these insiders described Reno's emerging identity as that of a "grind town," a destination dependent upon attracting large numbers of smaller betters, rather than the high rollers of days gone by. Not everyone meant the term to be derogatory. Referring to the Cal-Neva, of which he was a part-owner, Warren Nelson called it "a great grind joint. We cater to smaller players. Nickel slot machines are as important as dollar machines, and we just grind the money out of them. We're a high volume, low margin operation." He contrasted this to Caesars Palace and the Mirage in Las Ve-gas, with all their perks for the high rollers. At the Cal-Neva, Nelson ex-plained, "Up on the top floor you get a jumbo hot dog and a bottle of Heineken for $1.50, and that is our answer to 6,000-square-foot suites stacked with caviar and champagne."[79]

The grind town image might have worked for some, but on the whole, Reno's reputation in the 1980s was clearly in a downward spiral. Under the title, "Think of Reno, Nevada," a reporter for *Travel/Holiday* wrote in 1981, "Fast, what comes to mind? Perhaps a second-rate Las Vegas, where the bargain basement crowd goes because it can't afford the real thing?" Clearly, this was a rhetorical question, but the writer helpfully pointed out Reno's strengths: some of its hotels, like the MGM and Harrah's, were do-ing just fine, and the cost of Reno's dinner shows averaged $20 cheaper than those of Las Vegas.[80] An article in *Forbes* in 1984 outlined the problem in starker terms: "If ever there was a city with an image problem, it's Reno. It's got gambling, but even with the gambling, Las Vegas has the glitz and Reno is the pits." The report cited Reno's above average rape, burglary, and

murder rates for towns its size, as well as the instability of its casino properties. Reno's city manager Chris Cherches told the magazine, "In 1980,
1981, people here started to say, 'Hey, maybe we aren't recession-proof. . . .'
In council chambers people were saying, 'We'd better start to diversify
[and] go after more attractive industries.'"[81]

In order to spearhead this effort, a number of professional organizations were organized specifically to attract more diverse industries to the
Reno area. With legalized gambling already under way in Atlantic City,
Reno's civic and business leaders realized the continuing importance of
broadening the city's economic base. In the words of resident Harold Gorman, a primary goal was to bring some "so-called *clean* business in the
state." A group called Western Industrial Nevada (WIN) formed under the
auspices of the Sparks Chamber of Commerce to raise money for development of the region through private citizens and businesses. Members of
the board would "bring these people in to wine them and dine them, and
take them around and show them what we had to offer," selling them on
the quality of life and resources including the region's effective transportation network. The Economic Development Authority of Western Nevada
(EDAWN) also formed in the early 1980s in order to attract new, nongaming businesses to the region, including more freeport warehousing, an industry that had boomed through the 1970s. The developer of an industrial
park promised, "We'll bend over backwards to get that first high-techer in
here."[82]

As Barbara Bennett was aware, attracting these new industries would
require a commitment to redeveloping downtown and formulating concrete plans to manage the community's growth. Like other advocates of
growth management in cities throughout the West in the 1970s and 1980s,
Bennett advocated democratic processes in determining growth patterns,
rather than the powerful individual-led patterns of the past.[83] In her ongoing quest to increase civic participation in planning decisions, Bennett persuaded the city council and City Planning Commission to hold nine public
forums in Reno in the fall of 1981. With that input, the City of Reno Department of Planning and Community Development produced a Policy
Plan the following spring, incorporating four major goals—Economic Development, Growth Management, Community Design, and Environmental
Conservation—into a Master Plan for the city.[84]

The plan, when completed, was notable for identifying, and celebrating, precisely what made Reno distinct. It promoted "the type of growth in

the tourism sector of the economy which expands Reno's image as a beautiful, multi-purpose, and family-oriented destination." Significantly, the goal was not simply to duplicate the tourist offerings of Las Vegas. As Bennett later explained, "I had always hoped that we would never become a city like Las Vegas. I think that's why a lot of us love the place [Reno], and we didn't want to see another Las Vegas here. Yet, today we're seeing this comparison between how much Las Vegas is growing and how many hotel-casinos they have, compared to our somewhat slower rate of growth. I think the comparisons are very unfair. The population down there wants this kind of expansion."[85]

In Reno, growth had brought problems to a downtown unprepared to deal with it. In the public forums, residents frequently expressed concern about the state and future of downtown and enthusiastically supported plans for downtown beautification and general clean-up, as well as specific ideas to create a pedestrian plaza and to improve the Truckee River corridor. The 1982 policy plan reflected these concerns, stating a main objective to "ensure revitalization of the downtown by creating a climate for investment in residential, retail, and tourist-related functions with a more attractive pedestrian environment." In 1989, Bennett explained, "Early on in my administration I said—and I have said repeatedly—that to be healthy, every city has to have a healthy downtown core. Our downtown core happens to be hotel-casinos. That being the case, then we want it to be presentable and successful, because if you destroy downtown Reno, I don't know where you're going to go from there."[86]

The plan's support for the non-tourist-oriented components of the downtown landscape included the creation of "high rise mixed use buildings and projects" and "the development of medium and high density residential development in and adjacent to the downtown area," as well as landscaping, façade improvements, a network of pedestrian walkways and plazas, and even "expanded programs for preservation, renovation, and reuse of historic and architecturally unique structures."[87] Bennett's administration began to discuss the creation of a major downtown redevelopment project, at an estimated cost of $30 million, to be derived from property taxes levied on a "tax increment district" downtown. In 1982, the city council formed the Reno Redevelopment District and began plans to reinvigorate the downtown area once and for all.[88]

The following February, the city council approved a $28.6 million redevelopment package for downtown Reno. The plan included four separate components: improvement of the Truckee River, including "riverside walk-ways, cascades and garden-like settings"; the development of a "Retail Garden," with shops, restaurants, and "amusements" at the intersection of Sierra Street and the Truckee River, described as "Reno's reply to Ghirardelli Square in San Francisco"; construction of a Virginia Street Mall, intended to transform Virginia Street from Interstate 80 on the north to the so-called "Financial District" on the south into a "tree-lined, pedestrian oriented boulevard" and reducing the street from Commercial Row south-ward to a single lane of traffic; and the creation of a Civic Plaza, from the river south to the Financial District, with a renovated post office that included a "greenhouse-like River Room and wintergarden," room for an outdoor market and a "terraced and landscaped riverside amphitheater." A laser tower was also proposed, to stand 30 feet high and project light patterns off downtown buildings.[89]

It all sounded encouraging, but project delays went on and on. Two major obstacles were the high cost of downtown construction and the "fragmented ownership" of downtown lots, which made it difficult to plan large developments. Downtown business owners were particularly concerned about the plan to reduce Virginia Street to one lane, and voiced their concern at city council hearings.[90] With the constant delays, it often seemed that the scope of redevelopment had been reduced to garbage removal and street sweeping. In May 1983, Ron Watson, executive vice president of the Greater Reno-Sparks Chamber of Commerce, reported that "the chamber has made a commitment of manpower and resources to see that the downtown redevelopment plan is implemented. We will augment our efforts with a year-round clean-up/beautification program." In August, Tony Fiannaca, President of the Greater Reno-Sparks Chamber of Commerce announced the clean-up program, called "Operation Pride." A brochure for downtown business owners divided the district into four areas, assigned business leaders to be area chairpersons and block captains, and encouraged businesses to clean sidewalks and parking lots, empty trash receptacles, replace broken lights, and complete other basic maintenance.[91]

With the actual landscape of downtown still faltering, Reno proceeded to update its marketing machinery in the 1980s, as city marketing nation-wide became an increasingly professional business, increasingly oriented toward tourism.[92] This transition was signified by the subtle name change of the Reno-Sparks Convention Authority (formerly the Washoe County

Fair and Recreation Board) to the Reno-Sparks Convention and Tourism Authority. This organization took over the civic promotional activities formerly handled by the Greater Reno-Sparks Chamber of Commerce, which changed its focus to downtown improvements. The large hotel-casinos supported removing promotional responsibilities from the Chamber of Commerce in order to reduce the dues they had had to pay to the chamber. A convention authority could be financed through room taxes and give them the same benefits.

In addition to a new tourism bureau, the Convention and Tourism Authority gained a facilities director, a convention director, and an executive director, as well as a $6.6 million budget. In 1984, the Reno News Bureau was formed "to assist travel writers prepare articles about the Reno area, provide photographs to newspapers and magazines and provide positive publicity about the area, its attractions and events."[93] Roy Powers, a publicity director for Harolds Club, became the director of this bureau. The Convention and Tourism Authority, eventually renamed the Reno-Sparks Convention and Visitors Authority (RSCVA), operated out of the Centennial Coliseum, miles from downtown on South Virginia Street, strangely separating the city's promotional machinery from the city's own physical center.[94] The Chamber of Commerce complemented the work of the Reno News Bureau, asserting in 1984 that "Reno is rapidly building a reputation as one of the nation's finest family vacation areas" and touting assets including Lake Tahoe, area ski resorts, and Virginia City. One Nevadan admitted that "Old time Nevadans will be shaking their heads at all the changes," but asserted, "If you are new to Reno you will see a pleasantly-situated western city of middle age, stretched somewhat at the seams, but still quite attractive."[95]

With redevelopment yet to begin, committees, like the earlier array of growth studies, continued to proliferate. The Chamber of Commerce introduced a new program in 1987 with the formation of the Downtown Renovation Association (DRA), an "administrative organization" that asked downtown business owners to join its action committees. Members would work with the Reno Redevelopment Agency to "create projects to improve [the] image of downtown to tourists and local residents" and to "coordinate completion of [the] Downtown Redevelopment project." Its action committees were devoted to projects including "redevelopment, maintenance, clean-up, transients, promotions/special events, the new arch, the William F. Harrah Automobile Museum, and legislative issues."[96]

The Biggest Little City Committee formed in 1987 to "build the community's awareness and appreciation of its unique assets and qualities," focusing on "regenerating a spirit and pride in the community." Under the slogan "Renew the Spirit—Restore the Pride," the group was given permission to use the resources of the Chamber of Commerce and shared an executive director with the Downtown Renovation Association. They took credit for the revival of the "Biggest Little City in the World" slogan by the Reno-Sparks Convention Authority, the creation of a promotional poster, and the redesign and replacement of the Reno arch in 1987.[97]

That Reno was now a city in transition was clear, but its ultimate destination was not. Over the past three decades, the city's residential and tourist landscapes had separated in a way that seemed largely irreversible, with the demolition of businesses that had served generations of local residents and created the appearance, to visitors, of a respectable and stable civic presence. The combination of economic competition and aesthetic deterioration had sent Reno's national reputation in a tailspin, in turn leading to further deterioration of the landscape. Casino growth clearly had outpaced market demand, and yet momentum and the profit motive were not easily derailed. Plans for redevelopment and growth management had gained many supporters, but so far spurred no concrete achievements. Without a thriving tourist landscape, Reno seemed to lack a concrete public identity beyond that of a city in decline.

On 22 November 1989, Las Vegas gaming impresario Steve Wynn threw open the doors of his spectacular Mirage, a resort of almost unimaginable scale and expenditure on the Las Vegas Strip. Constructed for the high rolling crowd at a cost exceeding $630 million, the Mirage featured an outdoor volcano, an elaborate indoor tropical forest complete with waterfalls, and more than 3,000 rooms. Defying all skeptics, the colossal resort averaged revenues of a staggering $2 million per day in its first year. Crowds simply could not get enough. As Reno struggled to regain its footing, the age of the megaresort was under way.[98]

CHAPTER SIX

A New Reno for the New Millennium

*Until you've lost your reputation, you never realize
what a burden it was or what freedom really is.*
Rhett Butler, in Margaret Mitchell's *Gone with the Wind*, 1936

*While Las Vegas to the south tears down casinos to make way for
bigger casinos, Reno has been trying to reinvent itself as competition
for gamblers has increased. At the same time, Reno's experience
shows how a city can grow beyond gambling.*
Philadelphia Inquirer, January 2006

In the 1992 movie *Sister Act*, comedian Whoopi Goldberg plays a second-rate casino lounge singer named Deloris Van Cartier who performs for listless crowds at Reno's Nevada Club. The majority of the plot unfolds in a San Francisco convent where Deloris is sent by the feds to hide after witnessing her mobster boyfriend, the casino's owner, shoot a squealer, but the Reno scenes that bookend that storyline are clearly identified through prominent shots of local landmarks including Harolds Club and the blazing neon Reno arch. Even so, the setting apparently did not register to some; upon the film's release, a reviewer for the *Washington Post* described Goldberg's character as "a singer of tacky Supremes-type medleys at a Vegas club."[1]

The easy substitution of Las Vegas for Reno was not confined to the reviewer. In fact, the original screenplay for the movie was not set in Reno at all, but in Atlantic City, and intended as a vehicle for Bette Midler. In scouting potential locations for the shoot, director Emilio Ardolino considered all three major American gambling cities—Atlantic City, Vegas, and Reno—requiring only that the setting be a casino town located near a major metropolitan center where Deloris could hide out. The Atlantic City angle helps to explain the odd placement of a "major underworld figure" like the boyfriend, played by Harvey Keitel as a slick, money-laundering wiseguy, in the Biggest Little City, a town never much known for its mafia ties. Ultimately, as producers concluded, general audiences weren't well versed in the history of organized crime and supposedly would not know the difference. In fact, through the years, numerous films with mobster themes, originally written for Vegas, were set in Reno when they finally hit the screen. In the minds of Hollywood executives, it seemed, the days when celluloid Reno could be mistaken for nowhere else were clearly over.[2]

As the *Sister Act* example shows, Americans in the late twentieth century increasingly considered Reno, if they considered it at all, as a second-rate, smaller-scale version of Las Vegas, rather than a distinct destination that had preceded Las Vegas by decades as a wedding, divorce, and gambling capital. The decades since 1960 had seen a complete role reversal between Nevada's two primary resort towns, as Las Vegas evolved from Reno's primary competition to an international tourist destination in a class all its own. The numbers bore this out. In 1990, 4.9 million tourists visited Washoe County, while Clark County attracted a staggering 24.2 million.[3] That same year, the thirty-three top Reno/Sparks casinos earned total revenues of approximately $1.16 billion, while the forty-one major casinos on the Las Vegas Strip alone took in more than triple that amount, at just over $3.9 billion.[4]

Even with the investment of major gaming companies like Mandalay Bay and Harrah's—by now a national casino chain—Reno's infrastructure simply could not support such a massive scale. The newest trend-setting Las Vegas resorts funneled millions of dollars into their exotically themed structures, from the $630 million tropical Mirage, to the $290 million medieval-themed Excalibur (opened in 1990), the $430 million pirate-themed Treasure Island (1993), and the $365 million Egyptian-themed, pyramid-shaped Luxor (1993). The new MGM Grand became the largest hotel in the world when it opened on the Strip in 1993, with more than 5,000 rooms and suites.[5]

The marketing masterminds of Las Vegas complemented the construction of these gaming goliaths with a striking shift in their sales pitch. In the late 1980s, promoters began to sell the town as a "family-friendly" resort rather than a "sin city," a clear attempt to embrace a broader audience in a relatively conservative era. The new generation of visitors to Las Vegas were less serious about gambling and more interested in recreation of all sorts, a trend that casino operators catered to in a number of ways, ranging from the installation of computerized video poker and slot machines to the development and promotion of elaborate buffet dinners, landscaped pools, magic shows, and dramatic spectacles like jousting tournaments at the Excalibur and full-scale shipwrecks at the entrance to Treasure Island. The Strip had become, as a *New York Times* reporter wrote in 1990, "a playground where the American middle class can indulge its fantasies."[6]

There was no competing with the spectacular temple of excess that Las Vegas had become. However, its success, along with the prospect of taxing casino revenues to fill city coffers, prompted a wide range of communities across the country to introduce gambling in the late 1980s and early 1990s. During the same period, as Donald Trump was opening his Taj Mahal Casino Resort in Atlantic City, new competition sprang from unexpected places. Legal gaming began in Deadwood, South Dakota, in 1989 and in the Colorado mountain towns of Black Hawk, Central City, and Cripple Creek in 1991, the same year that riverboat casinos began to travel along the Mississippi River in Iowa and Illinois. Three years later, fifty-seven riverboats were operating off the banks of those two states as well as in Mississippi, Missouri, and Louisiana. In addition, the 1988 passage of the Indian Gaming Regulatory Act, which enabled Native American tribes to operate casinos on their lands, meant that tribal casinos could be legalized in any state that allowed gaming. With backing from some of the largest gaming companies in the country, such casinos could offer their patrons a range of amenities similar to those offered in Reno. And if tribal casinos began to appear on reservations within range of Reno's traditional drive-up feeder markets from northern California to the Pacific Northwest, they could give the city's institutions a serious run for their money.[7]

As a result of this increased availability, and more inclusive marketing strategies, gambling was becoming more popular than ever. As the *New York Times Magazine* reported in 1994, "Gambling is now bigger than baseball, more powerful than a platoon of Schwarzeneggers, Spielbergs, Madonnas and Oprahs. More Americans went to casinos than to major league ballparks in 1993. Ninety-two million visits!"[8] Over the course of six decades, gambling had undergone a remarkable transformation from a widely criticized sign of moral failing to an acceptable mainstream American pastime. Accordingly, discussions accompanying the introduction of legalized gambling to a state or local jurisdiction centered less on the morality of the activity itself and more on the impact of such businesses on a given community's physical and economic infrastructure. The industry's critics bemoaned the potential damage inflicted upon communities by the introduction of extreme economic disparities between casino owners and locals, as well as the physical destruction of historic properties. In 1996, calling the onset of increased gaming development "the great social experiment of the late twentieth century," Patricia Stokowski blamed the arrival of casinos in the small Colorado towns of Black Hawk and Central City for destroying their unique sense of place.[9]

Such concerns were not at the forefront of public discussions in Reno, where the physical and economic impact of the gaming industry, particularly in the downtown area, had been so gradual and so largely unquestioned as to seem almost part of the natural course of urban development. But the growing competition for America's gambling dollars in the 1990s presented a stark challenge both to Reno's economy and to the soundness of past civic decisions. Although the gradual devotion of central Reno to the tourist trade, accelerated in the late 1970s, had seemed a reasonable gamble at the time, that decision now revealed some negative repercussions beyond the overbuilding that had led to the casino closures of the early 1980s. The construction of block-sized casinos, like the malls or big box retail stores of other cities, had driven out small businesses, and with them, the majority of residential patronage, a trend that continued in 1991 as the last downtown department store, J. C. Penney's, moved from its downtown location to outlying Meadowood Mall. The brilliant row of casinos captured on film in *Sister Act* clustered together on a few busy blocks of Virginia Street, but on its frayed edges, Reno's downtown teetered precariously on the brink of seediness, dragged down by spiritless rows of pawnshops, souvenir stores, and boarded-up buildings, including the once-proud Mapes and Riverside hotel casinos.

Those two structures, facing each other on opposite sides of the river, seemed to encapsulate Reno's developmental paralysis. When Reno's city government approved its first redevelopment plan, back in 1983, all eyes had turned to the city's closed casinos as targets for renewal. Demolition of the Mapes seemed a possibility almost immediately, considering the need to retrofit the building with a sprinkler system as well as new heating and air conditioning ducts. State preservationists tried to gain recognition for the site as soon as they could and successfully ensured the building's inclusion as a structure of "special significance" by the National Register of Historic Places in 1984, even though it was not yet fifty years old. In 1988, local businessmen George Karadanis and Robert Maloff bought the Mapes for an undisclosed sum, and almost immediately put it up for sale. There were no takers. Things were also not going well across the river, at the Riverside Hotel. Its owner, Pick Hobson, filed for bankruptcy in 1986, closing the casino that December, and the restaurant and hotel rooms the following November. For the rest of the decade, the two buildings had stood vacant, reminders of a glamorous era that seemed irretrievably lost.[10]

As more struggling casinos closed their doors, the sight of so many shuttered businesses further discouraged both visitation and new investment, spurring a relentless downward spiral as the appearance of Reno's central district mirrored the financial strain. Bucking the downtown trend, a handful of new casinos flourished outside of the downtown area; besides the MGM Grand, which became Bally's in 1986, these included the Peppermill, which had begun as a coffee shop in 1971, opened a small casino and motor lodge in 1980, and continued to benefit from its proximity to the Reno-Sparks Convention Center, formerly known as the Centennial Coliseum.

In this troubled context, public memory of a time when Reno had cornered the market on legal gambling was rapidly evaporating, leaving a void of attention that city leaders were uncertain how to fill. To regain both positive press and a strong tourist economy would require a complete reevaluation of the city's strengths and weaknesses. Accordingly, the tune sung by Reno's officials in the early 1990s was reinvention. Restoring the city's reputation now seemed linked more than ever to the restoration of an attractive urban landscape, along with the creation of amenities to appeal to a full spectrum of visitors and residents alike. As a result, every downtown construction project from the 1990s onward was subjected to the intense scrutiny of casino executives, public officials, and residents, all of whom were deeply invested, both literally and figuratively, in Reno's future. Every building that went up—or came down—seemed absolutely critical to the whole matter of creating a successful new civic identity.

In their effort to determine the perfect route to reinvention, city officials continued a longstanding pattern of embarking upon further studies and plans. From 1983 to 2000, the city sponsored at least sixteen different redevelopment plans for its downtown area.[11] All were dedicated, at least in part, to improving the appearance of central Reno and bringing residents back downtown. The city's business organizations reassured the community that this was their priority, as well. In 1990, the Downtown Renovation Association sponsored an advertising supplement in the *Reno Evening Gazette* with the optimistic title, "Changes: Renovation Is Working in Downtown Reno." The organization's president was Bill Thornton, chairman of the board of Club Cal-Neva. Although admitting that his gaming industry ties might cause local residents to label him as "a slick, casino type intent on sacrificing Reno's quality of life for more tourist dollars," Thornton assured Reno's citizens that "downtown Reno belongs to the people of Reno." He continued, "We have to let them know that we are not working our tails off just to please the tourist. We want a downtown that's attractive to locals, as well." His statement clearly revealed, perhaps unintentionally, an acknowledgment that the majority of local residents felt alienated from their own downtown.[12]

Jud Allen, now a Reno city councilman, added that Reno still had a chance to avoid the decay that had affected so many other cities. Although at one time an unabashed advocate of unrestrained growth, Allen seemed to have changed his tune; the key to this civic health, he now stated, would be the long-awaited Truckee River beautification. "Once the river project is completed, with a variety of family attractions," he wrote, "Reno will be unique, offering daytime family fun and nighttime adult entertainment, all within walking distance." As a result, he assured residents, "Reno will, at last, have a permanent identity that is different from Las Vegas, but to many, more appealing. And it doesn't have to pursue runaway growth in order to enjoy economic vitality. . . . Reno should strive to capitalize on our differences from Las Vegas instead of being identified as a 'poor man's Las Vegas.'"[13] Like Allen, many others focused on this question of "uniqueness," highlighting the need for Reno to avoid relegation to a second-class status and regain the national attention it had received for so long without even trying.

As Allen hoped, the first feature to receive a sanctioned civic overhaul was the Truckee River, an asset long neglected in favor of the bustling businesses of Commercial Row and, later, Virginia Street. Only the various incarnations of the Riverside Hotel truly had taken advantage of the riverfront with a combination of verandas and picture windows. In 1990, seven years after the first redevelopment plan had promised the creation of "riverside walkways, cascades and garden-like settings," the Reno Redevelopment Agency spent $7.8 million on materials to complete the Raymond I. Smith Truckee River Walk, named for the Harolds Club patriarch. Completed in 1991, the River Walk, with its wide sidewalks, fountains, sculptures, and pavilion area, all in a mauve color scheme, was intended to encourage pedestrians to stroll along the riverside, taking advantage of the natural beauty running through the center of town.[14] However, unlike San

Antonio's successful Riverwalk, Reno's version of riverside development featured no accompanying restaurants, bars, clubs, or shops alongside the river to entertain and sustain those who chose to stroll there. It did improve access to the river but would require complementary development in order to become a truly successful attraction, and few developers were ready to invest in the downtown district.

Reinvention was the intention of another early redevelopment project that hoped to attract a completely new tourist demographic, reinventing Reno as a bowling mecca. In 1993, espousing the philosophy that extremely narrow target marketing could guarantee a constant stream of revenue for the city, the RSCVA borrowed $6.7 million from the city's redevelopment agency to buy the land to construct an enormous, eighty-lane, professional-level bowling stadium. It was built to host tournaments, specifically the tens of thousands of bowlers attending the American Bowling Congress and Women's International Bowling Congress championships, for periods of five months each, two of out every three years. The plan raised many eyebrows, not least for its 80-foot aluminum geodesic dome, housing a 172-seat IMAX theater. The National Bowling Stadium, located one block east of the casinos on Virginia Street, was completed in 1995 at a cost of $50.2 million, approximately twice as much as originally estimated. Civic hopes were high; at the grand opening, a priest delivered a prayer that "this Biggest Little City [will] become the bowling capital of the nation and the world." His prayers seemed answered as the first major event brought in a record 17,285 teams. Brilliantly illuminated at night in vivid, casino-worthy hues of pink and purple, the stadium hit the spotlight the following year in the movie, *Kingpin*, which starred Woody Harrelson as a one-handed bowler who brings his protégé, an Amish bowling phenomenon, to Reno for the world championship. In its contemporary state, Reno seemed destined to serve as a setting for comedy rather than the glamour of a previous era.[15]

Targeting bowlers came as something of a surprise to many Reno residents, but not so surprising as the decision by a group of investors to construct an entirely new casino from the ground up. Despite the economic uncertainties of such a venture, plans for the so-called "Project C" began in 1993. A joint project of the Las Vegas–based Mandalay Bay Resort Group—owners of Reno's Circus Circus—and the Eldorado Hotel Casino, located two blocks to the south, the $310 million project, intended to link the two together, was touted proudly as the first "Las Vegas–style," or completely

themed resort casino, in Reno. The city stood to receive additional funding
from property taxes on the new resort through a tax increment financing
arrangement, an extremely popular strategy for financing urban redevelopment nationwide.[16]

Long before construction began, the structure was charged with symbolic meaning for the community as part of its civic resuscitation. As a gas
station employee working one block away from the future site of the project noted in May 1993, "This part of town is dead. We've got all the transients and the hookers downtown." Of the projected new casino, he suggested, "Not only will it have a financial impact . . . but I think it will help
class up this part of town." The influence of Las Vegas was clearly seen in
the initial thematic concept: a sixteenth-century Spanish Lost City of Gold,
featuring a massive castle nestled underneath a giant dome. However, not
everyone was sold on the idea; as one of the partners explained the following June, the Lost City was an exciting theme, but he "couldn't get his arms
around a castle." Neither could the other collaborators, leading to the introduction of an entirely new concept in the summer of 1994, with the new
structure already in mid-construction.[17]

The change was prompted not only by personal preference, but by a
reevaluation of the local context. According to Arthur Valdes, a conceptual
consultant for the project, the adoption of the new theme, an Old West silver mine, provided a meaningful connection both to local history and to
the broader heritage of the American West. As one of the city's redevelopment officers maintained, the design "takes us back to the roots of our
community, founded in mining, gaming and cattle country." This mining
of the city's roots was intended to be more than figurative. In employing a
narrative of the Old West, the casino's owners were attempting something
of a boom-by-association, essentially invoking an historic economic bonanza in the hopes of securing a contemporary one.[18]

The decision to connect Reno's newest casino to the region's mining
heritage met with widespread approval, especially from members of the local construction and casino industries. Bob Jones, executive director of the
Builders Association of Northern Nevada, commented, "Keying into our
own history is great. We cannot out-Las Vegas Las Vegas. It's silly to try."
Circus Circus president and CEO Clyde Turner expressed his satisfaction
that "we have finally got something that is really Reno," and Eldorado CEO
Don Carano agreed that the resort's theme was "uniquely Nevada,
uniquely Reno." The use of local heritage had certainly been successful in

other urban tourist destinations, from San Francisco's Fisherman's Wharf and Baltimore's Harbor Place to lower Manhattan's South Street Seaport.[19]

It was curious, however, that in their quest to create an attraction that was "uniquely Reno," its creators would have chosen a practice, silver mining, that never actually occurred in Reno proper. Not only that, but they also composed an elaborate founding myth for the resort, beginning "when a young man named Sam Fairchild traveled west in search of a dream." Fairchild, the story continued, found his fortune in the mines of Nevada in the late nineteenth century, ultimately became "the wealthiest of all the Silver Barons," and built this hotel as a showcase for his accumulated riches. Inside, the casino's centerpiece and main attraction was a giant, 120-foot-high "mining rig," said to mark the site of Fairchild's original silver mine. This rig, an oversized head frame, stood underneath a 180-foot diameter composite dome, advertised as the world's largest. Its curved surface depicted a lightly-clouded sky and served as an enormous screen for occasional light and laser shows. Signs posted on the rig and its attached "claims office" advertised the Nevada Central Railroad, the Gold Bullion Theatre, and other western-tinged sites and attractions—some real, some fictional.[20]

Having settled on a reinvented heritage intended to distinguish Reno from Las Vegas once and for all, the pressure was on for the project to make an enormous impact. While the structure was still under construction, Reno councilman Jim Pilzner admitted that if the new hotel-casino did not "jumpstart" downtown, "we're going to have terrible problems." On either side of the site stretched the windowless, modern facades of the Eldorado and Circus Circus hotel casinos, both built in the 1970s. Directly across the street, jewelry and loan, liquor, and T-shirt stores, a taco shop, and a dilapidated bar shared the block with a dusty empty lot and an economy motel. The casino's owners embraced the enormous economic and social responsibility that had been placed on their shoulders. At a highbrow ceremony in December 1994, when the casino's name, the Silver Legacy, was first revealed to the public, an actor playing the ghost of Sam Fairchild exclaimed, "This marks the rebirth of Reno. It's the renewal of the silver age . . . a Reno-vation of Reno," recycling a play on words that had previously been used to refer to an urban renewal program of the 1960s, and before that, to the city's divorce industry. Indeed, renovation seemed to be Reno's most enduring trait, both in the new beginnings its various industries promised visitors, and in its own constantly shifting identity.[21]

The Silver Legacy Resort Casino mimics the appearance of a bustling Victorian-era business district with trees, benches, and false storefronts. (Max Chapman Photo)

The building's architects designed the Silver Legacy literally to reinvent Reno's downtown landscape by capturing the appearance of a busy Victorian retail district. On its front façade, an elegant arched stone edifice evoking a grand hotel entrance, three stories high, graced the center of an uninterrupted block of brick and stone Victorian storefronts. Large display windows on ground level faced Virginia Street, while those of the upper floors were shaded by brightly colored canopies. The entire streetscape, albeit charming, was on the surface only; the doors of these "storefronts" were in fact sealed shut, and their windows offered not glimpses of the building's interior, but shallow representations of Victorian era businesses including a railroad station and grocery. Iron lampposts, benches, and slender trees lined the sidewalk, but the intention behind these was not just aesthetic. Rather, such "people areas," developers predicted, would help to create not just a "pedestrian atmosphere," but a "world-class walking city," returning Reno to its earlier days when visitors from across the country delighted in the mix of people they encountered on the city's streets.[22]

And yet, despite its developers' voiced intentions to restore Reno to a "world-class walking city," the casino resort seemed unlikely to inspire strolls through the questionable downtown area. Linked by massive, opaque skyways to the flanking Eldorado and Circus Circus casinos and their accompanying hotel towers, the Silver Legacy, which opened to great fanfare on 28 July 1995, now formed the centerpiece of an "analogous city" that ultimately encompassed six city blocks. In this artificially illuminated world, described by Michael Branch as an "interiorized urban wilderness," guests of any of these three hotel casinos could visit a wide range of attractions without taking a single step outside.[23]

In 1999, the three linked casinos, all north of the railroad tracks, further consolidated their presence by promoting the "tri-plex" as "Uptown Reno," consciously invoking the term "uptown," as have other cities, to suggest an area more elegant and sophisticated than "downtown," and thereby manufacturing a distinction between their location and that of the surrounding businesses.[24] The combined attraction was described as "northern Nevada's unparalleled entertainment resort complex," containing "every amenity a guest may desire—all under one roof," including "more than 4,000 elegantly appointed rooms, 21 excellent restaurants, a health club and spa, a microbrewery, and nightly entertainment including top-name performers, world-class circus acts, a comedy club and a dazzling production show." By consolidating their resources, this new "tri-plex" had successfully bolstered the position of all three, hedging their bets in an unpredictable economy. At the same time, they provided their patrons with a patrolled, climate-controlled environment, safe from the elements as well as the denizens of the city's public streets.[25]

While the Silver Legacy was busy evoking its faux-historic narrative, other buildings central to Reno's true heritage were closing their doors. In 1994, the owners of the venerable Harolds Club, the institution that arguably put Reno's casinos on the map, announced plans to sell the historic club to an Atlantic City gaming corporation, which hoped to transform the cobbled together buildings into a $31 million Australian-themed hotel-casino called Harolds Club Down Under. The building closed for remodeling in 1995, but financing fell through, and Harolds Club never reopened. The next few years brought additional closures of both gaming and nongaming businesses. By April 1998, the vacant properties downtown included Gil's Casino, King's Inn Casino, Rivoli's Italian Restaurant, the Nevada Club, the Senator Hotel, Frontier Silver, the Virginian, Woolworth's, Jay's Jewelers, the Mapes, the Riverside, the Riverboat, the Holiday, and the Bundox Motel/Restaurant. In total, more than a dozen vacant hotels, restaurants, casinos, and stores could be found in the central 30-block area.[26]

Those who had witnessed Reno in brighter times were especially discouraged by this decline in Reno's "reputational capital," a marketing term that could be compared to Pierre Bourdieau's term "cultural capital," the desirable cultural attributes of a city, and yet applies also to attractions and attributes that might not fit under the traditional rubric of "culture," such as, in Reno's case, gambling or quick divorces.[27] In his 1997 memoir, former Chamber of Commerce head and tireless civic booster Jud Allen argued that Reno needed to diversify the city's tourist appeal and stabilize its existing attractions. "Otherwise," he predicted, "the closed Mapes, Riverside, Harolds Club and Horseshoe Club are a sign of things to come. It isn't too late to remedy the situation, but the clock does keep ticking." In mid-1999, Harry Spencer, a journalist and former casino promoter, reported, "That Reno probably bottomed out last year is the general consensus of those most involved in the crucial heart of Reno's image." Citing thirty-six vacant downtown businesses in January 1999, the *Gazette-Journal*'s John Stearns agreed, "Downtown no doubt needs a shot in the arm—a dose of something to halt the business decay. It contributes heavily to the city's image and personality."[28]

Their concerns were not unfounded; that March, an article in the *San Diego Union-Tribune* labeled Reno a "faded gambling town," referring to its visible homeless population and closed casinos. A large photograph accompanying the story depicted a homeless person peering into a garbage can on a deserted-looking Virginia Street. A writer for *Casino Executive*, a gaming industry publication, stated, "While Las Vegas has grown up to be the sophisticated big brother, Reno's image has remained rough-hewn. More the country cousin, it hasn't evolved far beyond the hub of dude ranches, quickie divorces, and dusty, rinky-dink casinos." He went on to criticize the city's "dingy, desultory properties . . . in which Reno's image as a grind town where the slot machine is God seems inescapable . . . and everywhere there are more low-slung, sleazy motels than you can shake a stickman at."[29]

With calls for renewal growing in both volume and vigor, the stage was set for more drastic measures, and soon the wrecking balls were making their way down Virginia Street, demolishing buildings that had lost their immediate utility to the city. After two years of negotiations, Harrah's completed its purchase of the neighboring Harolds Club and Nevada Club, where *Sister Act* had been filmed, in order to demolish the two and construct a "spectacular" addition. Of Harolds Club, a newspaper editorial asserted, "It is not architecturally significant. It no longer serves any useful business or tourist purpose, and this city desperately needs something new and exciting in this key location. Much the same can be said for the Nevada Club, which will also be torn down." With its enormous pioneer mural removed for safekeeping, demolition of Harolds began in August 1999.[30]

Other downtown properties seemed in clear danger of preemptive demolition to make way for future redevelopment projects, as the city had done in order to clear the property for the twelve-screen $10.5 million Century Riverside movie theater, which opened on the river in 1999. The strategy of clearing sites through condemnation and demolition in order to offer more attractive sites to prospective developers was common through the 1980s in urban sites from New York City's Times Square to the area in Baltimore where Camden Yards was going to be built. In Reno, demolition of closed riverside properties seemed increasingly likely in the mid-1990s as outside developers—including a group calling itself the River Renaissance Group and composed of developers from Newport Beach, California, Boise, and Seattle—began to express great interest in riverfront locations.[31]

Both the Mapes and the Riverside were natural targets; both had remained closed since the mid-1980s, both now stood boarded-up on highly desirable property, serving no economic purpose, and certainly bringing in no tourist revenue. In January 1996, a local newspaper article defining the two buildings as "The Heart of Reno's History" asked, "These grand dames have seen better days, but should the hotel-casinos be razed?" In separate interviews, Charles Mapes and Pick Hobson, the last owner of the Riverside, both predicted the end of the city's remaining small gaming operations with the opening of the Silver Legacy and the expansion of other large properties.[32]

In an attempt to resolve the stagnating situation, the city of Reno purchased the Mapes Hotel for $4 million in September 1996. Two years earlier, Mayor Pete Sferrazza, successor to Barbara Bennett, had asked the city council to do just that, through the use of redevelopment money from the new Silver Legacy project. It had been Sferrazza's hope that the city could then issue a request for proposals (RFP) to developers interested in renovating the building into an atrium hotel-casino, retaining its outer façade.[33] The city advertised an RFP in April 1997, setting the deadline for just two months later. On August 15, the National Trust for Historic Preservation suggested that a new RFP be targeted toward experts in rehabilitation, to no response. That September, the city awarded an exclusive negotiating contract to a San Diego–based development firm called OliverMcMillan, developers of the Century Riverside movie theater, and gave the company just sixty days to work with local preservationists to locate the estimated $7–10 million needed to make the existing building earthquake safe. The firm had already voiced skepticism over the feasibility of rehabilitation, expressing interest in replacing the Mapes with a $6 million retail and restaurant development.[34] When criticized by the State Historic Preservation Officer for setting such a short time frame and for favoring a developer with no restoration expertise, city manager Charles McNeely responded, "It will take substantial resources to save the Mapes. The question is: Who is going to pay for that? Everybody loves the building, but can we afford to do it?"[35]

Alerted that the clock was ticking, the National Trust for Historic Preservation placed the Mapes Hotel on its 1998 list of the Eleven Most Endangered Historic Places in America. It was the tenth anniversary of the list, which had in previous years included such diverse sites as the original Antietam Battlefield and the last original McDonald's restaurant in Downey, California. In the past, the national attention the list provided had encouraged cities to seek innovative solutions to preserve their threatened buildings, and no sites named to the list had been demolished. The trust described the Mapes as "a proud Art Deco landmark with excellent adaptive-reuse potential" and in June 1998, featured the building on a one-hour History Channel documentary called *America's Most Endangered Historic Places.*[36]

Supporters of the building's preservation breathed a collective sigh of relief that September, when Mayor Jeff Griffin announced that the future of the Mapes was finally secure, as OliverMcMillan and a Sparks construction company, QM Corp., announced a $46.6 million renovation plan. Griffin announced, "It is a historic day. It is a great day not only for the Mapes, it's a great day for the city of Reno. We will see the building reopened in its former glory." The announced renovation plans included retail shops and restaurants on ground level, a health club on the mezzanine, time share suites on floors two through nine, and a cocktail lounge and convention facilities on the top floor site of the original Sky Room.[37] *Sunset* magazine published a page-length celebratory feature reporting the successful efforts of local preservationists to save the building. The article evoked a golden era in Reno's history by recalling how "Reno's Mapes Hotel was always about more than gambling. Back when the Biggest Little City in the World truly was a little city, this art deco wonder . . . was Reno's premier place to see and be seen." Such references could do much to revive public memory of a time when Reno's elegance was unquestioned.[38]

Unfortunately, their celebrations were a bit premature. By February 1999, local preservationists were protesting the city's agreement with OliverMcMillan, who had announced that if the cost of renovation surpassed $22 million, his company planned to demolish the building. Word came that QM Corp. was finding the cost of renovation to be approximately $500,000 more than expected, with discoveries of additional amounts of asbestos, and contaminated water in the basement, as the result of a 1997 flood. According to a representative of OliverMcMillan, negative national publicity due to their possible plans to demolish the Mapes had had a "significant impact" on attracting tenants for their riverfront project.[39] Four months later, the company withdrew from the Mapes deal, saying it was just too expensive for a private company, and the city terminated the developer's agreement.

With the sudden demise of the renovation plan, supporters of the building's renovation realized that the Mapes was rapidly developing the reputation of a lost cause. As an editorial headline in the paper put it, "Mapes Needs a Savior: Now."[40] In June 1999, National Trust president Richard Moe pledged his support for the effort to secure funding and find a new, "preservation-minded" developer to restore the building. Referring to the trust's list of Endangered Historic Places, Moe reiterated, "The National Trust has not yet lost a site that has been named to this national listing—and we do not want the Mapes to become the first." The ire of the preservationists increased when they found that the city had not applied for $3 million in historic tax credits while blaming the loss of such credits, in part, for their inability to restore the building.[41]

The city council set a new deadline, just a month away, for submission of new proposals, requiring that a $100,000 deposit accompany any plans for development. Only two proposals submitted by the August deadline included the required $100,000 deposit, and three others that did not were eliminated immediately. The two acceptable submissions were both from California-based developers; one proposed transforming the building into a combination of gaming and apartment suites, luxury apartments, or senior housing; the other, Nationwide Capital Services, a San Francisco–area company that had previously renovated a 1920s era hotel in San Jose, proposed converting it into a 204-unit retirement home.[42]

The Reno City Council was not impressed. Acting as the redevelopment agency, the group met on 13 September, discussed the proposals, and rejected them all, voting 5–2 to demolish the Mapes. In his comments, Mayor Griffin said, "It's time to let go of this thing. There is no white knight." In response, Nationwide Capital Services offered the city a nonrefundable deposit of $100,000 in exchange for an extension of four months to complete a market study of its proposal. However, members of the council voiced their unwillingness to relive the experience of having a developer pull out after determining its plan to be unfeasible. Council member Dave Rigdon said that demolition and subsequent sale of the site would be the best way for the city to get back the money it had given to the redevelopment agency. An offer two weeks later by Nationwide to forgo the market study, purchase the Mapes outright, pay off the city's $2.5 million debt to the former owner, and commence construction of senior housing within four months was also rejected. Council members expressed a feeling of weariness with the process.[43]

Preservationists were shocked. In a telephone interview, Richard Moe said, "In over 10 years and 100 sites, we never lost one. This will be a black mark for Reno." Reno resident and preservation supporter Scott Gibson warned the council, "You're going to spend $1 million to create a vacant lot. Don't think this is going to open the floodgates of development." One Reno resident wrote in a letter to the editor, "The designers of the Silver Legacy built a whole façade of historic buildings along Virginia Street that are modern-day reproductions of an era. Isn't it a paradox that one group tries to reproduce a historic era while down the street others are trying to tear down the real thing?"[44]

Over the next few months, the controversy escalated into a dramatic series of lawsuits, temporary reprieves, editorial page debates, court-ordered delays, protests, and petitions, but the transformation of the building into a symbol of the city's past failures seemed complete. To many city leaders and residents, the Mapes had come to represent Reno's troubled past and deteriorating reputation, and the drive to destroy it and start afresh became something of a psychological need, in order for the city to embrace an unclouded future. A newspaper editorial voiced approval of the demolition plan, saying the Mapes had become "the city's albatross, an obstacle to every effort to restore life to its urban core, the source of never-ending arguments and a drain on the Reno Redevelopment Agency's finances—and the city's energy." Once the tides had turned, it seemed that any new proposals could only be interpreted negatively. Responding to a proposal from the Washoe County commissioners that they purchase the Mapes and renovate it into new offices, the *Gazette-Journal*'s editorial board wrote that there was "no guarantee" voters would have supported the financing in a public vote, and "there was no reason to believe" that the Nationwide plan would be any more successful than the previous developer's.[45] As City Councilman Tom Herndon said that December, "It's unfortunate that the Mapes has become the poster child for redevelopment, but the fact is, it's got to go."[46]

The building's symbolism was made even clearer in the discussion of its imminent demolition. In the 1990s, Las Vegas raised the marketing of destruction to a high art, accompanying the implosion of the Dunes in October 1993 with a fireworks display and securing hundreds of thousands of spectators, not to mention inclusion in the 1995 Martin Scorsese film, *Casino.*[47] Writing of plans to demolish Harolds Club in late 1999, John Stearns of the *Reno Gazette-Journal* commented, "Sounds like good TV to me. Downtown Reno needs all the out-with-the-old-in-with-the-new publicity it can get. Las Vegas has done well getting its implosions on TV. They're bigger blasts of bigger properties, but a good, old-fashioned explosion in Reno—no matter what size—ought to get its share of coverage."[48] Harolds Club went first, demolished just after 2:00 a.m. on 15 December. "It was time for Harolds to go," wrote Stearns, "and the implosion sent a powerful statement that change is in the air for a downtown in serious need of improvement."[49] City council member Sherrie Doyle advocated scheduling the demolition of the Mapes for New Year's Eve, saying "It would be symbolic. I see it as a celebration" that could possibly attract media attention and even Hollywood filmmakers.[50]

The imminent demolition did prompt a flurry of national press. The *New York Times* cited the impatience of Reno city officials at all the attention being paid to the Mapes rather than to Reno's successful redevelopment efforts. It was a complaint oddly reminiscent of a local businessman's claim, nearly 100 years earlier, that outsiders were focusing only on Reno's scandalous qualities rather than its new Y.M.C.A. building. Standing on an upper floor of the Mapes, Mayor Griffin announced, "This is not a grand building."[51] National critics of the demolition plan disagreed. In an "open letter to the people of Reno" published in the local paper, National Trust head Richard Moe wrote, "Great cities don't destroy great buildings; they certainly don't 'celebrate' the destruction with a party on Super Bowl Sunday. The Mapes is unquestionably a great building, a welcome grace-note in a downtown which, like that of too many other American cities, has seen much of its character smothered under a shroud of glass, aluminum and concrete." The editorial board of the *New York Times* appeared to agree. "The destruction of this building," they argued, "will mean a significant loss of architectural and community heritage in a city undergoing swift transformation, a transformation that should make a national landmark like the Mapes all the more valuable." The venerable paper's disapproving tone did not go unnoticed back in Reno; as city spokesman Chris Good stated a few days later, "We like the idea of getting on the New York Times editorial page, but not this way."[52]

Ultimately, the debate over the Mapes boiled down to a competition between two competing value systems, and the one with the most economic and political power won. On the morning of 30 January 2000—Super Bowl Sunday—an estimated crowd of ten thousand curious onlookers gathered on the streets of downtown Reno. Over a loudspeaker, a countdown began, and the crowd joined in, chanting down the numbers until they hit zero, at which point a series of explosions blasted the morning air. The Mapes remained standing for a few seconds, prompting cheers from a small group of people. But then it imploded, dramatically falling down, to massive cheering. Within fifteen seconds, it was over, all twelve stories reduced to a two-story pile of rubble.[53] Months later, in a haiku contest in the local paper, one citizen would capture the mood of the advocates of preservation that day in a morose haiku: "See the Mapes come down / It is Superbowl Sunday / Go Rams Go Rams Go."[54] Caught up in the redevelopment frenzy of the 1990s, the Mapes, like many historic buildings throughout the country, was ultimately deemed expendable in the desperate quest for reinvention.

With the building gone, both attention and symbolism now shifted to what would replace it on the prime riverfront property, and all agreed it should be something impressive. Advertising executive Mark Curtis wrote, "Why not make the Expo center or whatever goes on the Mapes site the next Sydney Opera House, the next Guggenheim? Every great city has at least a few beautiful buildings that literally define them." An editorial agreed, "At this stage in its history, Reno simply cannot afford mediocrity; it cannot afford to think small; it cannot afford a building that generates yawns instead of wows. Anything less than a building that excites—surprises, in fact—would be considered a failure and forever doom the city's efforts to bring people back to its downtown. To build a building that is not visionary would be to waste everything the city already has done to rebuild its downtown."[55]

Unfortunately for such idealists, and for the advocates of preemptive demolition, no such plans materialized. During a retreat in January 2003, almost three years to the day after the Mapes came down, and in the absence of any feasible revenue-generating development proposals for the site, the city council decided to construct a public plaza there, perhaps with an ice skating rink, fountains, trees, a small coffee shop or bookstore, and an extension of the River Walk. Construction of the plaza began in March 2005. By summer 2008, the site featured a smattering of grass and trees, a large concrete slab that housed a seasonal ice skating rink in the winter and a weekly farmers' market in the summer, and an art installation cosponsored by the city's Historical Resources Commission and Arts and Culture Commission, displaying images of the Mapes and other historical structures that had graced the immediate vicinity through the years. Plans to add one or more retail and restaurant buildings and a massive canopy atop the ice rink to the site remained stalled.[56]

The Riverside Hotel, located across the river, had better luck. Although slated for demolition by the city council in 1997 and put into the hands of the Reno Redevelopment Agency, local preservationists had been working independently to locate funding for the building's restoration. Beginning that year, the Sierra Arts Foundation, a local nonprofit, encouraged Artspace, Inc., a nonprofit developer located in Minneapolis, to look at the building. The company had previously worked on three artist loft projects and renovated a number of historic theaters, mostly in the Twin Cities area. Artspace embraced the opportunity, and in late 1997, went into partnership with OliverMcMillan, who planned to renovate the ground floor with restaurants and shops, while Artspace would convert the upper floors into artist lofts. The partners submitted a joint proposal in February 1998, and the Reno City Council, sitting in their role as the Reno Redevelopment Agency, accepted it.[57]

In 1999, the Sierra Arts Foundation bought the building from the city for $350,000 and entered into a $7.9 million partnership with Artspace to create artist lofts subsidized by the federal Housing and Urban Development department. This allowed the building's operators to charge rents ranging from $297 to $634 for lofts ranging in area from approximately 700 to 1,400 square feet. In their renovation work, the project's architects located and utilized the original 1920s-era plans by architect Frederick De-Longchamps. Funding came from a variety of sources; historic and low-income tax credits provided more than $4 million, and a federal disaster-recovery grant, state cultural grant, and federal home grant provided another $2.2 million. Construction began in 2000, and the thirty-five-unit Riverside Artist Lofts opened that November.[58] The building received the 2001 James C. Howland Award for Urban Enrichment from the National League of Cities and a 2000 Tourism Development Award at the 2000 Governor's Conference in Reno.[59]

This success ensured that the building would survive, but the public memory of the prominent role it had once played was clearly fading as the population aged. The Riverside, the Washoe County Courthouse, and the Virginia Street Bridge still clustered together at the southern edge of downtown, but their former status as nationally recognized icons of Reno's divorce trade was mostly forgotten. Unmarked at the site, their cultural significance mainly reemerged when writers summoned up their colorful past, or when they came in imminent danger of demolition. The Virginia Street Bridge, listed on the National Register of Historic Places in 1980, was increasingly threatened with demolition over concern that its low arches blocked the river's flow in the event of major downtown flooding, therefore contributing to water damage of surrounding properties. Five years after a major downtown flood in 1997, an article about statewide efforts to protect Reno's divorce landmarks, including a few remaining former divorce ranches, appeared on the front page of the *New York Times*. With references to the ring-flinging and column-kissing tales, Walter Winchell's "Reno-vation" columns, and scandalous ranch romances, the article demonstrated how an aspect of the city's history formerly considered controversial and even possibly immoral might be transformed through the course of time and changing national mores into a colorful, even quaint historical attraction. And yet, focused on its reinvention efforts, city officials seemed uninterested in pursuing such a course, while the bridge languished, neglected and crumbling.[60]

Of greater concern to Reno's city government and business community was the future of the local gaming industry. The fate of the Mapes and the Riverside had finally been resolved, but many of downtown's remaining casinos were in dire straits, as competition among the nation's gaming destinations became fierce. By March 2001, legalized gaming in some form had reached forty-eight states, and Indian gaming in particular was increasing at an exponential rate. Its competitive threat to Reno seemed immediate and irreversible, as demonstrated by an increasing visitor overlap. A 1998 profile study of visitors to Reno released in 1999 found that 25 percent of visitors had gambled in an Indian casino over the past year, in comparison to 19 percent in 1997 and only 3 percent in 1993. In 1999, California legalized casino-style gambling on the state's Indian reservations, and by January 2003, fifty Indian casinos were operating throughout the state of California. In autumn 2002, the United Auburn Indian Community began construction of its $215 million Thunder Valley Indian Casino near Sacramento, halfway between Reno and its primary drive-up market, the San Francisco Bay Area. The resort opened in June 2003.[61]

In the increasingly competitive climate of the new millennium, downtown Reno's smaller casinos continued to falter. After the Flamingo Reno closed in October 2001, reporter John Stearns wrote, under the headline "Downtown Is Like a Bad Halloween Movie," "Clearly, 604 empty rooms and a dark casino hurt a section of town already identified with worn surroundings, worn women of the evening and, as one former Flamingo employee put it, 'pharmaceutical' vendors." The Flamingo was the eleventh casino, and the largest, to close downtown since 1995. Besides Harolds Club and the Nevada Club, the others included the Pioneer Inn, the Colonial Inn Hotel and Casino, the Comstock, the Holiday, the Horseshoe Club, the Virginian, the Speakeasy, and the Riverboat. Within just a few years, many had either been demolished or converted to other uses. Harrah's Reno created an outdoor plaza on the former Nevada Club and Harolds Club sites, deferring the promised development of its "spectacular" addition; the Cal-Neva reopened the Virginian and turned the Riverboat into a convention center; the Colonial Inn Hotel and Casino became a timeshare; and the Comstock Hotel-Casino reopened as the Comstock Apartments, offering weekly rates, with an antiques emporium spanning the entire first floor.[62]

The Pioneer Inn Hotel and Casino closed its doors in 2000 after thirty-two years of business, remaining boarded up for seventeen months before being demolished to make room for a parking lot. (Photograph by the author)

Of the two older casino properties that reopened as new hotel-casinos, neither was doing especially well at the beginning of 2003. In July 2001, Barney Ng completed his $54 million renovation of the Holiday Hotel into an attractive "boutique" Tuscan-themed hotel casino, the Siena Hotel Spa Casino. Upscale, with an elegant restaurant, wine cellar, and extensive spa facilities, the Siena nonetheless suffered financially upon its opening. In the fiscal year that ended in June 2002, the Siena's casino department lost $2.4 million, making it the first hotel that the county appraiser had ever seen lose money in its casino.[63] The Golden Phoenix Hotel Casino and Resort, rising from the ashes of the Flamingo Reno, opened in November 2002, but by February 2003 was struggling, with income falling far below projected figures.[64]

However, not all the news was bad for Reno's gaming community. The larger operations were holding their own, from the "uptown" triumvirate, to Harrah's, to the Club Cal-Neva. Southeast of downtown, the former MGM Grand, which had become Bally's, changed owners again in 1992, becoming the Reno Hilton. A self-contained megalith, the Hilton housed its own conventions and events, along with a movie theater, boutiques, showrooms, and an array of popular restaurants. Further south, the hotel towers of the Clarion and the Peppermill rose high above the surrounding commercial district, thriving from their proximity to the Reno-Sparks Convention Center.

As one of the state's foundational industries, gambling was not going away, and yet city leaders were eager to convey the message that Reno offered so much more. Complementing the diversification goals of the city's redevelopment agency was the mission of the Reno-Sparks Convention and Visitors Authority (RSCVA) to promote outward recognition of this diversifying landscape. In an era of reinvention, Reno's marketing efforts achieved greater importance, and greater sophistication, than ever. Destination branding had become big business, and Reno's tarnished "brand" was in need of some serious rehabilitation. With a goal of establishing a more appealing, distinctly unique identity for Reno that did not begin and end with gaming, the rebranding effort got under way.[65] An important initial task was to determine precisely how the Biggest Little City was being perceived from the outside. In the late 1990s, a series of focus groups conducted in Los Angeles, Chicago, and Dallas, in addition to surveys of gamers in Reno's core markets of northern California and the Pacific Northwest, revealed to the RSCVA that governing perceptions of Reno/Lake Tahoe were both negative and inaccurate. As the study reported, "Respondents were unaware of the destination's outdoor activities, proximity to the Sierra Nevada Mountain range and seasonal climate."[66]

This gave the RSCVA a clear place to begin. In order to correct such oversights, the agency invited journalists from out of town to visit Reno, to explore the entire area, not just downtown, and hopefully, to become inspired to write positive stories about the city. During one such visit by eight journalists from Southern California markets in January 2000, many admitted to great surprise at how nice Reno was; one was shocked to find that Reno was not simply "the dirty cousin of Las Vegas that you don't talk about."[67] The series of studies also revealed one of Reno's most valuable, and least recognized, assets to be its natural setting. As Chamber of Commerce staff analyst Dave Howard noted, "What we have . . . that Vegas doesn't are mountains, clean air, snowy slopes, and more temperate weather." In order to promote these advantages, and the recreational opportunities they enabled, a Regional Marketing Committee made up of the RSCVA, the Incline Village/Crystal Bay Visitors Bureau, Reno-Sparks hotels, and other northern Nevada agencies formed in June 2001 to develop new markets for what they now referred to as the "Reno-Tahoe area." The conflation of Reno and Tahoe had a precedent in the 1994 naming of the Reno-Tahoe International Airport, formerly called the Reno-Cannon International Airport after former U.S. senator Howard Cannon. In a final assertion of confidence in the area's natural assets, fundraising began to support a Reno-Tahoe bid for the 2014 winter Olympics. Although far more sophisticated in its goals and strategies, this campaign made manifest Reno's efforts to link their town with Lake Tahoe more than a century earlier. At that time, outdoor recreation was in its infancy; now it was a multimillion dollar industry recognized as one of Reno's chief assets. Finally the interest matched the landscape's potential.[68]

New marketing strategies cleverly incorporated the new image with previous promotions. In 2001, the RSCVA introduced a tagline, "Bet You Didn't Know," replacing an earlier campaign that had labeled Reno "The Treasure of the Sierra Madre," a line that did not seem to resonate with prospective visitors. According to the RSCVA, the new slogan acknowledged Reno's dominant reputation as a gambling town, while encouraging visitors to "take another look at Reno/Lake Tahoe and all that this great area has to offer."[69] Variations of the print advertisements targeted different markets. For the San Francisco Bay Area, a photograph of Lake Tahoe's Emerald Bay tacked over an image of the Golden Gate Bridge featured the line, "Visit Our Bay Area." An advertisement targeting Palm Springs featured a photograph of a verdant golf course tacked over an image of prickly cactus, with the tagline "High Desert Golf without Low Desert Heat," a not-so-subtle dig at frequently-scorching Las Vegas.

The RSCVA described this de-emphasis of gaming as a "repositioning" of the "destination brand," adopting a "community vision" for 2010 "to become a premier, four-season, recreation, resort and meeting destination with the added value of gaming and entertainment." By framing gaming as an "added value," in what is known as a "gaming-plus" strategy, and not the primary attraction, the RSCVA implemented an interesting reversal of an increasingly common strategy pursued by other cities, in which casino attractions were added to existing tourist destinations as part of larger urban revitalization schemes.[70] Nationally, this urban trend toward the construction of so-called "fantasy cities" had begun to successfully incorporate, in the words of John Hannigan, "an infrastructure of casinos, megaplex cinemas, themed restaurants, simulation theaters, interactive theme rides and virtual reality arcades which collectively promise to change the face of leisure in the postmodern metropolis." With the National Bowling Stadium's IMAX theater, the Riverside movie megaplex, casinos, restaurants, themed attractions like the Silver Legacy, and other components including the river, the landscape of downtown Reno might begin to approximate a smaller scale version of cityscapes in Times Square, downtown Pittsburgh, and Toronto, where public-private partnerships transformed formerly rundown urban districts into dynamic, entertainment-oriented spaces. Although coming at it from opposite directions, the two trends both seemed likely to result in downtown areas featuring a similar mix of gaming and nongaming attractions.[71]

Further research into national travel trends inspired the RSCVA to take their de-emphasis of gaming even further. In 2001 its analysts noted studies that Americans were traveling more than ever with their families and were interested in outdoor recreation as well as art and cultural attractions.[72] They responded in April 2002 with the introduction of a new print and television campaign labeling the Reno-Tahoe area "America's Adventure Place," a phrase not much different from "The Recreational Center of America," Reno's slogan of choice in the 1920s and early 1930s. The new slogan was meant to encompass the area's offerings in four areas—skiing, golfing, arts and culture, and adventure sports—with gaming as an "added attraction." One of the "strategic objectives" of the 2002–2003 Marketing and Sales Plan was to "continue the RSCVA vision to change the positioning of Reno-Sparks/Lake Tahoe from a 'Gaming-Plus' destination in 2002–2003 to an 'Adventure-Plus' destination by 2004–2005 with gaming being positioned just as another kind of adventure."[73] Sensing the turning of the tide, some of Reno's casinos began to tap into the market for outdoor tourism by opening "adventure desks" in their casinos to promote activities like hiking, kayaking, river rafting, and mountain biking.

With three of the city's four new marketing themes revolving around outdoor recreation, Reno's promoters took full advantage of the complete reversal of nineteenth-century attitudes toward Nevada's environment. What was once a huge liability—the region's combination of wide open spaces and aridity—had become one of its most valuable attributes. The soaring popularity of outdoor recreation and adventure tourism had transformed northern Nevada's rugged, inhospitable, and largely uninhabited terrain into the biggest asset of all, attracting practitioners of kayaking, mountain biking, telemarking, rafting, trail running, soaring, and other outdoor sports. This trend seemed likely to continue as the relentless

"America's Adventure Place," a new campaign introduced in 2002 by the Reno-Sparks Convention and Visitors Authority (RSCVA), linked Reno with Lake Tahoe and highlighted the great outdoors. (Reno-Sparks Convention and Visitors Authority)

march of urbanization across the country only served to emphasize what made the Reno area so unique. A 2004 RSCVA travel planner tried to convey this singularity, with the expected hyperbole: "Day or night, indoors or out—winter, spring, summer or fall—Reno-Tahoe is filled with adventures. There's no other place like it on the planet."[74]

With its emphasis on outdoor activities, the branding of Reno-Tahoe as "America's Adventure Place" also intended to reverse a troubling demographic trend: a steady increase in the average age of visitors to the area. From 1994 to 2005, the percentage of visitors between the ages of 31–40 dropped 10 percentage points to a new low of 9 percent while the percent of visitors aged 61–70 rose 5 percentage points to 24 percent. By 2005, the average age of visitors to Reno was 57, two years older than that of the previous year.[75] Down south, Las Vegas was also adjusting its target demographic, with the adoption of the slogan, "What Happens Here Stays Here," in late 2002. Co-created by the Las Vegas Convention & Visitors Authority (LVCVA) and its marketing partners, the memorable campaign positioned Las Vegas as "a mecca of adult freedom" as opposed to the family destination of the previous decade.[76] With such distinct rebranding campaigns, the two Nevada resort towns were finally projecting distinctly different images; precisely how visitors would respond to both remained to be seen.

The official de-emphasis of gaming on the part of the RSCVA was in keeping with new findings that determined that only 14 percent of Reno's tourists in 2006 visited town primarily for the gambling (although 91 percent did gamble at some point during their trip). Of the remaining 86 percent of tourists not visiting Reno primarily to gamble, some came for business purposes or conventions, others to visit family members, and others for different reasons entirely. Even those staying at the casinos spent proportionately less on gambling than on other amenities.[77] In fiscal year 2006, only 54.4 percent of the profits for Washoe County's casino resorts derived from gambling; the rest was spent on restaurants, hotel rooms, gift shops, spas, entertainment, and the like.[78] Having long lost its status as the first name in gambling, Reno no longer placed gambling first.

With its other signature industries fading into the past, the city no longer summoned up a universal image. Reno's reputation, although frequently changing, had always proceeded in identifiable phases as the community catapulted from obscurity to fame to infamy. In the nineteenth century, the little junction was unfamiliar to most, a fleeting name glimpsed in block letters on a railroad station, or a brief reference in a newspaper story about a mining deal, or perhaps some fellow's irrigation plans. As the twentieth century barreled in, unhappy spouses and an avid public were drawn to the Biggest Little City in the World, that scandalous playground teeming with socialites and speakeasies, prizefights and prostitutes. With gambling legally sanctioned once and for all, Reno made headlines as an entertainment capital, all flashy casinos, lively divorce ranches, and glamorous showrooms. And then, as Reno's lights began to fade, the consensus was also clear: its days in the limelight were over—time to head to Vegas where the fun never ended. It was not necessary to visit Reno to know what Reno was all about, or so it was widely believed.

However, as the new millennium began, identifying governing perceptions of Reno became a bit more difficult. Reno's reputation had fractured, but not necessarily to the city's detriment. Instead, evidence now suggested that a splintered reputation, like a diversified economy, could perhaps be even more advantageous in the long run. Confirmation was found in the numbers of tourists visiting Reno for completely different reasons in the early 2000s than in decades past. In the late twentieth century, as the city's casinos struggled and redevelopment ground slowly onward, a number of local groups, working independently of each other, had concocted a spectrum of special events that together began to attract hundreds of thousands of visitors to Reno per year. The members of each group tended to view Reno primarily through the lens of a particular interest, something that had always been true, and yet now, more of these interests were shared by substantial numbers of visitors and residents alike, creating a convergence of outsider and insider impressions that was, perhaps for the first time, largely free of tension, conflict, or a local sense of injustice among residents for having been misunderstood yet again.

Almost invariably, the growing media coverage of Reno's newer attractions referred in some way to the city's quest for reinvention, increasingly describing that effort as successful. The offbeat Tour de Nez, a three-day "celebration of cycling," complete with a pro series and century rides, gained national attention for its origins as a party thrown by two avid cyclists who owned a coffeehouse in Reno called the Deux Gros Nez. In 2006, CNN called the festival, which prominently features mint juleps on the sidelines, "one of the most popular cycling events in the West" and interviewed one of its publicists who admitted, "It doesn't hurt that Reno is trying to reposition itself as an outdoor adventure place."[79]

The reinvention of the Truckee River as an outdoor adventure asset continued with the construction of the $1.5 million Truckee River Whitewater Park in 2004. Located on a stretch right in the middle of downtown Reno, the park boasts a class 2 to 3 kayak slalom racing course, eleven drop pools along its half-mile length, and an annual Reno River Festival that began to draw an estimated 30,000 attendees each May. In a March 2006 article titled "Reno Revival," a writer for *Canoe & Kayak* wrote, "The Truckee River Whitewater Park symbolizes the city's scrubbed-up new image," presenting that civic transformation as a done deal.[80]

Other area events capitalizing on Reno's climate and gaining favorable national publicity ranged from the Reno-Tahoe Open, a PGA tour event founded in 1999, to the Great Balloon Race, an event drawing approximately 100 hot air balloonists and more than 150,000 spectators to a northwest Reno park each September.[81] The National Championship Air

Races, founded in 1964, takes over a small airport 8 miles north of Reno every year, just a week after the balloon event, featuring races by six classes of aircraft, from biplanes and modified World War II fighters to high performance kit-built aircraft and Formula One speedsters.

To some, Reno has remained a place to experience the traditions of the Old West. Rodeo fans have come to know it as the site of the fourth richest Professional Rodeo Cowboys Association (PRCA) tour rodeo in the country. Founded in 1919, the Reno Rodeo draws over 120,000 fans each June. In 2006 the famous Harolds Club pioneer mural was reassembled and installed on the back of one of the rodeo grandstands, making it clearly visible to drivers along the interstate. Aficionados of another facet of the American West know Reno for the Coeur d'Alene art auction, the largest auction of western American art in the country. More than 800 collectors and dealers attend each July, and their pockets are deep; featuring works by such icons as cowboy artist Charles Russell and Albert Bierstadt, the 2007 auction sold just over $35 million worth of art. "Over the last two decades," wrote a reporter after covering the event for the *New York Times*, "it has become the most important annual event for collectors of Western art and a benchmark for this market as a whole."[82]

Other slices of the American population know Reno best through events ranging from Hot August Nights, an annual weeklong tribute to classic cars and culture of the 1950s and 1960s, to September's annual motorcycle rally, Street Vibrations. On the other side of the spectrum, the city serves as the supply station and jumping off point for the Burning Man Festival, a countercultural celebration of artistic and personal expression held each Labor Day weekend on the playa of the Black Rock Desert, approximately 100 miles to the north.

Many of these activities are relatively new, but some are long established and visible year-round. Reno is still home to the streamlined wedding, with marriage licenses available at the county courthouse from 8 a.m. to midnight, seven days a week, with no waiting period or blood test required for couples eager to tie the knot. The Park Wedding Chapel across from the courthouse has been torn down, but one need not look far to find a wedding chapel in the downtown area; some, like the Chapel of the Bells on Fourth Street, which opened in 1962, even offer drive-through ceremonies.

As more nationally recognized reasons to visit the city proliferated, gambling became even less central to Reno's overall tourism profile. At the same time, the visibility of gaming in downtown Reno was shrinking noticeably in the early 2000s. Although a direct result of economic hardship for the local casino industry, this trend also coincided with redevelopment goals. In December 2002, the city council endorsed a new 81-page comprehensive report that compiled all nineteen existing redevelopment plans under the title "Downtown—Putting It All Together." The plan identified, as its two fundamental principles, the need to diversify the economy and the need to make the downtown area attractive to both visitors and residents. In order to do this, the three areas given priority through 2005 were enhancement of the river corridor; development of an entertainment events center/retail complex; and promotion of increased residential activity downtown.[83]

All three goals were evoked in the emergence of an incipient cultural district just a few blocks west of the Riverside Artist Lofts by late 2000. Anchoring the modest district were a number of art galleries, coffeehouses, salons, and boutiques, one block removed from the river. Just as Reno had followed larger cities into periods of blight and redevelopment, it now joined the urban trend of nurturing and promoting a cultural arts district, as had cities like Tucson and Dallas back in the 1980s.[84] With the assistance of the city's Redevelopment Agency, local business owners compiled a shopping guide and map, naming the area the "River Walk" and labeling it "Reno's hippest downtown neighborhood." As the River Walk Merchants, the group began to organize events including a regular wine walk. Referring to their efforts as part of a "downtown revival," a local newspaper editorial lauded the district, saying "It's small business, after all, that gives a city its character, that lets it stand out from all the rest of the cities in the world, that makes it a community where people want to live, work and play."[85] This cultural mission was bolstered by the founding in 1996 of Artown, a monthlong, citywide summer arts festival held each July. In 2000, the Artown festival won the prestigious International Downtown Association "Redevelopment Event of the Year" award, as well as a Nevada's Governor's Arts Award.[86]

In the same cultural vein, Reno received a flurry of positive coverage with the opening of the new $16 million Nevada Museum of Art, located just a few blocks south of the river, in spring 2003.[87] Designed by Phoenix architect Will Bruder, the dramatic four-story structure was covered in black zinc sheets meant to evoke the Black Rock desert to the north. Under an astonished headline announcing, "Architecture in Reno (and Not a Casino)," a *New York Times* writer described the structure as "a spectacular chunk of black desert rock that mysteriously landed amid the patchwork of office blocks, parking lots and wedding chapels of downtown Reno." But his praise was not comprehensive, as he labeled the museum "a dark and elegant riposte to the garish, neon-lighted casino district less than half a mile away."[88]

However, that main casino district was undergoing some radical changes as well. The resident-initiated success of the Riverside Hotel and its concentration of the city's artistic community enabled a number of developments that began to reestablish a clear nongambling presence downtown, a presence that the city increasingly began to support. In March 2001, the *Christian Science Monitor* described Reno as a city where "a tree-lined river gurgles through a downtown brimming with redeveloped artists lofts, bohemian music venues, and first-rate galleries. It even has a serene university that could double for any in the Ivy League." The aesthetic value of the latter had long been recognized, as the original campus quadrangle, with its many nineteenth-century brick buildings, was designated a National Historic District in 1987, while the university itself had grown to approximately 16,000 students and nine degree-granting colleges. But just a few years earlier, locals might have doubted that the rest of Reno's central district could evoke such a glowing description.[89]

In a unique twist on adaptive reuse, developers began to transform some of Reno's failed hotel casinos into condominiums, as other postindustrial cities might do with spacious older warehouses or factory buildings. This new real estate trend breathed a second, and sometimes a third life into former casinos and their high-rise hotel towers. The Comstock Apartments, already altered from its previous incarnation as the Comstock Hotel and Casino, was completely overhauled and reopened in 2005 as the Riverwalk Towers condominiums. The Golden Phoenix, formerly the Flamingo Hilton, was completely gutted in 2007 in preparation for its transformation into a luxurious condominium property called the Montage. A new condo called the Palladio was built from the ground up along the river, and even the enormous Reno Hilton—the original MGM Grand—joined the trend after gaining new ownership and reopening as the Grand Sierra Resort, a hotel and casino featuring luxury condos high in its tower. Driven not by avid consumer demand but by the need to transform former casinos into something more in keeping with the city's new goals, it was not clear how successful this trend ultimately would be, but the improved aesthetics of those properties was noticed immediately.

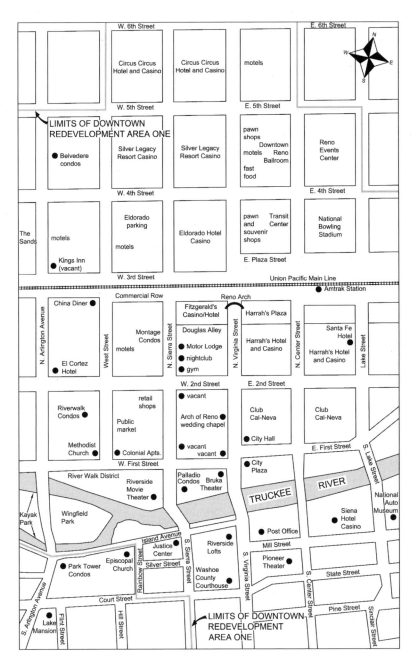

Selected landmarks of downtown Reno, 2008

Writers across the country continued to highlight Reno's diversifying downtown. In a January 2006 article, Suzette Parmley of the *Philadelphia Inquirer* highlighted Reno's new downtown casino-condo conversions, eight of which were either finished or in progress at the time. "While Las Vegas to the south tears down casinos to make way for bigger casinos," she wrote, "Reno has been trying to reinvent itself as competition for gamblers has increased. At the same time, Reno's experience shows how a city can grow beyond gambling."[90] That July, an article published nationwide through the Associated Press asserted, "Reno Has Much to Offer Besides Gambling," specifically mentioning Artown, outdoor recreational opportunities, and the city's proximity to Lake Tahoe. As a reporter for the *Sacramento Bee* explained, "while you weren't paying close attention, Reno blossomed beyond slot machines and blackjack tables. The 'biggest little city' has branched out with world-class attractions and festivals to add to the natural charms of its location along the Truckee River and within the mountains."[91]

More and more, major publications across the country picked up the theme of Reno's reinvention, citing the city's most familiar industries only in order to emphasize the shift away from them. In July 2003, the *New York Times* ran a short article with the headline, "In Reno; City Known for Gambling Works to Reinvent Itself."[92] Although cautioning, "Old reputations die slowly," a Reuters article instructed its readers, "Forget about casinos, quick divorces and legalized prostitution (permitted only in the adjacent counties anyway); Reno today promotes itself as a land of economic opportunity where the unemployment rate is just 3.5 percent." The story quoted a recent transplant from California who said, "Reno has still got this stigma," but continued, reassuringly, "once you come here and spend a couple of days here it goes away."[93]

Diversifying business had positive repercussions for the nontourist economy. For a long time, Reno's troubled reputation had forced executives to convince prospective employees that the residential population did not spend all their free time in the casinos. The local business community also suffered from published national rankings that regularly attributed to Nevada the highest rates of high school dropouts, suicide, firearms deaths, and teenage pregnancy. Such statistics were seen as damaging not just to Reno's tourism industry, but to its continuing effort to secure new residents.[94] Understandably, then, local businesses were thrilled when *Inc.* magazine ranked Reno first among 274 metropolitan areas for doing business in 2005. Rankings were based on a variety of factors including rates of job growth over the past decade, affordability of housing, low labor costs, and lower taxes. Calling Reno an "entrepreneurial hotbed," the article described a shift in the new economy from high-tech centers like Silicon Valley and Austin, Texas, to midsized cities like Reno and Boise (which ranked second). The same magazine ranked the Reno-Sparks area fifth for midsized cities and twenth-fifth overall in 2006.[95]

As others began to recognize Reno as an attractive site for business, the increasing cost of living on the Pacific coast prompted something of a migration from California to Nevada. The state that had for so long been criticized for its harsh physical climate was now receiving praise for its favorable economic climate. The Reno-Sparks area also did well in the annual "Best Performing Cities" ranking by the Milken Institute's Best Performing Cities Index, ranking number 21 out of 379 metropolitan areas in 2005, five slots higher than the previous year's ranking.[96]

Momentum seemed to be shifting in the desired direction, with increasingly favorable reviews of Reno not only as a tourist destination but as a place to live and work. The chorus was far from unanimous, of course; many observers continued to point out Reno's flaws, particularly its visible indigent population, its bane of seedy weekly-rate motels, and a tenacious methamphetamine problem. And yet, in comparison to the virtual dearth of positive press Reno had received over the preceding two decades, the overall refrain was heartening.

Residents were quick to attribute this encouraging trend to the combination of an intense rebranding campaign and successful redevelopment initiatives, and these processes did, no doubt, play a central role. With the downtown district representing the whole of Reno in so many minds, its gradually improving appearance could not help but reflect well upon perceptions of the entire city; likewise, the power of marketing in a media age could not be underestimated. At the same time, the cultivation of so many alternate reasons besides the old to visit Reno, and possibly even to stay there, brought impressions of the "real Reno" and the "tourist Reno" closer than they had been in a very long time. After a long and storied history in which Reno's reputation appeared to be the driving factor behind so many marketing and developmental decisions, perhaps that reputation had finally been tamed, and could finally be controlled.

Local officials claimed that the new branding campaign was working in 2007 after *National Geographic Adventure* magazine included a short feature on the many recreational activities available in Reno in January 2007.

The RSCVA estimated the article's worth at over $200,000, calculating that editorial coverage of Reno was worth three times the value of paid advertising. As an editorial in the *Gazette-Journal* boasted, "When a *National Geographic* publication says a place is worth visiting, its readers take it as truth, so unlike the skepticism with which they often view advertisements created and paid for by people and organizations tooting their own horns and trying to sell something."[97]

RSCVA officials responded even more enthusiastically to the publication of an article about Reno in *Esquire* magazine that fall, estimating "The Dirtiest Secret in Nevada," the tale of one man's trek through the city's core, to be worth $832,000. The article won raves from RSCVA officials, local gaming analysts, and even Reno's mayor, even while presenting Reno as a little rough around the edges. Most remarkably, the writer, Tom Chiarella, brought to light many of the characteristics Reno's residents and promoters had been trying to assert for decades:

> You cannot deconstruct Reno. It's ruddy and rock hard, self-evident and openhearted. Reno is of a whole. It is a city, not an event. It is clean; safe, small, open, easy to get around in, cheap, seedy in the right ways, elegant in its own small measures. The airport? Intensely easy. Crowds? None that you can't handle. Hotels? None over a hundred dollars. There are mountains—real ones—lush, snowcapped, visually magnetic, utterly proximate. In Vegas, the mountains are dead hills in the distance. You know where you are when you're in Reno. You are in the new Vegas.

In his low-key appreciation of everything from Reno's breakfast and burger joints, no-nonsense card dealers, and Basque restaurants to its kayak park, Chiarella made the case that Reno's time had arrived:

> It brings to mind any number of forgotten American cities where the reputation does not fit what you find. In Reno, you go for the sin and discover the food. Or for the mountains and discover the lake. Or for the seedy whorehouses that dot the perimeter of the city, only to find the solace of a classy, well-run cardroom like the one at the Peppermill. You're a long way from anywhere, and yet you can still find an upscale restaurant, a tony casino, and a well-stocked bar.

According to this writer, Reno was walkable, honest, and different from Vegas in all the right ways, and Reno couldn't have been happier.[98]

The debut of Reno 911! *on the Comedy Central cable network in 2003 prompted both amusement and outrage among Reno residents. (Reno 911! photo courtesy of Comedy Central © 2003)*

Another popular portrayal prompted a bit more concern. When the television series *Reno 911!* premiered on the Comedy Central cable channel in July 2003, Reno residents exhibited an array of responses, from amusement to dismay to outrage. The mostly improvised comedy, a loose parody of the long-running reality series *Cops,* was set in a fictionalized Reno Sheriff's Department staffed by a bumbling group of buffoons and bimbos. Opening shots taped in Reno established the ostensible setting, while the show itself was filmed in southern California, as evidenced by the occasional incongruous palm tree visible in the first few seasons. Members of the inept department regularly crashed into cars while attempting to interpret personalized license plates, were duped by criminals, wrangled an endless parade of prostitutes, strippers, and pimps, and conducted busts in a landscape of trailer parks, meth labs, dilapidated motels, and massage parlors.

When questioned about their choice of Reno for the show's setting, its creators offered a range of explanations. In an interview with *GQ* magazine, co-creator and star Thomas Lennon, who plays the role of Lieutenant Jim Dangle, said, "With all due respect to Reno, it's a disgusting trash pit. And I mean that with love," but when prodded later by a local reporter, backtracked to assert, "Totally, totally a joke," citing instead the "nice ring" of the Reno name and suggesting, "There's a certain rural quality and a very fancy quality sort of mixed. I don't think there's a town that's so high and so low altogether. . . . It could have been 'Phoenix 911!' or it could have been Denver, but there's a certain sexiness to Reno, I think, that is really a benefit to the show." He added, "I don't think we're taking any shots at Reno per se. I think we're taking shots at hillbillies and racists." Co-creator and actor Robert Ben Garant took the diplomatic approach, explaining, "It's a small town, but it's got all the big crime that you need for cops to be running around doing stuff," while the third creator and actor, Kerri Kenney, admitted, "We picked Reno just because it had a bit of a lame factor."[99] This was not exactly what the RSCVA or local government wanted to hear.

With the city's name in the national spotlight yet again, the show's debut quickly earned the attention of local residents, a number of whom were interviewed by local reporter and film critic Forrest Hartman for their reactions. Some were bemused, like Robin Holabird of the Nevada Film Office, who took the long view when it came to media depictions of the Biggest Little City. "Name recognition is always useful," she said. "A lot of people who will not see 'Reno 911!' will still be hearing Reno. So when it comes to thinking of places to go, it's a name that might just pop up, and they won't even be aware of why."[100] And indeed, if name recognition were the goal, maybe the old adage about no bad publicity still held true.

Other residents, weary of Reno's long Dangerfield-like struggle for respect, were clearly fed up with the continuing ridicule the show seemed sure to perpetuate. As a publicist for the Atlantis Casino Resort, formerly known as the Clarion, complained, "It doesn't do anything for the bad stigma that lies over Reno. A lot of people think Reno's a dirty gaming town with brothels everywhere. Living here, we know that's not true. . . . I would love to see Reno portrayed all the time the way I see it."[101] What the media gave, it was feared, the media could take away, a lesson Reno's promoters knew all too well. In a meeting revealing a new "business brand" for the region—"can do"—a member of the creative team behind the slogan asserted, "We've got to change people's minds, raise the level of positive talk about the region." He continued, "We're not 'Reno 911.' We're going to set the record straight and tell the truth about the region. People know they don't have the whole story. We've got to sing from one inspiring song sheet."[102] Meth labs and trailer parks were obviously not among his lyrics of choice; however, in October of 2007, the students of the University of Nevada–Reno chose to wear the show's notoriety as a badge of honor, inviting actor Thomas Lennon to serve as grand marshal of their campus homecoming parade, a role he gamely filled, jauntily posing on top of an open convertible in his character's signature skin-tight short shorts and a cowboy hat. Like fans of the gritty *Esquire* article, some residents increasingly seemed willing to embrace the satire as well as the praise, accepting Reno's emerging image as a slightly wacky, ultimately charming alternative, but not a runner-up, to Las Vegas or any other city.

The hyperbolically squalid world depicted in *Reno 911!* is just the latest version of Reno to hit the national stage; it is surely not the last. Like the magazine and newspaper articles of the past, the plays, movies, and songs, the gossip and the criticism, the thrill and the spectacle, the delight and the condemnation, it is just one of many images of Reno filtering through the collective consciousness to create an image of place that is as organic as ourselves. The vital nature of our own cognitive processes ensures that our impressions of the outside world remain unfixed, offering a place like Reno endless opportunity for reinvention and its reputation endless opportunity for improvement, deterioration, or both.

CONCLUSION

My reputation is a media creation.
John Lydon (a.k.a. Johnny Rotten), quoted in the *Observer,* 4 May 1986

A reputation is a curious and volatile thing. An intangible phenomenon with sometimes brutally tangible consequences, it operates largely outside the rules of logic and prediction. A reputation can at times seem impossible to rein in; one event, whether tragic or celebratory, or one popular media depiction has the potential to affect more opinions of a place than its official promoters ever could alone. And an ongoing series of events and depictions, all centering upon impressions of vice, rebellion, and depravity, can create an overall impression that is difficult to dislodge.

This predicament held as true for Reno in the days of Laura Corey, the pioneering socialite divorcée, as when the state legalized gambling in 1931, or when Reno's lights dimmed in the neon glare of a new Sin City, decades later. From "The Gentleman from Reno" to *Reno 911!,* outside observers long have profited from Reno's seemingly limitless potential to entertain, shock, and bemuse. Accordingly, each generation of residents, from Francis Newlands to Jud Allen, from the Bureau of Immigration to the RSCVA, has fought its own battles with the images thereby created, so divergent in most cases from what they have understood the "real Reno" to be.

Even today, nearly every Reno resident can offer a story of an acquaintance's shocked reaction to the news that he/she was from Reno, or was moving there, or perhaps relate his or her own initial dismay at being forcibly relocated to the Biggest Little City in the World. I have heard many of these stories; I have told some myself. They are, in a way, part of the process of bonding with other Reno residents, as is the effusive round of praise for Reno's positive qualities that invariably follows.

In a historical sense, however, local residents were complicit in creating the very reputation their successors now decry. Since 1868, an ever-shifting mélange of power dynamics and civic priorities has influenced what was

250

constructed, what was destroyed, and what was allowed to remain on the city's landscape. As the city's most consistent source of income and attention, the tourist industry has been the most determinative force in shaping that pivotal landscape. Rather than steel or paper mills, Reno had its divorce mill; instead of assembly lines, it produced gleaming lines of slot machines. Eyes fixed on market demand, and potential profits, Reno's leaders consistently chose to increase the city's supply of tourist amenities, ultimately sacrificing its only city center to that single goal.

Perhaps no other American city has linked both its economic fate and physical appearance so consistently to the vagaries of human nature, for better and for worse. With a service economy reliant on consumer demand almost from the beginning, Reno found a specialized niche in catering to the human desire for liberation, of one kind or another. The fact that the industries that earned Reno the most national attention were the very sort of industries that tended to detract from community stability, or to stand in seeming opposition to civic responsibility, was an unforeseen (or, in some cases, foreseen but largely unlamented) consequence of orienting the heart of the city to a transient population. When the city's business community suffered from these choices, it generally suffered not from having misjudged human nature, but from either overestimating consumer demand (as with the overbuilding trend of the 1970s) or failing to anticipate inevitable cultural shifts, including the rise of competition from other destinations.

While other cities across America have employed tourism to revitalize their postindustrial downtowns, Reno consistently has used its downtown—some might say, used it up—to revitalize its tourist industry, repeatedly reshaping its central district to match what visitors were believed to want at any given time. From a very early point, this desire to give the American public what it wanted, while quickly removing what it did not, established a pattern of enacting short-term, responsive moves rather than formulating any abiding long-term vision for the city. The current attempt to bring residents back downtown demonstrates a clear departure from the previous pattern, and its ultimate success will depend upon the same factors that influence an outward reputation: the attractiveness of the landscape and the correspondence of amenities to demand.

In that triumvirate of civic identity—reputation, sense of place, and promoted image—Reno's reputation has long reigned as the driving force, casting locals into a defensive position while requiring promoters repeatedly to counter that reputation with an alternate series of more respectable images, hoping that eventually one would stick. Finally, with its deliberate diversification of industries and tourist amenities, and the incipient return of residential spaces to downtown, Reno may yet accomplish the stability and reinvigorated identity its residents and promoters have always sought. The new image of "America's Adventure Place" has the advantage of appealing not only to a growing tourist demographic, but also to a wide swath of the local population who were attracted to Reno for the very recreational opportunities that the RSCVA is now so eager to promote. That the equation ultimately relies upon the presiding values of the broader culture is made abundantly clear by the realization that Reno's climate and topography, now considered so desirable, were once its greatest liabilities. Perhaps in this new era the city will be able to live it up without creating a civic reputation that it will only have to live down again.

In its extremes, Reno can perhaps be seen as a cautionary tale for destinations considering hitching their wagons to the latest consumer trend, or for places that currently bask in their success at doing so. But its history may also be considered in another, perhaps more forgiving light, as the tale of a small town that found national fame very early and has in a sense spent the subsequent years attempting to replicate and sustain that success while growing into a midsized city, like a child star battling both his own maturity and the short attention span of the American public.

The heart of downtown Reno clearly still faces some aesthetic challenges. While revitalization slowly proceeds from the outlying streets inward, the main casino strip on Virginia Street remains something of a dingy visual hangover in the light of day. A number of closed casinos attest to the continuing struggles of the local gaming industry, while its successful hotel casinos share space with pawn and souvenir shops, cheap motels, and neglected storefronts. A campaign to update the street's facades and the current inclusion of nearly the entire downtown core inside the redevelopment district demonstrate the city's intent to match its appearance to its ambitions. A trend towards demolition has proceeded as well, as the Reno City Council voted in spring 2007, amid much controversy, to replace the historic Virginia Street Bridge, citing flooding and budgetary concerns. And yet in early 2008, that same body approved the city's first Historic Preservation Master Plan. As of summer 2008, projects well under way and prompting great optimism for the downtown area included an indoor/outdoor urban market in the arts district, a 10,000-seat Triple-A baseball stadium and accompanying retail district, a children's museum, and more.

Driving into Reno at night via Interstate 80 still evokes a sense of the surreal, with a skyline lit up like a Christmas tree. The Eldorado's hotel tower radiates pink, while the Silver Legacy glows green, and Circus Circus beckons in brilliant gold. Like the early travelers who glimpsed Gambler's Row from their railroad berths, a traveler who sticks to the highway might gain a misleading impression of Reno from those brilliant lights alone, as the residential and commercial districts of the rest of the city stretch quietly away on either side. Reno owes its skyline and its enduring fame to the gaming industry, but its future remains elusive. A city, like the people who inhabit it, is a source of constant surprise. The story is never over.

NOTES

INTRODUCTION: BECOMING "THE BIGGEST LITTLE CITY"

1. Garrison Keillor, *A Prairie Home Companion*, performance and live radio broadcast, Lawlor Events Center, University of Nevada–Reno, Reno, Nevada, 19 June 1999. For stereotypes of Nevada, see Wilbur S. Shepperson with Ann Harvey, *Mirage-Land: Images of Nevada* (Reno: University of Nevada Press, 1992); and Wilbur Shepperson, ed., *East of Eden, West of Zion: Essays on Nevada* (Reno: University of Nevada Press, 1989).

2. James W. Hulse, *The Silver State: Nevada's Heritage Reinterpreted*, 2d ed. (Reno: University of Nevada Press, 1998), 196–209.

3. For elaboration on this point, see R. Timothy Sieber's essay on "Urban Tourism in Revitalizing Downtowns," in *Tourism and Culture: An Applied Perspective*, ed. Erve Chambers (Albany: State University of New York Press, 1997), 59–76.

4. Grady Clay, *Close Up: How to Read the American City* (Chicago: University of Chicago Press, 1980), 38–65.

5. "A River Runs through It," *Casino Executive*, May 1999, 30.

6. Yi-Fu Tuan, *Topophilia: A Study of Environmental Perception, Attitudes, and Values* (Englewood Cliffs, N.J.: Prentice-Hall, 1974); John Brinckerhoff Jackson, "A Sense of Place, a Sense of Time," in his *A Sense of Place, a Sense of Time* (New Haven, Conn.: Yale University Press, 1994), 151. See also Wallace Stegner, "The Sense of Place," in his *Where the Bluebird Sings to the Lemonade Springs* (New York: Penguin, 1992), 199–206; and Lucy Lippard, *The Lure of the Local: Senses of Place in a Multicentered Society* (New York: New Press, 1997).

7. Stephen P. Hanna, "Is It Roslyn or Is It Cicely? Representation and the Ambiguity of Place," *Urban Geography* 17, no. 7 (1996): 633; Peter Borsay, *The Image of Georgian Bath, 1700–2000: Towns, Heritage, and History* (Oxford and New York: Oxford University Press, 2000), 324.

8. See Briavel Holcomb, "Revisioning Place: De- and Re-constructing the Image of the Industrial City," in *Selling Places: The City as Cultural Capital, Past and Present*, ed. Gerry Kearns and Chris Philo (Oxford: Pergamon Press, 1993), 142.

9. M. Christine Boyer, *The City of Collective Memory: Its Historical Imagery and Architectural Entertainments* (Cambridge: MIT Press, 1994), 5; Dennis R. Judd and Susan S. Fainstein, ed., *The Tourist City* (New Haven, Conn.: Yale University Press, 1999), 4, 6.

10. See, for instance, David M. Wrobel, *Promised Lands: Promotion, Memory, and the Creation of the American West* (Lawrence: University Press of Kansas, 2002), 16.

11. For reputational capital, see Charles J. Fombrun, *Reputation: Realizing Value from the Corporate Image* (Boston: Harvard Business School Press, 1996), 10–13. For cultural capital, see Chris Philo and Gerry Kearns, "Preface," in Kearns and Philo, eds., *Selling Places,* ix; and Chris Philo and Gerry Kearns, "Culture, History, Capital: A Critical Introduction to the Selling of Places," in ibid., 3; For a list of some contemporary cities and their brand associations, see Briavel Holcomb, "Marketing Cities for Tourism," in Judd and Fainstein, eds., *Tourist City,* 55.

12. For a sociological approach to reputation, see Gary Alan Fine, "Reputational Entrepreneurs and the Memory of Incompetence: Melting Supporters, Partisan Warriors, and Images of President Harding," *American Journal of Sociology* 101 (March 1996): 1161. For collective memory, see Maurice Halbwachs, *On Collective Memory* (Chicago: University of Chicago Press, 1992); and Boyer, *City of Collective Memory.*

13. Yi-Fu Tuan, "Language and the Making of Place: A Narrative-Descriptive Approach," *Annals of the Association of American Geographers* 81 (December 1991): 684.

14. Kevin Lynch, *The Image of the City* (Cambridge, Mass.: MIT Press, 1960), 2–3.

15. Chris Wilson, *The Myth of Santa Fe: Creating a Modern Regional Tradition* (Albuquerque: University of New Mexico Press, 1997), 7–8; Mike Davis, *City of Quartz: Excavating the Future in Los Angeles* (1990; New York: Vintage Books, 1992), 23; Robert M. Fogelson, *The Fragmented Metropolis: Los Angeles, 1850–1930* (Cambridge, Mass.: Harvard University Press, 1967). For more on urban sprawl, see Kenneth T. Jackson, *Crabgrass Frontier: The Suburbanization of the United States* (Oxford: Oxford University Press, 1985); Joel Garreau, *Edge City: Life on the New Frontier* (New York: Anchor Books, 1991); and Richard Moe and Carter Wilkie, *Changing Places: Rebuilding Community in the Age of Sprawl* (New York: Henry Holt & Co., 1997).

16. See Hal K. Rothman, *Devil's Bargains: Tourism in the Twentieth-Century American West* (Lawrence: University Press of Kansas, 1998). Briavel Holcomb describes the process as a "Faustian bargain" in "Marketing Cities for Tourism," 69; Patricia Stokowski uses similar language in *Riches and Regrets: Betting on Gambling in Two Colorado Mountain Towns* (Niwot, Colo.: University Press of Colorado, 1996).

17. See Bonnie Christensen, *Red Lodge and the Mythic West: Coal Miners to Cowboys* (Lawrence: University Press of Kansas, 2002). For early tourist towns, see Catherine Cocks, *Doing the Town: The Rise of Urban Tourism in the United States, 1850–1915* (Berkeley: University of California Press, 2001).

CHAPTER ONE: "IN THE MIDDLE OF A FRIGHTFUL PLAIN":
THE QUEST FOR A REPUTATION

1. Anonymous reporter for the *San Francisco Times,* quoted in Phillip I. Earl, "Meandering along the Line of the Central Pacific Railroad, 1868," *Nevada Historical Society Quarterly* 21, no. 4 (1978): 279, 280.

2. Ibid., 280–281.

3. William D. Rowley, *Reno, Hub of the Washoe Country* (Woodland Hills, Calif.: Windsor Publications, 1984), 19.

4. Anonymous reporter for the *San Francisco Times,* quoted in Earl, "Meandering along the Line," 281.

5. Richard White, *It's Your Misfortune and None of My Own: A New History of the American West* (Norman: University of Oklahoma Press, 1993), 192.

6. See David M. Wrobel, *Promised Lands: Promotion, Memory, and the Creation of the American West* (Lawrence: University Press of Kansas, 2002), 157–158. On the reality of mining camps, see Susan Lee Johnson, *Roaring Camp: The Social World of the California Gold Rush* (New York: W. W. Norton, 2000).

7. Noah Brooks, "The Gentleman from Reno," *Overland Monthly,* October 1868, 380–381, 383.

8. *Nevada State Journal,* 10 December 1870, 3.

9. J. Hector St. John de Crevecoeur, *Letters from an American Farmer and Sketches of Eighteenth-Century America* (New York: Penguin Classics, 1981), 71.

10. Wilbur S. Shepperson, *Mirage-Land: Images of Nevada* (Reno: University of Nevada Press, 1992), xvii.

11. Ibid., 21, 23.

12. Mark Twain, *Mark Twain: The Innocents Abroad, Roughing It* (New York: Library of America, 1984), 642, 643.

13. Earl Pomeroy, *In Search of the Golden West: The Tourist in Western America* (Lincoln: University of Nebraska Press, 1990), 66.

14. Caroline M. Churchill, *"Little Sheaves" Gathered While Gleaning after Reapers. Being Letters of Travel Commencing in 1870, and Ending in 1873* (San Francisco: n.p., 1874), 59, available from Library of Congress, American Memory collection, http://hdl .loc.gov/loc.gdc/calbk.091 (2 November 2007).

15. U.S. Decennial Census Records, 1870 (Carson City: Nevada State Data Center); train schedule appearing in *Nevada State Journal,* 14 December 1872, 4; Churchill, *"Little Sheaves,"* 62.

16. Shepperson, *Mirage-Land,* 21. For discussion of California's long-standing reputation as a promised land, see Claire Perry, *Pacific Arcadia: Images of California, 1600–1915* (New York: Oxford University Press, 1999).

17. *Atlantic Monthly,* quoted in Shepperson, *Mirage-Land,* 41; Phil Robinson, *Sinners and Saints: A Tour across the States and round Them with Three Months among the Mormons* (London: Sampson Low, Marston, Searle, & Rivington, 1883), 261.

18. Gray Brechin, *Imperial San Francisco: Urban Power, Earthly Ruin* (Berkeley: University of California Press, 1999), 39.

19. Ronald M. James, *The Roar and the Silence: A History of Virginia City and the Comstock Lode* (Reno: University of Nevada Press, 1998), 230–231, 236, 244–245; U.S. Decennial Census Records, 1880 and 1890 (Carson City: Nevada State Data Center).

20. Quoted in C. C. Warner, *Products, Resources, Opportunities for Capital and Advantages to Emigrants of Nevada* (Reno: Gazette Book and Job Print, 1889), 5.

21. "A Question for Statesmen," *New York Times,* 25 March 1878, 4; "Nevada's Past and Future," *New York Times,* 22 January 1881, 5.

22. Quoted in "A Dying State," *New York Times,* 28 July 1889, 4.

23. J. W. Buel, *America's Wonderlands: A Pictorial and Descriptive History of Our Country's Scenic Marvels* (Boston: J. S. Round, 1893), 182.

24. Nevada State Bureau of Immigration, *Nevada and Her Resources* (Carson City, Nev.: State Printing Office, 1894), "Introductory."

25. "The Metropolis of Nevada," *San Francisco Call,* 31 March 1898, 13.

26. Warner, *Products, Resources, Opportunities,* 5; Nevada State Bureau of Immigration, *Nevada and Her Resources,* "Washoe County Agriculture."

27. *Nevada at the World's Fair: Accompanied by Illustrations of Its Home Interests* (Carson City, Nev.: J. A. Yerington, ca. 1893).

28. Fred Warren Parks, "Two Notable Exhibits," *Overland Monthly and Out West Magazine,* June 1894, 618, 621.

29. U.S. Decennial Census Records, 1880, 1890, 1900 (Carson City: Nevada State Data Center); Russell R. Elliott with William D. Rowley, *History of Nevada,* 2d ed., rev. (Lincoln: University of Nebraska Press, 1987), 404–405; "Washoe County," *Daily Nevada State Journal,* 25 January 1881, 2.

30. L. M. McKenney & Co., *McKenney's Business Directory of the Principal Towns of California, Nevada, Utah, Wyoming, Colorado and Nebraska* (Sacramento: H. S. Crocker, 1882), 649; "Reno's Surroundings," *Reno Evening Gazette,* 2 June 1879, 2.

31. Census Office, Department of the Interior, *Report on the Statistics of Agriculture in the United States at the Eleventh Census* (Washington, D.C.: U.S. Government Printing Office, 1890), 164, 298; Census Office, Department of the Interior, *Report on the Statistics of Agriculture in the United States at the Ninth Census* (Washington, D.C.: U.S. Government Printing Office, 1870), 202–203, 358.

32. "The Metropolis of Nevada," *San Francisco Call,* 31 March 1898, 13; Alan Trachtenberg, *The Incorporation of America: Culture and Society in the Gilded Age* (New York: Hill & Wang, 1982), 113. See also William Cronon, *Nature's Metropolis: Chicago and the Great West* (New York: W. W. Norton, 1991).

33. David Hamer, *New Towns in the New World: Images and Perceptions of the Nineteenth-Century Urban Frontier* (New York: Columbia University Press, 1990), 37, 131–134.

34. Wrobel, *Promised Lands,* 2; Gunther Barth, *Instant Cities: Urbanization and the Rise of San Francisco and Denver* (New York: Oxford University Press, 1975), 5–6.

35. *Reno Evening Gazette,* 14 November 1887; Warner, *Products, Resources, Opportunities,* Prefatory, 5.

36. See John M. Townley, *Tough Little Town on the Truckee* (Reno: Great Basin Studies Center, 1983), 73.

37. "Brief Journey in Scenic Nevada," *Nevada State Journal,* 3 December 1899, 3; "The Metropolis of Nevada," *San Francisco Call,* 31 March 1898, 13.

38. "Many Are Joining," *Nevada State Journal,* 21 October 1902, 1; "Exhibits Arrive Daily in Reno," *Nevada State Journal,* 12 September 1903, 1.

39. Perry, *Pacific Arcadia,* 137; Catherine Cocks, *Doing the Town: The Rise of Urban Tourism in the United States, 1850–1915* (Berkeley: University of California Press, 2001). For more on the development of tourism in the American West, see Hal K. Rothman, *Devil's Bargains: Tourism in the Twentieth-Century American West* (Lawrence: University Press of Kansas, 1998).

40. "Tourists Coming," *Reno Evening Gazette,* 11 April 1882, 2; Alfred Runte, *National Parks: The American Experience,* 3d ed. (Lincoln: University of Nebraska Press, 1997), 29–34. See also Anne Farrar Hyde, *An American Vision: Far Western Landscape and National Culture, 1820–1920* (New York: NYU Press, 1990).

41. Twain, *Roughing It,* 650; "The Pedestrian Fever," *Reno Weekly Gazette,* 14 August 1879, 1.

42. Advertisement in *Reno Evening Gazette*, 17 July 1879, 3; "Pacific Coast News," *Reno Evening Gazette*, 29 May 1880, 3; "Hints to Tourists," *Reno Evening Gazette*, 18 April 1889, 3.

43. George A. Crofutt, *Crofutt's New Overland Tourist and Pacific Coast Guide* (Omaha and Denver: Overland Publishing, 1882), 144.

44. "The Riverside Hotel," *Reno Evening Gazette*, 5 June 1888, 3; "The Riverside Hotel," *Reno Evening Gazette*, 23 June 1888, 3; "Jottings," *Reno Evening Gazette*, 26 December 1889, 3; Advertisement, *Reno Evening Gazette*, 21 September 1896, 3.

45. Pomeroy, *In Search of the Golden West*, 118–121.

46. Warner, *Products, Resources, Opportunities*, 7; Western Nevada Improvement Association, *Nature's Sanitarium: Reno, Nevada and Its Surroundings in the Sierras* (Reno: Journal Print, 1893), 4, 5; *Reno Evening Gazette*, 24 December 1891, 12.

47. Pomeroy, *In Search of the Golden West*, 118–119; Western Nevada Improvement Association, *Nature's Sanitarium*, 11.

48. James W. Hulse, *The University of Nevada: A Centennial History* (Reno: University of Nevada Press, 1974), 9; *Reno Evening Gazette*, 7 March 1885.

49. Hulse, *University of Nevada*, 29–30, 32.

50. "A Valuable Acquisition," *Reno Weekly Gazette and Stockman*, 23 May 1889, 2; William D. Rowley, *Reclaiming the Arid West: The Career of Francis G. Newlands* (Bloomington and Indianapolis: Indiana University Press, 1996), 22; "Wedding in San Francisco," *New York Times*, 28 November 1874, 6.

51. Rowley, *Reclaiming the Arid West*, 38, 40–43.

52. "A Valuable Acquisition," 2.

53. Rowley, *Reclaiming the Arid West*, 38–39. The promotional publications included Southern Pacific Railroad Passenger Department, *The New Nevada: What It Is and What It Is to Be* (San Francisco: Southern Pacific Railroad Passenger Department, 1903); and Clay Peters, "Reno of the Silver State," *Sunset*, November 1904, 81.

54. James W. Hulse, *The Silver State: Nevada's Heritage Reinterpreted*, 2d ed. (Reno: University of Nevada Press, 1998), 197–198; Rowley, *Reno: Hub of the Washoe Country*, 51.

55. Townley, *Tough Little Town*, 158; "Silver Convention," *Reno Weekly Gazette and Stockman*, 5 December 1889, 2.

56. "Francis G. Newlands," *Reno Evening Gazette*, 24 December 1891, 7.

57. "'Buds' Not Numerous," *New York Times*, 1 December 1895, 11.

58. Francis G. Newlands, "The Future of Nevada," *Independent*, 18 April 1901, 888; Shepperson, *Mirage-Land*, 65.

59. Hulse, *The Silver State*, 227–229. See also Donald Worster, *Rivers of Empire: Water, Aridity, and the Growth of the American West* (New York: Random House, 1985).

60. William E. Smythe, *The Conquest of Arid America* (New York: Harper & Brothers Publishers, 1900), 194, 199, 201; Shepperson, *Mirage-Land*, 75–76.

61. Elliott, *History of Nevada*, 211; Peters, "Reno of the Silver State," 83.

62. *Nevada State Journal*, 14 May 1903, 3; *Nevada State Journal*, Roosevelt Edition, 19 May 1903, 1.

63. "President's Trip in Nevada," *Reno Evening Gazette*, 19 May 1903, 1; Southern Pacific Railroad Passenger Department, *New Nevada*, 18; Pomeroy, *In Search of the Golden West*, 122; Peters, "Reno of the Silver State," 83.

64. Southern Pacific Railroad Passenger Department, *New Nevada,* 35; "The New West: A Social Study of Life in Nevada Towns Today," *Sunset,* February 1907, 296.

65. On the relationship of western cities to the frontier identity, see Carl Abbott, *The Metropolitan Frontier: Cities in the Modern American West* (Tucson: University of Arizona Press, 1993), xvii–xviii; Pomeroy, *In Search of the Golden West,* 2–3, 132, 135; and Hamer, *New Towns,* 85, 130–138. As historian David Wrobel has noted, this conundrum over the word "frontier" often resulted in a "delicate balancing act" in which boosters promoted "frontiers of opportunity" unaccompanied by "frontier hardships." See Wrobel, *Promised Lands,* 24–25; Henry Nash Smith, *Virgin Land: The American West as Symbol and Myth* (Cambridge, Mass.: Harvard University Press, 1950), 176; Frederick Jackson Turner, "The Significance of the Frontier in American History," in *Rereading Frederick Jackson Turner: "The Significance of the Frontier in American History" and Other Essays,* ed. John Mack Faragher (New York: Henry Holt, 1994), 31–60; and Charles F. Lummis, "The Right Hand of the Continent," *Out West,* March 1903, 307–308.

66. "Thriving Reno Expects Boom by Reason of the Wedekind Find and the Promise of Glittering Treasures," *San Francisco Call,* 9 November 1901, 10; "Flourishing Nevada," *San Francisco Call,* 11 November 1901, 4.

67. "The Gateway to Nevada," *Harper's Weekly,* 20 June 1903, 1031, 1032.

68. "Nevada Is Dead Easy," *Reno Evening Gazette,* 9 July 1903, 6; "Is Misleading Literature," *Nevada State Journal,* 12 July 1903, 3.

69. "Is Misleading Literature," 3.

CHAPTER TWO: "A FRONTIER POST OF CIVILIZATION":
CHASING MODERNITY IN THE PROGRESSIVE ERA

1. *Daily Nevada State Journal,* 21 May 1903, 1; Philip I. Earl, "100 Years Ago, First Motorcycle Crossed the Sierra," *Reno Gazette-Journal,* 25 August 2002, 1B.

2. John M. Findlay, *People of Chance: Gambling in American Society from Jamestown to Las Vegas* (New York: Oxford University Press, 1986), 108; *Daily Nevada State Journal,* 27 February 1902, 1.

3. *Nevada State Journal,* 7 December 1901, 4.

4. William D. Rowley, *Reno: Hub of the Washoe Country* (Woodland Hills, Calif.: Windsor Publications, 1984), 31, 38.

5. Findlay, *People of Chance,* 99.

6. *Nevada State Journal,* 25 November 1900, 3.

7. U.S. Decennial Census Records, 1900 (Carson City: Nevada State Data Center); *Nevada State Journal,* 19 May 1903, 4.

8. *Nevada State Journal,* 19 May 1903, 4.

9. Ibid.; *Daily Nevada State Journal,* 5 November 1903, 5; Rowley, *Reno: Hub of the Washoe Country,* 32.

10. "First Steps toward a Chamber of Commerce," *Nevada State Journal,* 4 October 1902, 1.

11. Paul Boyer, *Urban Masses and Moral Order in America, 1820–1920* (Cambridge,

Mass.: Harvard University Press, 1978), 164–165, 193. Material and moral progress were intertwined in the minds of the bourgeois morality, according to T. J. Jackson Lears, *No Place of Grace: Antimodernism and the Transformation of American Culture, 1880–1920* (New York: Pantheon Books, 1981), 12.

12. "Should Be Remedied," *Nevada State Journal*, 10 December 1902, 1.

13. "Public Parks a Necessity," *Reno Evening Gazette*, 13 October 1906, 2; "Reno Is Waking Up," *Nevada State Journal*, 12 October 1906, 10.

14. "The Revolt against an Infamous Project," *Nevada State Journal*, 14 October 1906, 10; "Century Club to Appeal to City," *Nevada State Journal*, 31 October 1906, 3.

15. "Bunco Men," *Reno Evening Gazette*, 1 June 1903, 1.

16. James W. Hulse, *The University of Nevada: A Centennial History* (Reno: University of Nevada Press, 1974), 32.

17. *Reno Evening Gazette*, 19 February 1903, 2; *Reno Evening Gazette*, 4 June 1904, 1.

18. *Reno Evening Gazette*, 21 February, 1903, 5; "Far from the Maddening Crowd," *Nevada State Journal*, 30 May 1903, 1; *Reno Evening Gazette*, 29 October 1903, 4.

19. "World's Fair," *Nevada State Journal*, 4 September 1904, 5; "Passengers Got Left," *Nevada State Journal*, 8 September 1904, 4.

20. *Reno Evening Gazette*, 24 February 1905, 1.

21. *Reno Evening Gazette*, 11 June 1904, 3; *Daily Nevada State Journal*, 15 September 1904, 7; *Reno Evening Gazette*, 22 June 1904, 5.

22. "Will Have Gaming Tables," *Daily Nevada State Journal*, 16 March 1905.

23. *Daily Nevada State Journal*, 11 March 1905, 1.

24. Quoted in ibid.

25. "Favors Wide Open State," *Nevada State Journal*, 12 March 1905, 8.

26. "Another Outside View of Local Situation," *Reno Evening Gazette*, 11 April 1905, 2.

27. *Reno Evening Gazette*, 8 February 1908, 1.

28. *Reno Evening Gazette*, 6 December 1905, 1; *Nevada State Journal*, 6 December 1905, 1.

29. "Expects a Divorce," *Altoona* (Pa.) *Mirror*, 7 December 1905.

30. Rowley, *Reno: Hub of the Washoe Country*, 36.

31. John M. Townley, *Tough Little Town on the Truckee* (Reno: Great Basin Studies Center, 1983), 225; "The Metropolis of Nevada," *San Francisco Call*, 31 March 1898, 13.

32. See Karen Dubinsky, *The Second Greatest Disappointment: Honeymooning and Tourism at Niagara Falls* (New Brunswick, N.J.: Rutgers University Press, 1999); Nelson Manfred Blake, *The Road to Reno: A History of Divorce in the United States* (New York: Macmillan, 1962), 116–123; and Anita J. Watson, "Tarnished Silver: Popular Image and Business Reality of Divorce in Nevada, 1900–1939" (M.A. thesis, University of Nevada–Reno, 1989), 23.

33. *New York Times*, 31 July 1906, 1; 17 November 1906, 1; 23 November 1923, 1.

34. *Nevada State Journal*, 6 December 1906, 3; "The New Divorce Centre," *New York Times*, 18 July 1909, sec. 5, 5; Allen D. Albert, Jr., "Reno, the Refuge of Restless Hearts," *Munsey's Magazine*, October 1909, 3.

35. Arthur Ruhl, "Reno and the Rush for Divorce," *Collier's*, 1 July 1911, 20; Blake, *Road to Reno*, 153.

36. *Reno Evening Gazette,* 13 February 1908, 1; *Reno Evening Gazette,* 8 October 1910, 2.

37. "Who Wrote Treatise on Divorce?" *Nevada State Journal,* 24 October 1910, 1; "Schnitzer Has Word about Reno," *Nevada State Journal,* 14 November 1910, 6; Blake, *Road to Reno,* 154.

38. *Washington Post,* 13 August 1910, 1.

39. "I'm on My Way to Reno," quoted in Rowley, *Reno: Hub of the Washoe Country,* 37.

40. Willard Huntington Wright, "Reno, City of Easy Divorce, Most 'Wide-Open' of Towns," *Los Angeles Times,* 19 June 1910, sec. 2, 1; "Reno Copes with Twin Evils, Divorce and Gambling," *New York Times,* 8 January 1911, sec. 5, 4; Albert, "Reno, the Refuge of Restless Hearts," 3.

41. Wright, "Reno, City of Easy Divorce," sec. 2, 1.

42. "New Divorce Centre," sec. 5, 5; Albert, "Reno, the Refuge of Restless Hearts," 9.

43. Ruhl, "Reno and the Rush for Divorce," 19.

44. Mella Harmon, "Divorce and Economic Opportunity in Reno, Nevada during the Great Depression" (M.S. thesis, University of Nevada–Reno, 1998), 75–77.

45. Albert, "Reno, the Refuge of Restless Hearts," 9; "Broker's Wife Tired of Him," *Los Angeles Times,* 2 July 1909, 13.

46. "Miss Illington Joins Colony," *Los Angeles Times,* 5 June 1909, sec. 1, 1; "After Divorce on Engine," *Los Angeles Times,* 2 November 1909, sec. 1, 3.

47. "Ring Twice for a Divorce," *Los Angeles Times,* 11 October 1908, sec. 2, 5; "Nat Asks for Divorce," *Los Angeles Times,* 23 September 1908, sec. 1, 1; "Features Farce of Divorce Law," *Los Angeles Times,* 30 May 1910, sec. 1, 3; "Reno's Divorce Colony Gets a Glimpse of Itself," *San Francisco Sunday Call,* 10 July 1910, magazine section, 1.

48. *Nevada State Journal,* 12 July 1910, 1; "Explanations in Order out There," *New York Times,* 18 July 1910, 6.

49. "Reno Reveries Is Worth the Price," *Nevada State Journal,* 24 November 1910, 3; *Nevada State Journal,* 24 May 1911, 8; "Miss Curtis Is to Issue a New Book," *Reno Evening Gazette,* 21 March 1911, 5.

50. Ruhl, "Reno and the Rush for Divorce," 19.

51. Albert, "Reno, the Refuge of Restless Hearts," 4.

52. "The Togo Tourists Visit Reno's Divorce Factory," *New York Times,* 10 July 1910, sec. 5, 12.

53. "New Divorce Centre," sec. 5, 5; Ruhl, "Reno and the Rush for Divorce," 19.

54. *New York Times,* 18 July 1909, sec. 5, 5.

55. "Enormous Progress in Reno Building," *Reno Evening Gazette,* 3 April 1907, 8; Stephen L. Hardesty, *The Site of Reno's Beginning: The Historical Mitigation of the Riverside Hotel/Casino* (Reno: City of Reno Redevelopment Agency, August 1997), State Historic Preservation Office, Carson City, Nev., 11–12; Ruhl, "Reno and the Rush for Divorce," 19.

56. "Two Hundred Thousand Dollars to Be Used for New Buildings," *Reno Evening Gazette,* 20 June 1907, 1; "Enormous Progress in Reno Building," 8.

57. "Fight Bugs Raid Reno," *Los Angeles Times,* 3 July 1910, sec. 7, 3; "Reno Copes with Twin Evils," sec. 5, 4; Ruhl, "Reno and the Rush for Divorce," 19.

58. Glenda Riley, *Divorce: An American Tradition* (New York: Oxford University Press, 1991), 108–109.

59. "Reno's Sensitive Judge," *New York Times*, 16 November 1909, 8; U.S. Department of Commerce and Labor, Bureau of the Census, *Marriage and Divorce 1887–1906* (Washington, D.C.: U.S. Government Printing Office, 1908), 11.

60. U.S. Department of Commerce and Labor, Bureau of the Census, *Marriage and Divorce 1887–1906*, 21; Riley, *Divorce: An American Tradition*, 108.

61. George Elliott Howard, "Is the Freer Granting of Divorce an Evil?" *American Journal of Sociology* 14, no. 6 (May 1909): 767, 775.

62. George Elliott Howard, review of *Divorce: A Study in Social Causation*, by James P. Lichtenberger, *American Political Science Review* 4 (May 1910): 303.

63. Howard, "Is the Freer Granting of Divorce an Evil?" 789; "The New Doctrine of Divorce," *New York Times*, 30 May 1909, 8.

64. *Reno Evening Gazette*, 8 October 1910, 2.

65. *Reno Evening Gazette*, 19 April 1910, 4.

66. "The Situation in Reno," *New York Times*, 5 April 1910, 10; *Reno Evening Gazette*, 19 April 1910, 4.

67. *Nevada State Journal*, 14 February 1908, 3.

68. *Reno Evening Gazette*, 8 October 1910, 4.

69. *Nevada State Journal*, 13 February 1908, 3; *New York Times*, 18 July 1910, 6.

70. "Beautiful Book from Gazette Plant," *Reno Evening Gazette*, 19 December 1907, 5; *Reno Evening Gazette*, 11 February 1908, 7.

71. Albert, "Reno, the Refuge of Restless Hearts," 6; "Reno, City of Easy Divorce, Most Wide-Open of Towns," *Los Angeles Times*, 19 June 1910, sec. 2, 1.

72. *San Francisco Call*, 15 June 1908, 4.

73. *Reno Evening Gazette*, 31 January 1908, 1.

74. *Reno Evening Gazette*, 3 February 1908, 2.

75. *San Francisco Call*, 10 February 1908, 3; *Reno Evening Gazette*, 31 March 1908, 2.

76. *Reno Evening Gazette*, 8 February 1909, 1; *Reno Evening Gazette*, 24 February 1909, 1; *Nevada State Journal*, 25 March 1909, 1.

77. Jeffrey T. Sammons, *Beyond the Ring: The Role of Boxing in American Society* (Urbana and Chicago: University of Illinois Press, 1988), 10.

78. Lears, *No Place of Grace*, 7.

79. Sammons, *Beyond the Ring*, 16, 19.

80. Ibid., 24; "Nevada for Nevadans," *Reno Evening Gazette*, 1 October 1900, 3.

81. Rowley, *Reno: Hub of the Washoe Country*, 37; Guy L. Rocha and Eric N. Moody, "Hart vs. Root: Reno's First Championship?" *Nevadan*, 6 April 1980, 6J; "Champion Hart May Fight Wrestler Gotch," *Reno Evening Gazette*, 6 July 1905, 8; "Knockout in Twelfth," *Reno Evening Gazette*, 3 July 1905, 1.

82. *Washington Post*, 6 January 1907, 2.

83. Rowley, *Reno: Hub of the Washoe Country*, 37.

84. "Mayor's Mail Grows Larger," *Nevada State Journal*, 28 June 1910, 8; Robert Greenwood, *Jack Johnson vs. Jim Jeffries: The Fight of the Century* (Reno: Jack Bacon, 2004), 68.

85. "Auto Owners Chug to Fight," *Los Angeles Times*, 3 July 1910, sec. 7, 10.

86. "Reno Banker Here, Defends His City," *New York Times*, 3 July 1910, 5; Nevada Directory Company, "City of Reno," *Directory of Reno, Sparks and Carson* (Reno: Nevada Directory Company, 1910).

87. "Fight Bugs Raid Reno," sec. 7, 3.

88. Greenwood, *Jack Johnson vs. Jim Jeffries,* xi, 103–104, 121–125.

89. Quoted in *Reno Evening Gazette,* 3 October 1910, 2.

90. Ibid.

91. *Reno Evening Gazette,* 19 September 1910, 3; City Directory Publishing Company, *1911–1912 Directory of Reno and Sparks* (Reno: City Directory Publishing Company), 12. The cartoon appeared in the *Reno Evening Gazette,* 1 October 1910, 2.

92. *Reno Evening Gazette,* 1 October 1910, 4; *Reno Evening Gazette,* 4 October 1910, 6.

93. Jeanne Elizabeth Wier, "The Work of the Western State Historical Society as Illustrated by Nevada," paper read at the annual meeting of the Pacific Coast branch of the American Historical Association, University of California, 19 November 1910, Special Collections, University of Nevada–Reno Library.

94. *Reno Evening Gazette,* 30 July 1910, 4.

CHAPTER THREE: SELLING RENO IN THE CONSUMER AGE

1. Leslie Curtis, "Oh, Hash of Life, Thy Name Is Reno!" *Washington Post,* 4 June 1911, 4–5.

2. Arthur Ruhl, "Reno and the Rush for Divorce," *Collier's,* 1 July 1911, 20.

3. "Reno Divorcons at Secret Hop," *Los Angeles Times,* 12 December 1910, sec. 1, 3; Edith Wharton, *The Custom of the Country* (London: Penguin Books, 1987), 329–330.

4. See Edward Hungerford, *The Personality of American Cities* (New York: McBride, Nast, 1913); and Catherine Cocks, *Doing the Town: The Rise of Urban Tourism in the United States, 1850–1915* (Berkeley: University of California Press, 2001), 145–146.

5. Delos F. Wilcox, *Great Cities in America: Their Problems and Their Government* (New York: Macmillan, 1910), 2.

6. U.S. Decennial Census Records, 1900 and 1910 (Carson City: Nevada State Data Center); C. T. Stevenson, "Reno, 'Biggest Little City on the Map,' Metropolis of Nevada," *Reno Evening Gazette,* development section, 1 January 1912.

7. "Sensitive Reno," *New York Times,* 17 October 1911, 10; "Reno Will Thrive Once More," *New York Times,* 19 February 1915, 8.

8. "Crusade Coming in Divorce City?" *Los Angeles Times,* 18 December 1910, sec. 5, 17.

9. "Roosevelt Assails Reno," *New York Times,* 4 April 1911, 1; *Goldfield Daily Tribune,* 11 April 1912.

10. "The New Divorce Centre," *New York Times,* 18 July 1909, sec. 5, 5.

11. Allen D. Albert, Jr., "Reno, the Refuge of Restless Hearts," *Munsey's Magazine,* October 1909, 11–12.

12. *Nevada State Journal,* 21 January 1913, 8.

13. "Farewell to Reno's Supremacy as a Divorce Centre," *New York Times,* 11 January 1914, 5; George Wharton James, "What's the Matter with Nevada?" *Out West,* April 1914, 182.

14. Effie Price Gladding, *Across the Continent by the Lincoln Highway* (New York: Brentano's, 1915), 117, 118.

15. "Governor Boyle Signs Divorce Bill," *Reno Evening Gazette*, 24 February 1915, 11.

16. David G. Schwartz, *Roll the Bones: The History of Gambling* (New York: Gotham Books, 2006), 353; John M. Findlay, *People of Chance: Gambling in American Society from Jamestown to Las Vegas* (New York: Oxford University Press, 1986), 118; "Nevada Is Outlet of Pent Up Urban Feeling," *Oakland Tribune*, 18 April 1915, 29.

17. "Addresses Delivered at the Nevada State Business Men's Convention, Held at the Reno Commercial Club Rooms, Reno, Nevada, Friday and Saturday, June 16–17, 1916" (Reno: Nevada Press, 1916), Special Collections, University of Nevada–Reno Library, 44.

18. "Driving Auto across U.S." *Reno Evening Gazette*, 15 April 1913, 4.

19. Hal K. Rothman, *Devil's Bargains: Tourism in the Twentieth-Century American West* (Lawrence: University of Kansas Press, 1998), 146; Earl Pomeroy, *In Search of the Golden West: The Tourist in Western America* (Lincoln: University of Nebraska Press, 1990), 127–130.

20. Annie Estelle Prouty, "The Development of Reno in Relation to Its Topography" (M.A. thesis, University of Nevada, 1917), 98.

21. *Reno Evening Gazette*, 14 February 1914, 2; *Reno Evening Gazette*, 10 January 1920, 3.

22. "Reno—Famed for Life and Beauty," in *Reno: The Gem of the West, without Equal in America for Beauty and Promise, Special Edition of Nevada Newsletter*, 10 January 1920.

23. George W. Bond, *Six Months in Reno* (New York: Stanley Gibbons, 1921); Lilyan Stratton, *Reno: A Book of Short Stories and Information* (Newark, N.J.: Colyer Printing, 1921).

24. *Reno Evening Gazette*, 25 June 1921, 2.

25. *Carson Appeal* quoted in *Reno Evening Gazette*, 12 March 1920, 4; *Reno Evening Gazette*, 19 March 1921, 3.

26. Lary May, *Screening Out the Past: The Birth of Mass Culture and the Motion Picture Industry* (New York: Oxford University Press, 1980), 119, 145.

27. Grace Hegger Lewis, "Just What Is Reno Like," *Scribner's*, January 1929, 38; "Reno Is Found Interesting and Human by Writer Who Spent 3 Months Here," *Reno Evening Gazette*, 27 December 1928, 8.

28. Sherwood Anderson, "So This Is Reno," *Nevada Newsletter*, 5 April 1924, 21.

29. Katharine Fullerton Gerould, "Reno," *Harper's*, June 1925, 47, 48–49, 57.

30. Stratton, *Reno*, 9.

31. William W. Greene, "Reno," *Travel*, July 1922, 26, 29, 40.

32. Bond, *Six Months in Reno*, 5–6, 43.

33. Stratton, *Reno*, 47–48, 164.

34. John M. Townley, *Tough Little Town on the Truckee* (Reno: Great Basin Studies Center, 1983), 223; Pomeroy, *In Search of the Golden West*, 175–177.

35. William D. Rowley, *Reno: Hub of the Washoe Country* (Woodland Hills, Calif.: Windsor Publications, 1984), 39; Philip I. Earl, "Reno Rodeo Has Long and Rich History Dating Back to 1919," n.d., "Reno History" file, Nevada Historical Society.

36. Tom Gilbert, *Reno! "It Won't Be Long Now"* (Reno: Gilbert & Shapro, 1927), 17, 35.

37. Greene, "Reno," 26; Ramona Park Brockliss, "Reno Has a Personality," *Sunset Magazine*, September 1926, 44.

38. See John Urry, *The Tourist Gaze: Leisure and Travel in Contemporary Societies* (London: Sage, 1990); Greene, "Reno," 27.

39. Genevieve Parkhurst, "In Reno—Where They Take the Cure," *Pictorial Review*, February 1929, 2.

40. Lewis, "Just What Is Reno Like," 38.

41. Stratton, *Reno*, 266; Greene, "Reno," 28.

42. Stratton, *Reno*, 152–153.

43. Gilbert, "*Reno!*" 7; Lewis, "Just What Is Reno Like," 43.

44. Mary Day Winn, *The Macadam Trail: Ten Thousand Miles by Motor Coach* (New York: Alfred A. Knopf, 1931), 74; Gilbert, *Reno!* 9.

45. Gilbert, *Reno!* 7. Nevada state archivist discusses the myth in Guy Rocha, "Does Divorce Legend Have the Ring of Truth?" *Reno Gazette-Journal*, 27 March 2005, 8B.

46. Roland Marchand, *Advertising the American Dream: Making Way for Modernity, 1920–1940* (Berkeley: University of California Press, 1985), 118.

47. Gilbert, *Reno!* 17, 35, 37, 39.

48. Bond, *Six Months in Reno*, 6, 11, 41.

49. Stratton, *Reno*, 45; Parkhurst, "In Reno," 2; Henry F. Pringle, "Reno the Wicked: The American Capital of Divorce and Gambling," *Outlook*, 29 July 1931, 396.

50. Bond, *Six Months in Reno*, 16, 20, 28, 50.

51. Bond, *Six Months in Reno*, 31, 34; James H. Bolin, *Reno, Nevada; "Holy City" of the World* (Reno: Bolin Publishing, 1924), 7; Gerould, "Reno," 50.

52. Dwayne Kling, *The Rise of the Biggest Little City: An Encyclopedic History of Reno Gaming, 1931–1981* (Reno: University of Nevada Press, 2000), 176; "Reno, in Full Dress, Gambles All Night; 'Divorce Cure' Patrons Hailed in Resort Song," *New York Times*, 23 March 1931, 14; Basil Woon, *Incredible Land: A Jaunty Baedeker to Hollywood and the Great Southwest* (New York: Liveright Publishing, 1933), 232.

53. Kling, *Rise of the Biggest Little City*, 4, 123; Greene, "Reno," 29.

54. *R. L. Polk & Co.'s 1920–21 Reno City Directory* (R. L. Polk & Co., 1920), 15; Greene, "Reno," 26, 40; "What the Folks Are Thinking About—In Reno, Nevada," *Collier's*, 28 April 1923, 33.

55. James W. Hulse, *The Silver State: Nevada's Heritage Reinterpreted*, 2d ed. (Reno: University of Nevada Press, 1998), 168; Rowley, *Reno: Hub of the Washoe Country*, 43–44; Elizabeth C. Raymond, *George Wingfield: Owner and Operator of Nevada* (Reno: University of Nevada Press, 1992), 34, 59.

56. Rowley, *Reno: Hub of the Washoe Country*, 43–44.

57. Hulse, *Silver State*, 168–171; Rowley, *Reno: Hub of the Washoe Country*, 43–44.

58. *Nevada State Journal*, 6 November 1922, 5; Anita Ernst Watson, "Fading Shame: Divorce Stigma in American Culture, 1882–1939" (Ph.D. diss., University of Nevada–Reno, 1997), 250–251.

59. Rowley, *Reno: Hub of the Washoe Country*, 51–52.

60. Ibid.

61. "When Reno Began to Spread," *Reno Evening Gazette*, 30 April 1923, 5.

62. "Stewart in Race for Re-election," *Reno Evening Gazette*, 20 March 1923, 6.

63. "No Monte Carlo yet Awhile," *Nevada State Journal,* 6 May 1923, 4.

64. "Roberts Swamps Opponents in Municipal Contest," *Reno Evening Gazette,* 9 May 1923, 1; "'We Must Pull Together and Make Reno a Bigger City,' Is Statement of Newest Mayor," *Nevada State Journal,* 10 May 1923, 8; "Reno Mayor Talks to Sparks' Lions," *Nevada State Journal,* 22 August 1923, 2.

65. Parkhurst, "In Reno," 2.

66. *Nevada State Journal,* 28 November 1923, 7.

67. Eric N. Moody and Guy Louis Rocha, "The Rise and Fall of the Reno Stockade," *Nevada,* April/May/June 1978, 29.

68. Bolin, *Reno, Nevada,* 11–12.

69. Alfred Holman, "Nevada Set Firmly against Prohibition," *New York Times,* 27 June 1926, sec. 2, 3; Alfred Holman, "Nevada Campaign Under Way," *New York Times,* 22 August 1926, sec. 2, 3.

70. Parkhurst, "In Reno," 71.

71. "Bar Association Head Assails Bill," *Reno Evening Gazette,* 18 March 1927, 1, 3; "Reno Divorces, 1927 Model," *Literary Digest,* 9 April 1927, 13.

72. "Trick of Lobby Leads Nevada Legislators to Cut Divorce Residence Time in Half," *New York Times,* 19 March 1927, 1; "Divorce Suit Every Hour," *New York Times,* 24 March 1927, 12; "Cornelius Vanderbilt Jr. on Way to Reno; He Is Reported to Be Seeking a Divorce," *New York Times,* 11 July 1927, 1; U.S. Department of Commerce, *Statistical Abstract of the United States, 1929* (Washington, D.C.: U.S. Government Printing Office, 1929), 92; U.S. Department of Commerce, *Statistical Abstract of the United States, 1931* (Washington, D.C.: U.S. Government Printing Office, 1931), 93.

73. Swift Paine, "As We See It in Reno," *North American Review,* June 1930, 726.

74. See Thorstein Veblen, *The Theory of the Leisure Class: An Economic Study of Institutions* (New York: Macmillan, 1905).

75. Stephen L. Hardesty, *The Site of Reno's Beginning: The Historical Mitigation of the Riverside Hotel/Casino* (Reno: City of Reno Redevelopment Agency, August 1997), 13–15; "Trick of Lobby," 1.

76. Winn, *Macadam Trail,* 74; Pringle, "Reno the Wicked," 395.

77. Woon, *Incredible Land,* 225–226; Lewis, "Just What Is Reno Like," 39.

78. R. L. Polk & Co., *Polk's Reno City, Washoe County and Carson City Directory, 1925–26* (Oakland, Calif.: R. L. Polk & Co., 1925), 63, 64.

79. *R. L. Polk & Co.'s Reno City Directory, 1927–1928* (San Francisco: R. L. Polk & Co., 1927), 5.

80. W. M. David, "Ramblings through the Pines and Sage: A Series of One Day Tours out of Reno" (n.p.: Nevada State Automobile Association, ca. 1928), Autry Library, Autry National Center, Los Angeles.

81. Rowley, *Reno: Hub of the Washoe Country,* 55; "Air Service for Shopping Boon to Reno Divorce Colony," *New York Times,* 21 July 1929, sec. III, 2; "Nevada Divorce and Marriage Laws Bring Airline Patrons," *New York Times,* 8 December 1929, sec. XI, 10.

82. Mary B. Mullett, "Mary B. Mullett Tells the Truth about Reno," *American Magazine,* October 1930, 26, 152.

83. "Slump Knocks Cupid Dizzy," *Los Angeles Times,* 27 June 1931, 3.

84. "Will Rogers Remarks," *Los Angeles Times,* 11 March 1931, 1; Leo D. Martin and

Joe McDonald, "Arkansas and Nevada in War for the Divorce Capital of the United States," *Danville* (W. Va.) *Bee,* 6 March 1931, 5.

85. "Speakers Rap Proposed Law at Gathering," *Nevada State Journal,* 5 February 1931, 1.

86. Findlay, *People of Chance,* 119.

87. "Not So Very Different from the Old 'Wild West' Days," *San Antonio Light,* 12 April 1931, 9.

88. Carol W. Cross, "Divorce Called 'Social Necessity,'" *Simpson's Daily Leader-Times* (Kittaning, Pa.), 11 May 1931, 5.

89. "'Old West' Returns in Nevada Gambling," *New York Times,* 21 March 1931, 3.

90. Ibid.

91. Daniel J. Boorstin, *The Americans: The Democratic Experience* (New York: Vintage Books, 1974), 64–77.

92. Schwartz, *Roll the Bones,* 355.

93. Kling, *Rise of the Biggest Little City,* 4, 123, 139.

94. "Streets Given Carnival Air; Rooms Needed," *Nevada State Journal,* 31 May 1931, 1.

95. Pringle, "Reno the Wicked," 402.

96. "Not So Very Different," 9.

97. "'Old West' Returns in Nevada Gambling," 3.

98. "Nevada's New Scheme," *Portsmouth* (Ohio) *Times,* 23 March 1931, 6.

99. Pringle, "Reno the Wicked," 403.

100. Paul Hutchinson, "Reno—A Wide Open Town," *Christian Century,* 2 December 1931, 1519–1520.

101. Paul Hutchinson, "Nevada—A Prostitute State," *Christian Century,* 25 November 1931, 1488.

102. Hutchinson, "Reno—A Wide-Open Town," 1520; Hutchinson, "Nevada—A Prostitute State," 1488.

103. Pringle, "Reno the Wicked," 403.

104. "Reno Is Denounced to Endeavorers," *New York Times,* 14 July 1931, 2; "With Its Gambling Legalized, Reno Becomes Even More Like 'Sodom, Gomorrah and Hell,'" *Kansas City Star,* 26 April 1931, 1C.

105. "Roberts Given Invitation as Defense Made," *Nevada State Journal,* 27 March 1931, 1–2.

106. "Reno Mayor Draws Throng to Church," *Nevada State Journal,* 30 March 1931, 1–2; "Reno Defender Goes It Alone," *Los Angeles Times,* 31 March 1931, 3.

107. "With Its Gambling Legalized," 2C.

108. "Why Laugh at Nevada?" *Helena* (Mont.) *Independent,* 29 March 1931, 14.

CHAPTER FOUR: "CITY OF SINFUL FUN": RENO HITS THE MAINSTREAM

1. "The Motion Picture Production Code of 1930," quoted in *The Dame in the Kimono: Hollywood, Censorship, and the Production Code from the 1920s to the 1960s,* ed. Leonard J. Jeff and Jerold Simmons (New York: Grove Wiedenfeld, 1990), 283–286.

2. Grace Kingsley, "Reno Subject of New Films," *Los Angeles Times*, 20 May 1931, A9.

3. Margaret Reid, "Day of Recognition for Reno Dawns in Hollywood," *Los Angeles Times*, 24 May 1931, B11.

4. Henry Pringle, "Reno the Wicked: The American Capital of Divorce and Gambling," *Outlook*, 29 July 1931, 395.

5. Russell R. Elliott with William D. Rowley, *History of Nevada*, 2d ed., rev. (Lincoln: University of Nebraska Press, 1987), 281.

6. U.S. Department of Commerce, *Statistical Abstract of the United States, 1933* (Washington, D.C.: U.S. Government Printing Office, 1933), "Vital Statistics," 91.

7. Elliott, *History of Nevada*, 285.

8. Harry Carr, "The Lancer," *Los Angeles Times*, 10 May 1931, A1.

9. Anne O'Hare McCormick, "Reno, Child of the Fabulous Frontier," *New York Times Magazine*, 1 November 1931, 4.

10. Anita Ernst Watson, "Fading Shame: Divorce Stigma in American Culture, 1882–1939" (Ph.D. diss., University of Nevada–Reno, 1997), 270.

11. "Reno's Mill Speeds Up," *Los Angeles Times*, 3 May 1931, 1; "Suit Filed at Reno Every Two Minutes," *New York Times*, 3 May 1931, 1.

12. Mark Curtis, *It Was Great While It Lasted: A PR Man's Reflections on Nevada's Entertainment Heyday* (Reno: Black Rock Press, 2001), 29–30.

13. Katherine T. Von Blon, "Latest Studio and Theater Gossip," *Los Angeles Times*, 5 February 1939, C2.

14. Neal Gabler, *Winchell: Gossip, Power, and the Culture of Celebrity* (New York: Knopf, 1994), xii–xiii.

15. Mollie Merrick, "Hollywood in Person," *Los Angeles Times*, 6 May 1931, 11; Hedda Hopper, "Why Hollywood Can't Stay Married," *Los Angeles Times*, 22 March 1931, H3.

16. Alma Whitaker, "Hollywood Divorces Rock Dan Cupid," *Los Angeles Times*, 1 March 1931, B9.

17. Robert Sklar, *Movie-Made America: A Cultural History of American Movies* (New York: Vintage Books, 1994), 161.

18. *The Road to Reno*, Richard Wallace, dir. (Paramount, 1931).

19. "Reno," *Variety*, 6 December 1923, in *Variety Film Reviews*, vol. 2 (New York: Garland Publishing, 1983); "Divorce," *New York Times*, 8 January 1924, 27.

20. "A Reno Divorce," *Variety*, 25 January 1928, in *Variety Film Reviews*, vol. 3 (New York: Garland Publishing, 1983); "Road to Reno," *Variety*, 13 October 1931, in *Variety Film Reviews*, vol. 4 (New York: Garland Publishing, 1983).

21. Grace Kingsley, "Heard on the Boulevard," *Los Angeles Times*, 27 July 1931, A9; *Life*, 21 June 1937.

22. Charles J. McGuirk, "Betrayal," *Los Angeles Times*, 26 April 1931, K9.

23. Mary Day Winn, *The Macadam Trail: Ten Thousand Miles by Motor Coach* (New York: Alfred A. Knopf, 1931), 75.

24. Winn, *Macadam Trail*, 71.

25. J. B. Griswold, "Wild West," *American Magazine*, May 1938, 14; Quentin Reynolds, "Relax in Reno," *Collier's*, 28 December 1935, 22.

26. Kendrick Johnson, *Rabelaisian Reminiscences of Reno by a Bachelor Lawyer* (Los Angeles: Gem Publishing, 1934); Con Ryan, "The City That Sex Built," *Real Detective,* November 1936, 14, 16.

27. See Michael R. Asimow, "Divorce in the Movies: From the Hays Code to *Kramer vs. Kramer,*" *Legal Studies Forum* 24 (2000): 221–267; and Ann Ronald, "Reno: Myth, Mystique, or Madness?" in *East of Eden, West of Zion: Essays on Nevada,* ed. Wilbur S. Shepperson (Reno: University of Nevada Press, 1989), 145. Some of these works of fiction and nonfiction include John Hamlin, *Whirlpool of Reno* (New York: Dial Press, 1931); Dorothy Wadsworth Carman, *Reno Fever* (New York: Ray Long & Richard R. Smith, 1932); Earl Derr Biggers, *Keeper of the Keys* (Indianapolis: Bobbs-Merrill, 1932); Faith Baldwin, *Temporary Address: Reno* (New York: Farrar & Rinehart, 1941); and Max Miller, *Reno* (New York: Dodd, Mead, 1941).

28. *The Women,* George Cukor, dir. (MGM, 1939).

29. Norbert Lusk, "'Wallingford' Proves Smash," *Los Angeles Times,* 18 October 1931, B13.

30. "Story of Reno Next at Warner," *Los Angeles Times,* 22 May 1934, 12; John Scott, "Humorous Story Now at Warner," *Los Angeles Times,* 25 May 1934, 13; "Films Classified in Catholic List," *New York Times,* 8 July 1934, 8.

31. "The Screen," *New York Times,* 24 December 1931, 22.

32. "Chan Solves Reno Murder," *Los Angeles Times,* 27 May 1939, A7.

33. "The Screen," *New York Times,* 29 September 1944, 18; "Maisie Goes to Reno," *Variety,* 16 August 1944, in *Variety Film Reviews,* vol. 7 (New York: Garland Publishing, 1983).

34. William Teeling, *American Stew* (London: Herbert Jenkins, 1933), 97–98.

35. Dwayne Kling, *The Rise of the Biggest Little City: An Encyclopedic History of Reno Gaming, 1931–1981* (Reno: University of Nevada Press, 2000), 18, 45, 140, 176.

36. "Reno," *Life,* 21 June 1937, 40; "Day of a Divorcee," *Saturday Evening Post,* 11 December 1937, 22–23, 88.

37. Harry Carr, "Reno's Divorce Courts Share Time with Races," *Los Angeles Times,* 2 July 1931, 1.

38. Griswold, "Wild West," 172.

39. On dude ranches, see Earl Pomeroy, *In Search of the Golden West: The Tourist in Western America* (Lincoln: University of Nebraska Press, 1990), 100, 168, 171; G. Edward White, *The Eastern Establishment and the Western Experience: The West of Frederic Remington, Theodore Roosevelt, Owen Wister* (Austin: University of Texas Press, 1968); and Robert Athearn, *The Mythic West in Twentieth-Century America* (Lawrence: University Press of Kansas, 1986), 131–140.

40. Philip E. Siggers, *The Truth about Reno* (Reno: privately printed, 1934), 13; Reynolds, "Relax in Reno," 35.

41. Anthony M. Turano, "Reno the Naughty," *American Memory,* February 1936, 186.

42. For more on the idea of "staged authenticity," see Dean MacCannell, *The Tourist: A New Theory of the Leisure Class* (New York: Schocken, 1976).

43. *Nevada State Journal,* 30 October 1931.

44. Cornelius Vanderbilt, Jr., *Ranches and Ranch Life in America* (New York: Crown Publishers, 1968), 251–253.

45. "Nevada Dude Ranch Association" brochure (Reno: Nevada Dude Ranch Association, ca. 1936), "Dude Ranches" file, Nevada Historical Society.

46. Reynolds, "Relax in Reno," 35.

47. "Reno," 40.

48. Ed Cray, *Ramblin' Man: The Life and Times of Woody Guthrie* (New York: W. W. Norton, 2004), 110.

49. Basil Woon, *Incredible Land: A Jaunty Baedeker to Hollywood and the Great Southwest* (New York: Liveright Publishing, 1933), 230; Turano, "Reno the Naughty," 186–187.

50. Johnson, *Rabelaisian Reminiscences,* 53.

51. David F. Cavers, "Migratory Divorce," *Social Forces* 16 (October 1937): 97.

52. "Nevada Dude Ranch Association" brochure.

53. Kling, *Rise of the Biggest Little City,* 9–10, 20, 39–41.

54. Guy Clifton, *Reno Rodeo: A History—The First 80 Years* (Reno: Reno Rodeo Foundation, 2000), 13–14.

55. "Streets Packed with Visitors Here for Climax of Premiere," *Reno Evening Gazette,* 16 March 1940, 1.

56. *Nevada State Journal,* 28 June 1939; Gladys Rowley, "Reno Revue," *Nevada State Journal,* 29 June 1938, 2; Clifton, *Reno Rodeo,* 15, 17, 61, 151.

57. Gladys Rowley, "Reno Revue," *Nevada State Journal,* 15 March 1939, 3.

58. Reno Chamber of Commerce, *Reno, Land of Charm* (Reno: Reno Chamber of Commerce, ca. 1930), Special Collections, University of Nevada–Reno Library; "Recreational Center of America" ad through 1935 Polk directory; "Year 'Round Playground" ad in 1940, 1941, 1942, 1944 Polk's directories; Virginia Kellogg, "The Real Reno," *Literary Digest,* 27 November 1937, 27–28.

59. Kling, *Rise of the Biggest Little City,* 5.

60. Mella Harmon, *Divorce and Economic Opportunity in Reno, Nevada during the Great Depression* (Ph.D. diss., University of Nevada, Reno, 1998), 41–48.

61. Woon, *Incredible Land,* 230; George Hellman, "Reno Revue," *Nevada State Journal,* 18 July 1939, 3.

62. Siggers, *Truth about Reno,* 14.

63. Mary B. Mullett, "Mary B. Mullett Tells the Truth about Reno," *American Magazine,* October 1930, 26.

64. Ronald, "Reno," 139.

65. Gladys Rowley, "Reno Revue," *Nevada State Journal,* 26 March 1938, sec. 2, 1.

66. Gladys Rowley, "Reno Revue," *Nevada State Journal,* 11 May 1938, sec. 2, 1; 7 October 1938, 3.

67. Rowley, "Reno Revue," *Nevada State Journal,* 8 January 1939, 3.

68. Rowley, "Reno Revue," *Nevada State Journal,* 15 March 1939, 3.

69. Rowley, "Reno Revue," *Nevada State Journal,* 13 September 1938, 2.

70. Griswold, "Wild West," 172.

71. Frank J. Taylor, "Rich Man's Refuge," *Collier's,* 19 February 1938, 14.

72. Griswold, "Wild West," 173.

73. First National Bank, *One Sound State* (Reno: First National Bank in Reno, 1936), Special Collections, University of Nevada–Reno Library.

74. Elliott, *History of Nevada,* 289; Taylor, "Rich Man's Refuge," 14. See Gladys Rowley, "Reno Revue," *Nevada State Journal,* 11 May 1938, sec. 2, 1.

75. Christian Arthur Wellesley, "Why I Chose Nevada," in First National Bank, *One Sound State*, 5–6.

76. Nevada Information Division, Reno Chamber of Commerce, *Nevada, the Last Frontier* 1 (Summer 1939): 12, 31.

77. Kling, *Rise of the Biggest Little City*, 61.

78. *Nevada State Journal*, 30 July 1939, 15.

79. Thomas Cave Wilson, *Reminiscences of a Nevada Advertising Man, 1930–1980, or Half a Century of Very Hot Air, or I Wouldn't Believe It If I Hadn't Been There* (Reno: Oral History Program, University of Nevada–Reno, 1982), 507.

80. Wilson, *Reminiscences*, 478.

81. Ibid., 339, 463–467, 479–481.

82. Ibid., 494; *Nevada State Journal*, 1 September 1941, 10; *Nevada State Journal*, 14 April 1941, 16.

83. Nevada State Historical Society, *Nevada: A Guide to the Silver State* (Portland, Oreg.: Binfords & Mort, 1940), 183.

84. James W. Hulse, *The Silver State: Nevada's Heritage Reinterpreted*, 2d ed. (Reno: University of Nevada Press, 1998), 211; John M. Findlay, *People of Chance: Gambling in American Society from Jamestown to Las Vegas* (New York: Oxford University Press, 1986), 124.

85. "A Rival Divorce Colony," *New York Times*, 30 August 1911, 6.

86. Eugene P. Moehring, *Resort City in the Sunbelt: Las Vegas, 1930–2000*, 2d ed. (Reno: University of Nevada Press, 2000), 29–30.

87. "Reno Challenged," *Business Week*, 14 July 1945, 26.

88. Paul Hutchinson, "Reno—A Wide Open Town," *Christian Century*, 2 December 1931, 1520; Wesley Stout, "Nevada's New Reno," *Saturday Evening Post*, 31 October 1942, 68–69.

89. Findlay, *People of Chance*, 154.

90. Max Miller, "Reno: Honky-Tonk and Trading Post," *Reader's Digest*, August 1941, 89.

91. Wilson, *Reminiscences*, iv, 269, 271, 274; Daniel J. Boorstin, *The Image: A Guide to Pseudo-events in America*, twenty-fifth anniversary ed. (New York: Atheneum, 1987).

92. Wilson, *Reminiscences*, 276, 559, 272.

93. "Reno Publicity Plans Outlined," *Western Advertising*, October 1945, "Reno Publicity" print file, Nevada Historical Society; "Reno Challenged," 24, 26; Moehring, *Resort City in the Sunbelt*, 66.

94. "Reno Challenged," 26; Erskine Johnson, "In Hollywood," *Daily Times-News* (Burlington, N.C.), 29 May 1947, 17.

95. David G. Schwartz, *Suburban Xanadu: The Casino Resort on the Las Vegas Strip and Beyond* (New York: Routledge, 2003), 52–53.

96. Kevin Wallace, "The Biggest Little City in the World," *San Francisco Chronicle*, 6 September 1948.

97. *Romantic Nevada*, produced by James A. Fitzpatrick (Metro-Goldwyn-Mayer, 1943).

98. Walter Van Tilburg Clark, *The City of Trembling Leaves*, reprint (Garden City, N.Y.: Sun Dial Press, 1946), 12.

99. Walter Van Tilburg Clark, "Reno: The State City," in *Rocky Mountain Cities,* ed. Ray B. West, Jr. (New York: W. W. Norton, 1949), 30, 31, 51.

100. U.S. Decennial Census Records, 1940, 1950 (Carson City: Nevada State Data Center); Clarence K. Jones, *Clarence K. Jones: From Paperboy to Philanthropist* (Reno: Oral History Program, University of Nevada–Reno, 1988), 77, Special Collections, University of Nevada–Reno Library.

101. "Reno Houses of Vice May Be Reopened," *Nevada State Journal,* 18 March 1942, 12; "Board Agrees to Ban Vice Houses Here," *Nevada State Journal,* 6 May 1942, 12.

102. "Pittman Vetoes Vice Bill," *Reno Evening Gazette,* 22 March 1949, 11; "Bother over Brothels," *Newsweek,* 30 August 1948, 19.

103. "Reno Becomes Pure as Snow," *Dunkirk* (N.Y.) *Evening Observer,* 5 June 1942, 17.

104. Elliott, *History of Nevada,* 316.

105. Roger Butterfield, "Harold's Club," *Life,* 15 October 1945, 131; Wilson, *Reminiscences,* 560.

106. Meyer Berger, "The Gay Gamblers of Reno," *Saturday Evening Post,* 10 July 1948, 22.

107. Rainshadow Associates, *National Register of Historic Places Nomination Form, Mapes Hotel and Casino* (Reno: Rainshadow Associates, 1983), State Historic Preservation Office, Carson City, Nevada; "New Mapes Hotel Towers over Other Buildings in Reno," *Nevada State Journal,* 18 December 1947, 10.

108. Rollan Melton, *101 Nevada Columns* (Reno: Nevada Humanities Committee, 2001), 228; Mapes Advertisement, *Nevada State Journal,* 17 December 1947, 8.

109. Herb Caen, "It's News to Me," *San Francisco Chronicle,* 22 December 1947; "Good Luck," *Nevada State Journal,* 18 December 1947, 4.

110. Wilson, *Reminiscences,* 488–490; Kling, *Rise of the Biggest Little City,* 64–65, 143–144; Pomeroy, *In Search of the Golden West,* 189–190.

111. Kling, *Rise of the Biggest Little City,* 61–66; *Nevada State Journal,* 14 January 1953, 3.

112. Daniel J. Boorstin, *The Americans: The Democratic Experience* (New York: Vintage Books, 1974), 74; Wilson, *Reminiscences,* 479.

113. Ernest Havemann, "Gamblers Paradise Lost," *Life,* 25 October 1954, 67–68.

114. "There Is a Limit," *Nevada State Journal,* 7 June 1946, 4.

115. "Counties Take Heed," *Nevada State Journal,* 26 June 1946, 4; "Reno Merchants Urge Gambling Zone Limit," *Nevada State Journal,* 13 September 1951, 12.

116. "Reno Council Upheld in Refusal of License," *Reno Evening Gazette,* 21 January 1953, 11; "Primm to Open Casino, Build His Hotel Later," *Nevada State Journal,* 23 June 1955, 8.

117. Kling, *Rise of the Biggest Little City,* 140–141; Stephen L. Hardesty, *The Site of Reno's Beginning: The Historical Mitigation of the Riverside Hotel/Casino* (Reno: City of Reno Redevelopment Agency, August 1997); Kling, *Rise of the Biggest Little City,* 73.

118. Kling, *Rise of the Biggest Little City,* 80.

119. Curtis, *It Was Great While It Lasted,* 4, 20, 47, 56; Melton, *101 Nevada Columns,* 228–230.

120. Kling, *Rise of the Biggest Little City,* 60–61.

121. Moehring, *Resort City in the Sunbelt,* 52; Elliott, *History of Nevada,* 328–333.

122. Jud Allen, *Life without a Safety Net: An Insider's View of War, Hollywood and Reno* (Marceline, Mo.: Walsworth, 1997), 146–148; William D. Rowley, *Reno: Hub of the Washoe Country* (Woodland Hills, Calif.: Windsor Publications, 1984), 69.

123. Allen, *Life without a Safety Net,* 143–148; Robert Warren, "'New Reno' Plan Set by C of C," *Nevada State Journal,* 27 September 1959, 25.

CHAPTER FIVE: BIG CITY STRUGGLES IN THE BIGGEST LITTLE CITY

1. Mark Curtis, *It Was Great While It Lasted: A PR Man's Reflections on Nevada's Entertainment Heyday* (Reno: Black Rock Press, 2001), 124, 127.

2. Ray Duncan, "Marilyn's Men Conquer Family Fear," *Independent Star-News* (Pasadena, Calif.), 5 February 1961, scene sec., 5.

3. Carl Abbott, *The Metropolitan Frontier: Cities in the Modern American West* (Tucson: University of Arizona Press, 1993), 71.

4. Eugene Moehring, *Resort City in the Sunbelt: Las Vegas, 1930–2000,* 2d ed. (Reno: University of Nevada Press, 2000), 73–85.

5. Russell R. Elliott with William D. Rowley, *History of Nevada,* 2d ed., rev. (Lincoln: University of Nebraska Press, 1987), 404.

6. Jud Allen, *Life without a Safety Net: An Insider's View of War, Hollywood and Reno* (Marceline, Mo.: Walsworth, 1997), 171; Abbott, *Metropolitan Frontier,* 184.

7. Elliott, *History of Nevada,* 329–333, 408–409; Edward F. Sherman, "Nevada: The End of the Casino Era," *Atlantic Monthly,* October 1966, 112–116.

8. Dwayne Kling, *The Rise of the Biggest Little City: An Encyclopedic History of Reno Gaming, 1931–1981* (Reno: University of Nevada Press, 2000), 141; "Where's the Action?" *Newsweek,* 14 January 1963, 26; Horace Sutton, "Gamesmanship in Nevada," *Saturday Review,* 4 November 1967, 54.

9. Allen, *Life without a Safety Net,* 158.

10. Ibid., 206.

11. Ibid., 148–149.

12. Ibid., 152, 154; Rollan Melton, *101 Nevada Columns* (Reno: Nevada Humanities Committee, 2001), 213.

13. Glenda Riley, *Divorce: An American Tradition* (New York: Oxford University Press, 1991), 156–157.

14. Robert Wernick, "Last of the Divorce Ranches," *Saturday Evening Post,* 17 July 1965, 32; Wendy Miller, "Divorce Ranch Owners Take Issue with Magazine Story," *Nevada State Journal,* 8 July 1965, 16; Michael Strauss, "Reno Divorcing Itself from Divorce," *New York Times,* 12 May 1968, resorts and travel sec., XX27.

15. Norman Weber, "A Cultural Geography of Reno," in *Twelve Doors to Reno,* ed. John A. Price (San Diego, 1970), Ethnological Archives, Special Collections, University of Nevada–Reno Library, 130.

16. Business and Industrial Development Department, Greater Reno Chamber of Commerce, *Greater Reno Area Profile* (Reno: Greater Reno Chamber of Commerce, 1969–1970).

17. Kling, *Rise of the Biggest Little City,* 134.

18. "Peace Terms Signed; Gaming Will Expand," *Nevada State Journal,* 27 December 1961, 8; David G. Schwartz, *Suburban Xanadu: The Casino Resort on the Las Vegas Strip and Beyond* (New York: Routledge, 2003), 39–40.

19. Kling, *Rise of the Biggest Little City,* 67, 73–74; Charles R. Bell, ed., *Nevada Official Centennial Magazine* (Las Vegas: Charles R. Bell, 1964), 152.

20. Graham Erskine, "Reno, Haven or Hovel?" (four-part lecture series sponsored by the University of Nevada, Reno, General University Extension and the Department of Art, April 1965), Special Collections, University of Nevada–Reno Library, lecture 1, 7; "The Rites of Reno," *Holiday,* June 1965, 62.

21. Erskine, "Reno," lecture 1, 7–8.

22. Ibid., lecture 4, 10.

23. Kling, *Rise of the Biggest Little City,* 68–69.

24. Elliott, *History of Nevada,* 335; Schwartz, *Suburban Xanadu,* 149–150.

25. Silvio Petricciani, *The Evolution of Gaming in Nevada: The Twenties to the Eighties* (Reno: Oral History Program, University of Nevada–Reno, 1982), 279.

26. Kling, *Rise of the Biggest Little City,* 75.

27. "Gambling in America," final report of the Commission on the Review of the National Policy toward Gambling (Washington, D.C.: U.S. Government Printing Office, 1976), 86.

28. Kling, *Rise of the Biggest Little City,* 141–142, 74.

29. Elliott, *History of Nevada,* 408.

30. Harold Gorman, *Recollections of a Nevada Banker and Civic Leader* (Reno: Oral History Project, University of Nevada, Reno, 1976), 226–227; Robert A. Ring, *Recollections of Life in California, Nevada Gaming, and Reno and Lake Tahoe Business and Civic Affairs* (Reno: Oral History Project, University of Nevada, Reno, 1973), 96–97.

31. Gloria G. Cole, "Reno Gambling," in Price, ed., *Twelve Doors to Reno,* 32–33; Jack McFarren and Burton Swope, "A Planning Dilemma," *Nevada State Journal,* 13 April 1978, 8.

32. "Council Passes Ordinance to Eliminate Red Line," *Reno Evening Gazette,* 11 May 1970, 1; "Local Chamber Joins in Condemning Recall," *Nevada State Journal,* 6 July 1970, 4.

33. U.S. Decennial Census Records, 1960, 1970, 1980 (Carson City: Nevada State Data Center).

34. On suburban sprawl, urban blight, and urban renewal in the American West, see Robert M. Fogelson, *Downtown: Its Rise and Fall, 1880–1950* (New Haven, Conn.: Yale University Press, 2001), 318–320; Abbott, *Metropolitan Frontier,* 48–49; Kenneth T. Jackson, *Crabgrass Frontier: The Suburbanization of the United States* (New York: Oxford University Press, 1985).

35. David L. Wilson, "The Social Organization of Black Pimps and Prostitutes in Reno," in Price, ed., *Twelve Doors to Reno,* 53.

36. Gloria G. Cole, "Reno Gambling," in Price, ed., *Twelve Doors to Reno,* 33.

37. Curtis, *It Was Great While It Lasted,* 15.

38. Phyllis Zauner, "Finding the Real Reno," *Travel,* December 1971; Sutton, "Gamesmanship in Nevada," 54; Robert Ring, *Recollections of Life,* 54; Lucius Beebe,

"Reno: Specialization and Fun," in *The American City: A Sourcebook of Urban Imagery*, ed. Anselm L. Strauss (Chicago: Aldine, 1968), 431.

39. "Introduction," *Reno Gazette-Journal*, 2 April 1978, 5; Washoe County Blue Ribbon Task Force on Growth, *Blue Ribbon Task Force Program: Growth and Development, Reno, Sparks and Washoe County, Nevada* (Reno: Regional Planning Commission of Reno, Sparks and Washoe County, 1973–1974).

40. "Government Should Guide Growth," *Nevada State Journal*, 8 April 1978, 4.

41. William Eadington et al., Final Report I, December 1973, Committee on Economics of Growth, Report VII, in Washoe County Blue Ribbon Task Force on Growth, *Blue Ribbon Task Force Program: Growth and Development, Reno, Sparks and Washoe County, 1973–74*, i–ii, 2–4, 23–24.

42. Wayne Dennis et al., Final Report II, 30 January 1974, Committee on Economics of Growth, Report VII, in Washoe County Blue Ribbon Task Force on Growth, *Blue Ribbon Task Force Program*, 44, 45–46, 82–102.

43. Jack McFarren and Burton Swope, "Planning: Missed Opportunities," *Nevada State Journal*, 11 April 1978, 10.

44. "Government Should Guide Growth," *Nevada State Journal*, 8 April 1978, 4; Jack McFarren and Burton Swope, "Grasping Growth's Future," *Nevada State Journal/Reno Evening Gazette*, 9 April 1978, 1; "Slow, Steady Action on Blue Ribbon Report," *Nevada State Journal*, 3 March 1975, 4.

45. "RUDAT in Reno," *Nevada State Journal*, 18 September 1975, 4; "Growth Plan Urged for Reno," *Nevada State Journal*, 21 September 1975, 1; "RUDAT Zeroes In," *Reno Evening Gazette*, 19 September 1975, 4; "Reno—What Better Spot for a City?" *Nevada State Journal*, 18 September 1975, 12.

46. "RUDAT in Reno," 4.

47. Elliott, *History of Nevada*, 408–409. Many studies have since determined that the effects on Atlantic City were more negative than positive. See, for example, George Sternlieb and James W. Hughes, *The Atlantic City Gamble* (Cambridge, Mass.: Harvard University Press, 1983).

48. Kling, *Rise of the Biggest Little City*, 46.

49. Curtis, *It Was Great While It Lasted*, 149; "The Lion: A Roar That Was Heard in Reno," *Nevada State Journal*, 12 April 1978, 9. Patricia Stewart wrote of "the few 'Native Americans,' the Indians who live in squalid conditions on a tiny reservation they have been desperately trying to hang onto in industrial east Reno." See Patricia Stewart, "Reno Still the Biggest Little City in the World," *Nevadan*, 14 April 1974, 5.

50. Jack McFarren and Burton Swope, "A Planning Dilemma," *Nevada State Journal*, 13 April 1978, 8; Jack McFarren and Burton Swope, "Planning: Missed Opportunities," *Nevada State Journal*, 11 April 1978, 11.

51. Wallace Turner, "A Changing Reno Will Get a 'Grand Hotel,'" *New York Times*, 20 January 1977, 18; Les Ledbetter, "Reno Discovers the Price of Prosperity," *New York Times*, 4 March 1978, 6.

52. Burton Swope, "Goliath Comes and Brings a Price," *Nevada State Journal*, 12 April 1978, 8; "Good-bye Las Vegas . . . Reno, Hello?" *Forbes*, 29 May 1978, 34.

53. "A Planning Dilemma," *Nevada State Journal*, 13 April 1978, 8.

54. Allen, *Life without a Safety Net*, 164–165.

55. Sam Bass Warner, Jr., *The Urban Wilderness: A History of the American City* (New York: Harper & Row, 1972), 242–243.

56. Kling, *Rise of the Biggest Little City,* 46, 50, 75–76, 125.

57. Jack McFarren and Burton Swope, "Grasping Growth's Future," *Nevada State Journal/Reno Evening Gazette,* 9 April 1978, 1; "The Future—A Time for Decisions," *Nevada State Journal,* 18 April 1978, 11.

58. R. L. Polk & Co., *Reno-Sparks City Directory* (El Monte, Calif.: R. L. Polk & Co., 1975), ix.

59. Swope, "Goliath Comes and Brings a Price," 8; "Reno Business 'Task Force' Visits St. Paul," *Nevada State Journal,* 1 May 1978, 14.

60. "Media Spotlight on MGM, Reno," *Nevada State Journal,* 2 May 1978, 7.

61. "Wrecker's Ball," *Reno Evening Gazette,* 18 December 1977, 4; Eric Moody and Guy Rocha, "The Rise and Fall of the Reno Stockade," *Nevada,* April/May/June 1978, 28–30.

62. "Media Spotlight on MGM, Reno," 7.

63. "Reno Hits the Big Time," *Nevada State Journal,* 4 May 1978, 1; "Good-bye Las Vegas. . . . Reno, Hello?" 34; Yvette Cardozo, "Think of Reno, Nevada," *Travel/Holiday,* February 1981, 10.

64. Les Ledbetter, "Reno Area Pins Its Hopes on a New Casino," *New York Times,* 6 May 1978, 10.

65. Jud Allen, "Let's Stop Belittling Our Success," *Reno Gazette-Journal,* 9 April 1978, 5.

66. "Good-bye Las Vegas . . . Reno, Hello?" 34.

67. "Community Leaders React with Awe, Wonder," *Nevada State Journal,* 4 May 1978, 10; "MGM Grand Epic," *Nevada State Journal,* 3 May 1978, 4.

68. Jack Douglass as told to William A. Douglass, *Tap Dancing on Ice: The Life and Times of a Nevada Gaming Pioneer* (Reno: Oral History Program, University of Nevada–Reno, 1996), 202–205; Kling, *Rise of the Biggest Little City,* 31.

69. Hilton took the Sahara Reno over in 1981, and it later became the Reno Flamingo Hilton; Kling, *Rise of the Biggest Little City,* 22, 110–111, 146.

70. Barbara Bennett, *Barbara Bennett: Mayor of Reno and Community Activist,* ed. Helen M. Blue and R. T. King (Reno: Oral History Program, University of Nevada–Reno, 1989), 41–44.

71. Bennett, *Barbara Bennett,* 40; Petricciani, *Evolution of Gaming,* 12.

72. Kling, *Rise of the Biggest Little City,* 25, 46, 147, 163; Douglass, *Tap Dancing,* 173–175.

73. Elliott, *History of Nevada,* 328; "How the West Was Won," *Newsweek,* 5 November 1984, 81.

74. Susan Voyles, "Mapes Goes for Nostalgia," *Nevada State Journal,* 23 June 1981, 19.

75. Kling, *Rise of the Biggest Little City,* 103, 111; Susan Voyles, "Money Tree Started Mapes' Money Woes," *Nevada State Journal,* 12 August 1980, 5.

76. Kling, *Rise of the Biggest Little City,* 54; Douglass, *Tap Dancing on Ice,* 213.

77. Thomas Cave Wilson, *Reminiscences of a Nevada Advertising Man, 1930–1980, or Half a Century of Very Hot Air, or I Wouldn't Believe It If I Hadn't Been There* (Reno: Oral History Program, University of Nevada–Reno, 1982), 539–540.

78. Curtis, *It Was Great While It Lasted,* 57; Jim Mort, "If Paranoiac-Schizophrenic Reno Doesn't Continue to Grow, It Will Die," *Nevada State Journal,* 19 July 1983, 11A.

79. Petricciani, *Evolution of Gaming,* 271; Warren Nelson, *Always Bet on the Butcher: Warren Nelson and Casino Gaming, 1930s–1980s* (Reno: Oral History Program, University of Nevada–Reno, 1994), 149.

80. Cardozo, "Think of Reno," 10, 14.

81. Roger Neal and Ellen Paris, "As They Say in Craps, It's a Hard Point," *Forbes,* 5 November 1984, 74.

82. Gorman, *Recollections of a Nevada Banker,* 114; Clarence K. Jones, *Clarence K. Jones: From Paperboy to Philanthropist* (Reno: Oral History Program, University of Nevada–Reno, 1988), 105–106; Neal and Paris, "As They Say in Craps," 80; "Downtown Won't Go Away," *Reno Gazette-Journal,* 22 May 1983, 5E.

83. Abbott, *Metropolitan Frontier,* 145–147; Bennett, *Barbara Bennett,* 64–65.

84. Reno Department of Planning and Development, *Reno Policy Plan: [A Report] to the Reno City Planning Commission* (Reno: Reno Department of Planning and Development, 1982).

85. Reno Department of Planning and Development, *Reno Policy Plan,* PP-10; Bennett, *Barbara Bennett,* 123.

86. Reno Department of Planning and Development, *Policy Plan,* PP-44; Bennett, *Barbara Bennett,* 91.

87. Reno Department of Planning and Development, *Policy Plan,* PP-29-30, PP-44, PP-48.

88. Bennett, *Barbara Bennett,* 72.

89. The Downtown Foundation, *Reno: Downtown Redevelopment* (The Downtown Foundation, Reno, n.d., ca. 1983), Drackert Collection, Special Collections, University of Nevada–Reno Library; Richard Moreno, "Reno Redevelopment: Where It's Going," *Reno Gazette-Journal,* 11 December 1983, 7C.

90. "RUDAT in Reno," 4; Moreno, "Reno Redevelopment," 1C, 7C.

91. "Downtown Won't Go Away," 5E; Tony Fiannaca, Greater Reno Sparks Chamber of Commerce, to Downtown Business Leaders, 19 August 1983, Drackert Collection, Special Collections, University of Nevada–Reno Library; Greater Reno-Sparks Chamber of Commerce, *Operation Pride: Downtown Revitalization Plan* (Reno: Greater Reno-Sparks Chamber of Commerce, 1983), Drackert Collection, Special Collections, University of Nevada–Reno Library.

92. For the professionalization of city marketing, see Stephen V. Ward, *Selling Places: The Marketing and Promotion of Towns and Cities, 1850–2000* (London: Routledge, 1998), 199; and Dennis R. Judd, "Constructing the Tourist Bubble," in *The Tourist City,* ed. Dennis R. Judd and Susan S. Fainstein (New Haven, Conn.: Yale University Press, 1999), 40–43.

93. Allen, *Life without a Safety Net,* 155; Carol Infranca, *Reno Sparks Convention and Visitors Authority, a Brief History* (Reno: Reno-Sparks Convention and Visitors Authority, ca. 1996), 13, 15. Special Collections, University of Nevada–Reno Library.

94. Kling, *Rise of the Biggest Little City,* 69, 127–128.

95. R. L. Polk & Co., *Reno-Sparks City Directory* (El Monte, Calif.: R. L. Polk & Co., 1984); David W. Toll, *The Compleat Nevada Traveler: A Guide to the State* (Gold Hill, Nev.: Gold Hill, 1981), 78.

96. Downtown Renovation Association, *Downtown Renovation Association: A New Voice for Downtown Reno* (Reno: Downtown Renovation Association, ca. 1987); Bob Rusk, chairman, Downtown Renovation Association to Downtown Business Owners, March 1987, Drackert Collection, Special Collections, University of Nevada–Reno Library.

97. The Biggest Little City Committee, *The Biggest Little City in the World,* brochure, ca. 1983, Drackert Collection, Special Collections, University of Nevada–Reno Library; Barbara Land and Myrick Land, *A Short History of Reno* (Reno: University of Nevada Press, 1995), 120.

98. Hal K. Rothman, *Devil's Bargains: Tourism in the Twentieth-Century American West* (Lawrence: University Press of Kansas, 1998), 329.

CHAPTER SIX: A NEW RENO FOR THE NEW MILLENNIUM

1. Desson Howe, "Sister Act," *Washington Post,* 29 May 1992, WW49.

2. Robin Holabird, "re: Sister Act," personal e-mail to author (27 August 2007).

3. Nevada Commission on Tourism, *Promoting Both Sides of Nevada for 15 Years* (Carson City: Commission on Tourism, ca. 1998), U.S. Library of Congress, Washington, D.C., 26.

4. Center for Gaming Research, University of Nevada, Las Vegas, "UNLV Online Gaming Statistics," http://gaming.unlv.edu/abstract/stats.html#strip (8 October 2007).

5. Tate Snyder Kinsey Architects, "Las Vegas Strip and Downtown Tour: Casinos, as of 2000," Architecture Studies Library, University of Nevada–Las Vegas Libraries, http://www.library.unlv.edu/arch/lasvegas/tatesnyderkimsey0tour1.html (9 October 2007).

6. Robert Reinhold, "Las Vegas Transformation: From Sin City to Family City," *New York Times,* 30 May 1989, 1; "Las Vegas: Day for Night," *New York Times,* 21 October 1990, *Sunday Magazine,* 25.

7. Ranjana Madhusudhan, "Betting on Casino Revenues: Lessons from State Experiences," *Fiscal Letter,* National Conference of State Legislatures, www.ncsl.org/programs/fiscal/tf196n5b.htm (14 February 2003).

8. Gerri Hirshey, "Gambling Nation," *New York Times Magazine,* 17 July 1994, 36.

9. Patricia Stokowski, *Riches and Regrets: Betting on Gambling in Two Colorado Mountain Towns* (Niwot: University Press of Colorado, 1996), 284. See also Cathy H. C. Hsu, ed., *Legalized Casino Gaming in the United States: The Economic and Social Impact* (Binghamton, N.Y.: Haworth Hospitality Press, 1999); Robert Goodman, *The Luck Business: The Devastating Consequences and Broken Promises of America's Gambling Explosion* (New York: Free Press, 1995); George Sternlieb and James W. Hughes, *The Atlantic City Gamble* (Cambridge, Mass.: Harvard University Press, 1983); and Katherine Jensen, *The Last Gamble: Betting on the Future in Four Rocky Mountain Mining Towns* (Tucson: University of Arizona Press, 1998). Historian Hal Rothman has claimed that Las Vegas is unique for having experienced a positive economic and social impact from gaming. See Hal K. Rothman, *Devil's Bargains: Tourism in the Twentieth-Century American West* (Lawrence: University Press of Kansas, 1998), and *Neon Metropolis: How Las Vegas Started the Twenty-First Century* (New York: Routledge, 2002).

10. Ronald M. James, deputy state historic preservation officer, to Bethel N. Van Tassel, 9 August 1989, State Historic Preservation Office, Carson City, Nevada; Edwin C. Bearss, chief historian, National Park Service, Department of the Interior, to Roland D. Westergard, director, Department of Conservation and Natural Resources, 30 March 1987, State Historic Preservation Office, Carson City, Nevada; Barbara F. Vucanovich to Ronald D. Westergard, 15 May 1987, State Historic Preservation Office, Carson City, Nevada; Dwayne Kling, *The Rise of the Biggest Little City: An Encyclopedic History of Reno Gaming, 1931–1981* (Reno: University of Nevada Press, 2000), 103.

11. These plans included the following: Downtown Redevelopment Plan (1983); Downtown Redevelopment Plan Amendment (1990); Plan Report—Downtown Redevelopment Area (1990); The Blueprint—A Revitalization Strategy for Downtown Reno (1992); A Revitalization Strategy for the Downtown River Corridor (1995); Center City Housing Strategy for the City of Reno (1995); Gateways Master Plan (1995); City of Reno Redevelopment District Streetscape Master Plan (1996); River Corridor Action Plan (1996); City of Reno Downtown Riverfront District Plan (1997); Entertainment Core Revitalization Plan (1999); Downtown Neighborhood Housing Action Plan (1999); Downtown Visioning Charette (1999); Downtown Office Core Action Plan (2000); Entertainment Core Master Plan (2000); Downtown Event Center and Retail District Parking Analysis (2000). City of Reno, "Downtown Redevelopment Plan Combines 19 Previous Plans," 10 December 2002, www.cityofreno.com/news/1039571874.html (30 April 2003).

12. "Bill Thornton," in Downtown Renovation Association, *Changes: Renovation Is Working in Downtown Reno,* advertising supplement, *Reno Gazette-Journal,* 28 July 1990, 18.

13. Jud Allen, "Reno's Future Is Downtown," in Downtown Renovation Association, *Changes,* 3.

14. "Does Reno Owe Downtown Agency Cash? Some Say No," *Reno Gazette-Journal,* 23 April 2001, 4A.

15. Susan Voyles, "Downtown Agency Could See Expansion," *Reno Gazette-Journal,* 2 May 2001, 7C; Bill Barol, "Lanes Paved with Gold," *Time,* 18 September 1995, 94; John Stearns, "RSCVA Giving Stadium a Facelift," *Reno Gazette-Journal,* 3 August 1999, 1C; "National Bowling Stadium Renews Ties with the ABC," *Bowling Digest,* Spring 2004, 8.

16. Susan Voyles, "Mega Resort Means Major Revenue Boost," *Reno Gazette-Journal,* 20 May 1993, 4A. On tax increment financing, see John Hannigan, *Fantasy City: Pleasure and Profit in the Postmodern Metropolis* (New York: Routledge, 1998), 136.

17. Mike Henderson, "Callers Mostly Favor Project, but Many Have Concerns," *Reno Gazette-Journal,* 20 May 1993, 4A; Susan Skorups, "Previous Themes Didn't Fit Reno's Western Image," *Reno Gazette-Journal,* 3 June 1994, 7A.

18. Skorups, "Previous Themes Didn't Fit Reno's Western Image," 7A; Susan Voyles, "Victorian Look Sparks Debate on Reno's Tone," *Reno Gazette-Journal,* 3 June 1994, 7A.

19. Gaye Delaplane, "Movers, Shakers Like Changes," *Reno Gazette-Journal,* 3 June 1994, 6A; Susan Skorups, "Project C Trading 16th-century Spain for Old West Look," *Reno Gazette-Journal,* 3 June 1994, 1A. On heritage tourism, see M. Christine Boyer, "Cities for Sale: Merchandising History at South Street Seaport," in *Variations on a*

Theme Park: The New American City and the End of Public Space, ed. Michael Sorkin (New York: Hill & Wang, 1992), 181–204.

20. Silver Legacy Hotel Casino, *Silver Legacy,* brochure (Reno: Silver Legacy Hotel Casino, ca. 1995); Silver Legacy Hotel Casino Web site, http://www.silverlegacyreno.com (10 December 2000).

21. Voyles, "Victorian Look," 7A; James Robbins, "Ghostly Host Announces Name for Project C," *Reno Gazette-Journal,* 16 December 1994, 1B.

22. Voyles, "Victorian Look," 7A.

23. Trevor Boddy describes the manner by which such "architectural devices" as pedestrian bridges and tunnels "render even the centers of the new corporate North American city sealed, separated, singular" in "Underground and Overhead: Building the Analogous City," in *Variations on a Theme Park,* ed. Michael Sorkin, 125. Michael P. Branch, "Cosmology in the Casino: Simulacra of Nature in the Interiorized Wilderness," in *The Nature of Cities: Ecocriticism and Urban Environments,* ed. Michael Bennett and David W. Teague (Tucson: University of Arizona Press, 1999), 189.

24. For more on such distinctions, see Robert M. Fogelson, *Downtown: Its Rise and Fall, 1880–1950* (New Haven, Conn.: Yale University Press, 2001), 3.

25. Eldorado Hotel Casino, Silver Legacy Resort & Casino, and Circus Circus Casinos, Inc., Uptown Reno, http://www.uptownreno.com (29 January 2002).

26. Kling, *Rise of the Biggest Little City,* 70; John Stearns, "Downtown 'Renaissance,'" *Reno Gazette-Journal,* 25 April 1998, 1E.

27. Charles J. Fombrun, *Reputation: Realizing Value from the Corporate Image* (Boston: Harvard Business School Press, 1996), 10.

28. Jud Allen, *Life without a Safety Net: An Insider's View of War, Hollywood and Reno* (Marceline, Mo.: Walsworth, 1997), 232; Harry Spencer, "Reno Returns to the Ranks as a Major Tourist City," *Reno Gazette-Journal,* 27 June 1999, 10B; John Stearns, "Reno Needs True Leader to Get on Track," *Reno Gazette-Journal,* 11 January 1999, 4A.

29. "Reno Hillbillies—TV's Jethro Has Colorful Plan for Faded Gambling Town," *San Diego Union-Tribune,* 3 March 1999, A1; "A River Runs through It," *Casino Executive,* May 1999, 30–32.

30. "Save Mural, Not Building," *Reno Gazette-Journal,* 3 August 1999, 9A; Robert Anglen, "Harolds, Nevada Clubs to Be Razed," *Reno Gazette-Journal,* 28 July 1999, 1A; Harry Spencer, "Once-Grand Harold's Club Slated for Demolition," *Reno Gazette-Journal,* 8 August 1999, 8B.

31. For preemptive demolition, see Hannigan, *Fantasy City,* 134–135.

32. Lenita Powers, "The Heart of Reno's History," *Reno Gazette-Journal,* 7 January 1996, 1B.

33. Susan Voyles, "It Made Reno a Destination," *Reno Gazette-Journal,* 17 December 1997, 4A; Susan Voyles, "Virginia Street Report to Face Judgment Day," *Reno Gazette-Journal,* 11 April 1994, 1C.

34. Truckee Meadows Heritage Trust, "Mapes Timeline," "Mapes" File, Nevada Historical Society.

35. "Reno City Manager Blasted over Plan for Landmark," *Las Vegas Sun,* 15 September 1997, 6A.

36. National Trust for Historic Preservation, "Mapes Hotel, Reno, Nev., America's

11 Most Endangered Historic Places," www.nthp.org/main/endangered/ mapes.htm (10 April 1999).

37. "Goodbye, Mapes," *Reno Gazette-Journal,* 31 January 2000, 4A; Robert Anglen, "Supporters See the Tide Turning in Old Hotel's Favor," *Reno Gazette-Journal,* 24 September 1998; Sandra Chereb, "Future Looking Bright for Mapes Hotel," *Las Vegas Sun,* 24 September 1998, http://www.lasvegassun.com/sunbin/stories/text/1998/sep/24/507781291.html (27 April 1999).

38. Peter Fish, "Window on the West: Betting on a Full House," *Sunset,* March 1999, 178.

39. "Mapes May Be Facing the End," *Reno Gazette-Journal,* 24 June 1999, 1A; Robert Anglen, "Asbestos Removal, Unexpected Contamination Add $500,000 to City Price Tag for Renovation," *Reno Gazette-Journal,* 6 February 1999, 1A.

40. "Mapes Needs a Savior: Now," *Reno Gazette-Journal,* 30 June 1999, 13A.

41. Sandra Chereb, "Trust for Historic Preservation Steps Up Fight to Save Mapes," *Reno Gazette-Journal,* 1 July 1999, 1B; Robert Anglen, "Preservationists Say Mapes Can Be Saved," *Reno Gazette-Journal,* 24 June 1999, 8A; Robert Anglen, "Tax Credits Never Sought for Mapes," *Reno Gazette-Journal,* 4 July 1999, 1A.

42. Robert Anglen, "3 Plans Offered to Save Mapes," *Reno Gazette-Journal,* 14 August 1999, 1A; Ken Alltucker, "Mapes Backers Rally for Historic Landmark," *Reno Gazette-Journal,* 4 December 1999, 1C.

43. Ken Alltucker, "Mapes Backers Rally for Historic Landmark," 1C. By September 1999, the city's General Fund had loaned the Reno Redevelopment Agency $2.8 million. This included $550,000 for downtown cleanup in advance of a U.S. mayors convention in April 1998; $300,000 to settle a lawsuit over the Riverside in June 1999; $1.2 million to purchase the old Riverside garage in 1997; and $818,000 to demolish the Mapes Hotel (loaned in September 1999). "Spending Decisions in Dispute," *Reno Gazette-Journal,* 27 September 1999, 1A; Robert Anglen, "Developer Wants Another Chance to Save the Mapes," *Reno Gazette-Journal,* 28 September 1999, 1B; Robert Anglen, "Panel Refuses to Reconsider Demolition of Mapes," *Reno Gazette-Journal,* 29 September 1999, 1C.

44. Susan Voyles, "Time's Up for the Mapes," *Reno Gazette-Journal,* 14 September 1999, 1A; Bobbi Brice, Letter to Editor, *Reno Gazette-Journal,* 27 July 1999, 9A.

45. "Decision Right, Hotel Had to Go," editorial, *Reno Gazette-Journal,* 15 September 1999, 11A.

46. Ken Alltucker, "Judge Won't Stop Mapes Demolition," *Reno Gazette-Journal,* 22 December 1999, 1A.

47. Rothman, *Devil's Bargains,* 334.

48. John Stearns, "Ka-boom! Downtown Could See a Couple Big Blasts in Coming Months," *Reno Gazette-Journal,* 3 October 1999, 1E.

49. John Stearns, "Harolds Implosion Removed a Blemish from Downtown Reno," *Reno Gazette-Journal,* 19 December 1999, 1E.

50. Robert Anglen, "Reno Still Hasn't Paid $2.2 Million on Mapes," *Reno Gazette-Journal,* 15 September 1999, 1A;

51. Evelyn Nieves, "In a Booming Reno, No Room for the Old Inn," *New York Times,* 25 January 2000, A12.

52. "It's not too late to save the Mapes," paid advertisement, National Trust for His-

toric Preservation, *Reno Gazette-Journal*, 26 January 2000, 7A; "The Fate of Reno's Mapes Hotel," editorial, *New York Times*, 27 January 2000, A26; Frank X. Mullen, Jr., "Mapes Saga Gets Big Apple Coverage," *Reno Gazette-Journal*, 30 January 2000, 9A.

53. "Goodbye, Mapes," 1A.

54. Ibid., 4A; Susan Voyles, "Implosion Adds Fuel to Preservationists' Fire," *Reno Gazette-Journal*, 31 January 2000, 6A; Forrest Hartman, "Winning Haiku," *Reno Gazette-Journal*, 5 May 2001, 3D.

55. "World-Class Buildings for Reno," *Reno Gazette-Journal*, 27 February 2001, 5A; "City's Next Step Is to Think Big," Editorial, *Reno Gazette-Journal*, 2 February 2000, 9A.

56. Reno City Council meeting minutes, 31 January 2003; "Reno Council Moves to Get Downtown Land Appraised," *Reno Gazette-Journal*, 12 February 2003, 8C.

57. Susan Voyles, "Artspace Proposes to Make Top Floors of Riverside Hotel into Lofts for Artists," *Reno Gazette-Journal*, 10 January 1998, 1B.

58. Lenita Powers, "Riverside Hotel Renovation on Track," *Reno Gazette-Journal*, 10 May 2000, 1C; Don Cox, "Old Landmark, New Lofts," *Reno Gazette-Journal*, 3 December 2000, 1A; Camille Hayes, "Lofty Living," *Reno Gazette-Journal*, 9 March 2001, 1E.

59. Cox, "Old Landmark, New Lofts," 1A.

60. Patricia Leigh Brown, "A Push to Preserve Reno's Landmarks as Divorce Capital," *New York Times*, 22 April 2002, A1, A24.

61. Reno-Sparks Convention & Visitors Authority, "Situational Analysis Summary," 2001, www.rscva.com/marketing/marketing/situation.html (1 March 2001); John Stearns, "Who's Visiting Reno?" *Reno Gazette-Journal*, 4 July 1999, 1E; Erica Werner, "Stakes High as Tribes Negotiate Contracts," *Reno Gazette-Journal*, 21 January 2003, 1D.

62. John Stearns, "Downtown Is Like a Bad Halloween Movie," *Reno Gazette-Journal*, 28 October 2001, 1E.

63. Susan Voyles, "Washoe County Cuts Value of Casinos," *Reno Gazette-Journal*, 21 February 2003, 1A.

64. Ryan Randazzo, "Phoenix Finances Far from Golden," *Reno Gazette-Journal*, 5 February 2003, http://www.rgj.com/news/printstory.php?id=33752 (6 February 2003).

65. For more on branding, see Marc Gobe, *Emotional Branding: The New Paradigm for Connecting Brands to People* (New York: Allworth Press, 2002); Daryl Travis, *Emotional Branding: How Successful Brands Gain the Irrational Edge* (Roseville, Calif.: Prima Venture, 2000); David E. Carter, *Branding: The Power of Market Identity* (New York: Watson-Guptill Publications, 1999); Travel and Tourism Research Association, *Travel Research Roundup: Branding the Travel Market* (Fort Worth, Tex.: Travel and Tourism Association, 1998).

66. Reno-Sparks Convention and Visitors Authority, *Sales & Marketing Plan Update, 2000–2001*, 29 January 2001, http://www.renolaketahoe.com/about/research/ (30 April 2003).

67. John Stearns, "Visiting Media Find a Northern Nevada They Didn't Expect," *Reno Gazette-Journal*, 30 January 2000, 1E.

68. Daniel B. Wood, "A Tale of How Two Cities Have Dealt with Growth," *Christian Science Monitor*, 13 March 2001, http://www.csmonitor.com/2001/0313/p12s1.html (1 December 2007); John Stearns, "Selling Northern Nevada," *Reno Gazette-Journal*, 22 November 2001, 1B.

69. Reno-Sparks Convention & Visitors Authority, "Media Campaign," http://rscva .com/marketing/marketing/media.html (1 March 2001).

70. Reno-Sparks Convention & Visitors Authority, "RSCVA Sales & Marketing Plan Update, 2000–2001"; Hannigan, *Fantasy City,* 56.

71. Hannigan, *Fantasy City,* 1.

72. Reno-Sparks Convention & Visitors Authority, "Situational Analysis Summary."

73. Reno-Sparks Convention & Visitors Authority, "RSCVA Marketing and Sales Plan, FY2002–2003," www.renolaketahoe.com/about/research/ (30 April 2003).

74. *Reno-Tahoe, America's Adventure Place: 2004 Visitor Planner* (Reno: Reno-Sparks Convention & Visitors Authority, 2004), 1.

75. Study conducted by Infosearch International in 2005 and reported in "Stretching for a Tourist Bump: Efforts to Attract Young Travelers Fall Short," *Reno Gazette-Journal,* 18 June 2006, 1E.

76. Advertising Research Foundation, "Las Vegas Alibi: A Campaign to Link the Brand's Benefits with Its Product Attributes," 2007, www.thearf.org/downloads/awards/ studies/Las_Vegas_2007_Ogilvy_Case_Study.pdf (5 June 2007).

77. RSCVA 2006 Visitor Profile Study, cited in "Who Are Reno Tourists?" *Reno Gazette-Journal,* 25 March 2007, 1E.

78. Gaming Control Board report for fiscal year 2006, cited in "Casinos Keep Diversifying," *Reno Gazette-Journal,* 5 January 2007, 1D.

79. "Tour de Nez Races onto Cycling's National Scene," CNN Web site, 15 June 2006, http://www.cnn.com/2006/TRAVEL/DESTINATIONS/06/09/sierra.cycling.ap/ index.html (10 September 2007).

80. Mike Kord, "Reno Revival," http://www.canoekayak.com/destinations/ westernus/renorevival/ (9 September 2007).

81. Great Reno Balloon Race fact sheet, http://www.renoballoon.com/media/ 2007/new_fact_sheet_07final.pdf (8 September 2007).

82. Jori Finkel, "The Fastest Gavel in the West," *New York Times,* 26 August 2007, Arts sec., 21.

83. The Community Visioning Workshop Outcomes (2002); Central City Master Circulation Plan (2002); California Avenue/Office Core Streetscape Concepts (2002); South Downtown Urban Design Plan (2002); City of Reno, "Downtown Redevelopment Plan Combines 19 Previous Plans."

84. See Derek Wynne, "Cultural Quarters," in *The Culture Industry: The Arts in Urban Regeneration,* ed. Derek Wynne (Brookfield, Vt.: Avebury, 1992).

85. Doresa Banning, "Downtown Merchants Team Up to Boost Foot Traffic to the Area," *Reno Gazette-Journal,* 15 November 2000, 2D; "Small Business Changing Reno," editorial, *Reno Gazette-Journal,* 5 September 2000, 5A.

86. Heritage Tourism Coalition, *Directory of Historic Organizations and Resources in Northwestern Nevada* (Reno: Heritage Tourism Coalition, 2002); GustinCurtis Advertising, "Our Community," http://gustincurtis.com/work/community.html (10 February 2003).

87. Bel Willem, "New Museum Will Be Work of Art," *Reno Gazette-Journal,* 12 November 2002, 1A.

88. Christopher Hall, "Architecture in Reno (and Not a Casino)," *New York Times,* 20 July 2003, AR30.

89. Wood, "A Tale of How Two Cities Have Dealt with Growth"; "About the University of Nevada, Reno," http://www.unr.edu/about/index.html#about (1 September 2007).

90. Suzette Parmley, "Settling Down," *Philadelphia Inquirer*, 29 January 2006, E01.

91. Mel Shields, "There's More to Visit in Reno than Just the Casinos," *Sacramento Bee*, travel sec., 15 July 2007, www.sacbee.com/374/v-print-story-269749.html (10 September 2007).

92. Melinda Ligos, "In Reno; City Known for Gambling Works to Reinvent Itself," *New York Times*, 15 July 2003, C6.

93. Adam Tanner, Reuters, "Casinos Fading, but Reno Enjoys Economic Boom," 6 August 2005.

94. Don Cox, "'Bleak'? Locals Don't Buy It," *Reno Gazette-Journal*, 26 May 2001, 1A, quoting *New York Times*, 19 May 2001; Robert Gavin, "Reno's Gamble on Development Pays Off Big," *Wall Street Journal*, 2 January 2002, A7, A8.

95. Joel Kotkin, "The Best Places for Doing Business in America 2005," *Inc.*, May 2005; "How the 2007 Best Cities Were Selected," *Inc.*, 13 April 2007, http://www.inc.com/articles/2007/04/methodology.html (10 September 2007).

96. Ross DeVol, Lorna Wallace, and Armen Bedroussian, "Best Performing Cities 2005: Where America's Jobs Are Created and Sustained," Milken Institute, February 2006, http://www.milkeninstitute.org/publications/publications.taf?function=detail& ID=478&cat=ResRep (3 November 2007).

97. Ryan Randazzo, "Reno Earns a Full Page in National Geographic Adventure," *Reno Gazette-Journal*, 11 January 2007, 1D; "Adventure Place Brand Taking Hold," *Reno Gazette-Journal*, editorial, 12 January 2007, 9A.

98. Ray Hagar, "Biggest Little Dirty Secret," *Reno Gazette-Journal*, 7 October 2007, 12A; Tom Chiarella, "The Dirtiest Secret in Nevada," *Esquire*, October 2007, 153, 156.

99. Forrest Hartman, "Protect, Serve and Spoof," *Reno Gazette-Journal*, 2 July 2003, 1E; Forrest Hartman, "Reno Stars in Pair of TV Shows Debuting This Month," *Reno Gazette-Journal*, 13 July 2003, 15A.

100. Hartman, "Reno Stars in Pair of TV Shows," 1A.

101. Ibid.

102. Bill O'Driscoll, "EDAWN Unveils New Brand," *Reno Gazette-Journal*, 25 April 2007, 7A.

BIBLIOGRAPHY

NEWSPAPERS

Altoona (Pa.) *Mirror*
Daily Nevada State Journal
Daily Times-News (Burlington, N.C.)
Danville (W.Va.) *Bee*
Dunkirk (N.Y.) *Evening Observer*
Goldfield Daily Tribune
Helena (Mont.) *Independent*
Independent Star-News (Pasadena, Calif.)
Kansas City Star
Las Vegas Sun
Los Angeles Times
Nevada State Journal
New York Times
Oakland Tribune
Philadelphia Inquirer
Portsmouth (Ohio)*Times*
Reno Evening Gazette
Reno Gazette-Journal
Reno Weekly Gazette
Reno Weekly Gazette and Stockman
Sacramento Bee
San Antonio Light
San Diego Union-Tribune
San Francisco Call
San Francisco Chronicle
San Francisco Sunday Call
Simpson's Daily Leader-Times (Kittaning, Pa.)
Wall Street Journal
Washington Post

ARCHIVAL MATERIALS

Autry Library, Autry National Center, Los Angeles

David, W. M. "Ramblings through the Pines and Sage: A Series of One Day Tours out of Reno." Nevada State Automobile Association, ca. 1928.

Nevada Historical Society, Reno, Nevada

Business and Industrial Development Department, Greater Reno Chamber of Commerce. *Greater Reno Area Profile*. Reno: Greater Reno Chamber of Commerce, 1969–70. "Reno Publicity" file.
Earl, Philip I. "Reno Rodeo Has Long and Rich History Dating Back to 1919," n.d. "Reno History" file.
"Nevada Dude Ranch Association." Brochure. Reno: Nevada Dude Ranch Association, ca. 1936. "Dude Ranches" file.
"Reno Publicity Plans Outlined." Western Advertising, October 1945. "Reno Publicity" print file.
Truckee Meadows Heritage Trust. "Mapes Timeline," n.d. "Mapes" file.

Nevada State Historic Preservation Office, Carson City, Nevada

Bearss, Edwin C., chief historian, National Park Service, director, Department of the Interior to Roland D. Westergard, Department of Conservation and Natural Resources, Carson City, Nevada, 30 March 1987. "Mapes" file.
James, Ronald M., deputy state historic preservation officer to Bethel N. Van Tassel. Carson City, Nevada, 9 August 1989. "Mapes" file.
Rainshadow Associates. *National Register Nomination Form, Mapes Hotel and Casino*. Reno: Rainshadow Associates, 1983.
Vucanovich, Barbara F., to Director Ronald D. Westergard, Department of Conservation and Natural Resources, Carson City, Nevada, 15 May 1987.

Special Collections, University of Nevada–Reno Library, Reno, Nevada

"Addresses Delivered at the Nevada State Business Men's Convention Held at the Reno Commercial Club Rooms, Reno, Nevada, Friday and Saturday, June 16–17, 1916." Reno: Nevada Press, 1916.
Bennett, Barbara. *Barbara Bennett: Mayor of Reno and Community Activist*, ed. Helen M. Blue and R. T. King. Reno: Oral History Program, University of Nevada–Reno, 1989.
The Biggest Little City Committee. *The Biggest Little City in the World*. Brochure. Reno: The Biggest Little City Committee, ca. 1983.
Cole, Gloria G. "Reno Gambling." In *Twelve Doors to Reno*, ed. John Price, 27–35. San Diego: Ethnological Archives, 1970.
Douglass, Jack, as told to William A. Douglass. *Tap Dancing on Ice: The Life and Times of*

a Nevada Gaming Pioneer. Reno: Oral History Program, University of Nevada–Reno, 1996.

The Downtown Foundation. *Reno: Downtown Redevelopment.* Brochure. Reno: The Downtown Foundation, ca. 1983. Drackert Collection.

Downtown Renovation Association. *Downtown Renovation Association: A New Voice for Downtown Reno.* Brochure. Reno: Downtown Renovation Association, ca. 1987.

Erskine, Graham. "Reno, Haven or Hovel?" Four-part lecture Series sponsored by the University of Nevada, Reno, General University Extension and the Department of Art, 1965.

Fiannaca, Tony, president, Greater Reno-Sparks Chamber of Commerce, to Downtown Business Leaders. Reno, 19 August 1983. Drackert Collection.

First National Bank. *One Sound State.* Reno: First National Bank, 1936.

Gorman, Harold. *Recollections of a Nevada Banker and Civic Leader.* Oral History Project, University of Nevada–Reno, 1976.

Greater Reno-Sparks Chamber of Commerce. *Operation Pride: Downtown Revitalization Plan.* Brochure. Reno: Greater Reno-Sparks Chamber of Commerce, 1983. Drackert Collection.

Infranca, Carol. *Reno-Sparks Convention and Visitors Authority, a Brief History.* Reno: Reno-Sparks Convention & Visitors Authority, ca. 1996.

Jones, Clarence K. *Clarence K. Jones: From Paperboy to Philanthropist.* Reno: Oral History Program, University of Nevada–Reno, 1988.

Nelson, Warren. *Always Bet on the Butcher: Warren Nelson and Casino Gaming, 1930s–1980s.* Reno: Oral History Program, University of Nevada–Reno, 1994.

Petricciani, Silvio. *The Evolution of Gaming in Nevada: The Twenties to the Eighties.* Reno: Oral History Program, University of Nevada–Reno, 1982.

Price, John A., ed. *Twelve Doors to Reno.* San Diego: Ethnological Archives, 1970.

Reno Chamber of Commerce. *Reno, Land of Charm.* Reno: Chamber of Commerce, ca. 1930.

Ring, Robert A. *Recollections of Life in California, Nevada Gaming, and Reno and Lake Tahoe Business and Civic Affairs.* Oral History Project, University of Nevada, Reno, 1973.

Rusk, Bob, Chairman, Downtown Renovation Association to Downtown Business Leaders, March 1987. Drackert Collection.

Siggers, Philip E. *The Truth about Reno.* Reno: privately printed, 1934.

Washoe County Blue Ribbon Task Force on Growth. *Blue Ribbon Task Force Program: Growth and Development, Reno, Sparks and Washoe County, Nevada.* Reno: Regional Planning Commission of Reno, Sparks and Washoe County, 1973–1974.

Weber, Norman. "A Cultural Geography of Reno." In *Twelve Doors to Reno,* ed. John A. Price, 127–132. San Diego: Ethnological Archives, 1970.

Wier, Jeanne Elizabeth. "The Work of the Western State Historical Society as Illustrated by Nevada." Paper read at the annual meeting of the Pacific Coast Branch of the American Historical Association, University of California, 19 November 1910.

Wilson, David L. "The Social Organization of Black Pimps and Prostitutes in Reno." In *Twelve Doors to Reno,* ed. John A. Price, 52–60. San Diego: Ethnological Archives, 1970.

Wilson, Thomas Cave. *Reminiscences of a Nevada Advertising Man, 1930–1980, or Half a Century of Very Hot Air, or I Wouldn't Believe It If I Hadn't Been There.* Reno: Oral History Program, University of Nevada–Reno, 1982.

OTHER SOURCES

Abbott, Carl. *The Metropolitan Frontier: Cities in the Modern American West.* Tucson: University of Arizona Press, 1993.
"About the University of Nevada, Reno," University of Nevada, Reno Web site. http://www.unr.edu/about/index.html#about (1 September 2007).
Advertising Research Foundation, "Las Vegas Alibi: A Campaign to Link the Brand's Benefits with Its Product Attributes," 2007, www.thearf.org/downloads/awards/studies/Las_Vegas_2007_Ogilvy_Case_Study.pdf (5 June 2007).
Albert, Allen D., Jr. "Reno, the Refuge of Restless Hearts," *Munsey's Magazine,* 42, no. 1, October 1909, 3–18.
Allen, Jud. *Life without a Safety Net: An Insider's View of War, Hollywood and Reno.* Marceline, Mo.: Walsworth, 1997.
Anderson, Sherwood. "So This Is Reno," *Nevada Newsletter,* 5 April 1924.
Asimow, Michael R. "Divorce in the Movies: From the Hays Code to *Kramer vs. Kramer.*" *Legal Studies Forum* 24 (2000): 221–267.
Athearn, Robert. *The Mythic West in Twentieth-Century America.* Lawrence: University Press of Kansas, 1986.
Baldwin, Faith. *Temporary Address: Reno.* New York: Farrar & Rinehart, 1941.
Barol, Bill. "Lanes Paved with Gold." *Time,* 18 September 1995.
Barth, Gunther. *Instant Cities: Urbanization and the Rise of San Francisco and Denver.* New York: Oxford University Press, 1975.
Beebe, Lucius. "Reno: Specialization and Fun." In *The American City: A Sourcebook of Urban Imagery,* ed. Anselm L. Strauss, 431–433. Chicago: Aldine, 1968.
Bell, Charles R., ed. *Nevada Official Centennial Magazine.* Las Vegas: Charles R. Bell, 1964.
Berger, Meyer. "The Gay Gamblers of Reno." *Saturday Evening Post,* 10 July 1948, 22.
Biggers, Earl Derr. *Keeper of the Keys.* Indianapolis: Bobbs-Merrill, 1932.
Blake, Nelson Manfred. *The Road to Reno: A History of Divorce in the United States.* New York: Macmillan, 1962.
Boddy, Trevor. "Underground and Overhead: Building the Analogous City." In *Variations on a Theme Park: The New American City and the End of Public Space,* ed. Michael Sorkin, 123–153. New York: Hill & Wang, 1992.
Bolin, James H. *Reno, Nevada; "Holy City" of the World.* Reno: Bolin Publishing, 1924.
Bond, George W. *Six Months in Reno.* New York: Stanley Gibbons, 1921.
Boorstin, Daniel J. *The Americans: The Democratic Experience.* New York: Vintage Books, 1974.
———. *The Image: A Guide to Pseudo-events in America.* Twenty-fifth anniversary edition. New York: Atheneum, 1987.
Borsay, Peter. *The Image of Georgian Bath, 1700–2000.* New York: Oxford University Press, 2000.

"Bother over Brothels." *Newsweek*, 30 August 1948, 19–20.

Boyer, M. Christine. "Cities for Sale: Merchandising History at South Street Seaport." In *Variations on a Theme Park: The New American City and the End of Public Space*, ed. Michael Sorkin, 181–204. New York: Hill & Wang, 1992.

———. *The City of Collective Memory: Its Historical Imagery and Architectural Entertainments*. Cambridge, Mass.: MIT Press, 1994.

Boyer, Paul. *Urban Masses and Moral Order in America, 1820–1920*. Cambridge, Mass.: Harvard University Press, 1978.

Branch, Michael P. "Cosmology in the Casino: Simulacra of Nature in the Interiorized Wilderness." In *The Nature of Cities: Ecocriticism and Urban Environments*, ed. Michael Bennett and David W. Teague. Tucson: University of Arizona Press, 1999.

Brechin, Gray. *Imperial San Francisco: Urban Power, Earthly Ruin*. Berkeley: University of California Press, 1999.

Brockliss, Ramona Park. "Reno Has a Personality," *Sunset Magazine*, September 1926, 44.

Brooks, Noah. "The Gentleman from Reno," *Overland Monthly*, 1, no. 4, October 1868, 379–384.

Buel, J.W. *America's Wonderlands: A Pictorial and Descriptive History of Our Country's Scenic Marvels*. Boston: J.S. Round, 1893.

Butterfield, Roger. "Harold's Club." *Life*, 15 October 1945, 116–118, 120, 122, 125–126, 128, 131.

Cardozo, Yvette. "Think of Reno, Nevada." *Travel/Holiday*, February 1981, 10–16.

Carman, Dorothy Wadsworth. *Reno Fever*. New York: Ray Long & Richard R. Smith, 1932.

Carter, David E. *Branding: The Power of Market Identity*. New York: Watson-Guptill Publications, 1999.

Cavers, David F. "Migratory Divorce." *Social Forces* 16 (1937): 96–107.

Census Office, Department of the Interior. *Report on the Statistics of Agriculture in the United States at the Eleventh Census*. Washington, D.C.: U.S. Government Printing Office, 1890.

Census Office, Department of the Interior. *Report on the Statistics of Agriculture in the United States at the Ninth Census*. Washington, D.C.: U.S. Government Printing Office, 1870.

Center for Gaming Research, University of Nevada, Las Vegas. "UNLV Online Gaming Statistics." http://gaming.unlv.edu/abstract/stats.html#strip (8 October 2007).

Chiarella, Tom. "The Dirtiest Secret in Nevada." *Esquire*, October 2007, 153–156.

Christensen, Bonnie. *Red Lodge and the Mythic West: Coal Miners to Cowboys*. Lawrence: University Press of Kansas, 2002.

Churchill, Caroline M. *"Little Sheaves" Gathered While Gleaning after Reapers. Being Letters of Travel Commencing in 1870, and Ending in 1873*. San Francisco: n.p., 1874. Available from Library of Congress, American Memory collection, http://hdl.loc.gov/loc.gdc/calbk.091 (2 November 2007).

City Directory Publishing Company, *1911–1912 Directory of Reno and Sparks*. Reno: City Directory Publishing Company, 1911.

City of Reno. "Downtown Redevelopment Plan Combines 19 Previous Plans." City of Reno, 10 December 2002, http://www.cityofreno.com/news/1039571874.html (30 April 2003).

Clark, Walter Van Tilburg. *The City of Trembling Leaves.* Reprint ed. Garden City, N.Y.: Sun Dial Press, 1946.

———. "Reno: The State City." In *Rocky Mountain Cities,* ed. Ray B. West, Jr., 29–53. New York: W. W. Norton, Inc., 1949.

Clay, Grady. *Close Up: How to Read the American City.* Chicago: University of Chicago, 1980.

Clifton, Guy. *Reno Rodeo: A History—The First 80 Years.* Reno: Reno Rodeo Foundation, 2000.

Cocks, Catherine. *Doing the Town: The Rise of Urban Tourism in the United States, 1850–1915.* Berkeley: University of California Press, 2001.

Cray, Ed. *Ramblin' Man: The Life and Times of Woody Guthrie.* New York: W. W. Norton, 2004.

Crevecoeur, J. Hector St. John de. *Letters from an American Farmer and Sketches of Eighteenth-Century America.* New York: Penguin Classics, 1981.

Crofutt, George A. *Crofutt's New Overland Tourist and Pacific Coast Guide.* Omaha: Overland Publishing, 1882.

Cronon, William. *Nature's Metropolis: Chicago and the Great West.* New York: W. W. Norton, 1991.

Curtis, Leslie. "Oh, Hash of Life, Thy Name Is Reno!" *Washington Post,* 4 June 1911, 4–5.

Curtis, Mark. *It Was Great While It Lasted: A PR Man's Reflections on Nevada's Entertainment Heyday.* Reno: Black Rock Press, 2001.

Davis, Mike. *City of Quartz: Excavating the Future in Los Angeles.* First Vintage Books ed. New York: Vintage Books, 1992.

"Day of a Divorcee." *Saturday Evening Post,* 11 December 1937, 22–23, 88.

DeVol, Ross, Lorna Wallace, and Armen Bedroussian, "Best Performing Cities 2005: Where America's Jobs Are Created and Sustained," Milken Institute, February 2006, http://www.milkeninstitute.org/publications/publications.taf?function=detail&ID=478&cat=ResRep (3 November 2007).

Dubinsky, Karen. *The Second Greatest Disappointment: Honeymooning and Tourism at Niagara Falls.* New Brunswick, N.J.: Rutgers University Press, 1999.

Earl, Philip I. "Meandering along the Line of the Central Pacific Railroad, 1868." *Nevada Historical Society Quarterly* 21, no. 4 (1978): 279–285.

———. "100 Years Ago, First Motorcycle Crossed the Sierra," *Reno Gazette-Journal,* 25 August 2002, 1B.

Eldorado Hotel Casino, Silver Legacy Resort & Casino, and Circus Circus Casinos. Uptown Reno. 1999, http://www.uptownreno.com (29 January 2002).

Elliott, Russell R., with William D. Rowley. *History of Nevada.* 2d ed., rev. Lincoln: University of Nebraska Press, 1987.

Findlay, John M. *People of Chance: Gambling in American Society from Jamestown to Las Vegas.* New York: Oxford University Press, 1986.

Fine, Gary Alan. "Reputational Entrepreneurs and the Memory of Incompetence: Melting Supporters, Partisan Warriors, and Images of President Harding." *American Journal of Sociology* 101, no. 5 (1996): 1159–1193.

Fish, Peter. "Window on the West: Betting on a Full House." *Sunset,* March 1999, 178.

Fogelson, Robert M. *Downtown: Its Rise and Fall, 1880–1950.* New Haven, Conn.: Yale University Press, 2001.

————. *The Fragmented Metropolis: Los Angeles, 1850–1930.* Cambridge, Mass.: Harvard University Press, 1967.

Fombrun, Charles J. *Reputation: Realizing Value from the Corporate Image.* Boston: Harvard Business School Press, 1996.

Gabler, Neal. *Winchell: Gossip, Power, and the Culture of Celebrity.* New York: Knopf, 1994.

"Gambling in America." Final report of the Commission on the Review of the National Policy toward Gambling. Washington, D.C.: U.S. Government Printing Office, 1976.

Garreau, Joel. *Edge City: Life on the New Frontier.* New York: Anchor Books, 1991.

"The Gateway to Nevada." *Harper's Weekly,* 20 June 1903, 1031–1032.

Gerould, Katharine Fullerton. "Reno." *Harper's,* June 1925, 47–59.

Gilbert, Tom. *Reno! "It Won't Be Long Now."* Reno: Gilbert & Shapro, 1927.

Gladding, Effie Price. *Across the Continent by the Lincoln Highway.* New York: Brentano's, 1915.

Gobe, Marc. *Emotional Branding: The New Paradigm for Connecting Brands to People.* New York: Allworth Press, 2002.

"Good-Bye Las Vegas . . . Reno, Hello?" *Forbes,* 29 May 1978, 34.

Goodman, Robert. *The Luck Business: The Devastating Consequences and Broken Promises of America's Gambling Explosion.* New York: Free Press, 1995.

Great Reno Balloon Race fact sheet, http://www.renoballoon.com/media/2007/new_fact_sheet_07final.pdf (8 September 2007).

Greene, William W. "Reno." *Travel,* July 1922, 26–29, 40, 41.

Greenwood, Robert. *Jack Johnson vs. Jim Jeffries: The Fight of the Century.* Reno: Jack Bacon, 2004.

Griswold, J. B. "Wild West." *American Magazine,* May 1938, 14–15, 170–174.

GustinCurtis Advertising. *Our Community.* GustinCurtis Advertising Web site, http://www.gustincurtis.com/work/community.html (10 February 2003).

Halbwachs, Maurice. *On Collective Memory.* Chicago: University of Chicago Press, 1992.

Hamer, David. *New Towns in the New World: Images and Perceptions of the Nineteenth-Century Urban Frontier.* New York: Columbia University Press, 1990.

Hamlin, John. *Whirlpool of Reno.* New York: Dial Press, 1931.

Hanna, Stephen P. "Is It Rosyln or Is It Cicely? Representation and the Ambiguity of Place." *Urban Geography* 17, no. 7 (1996): 633–649.

Hannigan, John. *Fantasy City: Pleasure and Profit in the Postmodern Metropolis.* New York: Routledge, 1998.

Hardesty, Stephen L. *The Site of Reno's Beginning: The Historical Mitigation of the Riverside Hotel/Casino.* Reno: City of Reno Redevelopment Agency, August 1997.

Harmon, Mella. "Divorce and Economic Opportunity in Reno, Nevada during the Great Depression." M.S. thesis, University of Nevada–Reno, 1998.

Havemann, Ernest. "Gamblers Paradise Lost," *Life,* 25 October 1954, 67–68.

Heritage Tourism Coalition. *Directory of Historic Organizations and Resources in Northwestern Nevada.* Reno: Heritage Tourism Coalition, 2002.

Holabird, Robin. "re: Sister Act." Personal e-mail to author (27 August 2007).

Holcomb, Briavel. "Revisioning Place: De- and Re-Constructing the Image of the

Industrial City." In *Selling Places: The City as Cultural Capital, Past and Present,* ed. Gerry Kearns and Chris Philo, 133–143. Oxford: Pergamon Press, 1993.

"How the 2007 Best Cities Were Selected." *Inc.,* 13 April 2007, http://www.inc.com/articles/2007/04/methodology.html (10 September 2007).

"How the West Was Won." *Newsweek,* 5 November 1984, 81.

Howard, George Elliott. "Is the Freer Granting of Divorce an Evil?" *American Journal of Sociology* 14, no. 6 (May 1909): 766–796.

———. Review of *Divorce: A Study in Social Causation,* by James P. Lichtenberger. *American Political Science Review* 4 (May 1910): 302–305.

Hsu, Cathy H. C., ed. *Legalized Casino Gaming in the United States: The Economic and Social Impact.* Binghamton, N.Y.: Haworth Hospitality Press, 1999.

Hulse, James W. *The Silver State: Nevada's Heritage Reinterpreted.* 2d ed. Reno: University of Nevada Press, 1998.

———. *The University of Nevada: A Centennial History.* Reno: University of Nevada Press, 1974.

Hungerford, Edward. *The Personality of American Cities.* New York: McBride, Nast, 1913.

Hutchinson, Paul. "Nevada—A Prostitute State." *Christian Century,* 25 November 1931, 1488–1490.

———. "Reno—A Wide Open Town." *Christian Century,* 2 December 1931, 1519–1520.

Hyde, Anne Farrar. *An American Vision: Far Western Landscape and National Culture, 1890–1920.* New York: NYU Press, 1990.

Jackson, John Brinckerhoff. *A Sense of Place, a Sense of Time.* New Haven, Conn.: Yale University Press, 1994.

Jackson, Kenneth T. *Crabgrass Frontier: The Suburbanization of the United States.* Oxford: Oxford University Press, 1985.

James, George Wharton. "What's the Matter with Nevada?" *Out West,* April 1914.

James, Ronald M. *The Roar and the Silence: A History of Virginia City and the Comstock Lode.* Reno: University of Nevada Press, 1998.

Jeff, Leonard J., and Jerold Simmons, eds. *The Dame in the Kimono: Hollywood, Censorship, and the Production Code from the 1920s to the 1960s.* New York: Grove Weidenfeld, 1990.

Jensen, Katherine. *The Last Gamble: Betting on the Future in Four Rocky Mountain Mining Towns.* Tucson: University of Arizona Press, 1998.

Johnson, Kendrick. *Rabelaisian Reminiscences of Reno by a Bachelor Lawyer.* Los Angeles: Gem Publishing, 1934.

Johnson, Susan Lee. *Roaring Camp: The Social World of the California Gold Rush.* New York: W. W. Norton, 2000.

Judd, Dennis R. "Constructing the Tourist Bubble." In *The Tourist City,* ed. Dennis R. Judd and Susan S. Fainstein. New Haven, Conn.: Yale University Press, 1999.

Judd, Dennis R., and Susan S. Fainstein, eds. *The Tourist City.* New Haven, Conn.: Yale University Press, 1999.

Kearns, Gerry, and Chris Philo, eds. *Selling Places: The City as Cultural Capital, Past and Present.* Oxford: Pergamon Press, 1993.

Keillor, Garrison. *A Prairie Home Companion.* Performance and live radio broadcast. Lawlor Events Center, University of Nevada–Reno, Reno, Nevada, 19 June 1999.

Kellogg, Virginia. "The Real Reno, from 'Cosmopolitan.'" *Literary Digest,* 27 November 1937, 27–28.

Kling, Dwayne. *The Rise of the Biggest Little City: An Encyclopedic History of Reno Gaming, 1931–1981.* The Gambling Studies Series. Reno: University of Nevada Press, 2000.

Kord, Mike. "Reno Revival." http://www.canoekayak.com/destinations/westernus/renorevival/ (9 September 2007).

Kotkin, Joel. "The Best Places for Doing Business in America 2005." *Inc.,* May 2005, 93–104.

Land, Barbara, and Myrick Land. *A Short History of Reno.* Reno: University of Nevada Press, 1995.

Lears, T. J. Jackson. *No Place of Grace: Antimodernism and the Transformation of American Culture, 1880–1920.* New York: Pantheon Books, 1981.

Lewis, Grace Hegger. "Just What Is Reno Like." *Scribner's,* January 1929, 35–45.

Lippard, Lucy. *The Lure of the Local: Senses of Place in a Multicentered Society.* New York: New Press, 1997.

L. M. McKenney &. Co. *McKenney's Business Directory of the Principal Towns of California, Nevada, Utah, Wyoming, Colorado and Nebraska.* Sacramento: H. S. Crocker, 1882.

Lummis, Charles F. "The Right Hand of the Continent." *Out West,* March 1903, 307–308.

Lynch, Kevin. *The Image of the City.* Cambridge: MIT Press, 1960.

MacCannell, Dean. *The Tourist: A New Theory of the Leisure Class.* New York: Schocken, 1976.

Madhusudhan, Ranjana. *Betting on Casino Revenues: Lessons from State Experiences.* The Fiscal Letter, National Conference of State Legislatures, www.ncsl.org/programs/fiscal/tf196n5b.htm (14 February 2003).

Marchand, Roland. *Advertising the American Dream: Making Way for Modernity, 1920–1940.* Berkeley: University of California Press, 1985.

May, Lary. *Screening Out the Past: The Birth of Mass Culture and the Motion Picture Industry.* New York: Oxford University Press, 1980.

McCormick, Anne O'Hare. "Reno, Child of the Fabulous Frontier." *New York Times Magazine,* 1 November 1931, sec. V, 4–5, 16.

Melton, Rollan. *101 Nevada Columns.* Reno: Nevada Humanities Committee, 2001.

Miller, Max. *Reno.* New York: Dodd, Mead, 1941.

———. "Reno: Honky-Tonk and Trading Post." *Reader's Digest,* August 1941, 85–89.

Moe, Richard, and Carter Wilkie. *Changing Places: Rebuilding Community in the Age of Sprawl.* New York: Henry Holt, 1997.

Moehring, Eugene P. *Resort City in the Sunbelt: Las Vegas, 1930–2000.* 2d ed. Reno: University of Nevada Press, 2000.

Moody, Eric N., and Guy Louis Rocha. "The Rise and Fall of the Reno Stockade." *Nevada,* April/May/June 1978, 28–30.

Mullett, Mary B. "Mary B. Mullett Tells the Truth about Reno." *American Magazine,* October 1930, 26–29, 149–152.

"National Bowling Stadium Renews Ties with the ABC." *Bowling Digest,* Spring 2004.

National Trust for Historic Preservation. "Mapes Hotel, Reno, Nev., America's 11 Most

Endangered Historic Places. National Trust for Historic Preservation, 1999." www .nthp.org/main/endangered/mapes.htm (10 April 1999).

Neal, Roger, and Ellen Paris. "As They Say in Craps, It's a Hard Point." *Forbes,* 5 November 1984, 74–82.

Nevada at the World's Fair: Accompanied by Illustrations of Its Home Interests. Carson City, Nev.: J. A. Yerington, ca. 1893.

Nevada Commission on Tourism. *Promoting Both Sides of Nevada for 15 Years.* Carson City, Nev.: Nevada Commission on Tourism, ca. 1998. Library of Congress, Washington, D.C.

Nevada Directory Company. *Directory of Reno, Sparks and Carson.* Reno: Nevada Directory Company, 1910.

Nevada Information Division, Reno Chamber of Commerce. *Nevada, the Last Frontier* 1 (Summer 1939).

Nevada State Bureau of Immigration. *Nevada and Her Resources.* Carson City: Nevada State Printing Office, 1894.

Nevada State Historical Society. *Nevada: A Guide to the Silver State.* Portland, Oreg.: Binfords & Mort, 1940.

"The New West: A Social Study of Life in Nevada Towns Today." *Sunset,* February 1907, 296–298.

Newlands, Francis G. "The Future of Nevada." *Independent,* 18 April 1901, 885–888.

Paine, Swift. "As We See It in Reno." *North American Review,* June 1930, 720–726.

Parkhurst, Genevieve. "In Reno—Where They Take the Cure." *Pictorial Review,* February 1929, 2, 71–74.

Parks, Fred Warren. "Two Notable Exhibits." *Overland Monthly and Out West Magazine,* June 1894, 617–627.

Perry, Claire. *Pacific Arcadia: Images of California, 1600–1915.* New York: Oxford University Press, 1999.

Peters, Clay. "Reno of the Silver State." *Sunset,* November 1904, 78–83.

Pomeroy, Earl. *In Search of the Golden West: The Tourist in Western America.* Lincoln: University of Nebraska Press, 1990.

Pringle, Henry F. "Reno the Wicked: The American Capital of Divorce and Gambling." *Outlook,* 29 July 1931, 395–397, 402–403.

Prouty, Annie Estelle. "The Development of Reno in Relation to Its Topography." M.A. thesis, University of Nevada, Reno, 1917.

Raymond, Elizabeth C. *George Wingfield: Owner and Operator of Nevada.* Reno: University of Nevada Press, 1992.

"Reno." *Life,* 21 June 1937, 34–40.

"Reno Challenged." *Business Week,* 14 July 1945, 24–28.

Reno Department of Planning and Development. *Reno Policy Plan: [A Report] to the Reno City Planning Commission.* Reno: Reno Department of Planning and Development, 1982.

"Reno Divorces, 1927 Model." *Literary Digest,* 9 April 1927, 13–14.

Reno-Sparks Convention & Visitors Authority. "Media Campaign." Reno-Sparks Convention & Visitors Authority, 2001. http://www.rscva.com/marketing/marketing/ media.html (1 March 2001).

————. "RSCVA Marketing and Sales Plan, FY 2002–2003." Reno-Sparks Convention & Visitors Authority, 2002. www.renolaketahoe.com/about/research/ (30 April 2003).

————. "Sales & Marketing Plan Update, 2000–2001." Reno-Sparks Convention & Visitors Authority, 29 January 2001. http://www.renolaketahoe.com/about/research/ (30 April 2003).

————. "Situational Analysis Summary." Reno-Sparks Convention and Visitors Authority, 2001. www.rscva.com/marketing/marketing/situation.html (1 March 2001).

Reno-Tahoe, America's Adventure Place: 2004 Visitor Planner. Reno: Reno-Sparks Convention & Visitors Authority, 2004.

Reynolds, Quentin. "Relax in Reno." *Collier's,* 28 December 1935, 20–22, 35.

Riley, Glenda. *Divorce: An American Tradition.* New York: Oxford University Press, 1991.

"The Rites of Reno." *Holiday,* June 1965, 62–66.

"A River Runs through It." *Casino Executive,* May 1999, 30–32.

R. L. Polk & Co. *Polk's Reno City, Washoe County and Carson City Directory, 1925–26.* Oakland, Calif.: R. L. Polk & Co., 1925.

————. *Reno-Sparks City Directory.* El Monte, Calif.: R. L. Polk & Co., 1975.

————. *Reno-Sparks City Directory.* El Monte, Calif.: R. L. Polk & Co., 1984.

————. *R. L. Polk & Co.'s 1920–21 Reno City Directory.* R. L. Polk & Co., 1920.

————. *R. L. Polk & Co.'s Reno City Directory, 1927–1928.* San Francisco: R. L. Polk & Co., 1927.

The Road to Reno. Motion picture. Directed by Richard Wallace. Paramount Studios, 1931.

Robinson, Phil. *Sinners and Saints: A Tour across the States and round Them with Three Months among the Mormons.* London: Sampson Low, Marston, Searle & Rivington, 1883.

Rocha, Guy L., and Eric N. Moody. "Hart vs. Root: Reno's First Championship?" *Nevadan,* 6 April 1980, 6J.

Romantic Nevada. Documentary newsreel. Produced by James A. Fitzpatrick. Metro-Goldwyn-Mayer, 1943.

Ronald, Ann. "Reno: Myth, Mystique, or Madness?" In *East of Eden, West of Zion: Essays on Nevada,* ed. Wilbur S. Shepperson, 134–148. Reno: University of Nevada Press, 1989.

Rothman, Hal. *Neon Metropolis: How Las Vegas Started the Twenty-First Century.* New York: Routledge, 2002.

Rothman, Hal K. *Devil's Bargains: Tourism in the Twentieth-Century American West.* Lawrence: University Press of Kansas, 1998.

Rowley, William D. *Reclaiming the Arid West: The Career of Francis G. Newlands.* Bloomington and Indianapolis: Indiana University Press, 1996.

————. *Reno: Hub of the Washoe Country.* Woodland Hills, Calif.: Windsor Publications, 1984.

Ruhl, Arthur. "Reno and the Rush for Divorce." *Collier's,* 1 July 1911, 19–20.

Runte, Alfred. *National Parks: The American Experience.* 3d ed. Lincoln: University of Nebraska Press, 1997.

Ryan, Con. "The City That Sex Built." *Real Detective,* November 1936, 12–17, 79–82.

Sammons, Jeffrey T. *Beyond the Ring: The Role of Boxing in American Society.* Urbana and Chicago: University of Illinois Press, 1988.

Schwartz, David G. *Roll the Bones: The History of Gambling.* New York: Gotham Books, 2006.

———. *Suburban Xanadu: The Casino Resort on the Las Vegas Strip and Beyond.* New York: Routledge, 2003.

Shepperson, Wilbur S., ed. *East of Eden, West of Zion: Essays on Nevada.* Reno: University of Nevada, 1989.

Shepperson, Wilbur S., with Ann Harvey. *Mirage-Land: Images of Nevada.* Reno: University of Nevada Press, 1992.

Sherman, Edward F. "Nevada: The End of the Casino Era." *Atlantic Monthly,* October 1966, 112–116.

Sieber, R. Timothy. "Urban Tourism in Revitalizing Downtowns." In *Tourism and Culture: An Applied Perspective,* ed. Erve Chambers, 59–76. Albany: State University of New York Press, 1997.

Silver Legacy Hotel Casino. "Silver Legacy" brochure. Reno: Silver Legacy Hotel Casino, ca. 1995.

———. Silver Legacy Hotel Casino Web site. www.silverlegacyreno.com/generalinf02.php?id=4 (10 December 2000).

———. "Silver Legacy Resort Casino Fact Sheet." http://www.silverlegacyreno.com/fact_sheet.html (15 October 2001).

Sklar, Robert. *Movie-Made America: A Cultural History of American Movies.* New York: Vintage Books, 1994.

Smith, Henry Nash. *Virgin Land: The American West as Symbol and Myth.* Cambridge, Mass.: Harvard University Press, 1950.

Smythe, William E. *The Conquest of Arid America.* New York: Harper & Brothers Publishers, 1900.

Sorkin, Michael, ed. *Variations on a Theme Park: The New American City and the End of Public Space.* New York: Hill & Wang, 1992.

Southern Pacific Railroad Passenger Department. *The New Nevada: What It Is and What It Is to Be.* San Francisco: Southern Pacific Railroad Passenger Department, 1903.

Stegner, Wallace. "The Sense of Place." In *Where the Bluebird Sings to the Lemonade Springs.* New York: Penguin, 1992.

Sternlieb, George, and James W. Hughes. *The Atlantic City Gamble.* Cambridge, Mass.: Harvard University Press, 1983.

Stewart, Patricia. "Reno Still the Biggest Little City in the World." *Nevadan,* 14 April 1974, 3–5.

Stokowski, Patricia. *Riches and Regrets: Betting on Gambling in Two Colorado Mining Towns.* Niwot: University Press of Colorado, 1996.

Stout, Wesley. "Nevada's New Reno." *Saturday Evening Post,* 31 October 1942, 68–69.

Stratton, Lilyan. *Reno: A Book of Short Stories and Information.* Newark, N.J.: Colyer Printing, 1921.

Sutton, Horace. "Gamesmanship in Nevada." *Saturday Review,* 4 November 1967, 54–55.

Tate Snyder Kinsey Architects. "Las Vegas Strip and Downtown Tour: Casinos, as of

2000." Architecture Studies Library, University of Nevada, Las Vegas Libraries. http://www.library.unlv.edu/arch/lasvegas/tatesnyderkimsey0tour1.html (9 October 2007).

Taylor, Frank J. "Rich Man's Refuge." *Collier's,* 19 February 1938, 14, 55–56.

Teeling, William. *American Stew.* London: Herbert Jenkins, 1933.

Toll, David W. *The Compleat Nevada Traveler: A Guide to the State.* Gold Hill, Nev.: Gold Hill Publishing, 1981.

"Tour de Nez Races onto Cycling's National Scene." CNN Web site, 15 June 2006, http://www.cnn.com/2006/TRAVEL/DESTINATIONS/06/09/sierra.cycling.ap/index.html (10 September 2007).

Townley, John M. *Tough Little Town on the Truckee.* Reno: Great Basin Studies Center, 1983.

Trachtenberg, Alan. *The Incorporation of America: Culture and Society in the Gilded Age.* New York: Hill & Wang, 1982.

Travel and Tourism Research Association. *Travel Research Roundup: Branding the Travel Market.* Fort Worth, Tex.: Travel and Tourism Research Association, 1998.

Travis, Daryl. *Emotional Branding: How Successful Brands Gain the Irrational Edge.* Roseville, Calif.: Prima Venture, 2000.

Tuan, Yi-Fu. *Topophilia: A Study of Environmental Perceptions, Attitudes, and Values.* Englewood Cliffs, N.J.: Prentice-Hall, 1974.

———. "Language and the Making of Place: A Narrative-Descriptive Approach." *Annals of the Association of American Geographers* 81 (December 1991): 684–696.

Turano, Anthony M. "Reno the Naughty." *American Memory,* February 1936, 183–189.

Turner, Frederick Jackson. "The Significance of the Frontier in American History." In *Rereading Frederick Jackson Turner: "The Significance of the Frontier in American History" and Other Essays,* ed. John Mack Faragher, 31–60. New York: Henry Holt, 1994.

Twain, Mark. *Mark Twain: The Innocents Abroad, Roughing It.* New York: Library of America, 1984.

Urry, John. *The Tourist Gaze: Leisure and Travel in Contemporary Societies.* London: Sage, 1990.

U.S. Decennial Census Records, 1870–2000. Carson City: Nevada State Data Center.

U.S. Department of Commerce. *Statistical Abstract of the United States, 1929.* Washington: U.S. Government Printing Office, 1929.

U.S. Department of Commerce. *Statistical Abstract of the United States, 1931.* Washington: U.S. Government Printing Office, 1931.

U.S. Department of Commerce. *Statistical Abstract of the United States, 1933.* Washington: U.S. Government Printing Office, 1933.

U.S. Department of Commerce and Labor, Bureau of the Census. *Marriage and Divorce 1887–1906.* Washington: U.S. Government Printing Office, 1908.

Vanderbilt, Cornelius, Jr. *Ranches and Ranch Life in America.* New York: Crown Publishers, 1968.

Variety Film Reviews, vol. 2. New York: Garland Publishing, 1983.

Variety Film Reviews, vol. 3. New York: Garland Publishing, 1983.

Variety Film Reviews, vol. 4. New York: Garland Publishing, 1983.

Variety Film Reviews, vol. 7. New York: Garland Publishing, 1983.

Veblen, Thorstein. *The Theory of the Leisure Class: An Economic Study of Institutions.* New York: Macmillan, 1905.

Ward, Stephen V. *Selling Places: The Marketing and Promotion of Towns and Cities, 1850–2000.* London: Routledge, 1998.

Warner, C. C. *Products, Resources, Opportunities for Capital and Advantages to Emigrants of Nevada.* Reno: Gazette Book and Job Print, 1889.

Warner, Sam Bass, Jr. *The Urban Wilderness: A History of the American City.* New York: Harper & Row, 1972.

Watson, Anita Ernst. "Fading Shame: Divorce Stigma in American Culture, 1882–1939." Ph.D. diss., University of Nevada–Reno, 1997.

Watson, Anita J. "Tarnished Silver: Popular Image and Business Reality of Divorce in Nevada, 1900–1939." M.S. thesis, University of Nevada–Reno, 1989.

Wernick, Robert. "Last of the Divorce Ranches." *Saturday Evening Post,* 17 July 1965, 30–34.

Western Nevada Improvement Association. *Nature's Sanitarium: Reno, Nevada and Its Surroundings in the Sierras.* Reno: Journal Print, 1893.

Wharton, Edith. *The Custom of the Country.* London: Penguin Books, 1987.

"What the Folks Are Thinking About—In Reno, Nevada." *Collier's,* 28 April 1923, 33.

"Where's the Action?" *Newsweek,* 14 January 1963, 24–26.

White, G. Edward. *The Eastern Establishment and the Western Experience: The West of Frederic Remington, Theodore Roosevelt, Owen Wister.* Austin: University of Texas Press, 1968.

White, Richard. *It's Your Misfortune and None of My Own: A History of the American West.* Norman: University of Oklahoma Press, 1991.

Wilcox, Delos F. *Great Cities in America: Their Problems and Their Government.* New York: Macmillan, 1910.

Wilson, Chris. *The Myth of Santa Fe: Creating a Modern Regional Tradition.* Albuquerque: University of New Mexico Press, 1997.

Winn, Mary Day. *The Macadam Trail: Ten Thousand Miles by Motor Coach.* New York: Alfred A. Knopf, 1931.

The Women. Motion picture. Directed by George Cukor. MGM Studios, 1939.

Wood, Daniel B. "A Tale of How Two Cities Have Dealt with Growth." *Christian Science Monitor,* 13 March 2001, 12.

Woon, Basil. *Incredible Land: A Jaunty Baedeker to Hollywood and the Great Southwest.* New York: Liveright Publishing, 1933.

Worster, Donald. *Rivers of Empire: Water, Aridity, and the Growth of the American West.* New York: Random House, 1985.

Wrobel, David M. *Promised Lands: Promotion, Memory, and the Creation of the American West.* Lawrence: University Press of Kansas, 2002.

Wynne, Derek. "Cultural Quarters." In *The Culture Industry: The Arts in Urban Regeneration,* ed. Derek Wynne. Brookfield, Vt.: Avebury, 1992.

Zauner, Phyllis. "Finding the Real Reno." *Travel,* December 1971, 56.

Zukin, Sharon. *The Cultures of Cities.* Malden, Mass., and Oxford: Blackwell, 1995.

INDEX